☞ **Tom Robbins:**

"The brave neuronaut whom I believe to   possessed of considerable Irish blarney, which makes him all the more agreeable."

☞ **William S. Burroughs:**

"A true visionary of the potential of the human mind and spirit."

☞ **Allen Ginsberg:**

"A hero of American consciousness."

☞ **William Gibson:**

"The '90s are here, and the Doctor is in!"

☞ **Mondo 2000:**

"The cyberdelic guru. . . . The MVP (Most Valuable Philosopher) of the 20th Century."

☞ **Guide to Computer Living:**

"One of the intellectual giants of our time. . . . No one else had dared to publicly explore the metaphysical and evolutionary implications of the home computer."

☞ **Creem:**

"The Grandfather of Slacker Prophets."

☞ **Exposure:**

"Inner-space pioneer. Outer-space advocate. Computer enthusiast. Writer. Humorist. A West Point man. An ex-Harvard professor. A former political prisoner. A provocateur extraordinaire. A high cat with Cary Grant style and grace."

☞ **Magical Blend:**

"Dr. Timothy Leary: psychologist, iconoclast, prophet, outlaw, historian, and visionary."

☞ **Fad:**

"In Leary's 25–plus books and software one finds ideas pertinent to the present, not only to the 'new.' Touching on media and culture, politics and psychology, mind and chaos, his ideas open up possibilities for the present."

☞ **Time:**

"Yes, he's back. At 72, the ex-Harvard professor who encouraged a generation to 'turn on, tune in, and drop out' now counts himself as a cyberpunk. 'The PC is the LSD of the 1990s,' he says."

☞ **R. U. Sirius:**

"He's a visionary, theoretician, fighter for individual freedom, advocate of tolerance . . . but more importantly, Timothy Leary's lust for life always cheers us on."

☞ **Susan Sarandon:**

"He makes the chaos of our everyday lives sexy."

THE ACCELERATION OF BRAIN POWER

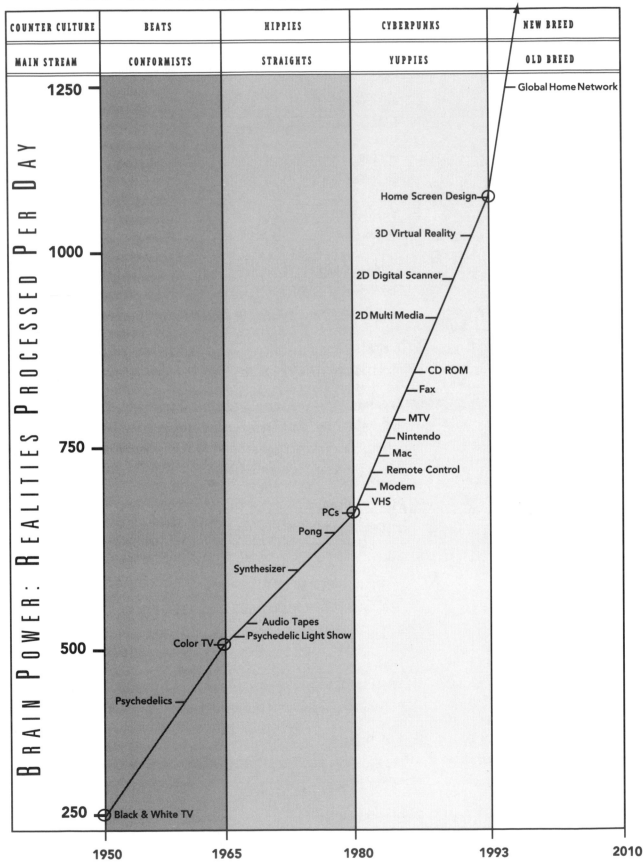

COUNTER CULTURE	BEATS	HIPPIES	CYBERPUNKS	NEW BREED
MAIN STREAM	CONFORMISTS	STRAIGHTS	YUPPIES	OLD BREED

BRAIN POWER: REALITIES PROCESSED PER DAY

1250 — Global Home Network

Home Screen Design ○

3D Virtual Reality —

2D Digital Scanner —

2D Multi Media —

1000

— CD ROM
— Fax

— MTV
— Nintendo
— Mac
— Remote Control
— Modem
— VHS

750

PCs ○
Pong —

Synthesizer —

Audio Tapes
Psychedelic Light Show

Color TV ○

500

Psychedelics —

250 ○ Black & White TV

1950   1965   1980   1993   2010

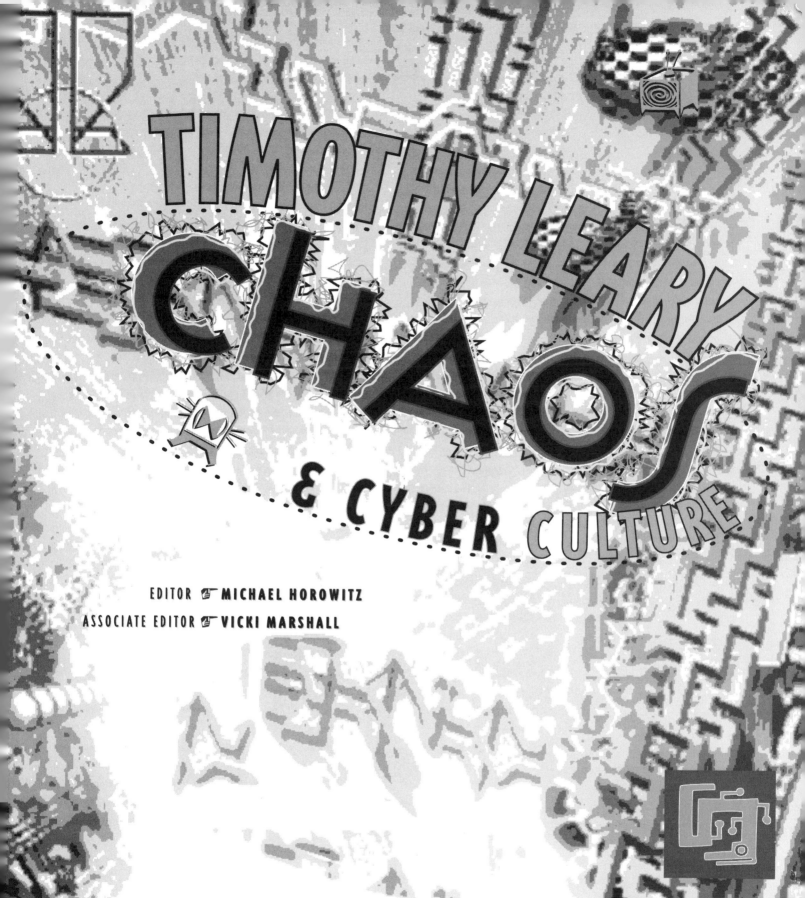

TIMOTHY LEARY
CHAOS
& CYBER CULTURE

EDITOR ☞ MICHAEL HOROWITZ
ASSOCIATE EDITOR ☞ VICKI MARSHALL

RONIN PUBLISHING, INC.
BOX 1035, BERKELEY, CALIFORNIA 94701

CHAOS & CYBER CULTURE
First Edition
ISBN: 0-914171-77-1

PUBLISHED BY
Ronin Publishing, Inc.
Post Office Box 1035
Berkeley, California 94701

Printed in the United States of America
First edition first printing: 1994

9 8 7 6 5 4 3 2

PROJECT EDITORS ....Sebastian Orfali, Beverly Potter, Ph.D.

BOOK EDITORS ....Michael Horowitz, Vicki Marshall

MANUSCRIPT EDITORS ....Aidan Kelly, Ginger Ashworth

ART DIRECTOR ....Carolyn Ferris

COVER DESIGN..........................Brian Groppe

BOOK DESIGN ....Judy July

TYPE·SCANS·PRODUCTION ......Generic Type

COVER ART ....Carolyn Ferris, Brummbaer, Vic Keller, Robert Williams

ILLUSTRATIONS ....Carolyn Ferris, Vic Keller, Andy Frith, Brummbaer

The material herein is presented in the spirit of the First Amendment for reference and informational purposes, and should in no way be construed as advocating the breaking of laws.

U.S. Library of Congress Cataloguing-in-Publication Data
    Leary, Timothy Francis, 1920– .
    Chaos & Cyber Culture / by Timothy Leary: with guest appearances by William S. Burroughs...[et al.]: editor Michael Horowitz. —1st ed.
       p.   cm.
    Includes bibliographical references and index.
    ISBN 0-914171-77-1: $19.95

    1. Popular culture—United States.   2. Subculture—United States.
    I. Burroughs, William S., 1914– . II. Horowitz, Michael, 1938– .
    III. Title.   IV. Title: Chaos and cyber culture.

E169.04.L463   994
306'.11'0973—dc20   94-29511
                                                                                   CIP

DEDICATIONS

DEFINITIONS: "DEDICATE"

☞ 1. To set apart and consecrate to a deity or to a sacred purpose.

☞ 2. To devote wholly and earnestly, as to some person or purpose.

☞ 3. To inscribe (a book, piece of music, etc.) to a person, cause or the like.

DESIGN TEAM

Sebastian Orfali
Carolyn Ferris
Mike Horowitz
Vicki Marshall
Brummbaer
Vic Keller
Andy Frith
Howard Hallis
Ginger Ashworth
Judy July

THE CHILDREN

Susan Martino
Jack Leary
Zach Chase
Dieadra Martino
Ashley Martino
Brett Leary
Annie Leary
Sarah Brown
Davina Suzanne
Sunyata Palmer
Jubal Palmer
Noni Horowitz
Uri Horowitz

DEAREST FRIENDS

Barbara Leary
Rosemary Woodruff
Denis Berry
Aileen Getty
Angela Janklow
Siobhan Cyr
Momoko Ito
Joi Ito
Mimi Ito
Donna Wilson
Barbara Fouch
Camella Grace
Betsy Berg
Janice Gardner
Louise Schwartz
Susan Sarandon
Diana Walstrom
Joey Cavallo
Vince de Franco
Don, Holly & Kenny
Greater Talent
Network
Marianne Leary
Anita Hoffman
Clementia
Jack Armstrong
Jerry Harrington
J. P. Barlow
Al Jourgenson
Tony Scott
John Roseboro
Chris Graves
Scott Fisher
Joel Fredericks
Eric Gardner
Alan Schwartz
Tim Robbins
George Milman
Jas Morgan
Mondo 2000
Dave & Andy
Ron Lawrence
Michael Shields

ACKNOWLEDGEMENTS

I. PHOTO CREDITS ....▶

Peter Booth Lee
Cindy Horowitz
Michael Shields
Jeremy Bigwood
Hi Leitz
Dana Gluckstein
Herb Ritts

II. PHOTOS USED TO RENDER PAINTINGS AND DRAWINGS...▶

Morgan Russell: William Gibson
Allen Ginsberg: William S. Burroughs
Yvette Roman: David Byrne

III. ILLUSTRATIONS ....▶

Carolyn Ferris
Vic Keller
Andy Frith
Brummbaer
Robert Williams
Keith Haring
Matt Gouig
Howard Hallis

IV. COMPUTER ART AND COLLECTION ARCHIVES........▶

Michael Witte
Michael Horowitz
Ronin Publishing, Inc.
Paul Kagan
Vicki Marshall
Mike Saenz
Mark Franklyn
Rick Griffin

V. SPECIAL THANKS.............▶

Special thanks for their help to the following:
Robin Kay
Ron Lawrence
Kenn Thomas
Joe Ranno
Flash Photo (San Anselmo, California)

MICHAEL WITTE

"We are mutating into another species—from Aquaria to the Terrarium, and now we're moving into Cyberia. We are creatures crawling to the center of the cybernetic world. But cybernetics are the stuff of which the world is made. Matter is simply frozen information. . . . The critics of the information age see everything in the negative, as if the quantity of information can lead to a loss of meaning. They said the same thing about Gutenberg. . . . Never before has the individual been so empowered. But in the information age you do have to get the signals out. Popularization means making it available to the people. Today the role of the philosopher is to personalize, popularize, and humanize computer ideas so that people can feel comfortable with them. . . . The fact is that a few of us saw what was happening and we wrestled the power of LSD away from the CIA, and now the power of computers away from IBM, just as we rescued psychology away from the doctors and analysts. In every generation I've been part of a group of people who, like Prometheus, have wrestled with the power in order to hand it back to the individual."

—TIMOTHY LEARY, <u>PATAPHYSICS</u> MAGAZINE (1990)

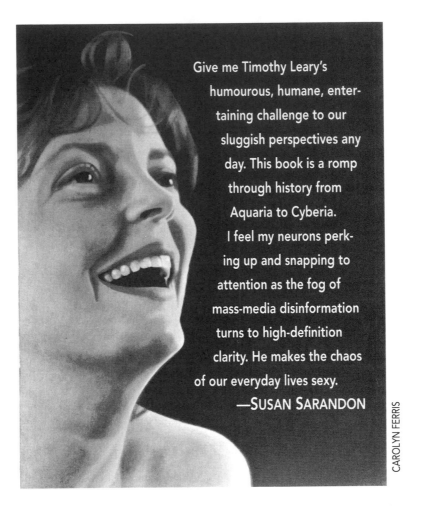

Give me Timothy Leary's humourous, humane, entertaining challenge to our sluggish perspectives any day. This book is a romp through history from Aquaria to Cyberia. I feel my neurons perking up and snapping to attention as the fog of mass-media disinformation turns to high-definition clarity. He makes the chaos of our everyday lives sexy.
—SUSAN SARANDON

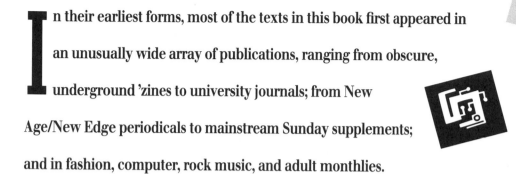

I n their earliest forms, most of the texts in this book first appeared in an unusually wide array of publications, ranging from obscure, underground 'zines to university journals; from New Age/New Edge periodicals to mainstream Sunday supplements; and in fashion, computer, rock music, and adult monthlies.

The ideas expressed in these articles were also put forth in spoken-word performances at hundreds of colleges, in Whole Life Expo workshops, at the Lollapalooza rock 'n' roll tour, from the stages of Sunset Strip comedy clubs, and large rave parties—often accompanied by computer-generated multimedia displays by some of the artists in this book.

A number of these texts were desktop-published and sold by mail order in the manner of samizdat (dissident, underground) publications from a "cyberdeli" called KnoWare—thanks to whom some of the buzzwords and soundbites in these pieces are sometimes worn as buttons and displayed as bumper stickers.

Like almost all of Timothy Leary's spoken and written transmissions since the 1960s, the works in this book—mostly published during the dull, repressive Reagan–Bush years—are marked by a tone of entertaining dissent and optimistic critique, fueled by humour and brimming with novel perceptions.

Welcome to a cyberdelic Be-In!

– M.H.

TABLE OF CONTENTS ....➤

BRUMMBAER

The Eternal Philosophy of Chaos

For several thousand years it has seemed obvious that the basic nature of the universe is extreme complexity, inexplicable disorder—that mysterious, tangled magnificence popularly known as Chaos.

The poetic Hindus believed the universe was a dreamy dance of illusion (*maya*). The paradoxical, psycho-logical Buddhists spoke of a void too complex— maybe a trillion times too complex—to be grasped by the human A–B–C–1–2–3 word-processing system (*mind*).

Chinese poet-philosopher Lao-tzu sardonically reminded us that the tao is forever changing complexities at light speed, elusive and inaccessible to our fingers and thumbs laboriously tapping letters on our alphanumeric keyboards and mind-operating systems.

Socrates, that proud, self-reliant Athenian democrat, indiscreetly blurted out the dangerous secret when he said, *"The aim of human life is to know thy selves."* This is surely the most subversive T-shirt flaunted over the centuries by humanists, the most confrontational bumper sticker on their neuro-auto-mobiles.

Individualistic thinking is the original sin of the Judæo–Christian–Islamic Bibles. It sabotages attempts by the authorities to order Chaos.

The first rule of every law-and-order system is to trivialize-dæmonize the dangerous concepts of Self, Individual Aims, and Personal Knowledge. Thinking for Your Selves is heretical, treasonous, blasphemous. Only devils and satans do it. Creative thinking, committed out loud, becomes a capital crime. It was "Three Strikes and You're Out" for several hundred thousand Protestant dissenters during the Inquisitions of the Roman papacy—not to forget the witch burnings performed by the Protestants when they took charge of the Chaos-control department.

It was all very simple to the law-and-order controllers. There are the immortal Gods and Goddesses up there in that Gated Community on Olympus Drive. And then there are us—meaningless mortals, slaving around down here in the low-rent flatlands.

The concept of individuals with choice and identity seemed total folly, the ultimate nightmare—not just of authoritarian bureaucrats, but of common-sense liberals. Chaos must be controlled!

The standard way to tame and domesticate the impossible complexity that surrounds us is to invent a few "tooth-fairy" Gods, the more infantile the better, and to lay down a few childish rules: Honour your father and your mother, etc. The rules are simple and logical. You passively obey. You pray. You sacrifice. You work. You believe.

And then, Praise the Bored, let there be no terrorizing notions about individuals hanging around this meaningless, disordered universe trying to figure how to design themselves some individual selves.

CHAOS ENGINEERING

The first Chaos engineers may have been the Hindu sages who designed a method for operating the brain called *yoga*. The Buddhists produced one of the great hands-on do-it-

---

THIS BOOK IS ABOUT

DESIGNING CHAOS

AND FASHIONING

YOUR PERSONAL DISORDERS

☞ ON SCREENS

☞ WITH CYBERNETIC TOOLS

☞ FROM COUNTERCULTURAL

PERSPECTIVES

☞ WITH INFORMATIONAL

CHEMICALS (CHAOS DRUGS)

☞ WHILE DELIGHTING IN CYBEROTICS

☞ AS GUERRILLA ARTISTS

☞ WHO EXPLORE DE-ANIMATION

ALTERNATIVES

☞ WHILE SURFING THE WAVES OF

MILLENNIUM MADNESS

TO GLIMPSE THE GLORIOUS WILD

IMPOSSIBILITIES AND

IMPROBABILITIES OF THE

CENTURY TO COME.

ENJOY IT!

IT'S OURS TO BE PLAYED WITH!

yourself manuals for operating the brain: *The Tibetan Book of the Dying*. Chinese Taoists developed the teaching of going with the flow—not clinging to idea-structures, but changing and evolving. The message was: Be cool. Don't panic. Chaos is good. Chaos creates infinite possibilities.

The wacko Socratic idea of Do It Yourself (D.I.Y.), which created modern democracy, was a practical, common-sense, sassy Athenian version of the Hindu–Buddhist–Taoist yogas. And remember where this foolishness got India, Tibet, and China? Know-where!

The most dangerous idea is this crazed, megalomaniac Socratic notion of

KNOW!

which defines the serf-human being as a thinker. Outrageous impudence! The slave is encouraged to become a philosopher! The serf strives to be a psychologist! A potential yogic sage!

This heresy predicts why later atheist evolutionists like Linnæus and Darwin defined our super-chimp species as *Femina (Homo) sapiens sapiens*.

> # The standard way to tame and domesticate the impossible complexity that surrounds us is to invent a few "tooth-fairy" Gods, the more infantile the better, and to lay down a few childish rules: Honour your father and your mother, etc. The rules are simple and logical. You passively obey. You pray. You sacrifice. You work. You believe.

THE CHAOS WITHOUT

For centuries there existed a fanatic taboo against scientific understanding. Why? Because of the fear of Chaos. The facts about our (apparently) insignificant place in the galactic dance are so insulting to the control freaks who try (so manfully and diligently and seriously) to manage Chaos that they forbade any intelligent attempts to look out there and dig the glorious *complexity*.

At one point consciousness-altering devices like the microscope and telescope were criminalized for exactly the same reasons that psychedelic plants were banned in later times. They allow us to peer into bits and zones of Chaos.

Galileo got busted and Bruno got the Vatican microwave for showing that the Sun did not circle the Earth. Religious and political Chaos-phobes naturally want the nice, tidy, comfy universe to cuddle around them.

In the last century science has developed technical extensions of the human sensorium that specify the truly spooky nature of the complexities we inhabit.

Stellar astronomy describes a universe of fantastic multiplicity: a hundred billion tiny star systems in our tiny galaxy, a hundred billion galaxies in our teeny universe.

THE CHAOS WITHIN

In the last decades of the 20th Century, scientists began to study the complexity within the human brain.

Talk about Chaos!

It turns out that the brain is a galactic network of a hundred billion neurons. Each neuron is an information system as complex as a mainframe computer. Each neuron is connected to ten thousand other neurons. Each of us is equipped with a universe of neurocomplexity that is inscrutable to our alphanumeric minds.

This brain power is at once the most humiliating fact about our current ignorance, and the most thrilling prospect of our potential divinity—once we start learning how to operate our brains.

HUMANISM: THE NAVIGATIONAL GAME PLAN

Chaos theory allows us to appreciate our assignment: the understanding, enjoyment, and celebration of the delightful nature of the whole universe—including the totally mad paradoxes within our brains.

Activating the so-called right brain eliminates one of the last taboos against understanding Chaos and provides a hands-on scientific basis for the philosophy of humanism—encouraging us to team up with others to design our own personal versions of Chaos.

◎ ◎ ◎

This book, as you will discover, covers a decade of recent writing. Looking over this verbal disorder so elegantly arranged by Michael, Vicki, Carolyn, Sebastian, Aidan, Ginger, and Judy, I get that special, pleasurable, dizzying head-hit so prized by us Chaos addicts.

For the last few months I have been obsessed by the extreme complexity of everything. We don't know who, why, where, what, when we are. What a frightmare! Ignorant, alienated agents sent on a mission with no instructions.

My thrilling bewilderment about the Great Disorder (Chaos) is due, of course, to the three symptoms of senility which I have diligently earned.

1. Short-term memory loss means you forget exactly what's happening and why you are here.
2. Long-term memory gain gives you the ambiguous perspective of what our cultures have come up with in the way of weird solutions to the Mystery.
3. This book is about redesigning Chaos and fashioning our personal disorders . . .

On screens
With cybernetic tools
From countercultural perspectives
With informational chemicals (Chaos drugs)
While delighting in cyberotics
As guerrilla artists
Who explore de-animation alternatives
While surfing the waves of millennium madness
to glimpse the glorious wild impossibilities and improbabilities
of the century to come.
Enjoy it! It's ours to be played with!

Signed with Love,

Timothy Leary

Galileo got busted and Bruno got the Vatican microwave for showing that the Sun did not circle the Earth. Religious and political Chaos-phobes naturally want the nice, tidy, comfy universe to cuddle around them.

I. SCREENS

I.1. HOW I BECAME AN AMPHIBIAN

In 1980 Ronald Reagan, a screen person, became the president of the United States. At the same time, the screen image of an Iranian mullah, the leader of a notoriously irritable fundamentalist sect, became the rallying point of the Islamic world. In the same year, surveys showed that the average American spent more than four hours a day neuronarcotized by the artificial realities and fake news-dramas on television screens—more time than is spent on any other waking activity in the flesh-material reality.

It was about then that I too found myself mutating gradually, imperceptibly, into an amphibious form. (The word "amphibian" comes from the Greek *amphi* [double] and *bios* [life].)

I began spending around four hours a day producing and scripting and directing the images on my personal screen. Some of these digitized words and images were my own. Some were encoded on disks. Others were phoned to me by friends and colleagues at almost the speed of light.

In this way I learned how to file, process, organize, clarify, store, retrieve, and transmit my digitized thoughts in the form of words and icons.

These exercises in translating thoughts to digital codes and screen images have helped me understand how my brain works, how the universe evolves in terms of information algorithms. And, in the most practical mode, to understand:

1. **How we can avoid television dictatorships, and**
2. **How we can democratize the cyberscreen politics of the future.**

My experiences, far from being original or unique, seem to be part of an enormous cultural metamorphosis. Like millions of others, I have come to feel as comfortable over there in Cyberia, Tubeland, on the other side of my electronic-reality window, as I do operating in the closed-in Terrarium of the material world. My brain, like yours, needs to be clothed in cyberwear and to swim, float, navigate through the oceans of electronic data.

Surely we can be forgiven if we are confused by all this. Organisms in the process of metamorphosis are forced to use the metaphors of past stages in order to anticipate future stages—an obviously risky business. "They'll never get me up in one of those," says the caterpillar to the butterfly.

So, let me venture some shaky allegories.

FROM AQUARIA TO TERRARIUM TO CYBERIA

In our early marine forms, we lived under water. Trapped in Aquaria we could peer up through the sea ceiling and sense a wide world up there.

In the Devonian period (400 million years ago) we started developing the technology needed to migrate to the shoreline. I am talking state-of-the-art terrawear: skin-tight dry suits to maneuver around in the land world. Thus we became amphibians, able to live both in Aquaria and in Terrarium.

During the Triassic period we evolved to the mammalian stage and lost our ability to inhabit Aquaria. For the last 225 million years, we mammals crawled and ran around the Earth's surface, nervously improving our Terrarium survival technologies.

Then, during the last million or so years, human beings developed enormous brains that we did not know how to operate. Our hairless primate ancestors, banded in social groups, living in caves, fashioning clubs to fight tigers, were equipped with the same brain model that we are just now learning how to manage.

And for thousands of years, the more poetic or neurologically advanced among us have gazed upward on starry nights, beginning to realize that another universe exists in space and that we are trapped in the Terrarium of Earth's surface. Or what's a heaven for?

Around 1900, physicists (Einstein, Heisenberg, etc.) demonstrated that the elements of all energy matter in the universe, out there or down here, consist of quanta of information. Light.

During the Roaring 20th Century, the equations of quantum physics led to the development of quantum appliances that allowed humans to receive, process, and transmit electronic images. Telephone, cinema, radio, television, computers, compact discs, fax machines; suddenly humans were creating digital realities that were accessed on living-room screens.

This universe of electronic signals, in which we now spend so much time, has been called Cyberia.

Just as the fish brain had to don dry-skin terra-suits to inhabit the Terrarium, so do our primate brains have to don Canaveral space suits in order to migrate into outer space. And use digital appliances in order to inhabit cyberspace.

> **During the Roaring 20th Century, the equations of quantum physics led to the development of quantum appliances that allowed humans to receive, process, and transmit electronic images.**

THE BRAIN AS A DIGITAL TRANSMITTER

As our brain evolves, it develops new vehicles and information-processing devices in order to feed its insatiable hunger for stimulation. Like any adolescent organ, the human brain requires an enormous, continual supply of chemical and electronic data to keep growing toward maturity.

In the last eight years, the dendritic metabolism of my information organ (brain) seems to have undergone a dramatic change. My eyes have become two hungry mouths pressed against the Terrarium window through which electronic pulses reach the receptive areas of my brain. My brain seems to require a daily input of several billion bytes of digital (light-speed) information. In this I am no different than the average, televoid American sluggishly reclining on the bottom of the Terrarium. My brain also requires regular diets of chemical foods. But my Very Personal Computer has transformed my brain into an output organ emitting, discharging digital information through the Terrarium window into ScreenLand.

Just as the heart is programmed to pump blood, my sinewy brain is now programmed to fire, launch, transmit, beam thoughts through the electronic window into Cyberia. The screen is the revolving glass door through which my brain both receives and emits her signals.

As a result of personal computers and video arcades, millions of us are no longer satisfied to peer like passive infants through the Terrarium wall into the ScreenLand filled with cyberstars like Bill and Hillary and Boris and Saddam and Madonna and Beavis and Butt-Head. We are learning how to enter and locomote in Cyberia. Our brains are learning how to exhale as well as inhale in the datasphere.

Of course, not all humans will make this move. Many of our finny ancestors preferred to remain marine forms. "You'll never get me up in one of those," said the tadpole to the frog.

Many humans will be trapped by gene-pool geography or compelled by repressive societies or seduced by material rewards and thus reside in the material-flesh world of mammalian bipeds. Oh, yeah. To escape from the boredom and to rest after their onerous, mech-flesh labors, they will torpidly ingest electronic realities oozing from their screens. But they will not don cybersuits and zoom into ScreenLand.

MICHAEL SHIELDS

We tri-brains who learn to construct and inhabit auto-realities spend some time in the cyberworld and some in the material-organic world. We zoom through the datmosphere like Donkey Kongs and Pac Women, scooping up info-bits and spraying out electronic-reality forms. And then we cheerfully return to the slow, lascivious, fleshly material world to indulge our bodies with sensory stimulation and to exercise our muscles by pushing around mechanical realities in sport or recreation.

On the skin-tissue plane, our left brains are limited to mechanical-material forms. But in ScreenLand our right brains are free to imagineer digital dreams, visions, fictions, concoctions, hallucinatory adventures. All these screen scenes are as real as a kick-in-the-pants as far as our brains are concerned. Our brains have no sense organs and no muscles. Our brains command our bodies and send spaceships to the Moon by sending signals in only one linguistic: the quantum language of zeros and ones.

NO MORE MIND-BODY PARADOX FOR TRI-BRAIN ORGANISMS

We tri-brain creatures seem to be resolving that most ancient philosophic problem. Forget the quaint, mammalian dualism of mind versus body. The interplay of life now involves digital brain—body matter—digital screen.

Everything—animal, vegetable, mineral, tangible, invisible, electric—is converted to digital food for the info-starved brain. And now, using the new digital appliances, everything that the brain–mind can conceive can be realized in electronic patterns.

To be registered in consciousness, to be "realized," every sensory stimulation must be deconstructed, minimalized, digitalized. The brain converts every pressure signal from our skins, tickles from our genitals, delectables from our tongues, photons from our eyes, sound waves from our ears, and, best of all, electronic buzziness from our screens into quantum realities, into directories and files of 0/1 signals.

We tri-brain amphibians are learning how to use cyberwear (computer suits) to navigate around our ScreenLands the way we use the hardware of our bodies to navigate around the material-mechanical world, and the way we use spaceships and space suits to navigate around the outer space.

There are some amusing and alluring philosophic by-products. Quantum psychology allows us to define, operationally, other terms of classical metaphysics.

A DEFINITION OF "SPIRITUAL" COULD BE "DIGITAL"

Recite to yourself some of the traditional attributes of the word "spiritual": *mythic, magical, ethereal, incorporeal, intangible, nonmaterial, disembodied, ideal, platonic.* Is that not a definition of the electronic-digital?

CAN WE ENGINEER OUR SOULS?

Can we engineer our souls? Can we pilot our souls?

The closest you are probably ever going to get to navigating your soul is when you are piloting your mind through your brain or its external simulation on cybernetic screens. Think of the screen as the cloud chamber on which you can track the vapor trail of your platonic, immaterial movements. If your digital footprints and spiritual fingerprints look less than soulful on the screen, well, just change them. Learning how to operate a soul figures to take time.

The quantum-electronic universe of information defines the new spiritual state. These "spiritual" realms, over centuries imagined, may, perhaps, now be realized! The more philosophic among us find this philosophically intoxicating.

AMPHIBIANS WILL NOT NEGLECT THE BODY

 Those of us who choose the amphibian option will spend some of our waking hours suited up and moving around in the cybernetic-psybernetic ScreenLand. But please don't fret about our neglecting the wonderful body.

The first point to register is this: We tri-brains should not use our precious fleshware to work. Is it not a sacrilegious desecration to waste our precious sensory equipment on toil, chore, drudgery? We are not pack animals, or serfs, or executive robots garbed in uniforms rushing around lugging briefcases to offices. Why should we use our priceless, irreplaceable bodies to do work that can be done better by assembly-line machines?

But who will plough the fields and harvest the grapes? The languorous midwestern farmer will don her cybersuit and recline in her hammock in Acapulco operating the automated plough on her Nebraska farm. The Mexican migrant will recline in his hammock in Acapulco using his cybergear to direct the grape-harvest machines.

When we finish our work, we will take off our cybersuits, our brain clothing, and don body clothes. When we platonic migrants sweat, it will be in athletic or sensual pleasure. When we exert elbow grease, it will be in some form of painterly flourish or musical riff. When we operate oil-gulping machines, we will joyride

for pleasure. The only mechanical vehicles we will actually climb into and operate by hand will be sports cars. Trains, planes, boats will be used only for pleasure cruising, and will transport our bodies for æsthetic, artistic, recreational purposes only. Our bodily postures will thus be graceful and proud, our body movements delightful, slow, sensual, lush, erotic, fleshly, carnal vacations from the accelerated, jazzy cyberrealities of cyberspace, where the brain work is done.

PERSONAL APPEARANCE IN THE PRECIOUS FLESH

Face-to-face interactions will be reserved for special, intimate, precious, sacramentalized events. Flesh encounters will be rare and thrilling. In the future each of us will be linked in thrilling cyberexchanges with many others whom we may never meet in person and who do not speak our phonetic-literal language. Most of our important creations will take place in ScreenLand. Taking off our cyberwear to confront another with naked eyeballs will be a precious personal appearance. And the quality of our "personal appearances" will be raised to a level of mythic drama.

> Learning how to operate a soul figures to take time.

COMMON-SENSE QUANTUM PSYCHOLOGY

Until 1983, when I acquired a personal computer, the principles of quantum physics always seemed, to my immature material mind, to be incomprehensible, bizarre, abstract, and totally impractical. Now that my digital brain lobes have been activated, quantum physics seems to make common sense and to define a practical psychology of everyday life in the tri-brain mode.

Einstein's theories of relativity, for example, suggest that realities depend on points of view. Instead of the static absolutes of space–time defined by material reality, quantum-brain realities are changing fields defined by quick feedback interchanges with other information sources. Our computer brainware allows us to perform Einsteinian-spiritual transformations on our laptops.

Werner Heisenberg's principle states that there is a limit to objective determinacy. If everyone has a singular viewpoint, constantly changing, then everyone creates his or her own version of reality. This gives the responsibility for reality construction not to a bad-natured biblical God, or to an impersonal, mechanical process

of entropic devolution, or to an omniscient Marxist state, but to individual brains. Subjective determinacy operates in ScreenLand. Our brains create our own spiritual worlds, as they say along the Ganges. We get the realities we deserve. Or preserve. Or construct.

And now our interactivated brains can project wonderland realities onto our screens and hurl them around the globe at light speed. Notice the political implications. Quantum psychology stressing singularity of viewpoint is the ultimate democratic perspective. The screen is the window to the new world. Who controls our screens programs the realities we inhabit. Therefore it behooves us to control our own reality screens.

These two notions, of relativity and self-determination, are street-smart common sense. But Einstein and Heisenberg and Max Planck and Niels Bohr lost the crowd when they said that the basic elements of the universe were bits of off/on (yin/yang) information. And that solid matter is temporary clusters of frozen information. And that when material structures are fissioned, they release energy: $E = mc^2$.

These brilliant physicists were explaining electronic ideas by using their hands to write with paleolithic chalk on a slab of black slate!

During the next twenty to eighty years, quantum appliances became household items. The application of quantum physics to engineering produced vacuum tubes, transistors, integrated circuits, lasers, radio, television, computers. These gadgets are not intended to move "matter-energy" around. Instead, they move information. Data-buzzes. Electronic means "informational." Sticks and stones may break your bones, but information can never hurt you. Although it can, alas, totally control your mind.

So it becomes clear that the basic "particles" that make up matter are bits of "information." Matter is frozen information. Energy is just the dumb smoke and sweat that matter releases in its lumbering transformations. The famous formula changes to: $I = mc^2$, where *"I" = information*.

At the quantum level the Newtonian "laws" turn out to be local ordinances. It turns out that the smaller the linguistic element, the greater the I.Q. (Information Quotient). The larger is always the lumbering vehicle for the miniaturized, platonic info-units it carries around. The universe is an intelligence system, and the elements of intelligence are quanta. And suddenly we understand that the brain is an organ designed to metabolize digital information.

THE POPULARIZATION AND PERSONALIZATION OF QUANTUM PSYCHOLOGY IN THE ROARING 20TH CENTURY

Except to those who had studied the brilliantly intuitive metaphors of oriental philosophy, these principles of quantum psychology sounded implausible and weird when they were first announced around A.D. 1900. But looking back we can see that every decade of the Roaring 20th Century has produced events that have confirmed and applied quantum principles.

The philosophy of our century, since Peirce and Saussure, is linguistic, semiotic, semantic. So is the psychology, and the politics. Modern art, modern writing, modern music made us feel comfortable in the quantum atmosphere. The great artists dissolved representational structure, freed elements to create new forms, word patterns, sounds, and accepted the responsibility of subjective reality-formation. As Walt Disney demonstrated, the brain loves to be electronized.

And now we have interpersonal computers, Nintendo power gloves, Sega CD-ROMS, electronic bulletin boards. All of these relatively inexpensive gadgets place the power to create platonic, electronic realities in the hands of interacting individuals.

THE DISCOVERY AND EXPLORATION OF THE BRAIN

The advent of psychedelic (mind-opening) drugs (1960–80) produced a widespread fascination with consciousness alteration, mind exploration, inner searching, brain-stimulation gadgets, oriental yoga—all based on quantum principles. The advent of personal and interpersonal computers, digital editors, and audio-video gear (1976–90) turned the average American home into an electronic-information center. At the same time, neurologists were publishing their discoveries about how neurotransmitter chemicals and electrical nets move information around the brain.

The convergence of these waves of information, the inner psychedelic and the ScreenLand cybernetic, made it possible for the first time for human beings to understand how the brain operates.

The human brain is, by auto-definition, the most powerful control communication unit in the known universe. A constellation of a hundred billion cells floating in an ocean of info-gel. The brain has no muscles and no sense organs. It is a shimmering sea swarming with microchip molecules packaged in enormous hardware neurons, all linked by chemical-electrical signals. We could not understand how the brain operates until our electrical engineers had built computers. And now we are learning how to beam our brain waves into the Cyberia of electronic reality, to think and play and work and communicate and create at this basic (0/1) level.

Our hundred-billion–neuron computers are designed to process digital signals at the rate of a hundred fifty million per second. Each neuron can unfold as many as ten thousand dendrite receptors to pick up information from its neighbors. Talk about local-area networks! Talk about Central Intelligence Activity! More information is probably exchanged per second at the site of one synapse than in the CIA headquarters in a day. If any.

This is the reality field that Plato described in the 4th Century B.C., that quantum mechanics intuited in 1900, and that we tri-brains have begun to inhabit at the end of this Roaring 20th Century.

QUANTUM POLITICS: POWER TO THE SINGULARITIES

 In the 1980s we saw how the fabrication of quantum realities empowered the monopolistic organizations that manage the careers of screen actors like Ronald Reagan and the Pope and Ayatollah Khomeini and Mikhail Gorbachev.

In 1989 the nature of the quantum politics of thought processing and the human-computer interaction was dramatically changed by the introduction and marketing of digital home appliances.

We can now create electronic realities on the other side of the screen not just with a keyboard or a joystick or a mouse. We wear the interface. We don cybergloves, cybergoggles, cybercaps, cybervests. Cybershorts! Our bodily movements create the images on our screens. We walk, talk, dance, swim, float around in digital worlds, and we interact on screens with others who are linked in our nets.

Cyberwear is a mutational technology that allows individual's brains to experience O.O.B. (out-of-body) experiences just as landware like legs and lungs permitted the fish to escape the water (O.O.W. experiences). Cyberwear will make it possible for individual Americans to cross the Merlin Wall and to meet and interact in cyberspace.

CAROLYN FERRIS

THE PIONEERS OF CYBERSPACE

The basic notion of O.O.B. artificial-reality appliances was introduced by Myron Kreuger and Ted Nelson in the 1970s. The nitty-gritty realities of creating and inhabiting digital universes were described in 1985 by William Gibson in his brilliant, epic trilogy *Neuromancer, Count Zero,* and *Mona Lisa Overdrive.* Gibson described the "matrix," the dataworlds created by human digital communication. By 1989 cybernauts like Jaron Lanier, Eric Gullichsen, Joi Ito, Brenda Laurel, and Rebecca Allen were developing cyberspace realities built for two. Or more.

REALITIES BUILT FOR TWO

Many people are understandably disturbed by the idea that in the future human beings will be spending more time in PlatoLand than in Flesh Play; piloting their brain-selves inside electronic realities, interacting with other electronic humans.

Like adolescents whose hormones suddenly awaken the unused sexual circuits of their brains, we tri-brains are just now discovering that the brain is an info-organ wired, fired, and inspired to process and emit electronic signals. The main function of a computer is interpersonal communication.

Within ten years many of us will be spending almost all our screen time actively zooming around digital oceans interacting and re-creating with other tri-brains.

Some industrial-age cynics say that humans are too lazy. They would rather sit back as sedentary couch slugs than be active. But we've been through these tech-jumps before in history.

Before Henry Ford, only big-shot engineers and captains employed by corporations drove mass-media vehicles such as trains and steamboats. Now we recognize (and often deplore) this genetic compulsion to grab the steering wheel, smoke rubber, and freely auto-mobilize that sweeps over every member of our species at puberty.

In ten years most of our daily operations—occupational, educational, recreational—will transpire in ScreenLands. Common sense suggests that we are more likely to find compatible brain-mates if we are not restricted to local geography. ◎

For thousands of years, since the dawn of tribal societies, most human beings have lived in drab caves, huts, shacks, igloos, houses, or apartments furnished and supplied with minimum information equipment—oral-body language. Stone tools.

In these shut-in, introverted, inward-looking, data-starved abodes occurred the practical maintenance functions that people had to perform to keep the gene pool going. For most people the plumbing was crude, the clothing hardly seductive. Cosmetics and perfumes were minimal—to say the most.

In the tribal culture there were no books, radios, or daily newspapers. No *Vogue* magazine loaded with five hundred slick pages of silk fashion, voluptuous models pouting with desire, straining to arouse, flashing wide-open, inviting legs in high-heeled shoes, and curving, suck-me tits. No, the survival information needed to maintain the tribal home was packaged in rote, monkey-like signals expressed by the body: oral grunts, gestures, bodily movements, crude artifacts.

THE MARKETING MESSAGE FROM THE PRODUCERS OF THE TRIBAL-CULTURE SHOW

 If we wanted to experience a bit of glamour, if we yearned to flirt around, looking for a sexual partner, or to check on what was happening, if we needed a battery recharge to keep us going as a loyal gene-pool serf-servant, we had to exit the home and amble up to the village square. There we could get the evening tribal news, pick up the local gossip, and make deals for skins or fur coats for our wives in exchange for a stone knife.

On designated occasions, our entire tribe would swarm together for ceremonies of celebration: Planting. Harvesting. Full moons. Solstice flings. Weddings. Funeral orgies. In agricultural societies the ingestion of psychotropic vegetables has always provided the sacramental energy for the gene-pool gatherings. Wines, fermented grains, brain-change vines, roots, leaves, flowers containing the precious neurotransmitters prepared and administered by alchemical shamans produced the "high," the venerable, sacred, precious transcendental state of chaotics, ecstasy, possession, revelation, trance—the mythic-genetic right-brain vision. The Holy Confusion.

You know what I'm talking about. What orgasm is to the body, this shuddering psychedelic experience is to the brain.

At these treasured high moments, we tribe members could escape the drab and activate our individual myths, our special inner talents, and we could communicate it to others who were navigating their own personal neurorealities. These intense communications, brain exchanges which Catholics call "Holy Communion," we call the Holy Confusion.

At these ceremonies we tribe members could express our visions in communal theatre. This one becomes a jokester. Another sings. Another dances. Suddenly tricksters, artists, mimes take the center stage to act out the emotions and the identifying themes that held the tribe together.

The sponsors of the tribal show time?

The clique that ran the tribe. The priests and the chieftains. The lovable grey beards, the stern, traditional Old Ones. The studio heads. Those responsible for holding the tribe together for their own fame and profit.

The task of luring the populace to listen to the sponsors' messages in the feudal–industrial ages was delegated to a special caste called: The talent. The painters. The directors. The shaman. The architects. The entertainers. The minstrels. The storytellers. Their function and duty in the tribal economy was to calm the fears of Chaos with delightful comforting fantasies, titillating ceremonies, and romantic dramas.

We could let our swollen, tumescent eyeballs pop wide open and our turgid, drooling peasant tongues dangle as we watched the belly dancers and muscular dudes wiggle, writhe, slither, jiggle, and quiver until our loins ached. When we were back in the dark cave/hut in fireplace flicker, our plain, glamourless, loyal mates suddenly turned into the Whores of Babylon! Krishnas with glowing hard-ons! Talk about pornography inciting desire!

The perennial problem with the directors and the talent is this. To attract and dazzle villagers to listen to the commercials, they had to allow the public to vicariously experience this steamy, smoking-hot, exciting, naughty stuff that was absolutely taboo for the people, but which could be acted out in morality plays, racy festival performances, sculptures of naked bodies. And here's where we talents come in.

To keep the folks tuning in, the sponsors needed us performers. The sexy musicians, well-endowed dancers, clowns, raunchy comedians telling risqué stories about adulteries and risky new sexual adventures, poets, X-rated storytellers, comics, mimes. It was the talent who per-

TURN ON
TUNE IN
BOOT UP

formed the safety-valve function, who gave the populace a fantasy taste of the rich and forbidden fruits.

Talents were selected for beauty, erotic charm, powerful emotion. We were expected to go too far, to push the envelope of taboo, to test the limits of good taste. Show our tits and asses. Act out wild copulatory sex dances. Scandalize. And we were required to suffer the consequences. We were banned. Blacklisted. Sold down the river. Forced into harlotry. Fired from Harvard. Forever shamed and exposed in the local version of the perennial *National Enquirer*. Denounced as devils from the pulpits of the orthodox preachers, and denounced as C.I.A. agents by Marxists.

The sponsors of the tribal show, the priests and the chiefs, were kept busy not only producing the event, but also watching and censoring and punishing to make sure that nothing got too far out of hand, or upset the sponsors.

And, of course, the gene-pool commercials were ever-present. We could never forget who owned the drums and the rattles and the spears and the shamanic talent, and the temples: The patrons who paid for the tribal show.

THANK GOD FOR FEUDALISM

Marshall McLuhan spoke wisely. "Change the media and you change the culture." Literacy upgraded the æsthetic level and the efficiency of the entertainment packaging. The growth of cities and nations by the 1st Century B.C. provided big budgets and big crews to distribute continual messages from the gene-pool sponsors.

The people, the average folk, the six-pack-Joe families, were now called plebes or serfs or peasants. Their role in the feudal-information economy was not that different from that of their tribal ancestors. The poor people are always seen as primitive because they are forced to live in tribal neighbourhoods, ghettos, in huts, shacks, windowless rooms, slum pads, shabby urban caves where the signal rate was limited to immediate biological data exchanges from first breath to death.

The cultural and political messages from the sponsors of the feudal age were popularized and disseminated in spectacular public broadcasts. The church in the central plaza was large, ornate, decorative, loaded with statues and paintings of truly inspired æsthetic genius. The mediæval crime-time show, both Christian and Islamic, was performed by miraculously gifted talent. The tiled mysteries of the Alhambra and the ceilings of the Vatican Chapel still inspire the breathless reflex reaction, "Wow! Praise the Lord for sponsoring this great show!"

Every day the commercial logos and mottos of the feudal culture were repeated. The muezzin's call, the church bell's sonorous clang, the chanting of the monks, the colourful garb of the priests and mullahs. Stained glass!

No wonder these feudal religions—fundamentalist, fanatic, furious, passionate, paranoid—swept the Hooper ratings! The fellaheen could leave their scruffy hovels and walk through cathedrals with golden ceilings stretching to the sky, while candles flickered on the statues of the Prophet. A panoramic mosque-church scene throbbing with colour, pomp, grandeur, wealth, and melodrama pouring into virginal eyeballs.

The palaces of the secular rulers, the kings and dukes, were equally stunning, and much more sexy. The priests may have preached sexual abstinence, but the nobles fucked anyone they wanted to and celebrated sexual beauty in the paintings they commissioned. The walls of the palaces glowed with flamboyant celebrations of naked wantonness. Greek goddesses with pink, swollen thighs and acres of soft, silky flesh sprawled on clouds of filmy desire, enticing their male counterparts to enjoy their favors.

You could stand humbly with cap in hand and cheer the swells dressed up in opulent lace and leather riding by in gold-decorated carriages. You loved the changing of the Guard, probably not realizing that the troops were there to protect the sponsors of the show from you, the people.

The shack you live in may be dreary, but ankle downtown to catch the big, spectacular God–King show.

 The same McLuhan trends continued in the industrial age. As usual, the populace was housed in small, dark rooms, but now that big is better, the rooms were stacked in enormous slum buildings.

The factory culture created the highest form of intelligent life on this planet, up until now: the mass-market consumer.

The sponsors of the factory economy didn't really plan to create an insatiable consumer class that would eventually overwhelm it with acquisitive desire. Quite the contrary. The sponsors of the industrial culture were those who belonged to the one class that easily survived the fall of feudalism: the engineer-managers. They were sometimes called Masons. They were white, anti-papist, Northern European mechanics, efficient and rational, with a scary hive mentality totally loyal to The Order. Stern puritans. They worked so hard, postponed so much pleasure, and got obsessed with engineering so efficiently that they ended up flooding the world with an unstoppable cascade of highly appealing products. Labor-saving devices. Better medicines to save lives. Better guns to snuff lives. Books. Radios. Televisions.

This cornucopian assembly line of everything that a tribal hunter or a feudal serf or a Holy Roman Emperor could possibly have lusted for required endless rotating armies of indefatigably industrious consumers willing to lift items from shelves, haul grocery carts, unpack bags, store in refrigerators, kick tires, read manuals of instruction, turn keys, drive away, and then religiously repair, until death, the appliances that rolled like an endless river of metal-rubber-plastic down Interstate 101 to the shopping malls and into our factory-made homes.

How can the sponsors keep the

people motivated to perform the onerous tasks of producing and consuming at a feverish pace? The same old way—by putting on a show and promising them a glimpse of the high life. But this time, in the mercantile culture, they can sell 'em tickets.

The cultural celebrations that got people out of the house in the industrial society were no longer religious-political ceremonies. They occurred in commercial venues. Public invited. Tickets at box office or street corner. Every community boasted a theatre, concert hall, art gallery, opera house, burlesque palace, vaudeville show, sports stadium, bullring. Et cetera. These entertainment factories were built to resemble the royal structures of the feudal age. Theatres were called the "Palace" and the "Majestic" and the "Royal."

In these plastic-fantastic whore-house temples, workers could escape the routine, drab signalry of the workday and lose themselves in lascivious, wet-dream, hypnotic states of erotic pleasure, tantalizing, carnal carnivals designed and produced by us, the shamanic profession, the counterculture entertainers.

The psycho-economics were clear-cut. The consumers wanted the show to last as long as possible, anything to get out of the hovel. More was better. The show-biz trick was to stretch out the scenes of the opera, stage play, concert as long as possible. Give 'em their money's worth.

FILMS PRESENT ELECTRIC REALITIES

 By the mid-20th Century, at the peak of the mechanical age, the relentless engineering search for labor-saving devices and mass distribution naturally extended to the entertainment industry. The new McLuhan media was electricity. Stage plays could be filmed, the films duplicated and sent to hundreds of theatres.

No wonder these feudal religions— fundamentalist, fanatic, furious, passionate, paranoid— swept the Hooper ratings! The fellaheen could leave their scruffy hovels and walk through cathedrals with golden ceilings stretching to the sky, while candles flickered on the statues of the Prophet. A panoramic mosque-church scene throbbing with colour, pomp, grandeur, wealth, and melodrama pouring into virginal eyeballs.

The effect was astounding. Farmer Brown could sit in the village theatre and there in front of him, thirty-feet high, was the face of Clara Bow, her bulging red lips glistening with moisture, her eyes beaming nymphomaniac invitation! Farmer Brown had never in his wildest fantasies dreamed of this sultry thang! Meanwhile, Mrs. Brown is breathing hard and leaking her precious bodily juices watching Rudolf Valentino licking his full lips with his sensual tongue!

THE INDUSTRIAL MIND WANTS BIG SERVINGS OF MECHANICALLY PRODUCED STIMULATION

Movies swept the world. The film industry naturally followed the commandment of the mechanical age—big is better. Cloned quantity is better. Feature films were made in two convenient sizes. The epic was very long. But the industry was run by clothing merchants from New York who knew how to sell, cut-rate, two pants to a suit. So most films were manufactured in the half-size "double-bill." If and when the people left their homes and traveled downtown to the theatre, they expected a good three or four hours of escape.

Over the last twenty-five thousand years, until yesterday, the sponsors had come and gone, and the technologies had improved from oral–gestural to hand–tool to mechanical–electric. But the goals, principles, and venues of human motivation and human communication hadn't really changed much, and the economics hadn't changed. Big was always better.

The talent in tribal, feudal, and industrial cultures had two "charm" tasks. The first, and most important, was to entice, beg, grovel, seduce, use our sexual wiles, go down on our knees to the sponsors to get the deal. The second job was to please the customers. This was easier, because the customers basically were begging to get titillated, turned on, aroused. They had paid money to adore the talent.

The sponsors, of course, got their

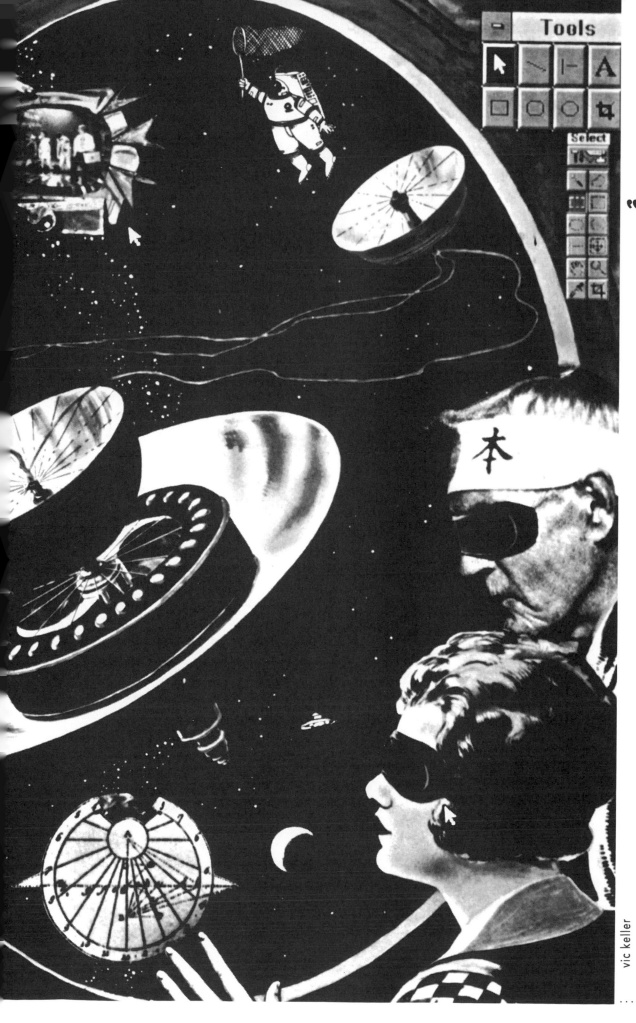

"They'll never get me up in one of those," says the caterpillar to the butterfly.

vic keller

kicks from fucking over everyone, especially the glamourous talent. When and if the entertainers became superstars, they, naturally, got off their knees, wiped off their mouths, and proceeded to take exquisite revenge on the sleazy producers, the grubby studio heads, the rodent-like agency executives, the greedy managers, and the assorted lawyer thieves with briefcases and fax machines who had formerly abused us.

"There's no business like show business!" As they were fond of saying.

INDIVIDUALS LEARN HOW TO CHANGE THE SCREENS

These ancient rituals, which endured through the tribal, feudal, industrial ages, amazingly enough, began to change dramatically in the last few years! Just before yesterday, around 1984, a combination of American creativity and Japanese precision suddenly mass-produced inexpensive, do-it-yourself home appliances for individuals to electronify, digitize, and transmit personal realities.

Digital communication translates the recording of any sound or photograph of any image into clusters of quanta or fuzzy clouds of off/on information. Any image digitized by an individual human can then be flashed on telephone lines around the world inexpensively at light speed.

BIGGER IS APPARENTLY NO LONGER BETTER

The basic elements of the youniverse, according to quantum-digital physics, can be understood as consisting of quanta of information, bits of compressed digital programs. These elements of pure (0/1) information contain incredibly detailed algorithms to program potential sequences for fifteen billion years—and still running. These information-jammed units have only one hardware-external function. All they do is flash off/on when the immediate environment triggers a complex array of "if-if-if-if . . . THEN!" algorithms.

Digital communication (i.e., the operation of the universe) involves massive arrays of these info-units, trillions of information pixels flashing to create the momentary hardware reality of one single molecule.

The Newtonian energy-matter equations of the industrial age (the 19th Century) defined a local-mechanical reality in which much bigger and more was very much better. You remember the catchphrases in the old Newtonian heavy-metal Dinosaur Marching Song? Force. Momentum. Mass. Energy. Work. Power. Thermodynamics.

In the information age we are coming to realize that in packaging digital data, much smaller is very much better.

The basic principle in light-speed communication is that so much more information is packed into so much smaller hardware units. For example, the 2-pound human brain is a digital organic computer that processes a hundred million times more information (r.p.m.) than the 200-pound body.

The almost invisible DNA code keeps programming and constructing improved organic computing appliances, i.e., generation after generation of better and more portable brains. A billion-year-old DNA megaprogram of invisible molecular size is much smarter than the shudderingly fragile, here-and-now brain!

And infinitely smaller. People are learning to deal with enormous stacks of digital-electronic information presented at light speeds. Telephone. Radio. Television. Computers. Compact discs. At home. In their "head" quarters. Electronic info pulled down from the sky and poured out of the portable stereophonic ghetto-blaster perched on shoulder, jacked into ear-balls as the body dances along the avenue. This "addiction" to electronic information has drastically expanded the reception scope and lessened the tar-pit attention span of the 19th Century.

THE CYBERNETIC BRAIN EXPECTS MORE DATA IN MUCH LESS TIME

 Folks in the mechanical age may be content to sit drinking tea and reading the London *Times* for two hours. But energetic smart people navigating a postindustrial brain move through an ocean of information, surfing data waves breaking at light speed and stereophonic CD (the current brand name here is Hypermedia or CD–I—compact disc–interactive).

This appetite for digital data, more and faster, can now be recognized as a species need. The brain needs electrons and psychoactive chemicals like the body needs oxygen. Just as body nutritionists list our daily requirements for vitamins, so will our brain-psyberneticians soon be listing our daily requirements for various classes of digital information.

By the year 2000, pure information will be cheaper than water and electricity. The average American home will be equipped to access trillions of bits of information per minute. The credit-card–size interpersonal computer will be able to scoop up any page from the Library of Congress, sift through the entire film library of MGM, sort through all the episodes of "I Love Lucy," and slice out (if it pleases you) paragraphs from the original Aramaic Bible.

On a typical Saturday way back in 1990, Los Angeles residents with a competitive itch could exercise the option to flick on seven major-league baseball games, nine college football contests, the Olympic games, two horse-racing tracks, etc.

By the year 2000, the poorest kid in the inner city will have a thumbnail-size chip (costing a dollar) with the storage and processing power of a billion transistors. He/she will also have an optic-fiber wall socket that will input a million times more signals than the current television set. Inexpensive virtual-reality suits and goggles will allow this youngster to interact with people all over the world in any environment he or she chooses to fabricate.

As George Gilder says, "The cultural limitations of television, tolerable when there was no alternative, are unendurable in the face of the new computer technologies now on the horizon—technologies in which the U.S. leads the world."

The home in the year 2000, thus equipped with inexpensive digital CD–I appliances, becomes our private television-film-sound studio that programs the digital universe we choose to inhabit, for as long as we want to inhabit it.

But is there not a danger of overload? The ability to scan and fish-net miniaturized, abridged, slippery bursts of essence-æsthetic information from the salty oceans of signals flooding the home becomes a basic survival skill in the 21st Century. Our bored brains love "overload." They can process more than a hundred million signals a second.

Of course, this acceleration and compression of information has already become state of the art in television. The aim of crime-time network television is to get people to watch commercials. A 30-second slot during the Super Bowl broadcast costs close to half a million dollars.

The advertising agencies were the first to pick up the handy knack of digital-miniaturization. They spurt dozens of erotic, shocking, eye-catching images into a half-minute info-slot convincing us that "the night belongs to Michelob." For that matter, we select our presidents and ruling bureaucrats on the basis of 30-second image clips, carefully edited by advertising experts.

BIGGER IS NO LONGER BETTER (EVEN IN MOVIES)

Slowly, reluctantly, the factory-based film industry is being forced to condense, speed up. Veteran, old-school movie directors don't want to do it. They are trapped in the antiquated industrial-age models of the opera and the "legitimate" stage play and the epic movie. And the prima-donna omnipotent director.

Before 1976, the bigger the movie the better. The long, leisurely, time-consuming film was the great epic. A director who came into the screening room with anything less than 2 hours (120 minutes or 7200 seconds) was considered a breezy lightweight.

Way back in 1966, before cable television, people loved long, slow films. They provided folks with a welcome escape from their info-impoverished homes. You went to the theatre to enter a world of technicoloured glamour and excitement that could not be experienced at convenience in the living room. In the theatre you could be Queen for a Night. The director, naturally enough, tried to stretch out the show as long as possible to postpone the customer's return to the home dimly lit by three black-and-white television networks.

MINIATURIZATION

By 1988, however, most American residences were equipped with cable inputs and VCRs and remote controls. Sitting like sultans in botanical torpor, we browse, graze, nibble as many multitone, flashing screen-flix as our warm little fingers can punch buttons.

We are no longer sensation-starved serfs pining in dark garrets, lusting, longing, craving, starved for the technicolour flash of soft curving flesh. On late-night television we can bathe in sexual innuendo. We can rent X-rated films of every erotic version and perversion ever dreamed. There is no longer that desperate appetite, that starved hunger, that yearning itch, that raw hankering for optical stimulation.

For this reason the long, slow, symphony-scored feature film has become a plodding line of 150 elephants trapped in the melodramatic swamp. Movies today are far too long. The information-age cyberperson simply will not sit for 150 minutes trapped in Cimino's wonderfully operatic mind or Coppola's epic intensities. For many of us, the best stuff we see on a movie screen are the trailers. A new art form is emerging—the production of 3-minute teasers about coming attractions. Electronic haikus! Most movies fail to live up to the trailers that hype them. The "high lights" of a smash-grab action flick can be fascinating for 3 minutes, but lethally boring for 2 hours. Indeed, most of the new breed of movie directors like Tony Scott,

This appetite for digital data, more and faster, can now be recognized as a species need. The brain needs electrons and psychoactive chemicals like the body needs oxygen. Just as body nutritionists list our daily requirements for vitamins, so will our brain-psyberneticians soon be listing our daily requirements for various classes of digital information.

Ridley Scott, Nelson Lyon, and David Lynch have learned their craft by making commercials or MTV clips, from which have come the new communication rhythms.

Filmmakers are learning the lesson of quantum physics and digital neurology: much more data in much smaller packages. It turns out that the brain likes to have digital signals jamming the synapses.

CUSTOM-SIZED MOVIES

In response to this obvious fact, some innovative filmmakers are beginning to experiment with customized movies, sized for length. The idea is this. If you go to a good restaurant, you don't want to sit trapped at a table for 150 minutes eating the same Italian dish. No matter how delicious. No matter how many Oscars the chef has won, most younger film buffs are not gonna sit still during a 2 1/2–hour spaghetti film by moody, self-absorbed auteur-directors from the operatic traditions.

But if long, slow flicks are what you want, if you really prefer to absorb electronic information like a python ingests a pig, if you want to stuff yourself and slowly digest a 150-minute film—why, no prob-

lem! You arrive at the cineplex and you make your menu selection when you buy your ticket. If you want the super-giant 150-minute version of *Last Temptation of Christ* you pay $15, visit the rest room, pack a lunch, cancel a few meetings, walk to the long-distance room, settle in, and let Scorcese leisurely paddle you down his cerebral canals. As a television person, your attention appetite at the visual banquet table probably gets satiated after an hour. So you'll tend to select the regular-size epic: *Christ*, $5 for 50 minutes.

But cyberpilots and brain jocks, with an eternity of digitized info-worlds at fingertip, tend to go for the nouvelle cuisine, gourmet buffet. You pay $5 and watch five 10-minute "best-of," haiku compressions of five films. Five "high lights" essence-teasers. Tastes great! Less filling!

If you are really taken by one of these specialite de maison and want more, you either go to the box office for a ticket or you stick your credit card in the dispenser cabinet, dial your choice, and out pops a custom-sized rental video to take home and scan at your convenience.

............................DO-IT-YOURSELF CYBERWEAR OFFERS PERSONAL ELECTRONIC REALITIES

So far you have been a busy consumer with many passive selective options.

But, suppose you want to move into the active mode? Change the film? Script and direct your own version? Put your personal spin on the great director's viewpoint? Heresy!

Suppose, for example, that you're a 14-year-old African or Asian girl and you dislike the movie *Rambo*, which cost $40 million, minimum, to make. You rent the video for $1 and scan it. Then you select the most offensive section. Maybe the one where Sly Stallone comes crashing through the jungle into the native village, naked to the waist, brandishing a machine gun with which he kills several hundred Asian men, women, and children.

To present your version, you digitize this 30-second scene, copy it into your $100 Nin-Sega-Mac computer, and use the

Director software program to re-edit. You digitize the torso of a stupid-looking gorilla, you scan a wilted celery stalk or the limp penis of an elephant, you loop in the voice of Minnie Mouse in the helium mode screaming the Stallone line: "You gonna let us win this time?"

You paste your version into the rented tape, pop it back in the box, and return it to the video store. The next person renting *Rambo* will be in for a laugh and a half! Within weeks this sort of viral contagion of individual choice could sweep your town.

In the cybernetic age now dawning, "Digital Power to the People" provides everyone the inexpensive option to cast, script, direct, produce, and distribute his or her own movie. Custom-made, tailorized, in the convenient sizes—mammoth, giant, regular, and byte-sized mini.

I.3. IMAGINEERING

I am viewing a videotape filmed by cyberspace researchers at Autodesk, a Sausalito computer-software company.

On the screen, a woman wearing tennis shorts leans ahead expecting a serve. On her head she wears a cap woven with thin wires. Her eyes are covered by opaque goggles. In her hand she holds a metal tennis racquet with no strings.

She dashes to her left and swings furiously at the empty air.

"Oh no!" she groans in disappointment. "Too low!"

She crouches again in readiness then runs forward, leaps up, slams a vicious volley at the empty air and shouts in triumph.

The videotape then changes point of view. Now I am seeing what the player sees. I am in the court. The ball hits the wall and bounces back to my left. My racquet smashes the ball in a low-angle winning shot.

This woman is playing virtual racquet ball. Her goggles are two small computer screens showing the digitized three-dimensional picture of a racquet-ball court. She is in the court. As she moves her head—left, right, up—orientation-direction sensors in her cap show her the left wall, the right wall, the ceiling. The movement of the ball is calculated to reflect "real-life" gravity and spin.

I am experiencing the current big trend in electronics. It is called artificial reality or virtual reality or electronic reality. Some literary computer folks call it platonic reality, in honor of the Socratic philosopher who described a universe of idealized or imagined forms more than two thousand years ago. Cynics call it virtual banality.

We no longer need to press our addicted optical nostrils to the television screen like grateful amoebas. Now, we can don cybersuits, clip on cybergoggles, and move around in the electronic reality on the other side of the screen. Working, playing, creating, exploring with basic particles of reality—electrons.

This technology was first developed by NASA. The idea was that technicians in Houston could use their gloves to direct robots on the moon. Architects and engineers are experimenting with an Autodesk device to walk around in the electronic projections of the buildings they are designing. Doctors can travel down arteries and veins, observing and manipulating instruments.

Does this sound too Star Trekky to be for real? Well, it's already happening. Way back at Christmas 1990 six hundred thousand American kids equipped with Nintendo power gloves were sticking their hands through the Alice Window moving ninja warriors around.

The implications of this electronic technology for work and leisure and interpersonal intimacy are staggering.

For example, within ten years many of us will not have to "go" to work. We will get up in the morning, shower, dress in our cyberwear suits, and "beam" our brains to work. No more will we have to fight traffic in our air-polluting 300-horsepower cars, hunt for parking spaces, take the elevator to our offices. No more flying, strapped in our seats in a monstrous toxic-waste–producing air-polluting jet-propelled sky-dinosaur, jammed with sneezing, coughing sardines, fighting jet lag to attend conferences and meetings.

Tomorrow our brains will soar on the wings of electrons into the offices of friends in Tokyo, then beam at light speed to a restaurant in Paris for a flirtatious lunch, pay a quick, ten-minute visit to our folks in Seattle—all without physically leaving our living rooms. In three hours of electronic, global house calls we can accomplish what would have taken three days or three weeks of lugging our brain-carrying bodies like slabs of inert flesh.

This is the information age, and the generator-producers of information are our delightful, surprise-packed brains. Just as the enormously powerful machines of the industrial age moved our bodies around, so, tomorrow, will our cybernetic appliances zoom our brains around the world at light speed.

We won't travel to play. We press two buttons and we are standing on the tee of the first hole at Pebble Beach. There to join us is sister Anita (who is actually standing on the lawn of her house in

ANDY FRITH

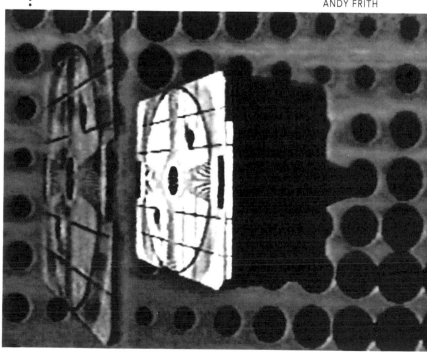

Atlanta) and our dearest, funniest, wonderful friend Joi, whom we have never met in the flesh (and who is actually standing in his backyard in Osaka). Each of us in turn "hits" the platonic golf ball and we watch them soar down the fairway. After finishing the first hole, we can dial-beam to Anita's patio to admire her garden, zap over to the tee of the second hole at St. Andrew's, then zoom to the Louvre to look at that Cezanne painting Joi was talking about.

Within ten years, most of us Americans will be spending half our waking hours zapping around in electronic environments with our friends. Any spot in the world we can think of can be dialed up on our screens with our friends. Any landscape, surrounding, setting, habitat we can think of or imagine can be quickly fabricated on our screens with our friends.

Some thoughtful critics are concerned by the prospect of human beings spending so much time trapped like zombies in the inorganic, plastic-fantastic electronic world. They fear that this will lead to a depersonalization, a dehumanization, a robotization of human nature, a race of screen-addicted nerds. This understandable apprehension is grounded in the horrid fact that today the average American spends around six hours each day passively reclining in front of the boob tube, and three hours a day peering docilely into Big Brother's computer screens.

The optimistic, human scenario for the future involves three common-sense steps:

1. **Cure the current apathetic, torpid television addiction,**

2. End the monopoly of top-down, spud-farm, mass-media centralized television, and

3. Empower individuals to actively communicate, perform, create electronic realities.

How? By means of inexpensive computer clothing.

Another example? A married couple, Tom and Jane, are walking down the Malibu beach. In material form, you understand. Real foot-massaging sand. Real skin-tanning sunshine blue sky. On loving impulse, they decide to spend a funny, loving minute or two with their daughter, Annie, who is in Boulder. They flip down their lens-goggles that look like sunglasses. Jane punches a few numbers on her stylish, designer wristwatch. Tom turns on the one-pound Walkman receiver-transmitter. In Boulder, Annie accepts their "visit" and dials them to a prefabricated pix-scene of her patio. She is smiling in welcome. She is actually in her living room, but electronically she is in her electronic patio. They see exactly what they would see if they were there. When they turn their heads, they see Annie's husband Joe walking out waving. He points out the roses that have just bloomed in the garden. Remember, at the same time Tom and Jane are "really" walking down the Malibu beach. They can look over the goggles and watch two kids in bathing suits chasing a dog.

The four people sharing the "patio" reality decide they want to be joined by sister Sue, in Toronto. They dial her and she beams over to the "patio" in Colorado. Sue wants to show them her new dress; so the gang beams up to Sue's living room.

It is logical for you, at this point, to wonder about the cost of this transcontinental home movie-making. Is this not another expensive toy for affluent yuppies playing while the rest of the world starves?

Happily, the answer is "no." The equipment used by this family costs less than a standard 1990 television set, that pathetic junk-food spud-box with no power to store or process electronic information. Designing and digitizing and communicating the electronic realities costs less than a phone call. In ten years fiber-optic wires will receive-transmit more information than all the clumsy air-wave broadcasting networks. A thumbnail-size brain-chip holding a billion transistors will allow us to store and process millions of three-dimensional signals per minute. Intense chaotics waiting to be re-created.

What will we possibly do with these inexpensive extensions of our brains? The answer is so down-to-earth human. We shall use these wizard powers to communicate with each other at unimaginable levels of clarity, richness, and intimacy. Reality designing is a team sport.

To help us imagine one dimension of the communication possibilities, let us consider the erotic interaction. Cyril Connolly once wrote, "Complete physical union between two people is the rarest sensation which life can provide—and yet not quite real, for it stops when the telephone rings."

Connolly's comment is useful because he distinguishes between "physical" communication, bodies rubbing, and neurological signals—words and thoughts transmitted electrically. The solution to his problem is simple. Electronic appliances are beautifully cooperative. (Hey, Cyril, if you don't want to be disturbed, just turn the gadget off when you head for the sack, and then turn it back on when you wish to.)

But let us examine a more profound implication. Connolly refers to "complete physical union" as "the rarest sensation which life can provide." Is he thereby denigrating the "union of minds and brains"? The interplay of empathy, wit, fantasy, dream, whimsy, imagination? Is he scorning "platonic love"? Is he implying that sex

> Intense chaotics waiting to be re-created . . . with our friends. Reality designing is a team sport.

should be mindless genital acrobatics? A grim, single-minded coupling that can be disturbed by the platonic rapture of metaphysical sex? Or a phone call?

Here is a typical episode of erotic play that could happen the day after tomorrow. The two lovers, Terry and Jerry, are performing bodily intercourse beautifully with elegance and sensual skill, etc. They are also wearing platonic lenses. At one point Jerry touches her/his watch, and suddenly they are bodysurfing twelve-foot rainbow waves that are timed to their physical erotic moves. Sounds of liquid magnificence flood their ears. Terry giggles and touches her/his watch, and the waves spiral into a tunnel vortex down which they spin and tumble. They intercreate reality dances. Terry is a seething volcano over whom Jerry soars as a fearless eagle, while birds sing and the Earth softly breathes.

Plato, it turns out, was magnificently on beam. He said that the material, physical expressions are pale, crude distortions of the idea forms that are fabricated by the mind, the brain, the "soul." We are talking about learning how to operate our minds, our brains, our souls. And learning the rudiments of mind-fucking, silky body juicy fucking, and . . . brain-soul fucking.

In fact, most physical sex, even the most "complete unions,"

We are talking about learning how to operate our minds, our brains, our souls. And learning the rudiments of mind-fucking, silky body juicy fucking, and . . . brain-soul fucking.

is no more than graceful motions unless enriched by brain-fucking imagination. And here is the charming enigma, the paradoxical truth that dares not show its face. Usually, even in the deepest fusions, neither partner really knows what is flashing through that delightful, adorable mind of the other.

In the future the wearing of cyberclothing will be as conventional as the wearing of body-covering clothing. To appear without your platonic gear would be like showing up in public stark naked. A new global language of virtual-signals, icons, 3-D pixels will be the lingua franca of our species. Instead of using words, we shall communicate in self-edited movie clips selected from the chaotic jungles of images stored on our wrists.

The local vocal dialects will remain, of course, for intimate communication. Nothing from our rich, glorious past will be eliminated. When we extend our minds and empower our brains, we shall not abandon our bodies, nor our machines, nor our tender, secret love whispers.

We will drive cars, as we now ride horses, for pleasure. We will develop exquisite bodily expressions, not to work like efficient robots, but to perform acts of grace.

The main function of the human being in the 21st Century is "imagineering" and electronic-reality fabrication; to learn how to express, communicate, and share the wonders of our brains with others. ◉

II. CYBERNETICS: CHAOS ENGINEERING

II.1.
CONVERSATION WITH
WILLIAM GIBSON

Timothy Leary: If you could put *Neuromancer* into one sentence, how would you describe it?

William Gibson: What's most important to me is that it's about the present. It's not really about an imagined future. It's a way of trying to come to terms with the awe and terror inspired in me by the world in which we live. I'm anxious to know what they'll make of it in Japan. Oh, God—I'm starting to feel like Edgar Rice Burroughs or something. I mean, how did Edgar Rice Burroughs finally come to feel about Tarzan in his own heart, you know? He got real tired of it. Wound up living in Tarzana, California.

TL: You'll end up living in a space colony called *Neuromancer.*

WG: That would be okay. I don't think we're going to have this kind of future. I think this book is so much *nicer* than what seems to be happening. I mean, this would be a cool place to *visit.* I wouldn't mind going there.

TL: Where?

WG: To the Sprawl, to that future.

TL: Going up the well?

WG: Yeah. Go up the well and all of that. A lot of people think that *Neuromancer* is a bleak book, but I think it's optimistic.

TL: I do, too.

WG: I think the future is actually gonna be more *boring.* I think some kind of Falwellian future would probably be my idea of the worst thing that could happen.

TL: Yeah. That was a wonderful scene where you have those Christians who were gonna mug those girls in the subway.

WG: It's not clear whether they're going to *mug* them or just try to force some *horrible pamphlet* on them or something. Personally, I have a real phobia about guys like that coming up to me on the street . . .

TL: That's a powerful scene! And you describe the girls as like hoofed animals wearing high heels.

WG: Yeah. The office girls of the Sprawl.

TL: Yeah, and they're wearing vaginas, and—Oh, God! That's a powerful scene.

WG: I like the idea of that subway. That's the state-of-the-art subway. It goes from Atlanta to Boston, *real fast.*

TL: You've created a world.

WG: What you're getting when you read that book—the impression is very complicated, but it's all actually one molecule thick. Some of it is still pretty much of a mystery to me. You know, the United States is never mentioned in the book. And there's some question as to whether the United States exists as a political entity or if, in fact, it's been Balkanized in some weird way. That's kind of a favorite idea of mine, that the world should be chopped up into smaller . . .

TL: Me too, boy.

WG: West-coast separatism and stuff. In *Count Zero*, I mention what's happening in California a little bit. One of the characters has a girlfriend who lives in a pontoon city that's tethered off Redondo. Kind of like a hallucinated . . . it's the Sprawl goes Sausalito—the Sprawl but mellower.

At the end of *Neuromancer*, the entire Matrix is sentient. It has, in some ways, one will. And, as it tells Case, kind of matter-of-factly, it's found another of its kind on Alpha Centuri or somewhere; so it's got something to talk to. *Count Zero* starts seven years later, and like Yeats's poem about how the center wouldn't hold, this sort of God-consciousness is now fragmented. It hasn't been able to keep it together. So the voodoo cultists in the Sprawl, who believe that they have contacted the voodoo pantheon through the Matrix, are in fact dealing with these fragmented elements of this God tiring. And the fragments are much more dæmonic and more human,

Case could be one of Burroughs's wild boys . . . in a way. I'm deeply influenced by Burroughs. . . . he found 'fifties science fiction and used it like a rusty can opener on society's jugular.

reflecting cultural expectations.

Anyway, I've got to do a different kind of book now, because I'm already getting some reviews saying, "Well, this is good, but it's more of the same stuff." I'm desperate to avoid that.

TL: Frank Herbert, who was a lovely guy, wrote a book that's entirely different from *Dune*. It's about humans who became insects up in Portland. Did you ever read it? It's a nice change. In some ways, I like that book as much as *Dune*. He got into an entirely different situation.

WG: Well, he *was* trapped! That's something I'm very worried about. I get flashes of "I don't want to be Frank Herbert." Because even as wealthy and as nice a guy as he was, I don't think he was happy with what had happened to him creatively. He did get trapped. It's different for somebody like Douglas Adams, where I think that the whole thing started off as such a goof for him that it was just a stroke of good luck that he built on. But Herbert was very serious, at a certain point. And then, gradually, he wound up having to do *more of the same*, because, I mean, how can you turn people down when something like that gets enough momentum?

TL: Douglas Adams told me that the three books were one book, and the publisher said to split them up into three. He made a million dollars on each one of them. And they're nice. It's a nice tour.

WG: Yeah. They're funny.

TL: These big books . . .

WG: I can't go for that.

TL: I'm glad about that. Norman Spinrad . . . by the way—I love Norman. But I have a terrible problem with him. He makes them too big. Did you read *Child of Fortune*?

WG: It was too big for me.

TL: Yeah. If he had divided it down the center. If he could only cut it in half.

WG: He wrote a book called *The Iron Dream*. It's a science-fiction novel by Adolf Hitler, in an alternate world where Hitler became a science-fiction writer. It's a critique of the innately fascist element in a lot of traditional science fiction. Very funny. For me, given the data in the books, the keys to Case's personality are the estrangement from his body, the meat, which it seems to me, he does overcome. People have criticized *Neuromancer* for not bringing Case to some kind of transcendent experience. But, in fact, I think he does have it. He has it within the construct of the beach, and he has it when he has his orgasm. There's a long paragraph there where he accepts the meat as being this infinite and complex thing. In some ways, he's more human after that.

TL: In some ways he reminds me of some of Burroughs's characters.

WG: *(Equivocally)* Yeah. Case could be one of Burroughs's wild boys . . . in a way. I'm deeply influenced by Burroughs. I always tell everybody that there's a very strong influence there. I didn't think I'd be able to put that over on the American science-fiction people, because they either don't know who Burroughs is or they're immediately hostile . . . he found 'fifties science fiction and used it like a rusty can opener on society's jugular. They never understood. But I was like 15 when I read *The Naked Lunch* and it sorta splattered my head all over the walls. And I have my megalomaniac fantasy of some little kid in Indiana picking up *Neuromancer* and pow!

TL: Well, that happens, dude. Don't worry. There's five hundred thousand copies already.

WG: I had to teach myself not to write too much like Burroughs. He was that kind of influence. I had to weed some of that Burroughsian stuff out of it. In an interview in London, in one of my rare lucid moments, I told this guy that the difference between what Burroughs did and what I

did is that Burroughs would just glue the stuff down on the page but I airbrushed it all.

TL: Burroughs and I are close friends. We've been through a lot together. I went to Tangier in 1961. I was in a hotel bar and Burroughs walks in with these two beautiful English boys. I started telling him about these new drugs and, of course, he knew much more about drugs than anyone in the world! I was just this childish Harvard professor doing my big research project on drugs. And Burroughs is saying, "Oh, shit. Here they come. Boy Scouts. And they're gonna save the world with drugs. Yeah, sure." We brought him back to Harvard. He came to the prison project and all. I got to know him very well. He couldn't stand us. We were much too goody-goody. It's

BRUMMBAER

implied that the crowd that Case hung out with is a drug crowd.

WG: Yeah. This seems to be a world where everybody is pretty much stoned most of the time.

TL: That first chapter . . . whew!

WG: I had to go over and over that. I must have rewritten it a hundred and fifty times.

TL: I'll bet. It's like a symphony or a fugue. This is the fifth line in the book: "It's like my body developed this massive drug deficiency. It was a Sprawl voice and a Sprawl joke." *(Laughs)* Of course, his life was jacking in.

WG: Oh yeah. He just lives for . . .

TL: Cyberspace.

WG: Yeah. For cyberspace.

TL: Would you describe cyberspace as the matrix of all the hallucinations?

WG: Yeah, it's a *consensual* hallucination that these people have created. It's like, with this equipment, you can agree to share the same hallucinations. In effect, they're creating a world. It's not really a place, it's not really space. It's notional space.

TL: See, we live in that space. We that are hooked up to *Neuromancer* are living in that consensual hallucination.

WG: I didn't think women would go for the Molly character very much. I've really been surprised at the number of women who have come up to me and said, "Molly's great. I really got off on her." I think America is ready for a female lead who

beats the shit out of everybody.

TL: Molly says, "You like to jack in. I've gotta tussle." That's a beautiful two-liner.

WG: I was originally gonna call this book *Jacked In.* The people at Ace said it sounded too much like "jacked off," but that was my first thought for a title. Molly's tougher than Case because Case is the viewpoint character, and I wanted an enigmatic character; so she's more shut off from me. It's the symbolism of the sunglasses. He never even finds out what colour her eyes are.

TL: And making love, she says . . .

WG: "No fingerprints." Yeah, she's a tough one for me to do, because that's some kind of image from my . . . She's a bushido figure. When she says she's street samurai, she means it quite literally. She has this code. And it may grow out of a sort of pathological personality, but it still is her code.

TL: What was that segment where she was like in hypnosis; so she didn't know what was going on?

WG: Oh, they use a sort of sensory cut-out, so that she isn't conscious when this stuff is happening, but her motor system was being run by a program. So, in effect, she became kind of a living sex-shop doll. Programmed. The people who write the program are in Berlin. She says, "They have some *nasty* shit there."

Actually, this starts in *Burning Chrome*. That's where it comes from. One of the key things in that story is when this guy realizes that his girlfriend is working in one of these places in order to buy herself an improved pair of artificial eyes. I described it a little more clearly in that story. The prostitutes aren't conscious. They don't remember. In *Burning Chrome*, the guy says the orgasms are like little silver flares right out at the edge of space, and that's the . . .

TL: That's the guy's orgasm, not hers. She's not even feeling it.

WG: Well, she can feel a little bit, maybe . . .

TL: What would you say about Riviera?

WG: Riviera is like some kind of terminal bag-person. He grows up in a radioactive pit, with cannibalism pretty much the only way to get along. It's like *Suddenly Last Summer*. Ever see that? Where the guy's ripped apart by the little Mexican children? Well, Riviera is like that, a feral child. He's smart, incredibly perverse. But all the stuff

WG: Yeah? Really? Well, I just try to reflect the world around me.

TL: I know. You're a mirror. Yes. How about Lucas Yonderboy?

WG: Lucas Yonderboy was my reaction to the spookier and more interesting side of punk. Kind of young and enigmatic. Cool to the point of inexplicability. And he's a member of the Panther Moderns. They're sorta like Marshall McLuhan's Revenge. Media

And I decided I didn't want to do it. I've said this to many people, so I should say it to you. Your book had the same effect on me as *Gravity's Rainbow*.

The way I read *Gravity's Rainbow* is pretty interesting. At one point, the American government was trying to get me to talk. They were putting incredible pressure on me. This FBI guy said if I didn't talk . . . "we'll put your name out at the federal prison with the jacket of a

I think America is ready for a female

that he does—the little projected hallucinations and things—are relatively low tech. He's just projecting holograms.

There's this amazing German surrealist sculptor named Hans Belmer who made a piece called "The Doll." He made a doll that was more his fetish object than a work of art, this totally idealized girlchild that could be taken apart and rearranged in an infinite number of ways. So I have Riviera call his piece "The Doll." Belmer's doll. Riviera also represents the fragmentation of the body. People see things like that, sometimes, out of the corners of their eyes.

TL: What about Armitage?

WG: He's a synthetic personality, a character utterly lacking *character*. As Molly says, "This guy doesn't do anything when he's alone." It's some kind of post-Vietnam state.

TL: I can see certain Gordon Liddy qualities in Armitage.

WG: Yeah, I saw a video of his *Miami Vice* performance without realizing it was Liddy. When I saw that, I thought of Armitage. This book's fraught with psychotics.

TL: (Laughing) You see, there are a few of us who think it's a very positive book in spite of that.

monsters. It's as though the worst street gang you ever ran into were, at the same time, intense conceptual artists. You never know *what* they're going to do.

TL: What recent book have you most enjoyed?

WG: Bruce Sterling is my favorite science-fiction writer. *Schismatrix* is the most visionary science-fiction novel of the last twenty years or so. Humanity evolves, mutates through different forms very quickly, using genetic engineering and biochemistry. It's a real mindfucker. When he first got it out and was getting the reviews back, he told me, "There are so many moving parts, people are scared to stick their heads in it." People will be mining that, ripping off ideas for the next thirty years.

TL: Like *Gravity's Rainbow*.

WG: Yeah. That's one of my personal favorites. Have you ever met Pynchon?

TL: Ohhhh . . . I had him tracked down and I could've. It was a deal where there was a *People* magazine reporter with an expense-paid thing. We were going to rent a car and pick up Ken Kesey. Pynchon was living up near Redding, Pennsylvania. We had him tracked there.

snitch." So I ended up in a prison called Sandstone. As soon as I got in there, there was a change of clothes and they said, "The warden wants to see you." So the warden said, "To protect you, we're going to put you here under a false name." And I said, "*Are* you crazy? Are you gonna put me on the main line with a fake name?" And he said "Yeah." I said, "What name are you going to give me?" He said, "Thrush." And you know what a thrush is? A songbird. So I said, "Uh-uh. In a prison filled with dopers, everybody's going to know that my name isn't Thrush. I refuse to do it." He says, "Okay. We'll have to put you in the hole." And I said "Do what you gotta do—but I want to be out there in my own name. I can handle any situation. I can deal with it. I've been in the worst fucking prisons and handled it so far. So I can handle it and you know it. So fucking put me out there!" And he said, "Sorry." He was very embarrassed because he knew.

He was a prison warden. His job wasn't to get people to talk or anything like that. He knew it was a federal-government thing. The reason they were trying to get me to talk was to protect the top FBI guys that had committed black-bag burglaries against the Weather

Underground; so they wanted me to testify in their defense. They actually went to trial, if you remember, and got convicted, and were pardoned by Carter.

Well, they put me in the worst lockup that I've ever been in, and I'd been in solitary confinement for over a year and a half. This was just a clean box with nothing but a mattress. The only contact I had with human beings was, five times a day, I could hear somebody with *Gravity's Rainbow.*

WG: It's got eight billion times more stuff in it than *Neuromancer* does. It's an *encyclopedic* novel.

TL: But there's a tremendous relationship, as you well know, between *Neuromancer* and Pynchon. Because Pynchon is into psychology. The shit he knows about! It's all about psychology. But you've taken the next step, because

Bruce said *(in laconic Southern drawl),* "beta-phenethylamine." It's in the book. Beta-P. Actually, some people have called me on how I spelled this in the book. I never checked it. So I may have misspelled the name of the *real* brain chemical. About a month after I finished the book, there was an article in *Esquire.* I think it was called, "The Chemistry of Desire." And they talked about beta-phenethylamine, which is structurally similar to amphetamine. And it's

lead who beats the shit out of everybody.

coming down the hall to open the "swine trough" and pass me my food. And I'd say, "Hey, can I have something to read?" And they'd say, "No." One of the guards was this black guy and, this one night, he came back. I could hear him walking—jingle, jingle, jingle—walking down the metal hall. He opens up the trough and says, "Here, man," and throws in a book. A new pocketbook. And it's dark, so I waited 'til dawn and picked it up. And it was *Gravity's Rainbow.*

WG: Perfect! Of all the books you could get, that'll last you a while.

TL: You should only read that book under those circumstances. It is not a book you could . . .

WG: It stopped my life cold for three months. My university career went to pot, I just sort of laid around and read this thing.

TL: What I did—first of all, I just read it. I read it all day until dark when they turned the lights out. I woke up the next morning and read it. For three days, I did nothing but read that book. Then I went back and I started annotating it. I did the same thing to yours. Yours is the only book I've done that with since. The film industry's never been able to do anything

you've done that whole thing to computers. You don't have any new drugs in *Neuromancer.*

WG: I've got the beta-phenethylamine. When that hits the street, watch out!

TL: That's the one that makes your teeth rattle the nerves.

WG: Yeah. That's actually a brain chemical. We all have a little bit, as we sit around the table. But you'd have to get it out of forty million people. Sort of like the Hunter Thompson story about adrenochrome. If you could eat somebody's pineal gland, or something . . .

TL: That's a very powerful drug experience that you describe, where he can feel it in his teeth.

WG: Yeah. I had a lot of fun writing that. *(Laughs)*

TL: I know you did. I appreciate the disciplined work that went into that!

WG: Beta-phenethylamine is the chemical that the brain manufactures; when you fall in love the level rises. I didn't know this when I wrote the book. I called Bruce Sterling in Texas, and I said, "This guy's been modified; so he can't do traditional stimulants. So, what can he get off on?" And

also present in chocolate. So there's some possibility . . .

TL: Ohhh! I'm a chocolate addict. Notice last night, how the waiter automatically brought me an extra plate during dessert? They know my weakness. Double-dose Tim.

WG: Japanese kids get high on big candy bars that are just sucrose and caffeine. They eat five or six of these things and go to concerts on this massive sucrose-and-caffeine high.

TL: One of the things that's wonderful about *Neuromancer* is that there is this glorious comradeship between Molly and Case. And he sings to her while she rubs her nipple and she's talking to him and telling him.

WG: How they gonna do that in the movie? There's no *Neuromancer Part II.*

TL: Case and Molly have children?

WG: *Son of Neuromancer.* People have children in *Count Zero,* which was a real breakthrough for me. I was trying to up the ante. I like *Count Zero* better. *Neuromancer,* for me, is like my adolescent book. It's my teenage book—the one I couldn't have written when I was a teenager. ◎

In the 1960s, Hermann Hesse was revered by college students and art rowdies as the voice of the decade. He was a megasage, bigger than Tolkien or Salinger, McLuhan or Bucky Fuller.

Hesse's mystical, utopian novels were read by millions. The popular, electrically amplified rock band Steppenwolf named themselves after Hesse's psyberdelic hero, Harry Haller, who smoked those "long, thin yellow . . . immeasurably enlivening and delightful" cigarettes, then zoomed around the Theatre of the Mind, ostensibly going where no fictional heroes had been before.

The movie *Steppenwolf* was financed by Peter Sprague, at that time the Egg King of Iran. I lost the male lead to Max Van Sydow. Rosemary's part was played by Dominique Sanda. But that story is filed in another data base.

Hesse's picaresque adventure, *The Journey to the East,* was a biggie too. It inspired armies of pilgrims (yours truly included) to hip-hike somewhere East of Suez, along the Hashish Trail to India. The goal of this Childlike Crusade? Enlightenment 101, an elective course.

Yes, it was that season for trendy Sufi mysticism, inner Hindu voyaging, breathless Buddhist searches for ultimate meaning. Poor Hesse, he seems out of place up here in the high-tech, cybercool, Sharp catalogue, M.B.A., upwardly mobile 1990s.

HERMANN HESSE: PROPHET OF THE COMPUTER AGE

But our patronizing pity for the washed-up Swiss sage may be premature. In the avant-garde frontiers of the computer culture, around Massachusetts Avenue in Cambridge, around Palo Alto, in the Carnegie–Mellon A.I. labs, in the back rooms of the computer-graphics labs in Southern California, a Hesse comeback seems to be

II.2. ARTIFICIAL INTELLIGENCE

happening. This revival, however, is not connected with Hermann's mystical, eastern writings. It's based on his last, and least-understood work, *Magister Ludi, or The Glass Bead Game.*

This book, which earned Hesse the expense-paid brain ride to Stockholm, is positioned a few centuries in the future, when human intelligence is enhanced and human culture elevated by a device for thought-processing called the glass-bead game.

Up here in the Electronic Nineties we can appreciate what Hesse did at the very pinnacle (1931–42) of the smoke-stack mechanical age. He forecast with astonishing accuracy a certain postindustrial device for converting thoughts to digital elements and processing them. No doubt about it, the sage of the hippies was anticipating an electronic mind-appliance that would not appear on the consumer market until 1976.

I refer, of course, to that Fruit from the Tree of Knowledge called the Apple computer.

THE ALDOUS HUXLEY–HERMANN HESSE FUGUE

I first heard of Hermann Hesse from Aldous Huxley. In the fall of 1960, Huxley was Carnegie Visiting Professor at MIT. His assignment: to give a series of seven lectures on the subject, "What a Piece of Work Is Man." A couple thousand people attended each lecture. Aldous spent most of his off-duty hours hanging around the Harvard Psychedelic Drug Research project coaching us beginners in the history of mysticism and the ceremonial care and handling of LSD, which he sometimes called "gratuitous grace."

Huxley was reading Hesse that fall and talked a lot about Hermann's theory of the three stages of human development.

1. The tribal sense of tropical-blissful unity,

2. The horrid polarities of the feudal-industrial societies, good–evil, male–female, Christian–Moslem, etc., and

3. The revelatory rediscovery of The Oneness of It All.

No question about it, Hegel's three authoritarian thumbprints (thesis–antithesis–synthesis) were smudged all over the construct, but Hesse and Huxley didn't seem to worry about it; so why should we untutored Harvard psychologists?

We all dutifully set to work reading Hesse.

Huxley claimed that his own spiritual-intellectual development in England followed the developmental lifeline of Hesse in

of Calw, Germany, the son of Protestant missionaries. His home background and education, like Huxley's, were intellectual, classical, idealistic. His life exemplified change and metamorphosis. If we accept Theodore Ziolkowski's academic perception, "Hesse's literary career parallels the development of modern literature from a *fin de siècle* æstheticism through expressionism to a contemporary sense of human commitment."

HESSE'S PROPHETIC GLASS BEAD GAME

Germany. Aldous delighted in weaving together themes from his life that paralleled Hesse's.

PARODIES OF PARADISE

Huxley's last book, *Island*, presents an atypical, tropical utopia in which meditation, gestalt therapy, and psychedelic ceremonies create a society of Buddhist serenity.

I spent the afternoon of November 20, 1963, at Huxley's bedside, listening carefully as the dying philosopher spoke in a soft voice about many things. He fashioned a pleasant little literary fugue as he talked about three books he called "parodies of paradise": his own *Island*, Orwell's *1984*, and Hesse's *Glass Bead Game*.

Aldous told me with a gentle chuckle that Big Brother, the beloved dictator of Orwell's nightmare society, was based on Winston Churchill. "Remember Big Brother's spell-binding rhetoric about the blood, sweat, and fears requisitioned from everyone to defeat Eurasia? The hate sessions? Priceless satire. And the hero's name is Winston Smith."

Aldous was, at that moment in time, fascinated by the *Tibetan Book of the Dying*, which I had just translated from Victorian English into American. The manuscript, which was later published as *The Psychedelic Experience*, was used by Laura Huxley to guide her husband's psychedelic passing.

Huxley spoke wryly of the dismal conclusions of *Island*, *The Glass Bead Game*, and Orwell's classic. His own idealistic island society was crushed by industrial powers seeking oil. Hesse's utopian Castalia was doomed because it was out of touch with human realities. Then the crushing of love by the power structure in *1984*. Unhappy endings. I timidly asked him if he was passing on a warning or an exhortation to me. He smiled enigmatically.

Two days later Aldous Huxley died. His passing went almost unnoticed, because John F. Kennedy also died on November 22, 1963. It was a bad day for utopians and futurists all over.

THE ONTOLOGICAL EVOLUTION OF HERMANN HESSE

Hermann Hesse was born in 1877 in the little Swabian town

VOICE OF ROMANTIC ESCAPISM, DISILLUSIONED BOHEMIAN, WAR RESISTER

Hesse's first successful novel, *Peter Camenzind* (1904), reflected the frivolous sentimentality of the Gay Nineties, which, like the Roaring Twenties, offered a last fun frolic to a class society about to collapse.

"From æstheticism he shifted to melancholy realism. . . . Hesse's novels fictionalize the admonitions of an outsider who urges us to question accepted values, to rebel against the system, to challenge conventional 'reality' in the light of higher ideals" (Ziolkowski).

In 1911 Hesse made the obligatory mystical pilgrimage to India, and there, along the Ganges, picked up the microorganisms that were later to appear in a full-blown Allen Ginsbergsonian mysticism.

In 1914 Europe convulsed with nationalism and military frenzy. Hesse, like Dr. Benjamin Spock in another time warp, became an outspoken pacifist and war resister. Two months after the "outbreak of hostilities," he published an essay titled "O Freunde, nicht dieser Töne" ["Oh Friends, Not These Tones"]. It was an appeal to the youth of Germany, deploring the stampede to disaster. His dissenting brought him official censure and newspaper attacks. From this time on, Hesse was apparently immune to the ravages of patriotism, nationalism, and respect for authority.

PROTO-BEATNIK? PROTO-HIPPY? FATHER OF NEW-AGE PSYCHOLOGY?

In 1922 Hesse wrote *Siddhartha*, his story of a Kerouac–Snyder manhood spent "on the road to Benares" performing feats of detached, amused, sexy one-upmanship.

In the June 1986 issue of *Playboy*, the Islamic yogic master and basketball superstar Kareem Abdul-Jabbar ("noble and powerful servant of Allah") summarized with his legendary cool the life stages he had experienced, using bead-game fugue techniques to weave together the strands of his biography: basketball, racism, religion, drugs, sex, jazz, politics. "In my senior year in high school," says Abdul-Jabbar, "I started reading everything I could get my hands on—Hindu texts, Upanishads, Zen, Hermann Hesse—you name it."

Playboy: "What most impressed you?"

Abdul-Jabbar: "Hesse's *Siddhartha*. I was then going through the same things that Siddhartha went through in his adolescence, and I identified with his rebellion against established precepts of love and life. Siddhartha becomes an æsthetic man, a wealthy man, a sensuous man—he explores all these different worlds and doesn't find enlightenment in any of them. That was the book's great message to me; so I started to develop my own value system as to what was good and what wasn't."

Steppenwolf (1927), observes Ziolkowski, was greeted as a "psychedelic orgy of sex, drugs, and jazz." Other observers with a more historic perspective (present company included) have seen *Steppenwolf* as a final send up of the solemn polarities of the industrial age. Hesse mocks the Freudian conflicts, Nietzschean torments, the Jungian polarities, the Hegelian machineries of European civilization.

Harry Haller enters "The Magic Theatre. Price of Admission: Your Mind." First he engages in a "Great Automobile Hunt," a not too subtle rejection of the sacred symbol of the industrial age. Behind the door marked "Guidance in the Building-Up of the Personality. Success Guaranteed!" H. H. learns to play a post-Freudian video game in which the pixels are part of the personality. "We can demonstrate to anyone whose soul has fallen to pieces that he can rearrange these pieces of a previous self *in what order he pleases* and so attain to an endless multiplicity of moves in the game of life."

This last sentence precisely states the basis for the many postindustrial religions of self-actualization. You learn how to put together the elements of your self *in what order pleases you!* Then press the advance key to continue.

The mid-life crisis of the Steppenwolf, his overheated Salinger inner conflicts, his Woody Allen despairs, his unsatisfied Norman Mailer longings, are dissolved in a whirling kaleidoscope of quick-flashing neurorealities. "I knew," gasps H. H., "that all the hundred pieces of life's game were in my pocket . . . One day I would be a better hand at the game."

THE GLASS-BEAD GAME CONVERTS THOUGHTS TO ELEMENTS

What do you do after you've reduced the heavy, massive boulder-like thoughts of your mechanical culture to elements? If you're a student of physics or chemistry you rearrange the fissioned bits and pieces into new combinations. Synthetic chemistry of the mind. Hesse was hanging out in Basel, home of Paracelsus. Alchemy 101. *Solve et coagule.* Recompose them in new combinations. You become a master of the bead game. Let the random-number generator shuffle your thought-deck and deal out some new hands!

Understandably, Hesse never gives a detailed description of this pre-electronic data-processing appliance called the bead game. But he does explain its function. Players learned how to convert decimal numbers, musical notes, words, thoughts, images into elements, glass beads that could be strung in endless abacus combinations and rhythmic-fugue sequences to create a higher level language of clarity, purity, and ultimate complexity.

A GLOBAL LANGUAGE BASED ON DIGITAL UNITS

Hesse described the game as "a serial arrangement, an ordering, grouping, and interfacing of concentrated concepts from many fields of thought and æsthetics."

In time, wrote Hesse, "the Game of games had developed into a kind of universal language through which the players could express values and set these in relation to one another."

In the beginning the game was designed, constructed, and continually updated by a guild of mathematicians called Castalia. Later generations of hackers used the game for educational, intellectual, and æsthetic purposes. Eventually the game became a global science of mind, an indispensable method for clarifying thoughts and communicating them precisely.

> **H**esse, of course, was not the first to anticipate digital thought-processing. Around 600 B.C. the Greek Pythagoras (music of the spheres) and the Chinese Lao (yin-yang) Tse were speculating that all reality and knowledge could and should be expressed in the play of binary numbers. . . . We reencounter here the age-long dream of philosophers, visionary poets, and linguists of a **universitas**, a synthesis of all knowledge, the ultimate data base of ideas, a global language of mathematical precision.

THE EVOLUTION OF THE COMPUTER

 Hesse, of course, was not the first to anticipate digital thought-processing. Around 600 B.C. the Greek Pythagoras (music of the spheres) and the Chinese Lao (yin–yang) -tzu were speculating that all reality and knowledge could and should be expressed in the play of binary numbers. In 1832 a young Englishman, George Boole, developed an algebra of symbolic logic. In the next decade Charles Babbage and Ada Countess Lovelace worked on the analytic thought-engine. A century later, exactly when Hesse was constructing his "game" in Switzerland, the brilliant English logician Alan Turing was writing about machines that could simulate human thinking. A.I.—artificial intelligence.

Hesse's unique contribution, however, was not technical, but social. Forty-five years before Toffler and Naisbitt, Hesse predicted the emergence of an information culture. In *The Glass Bead Game* Hesse presents a sociology of computing. With the rich detail of a World-Cup novelist (he won the Nobel Prize for Literature with this book) he describes the emergence of a utopian subculture centered around the use of digital mind-appliances.

Hesse then employs his favorite appliance, parody (psyber-farce), to raise the disturbing question of the class division between the computer hip and the computer illiterate. The electronic elite versus the rag-and-glue proles with their hand-operated Coronas. The dangers of a two-tier society of the information rich and the information have-nots.

GLORIFICATION OF THE CASTALIAN HACKER CULTURE

The Glass Bead Game is the story of Joseph Knecht, whom we meet as a brilliant grammar-school student about to be accepted into the Castalian brotherhood and educated in the intricacies of the authorized thought-processing system. The descriptions of Castalia are charmingly pedantic. The reverent reader is awed by the sublime beauty of the system and the monk-like dedication of the adepts.

The scholarly narrator explains:

> This Game of games . . . has developed into a kind of universal speech, through the medium of which the players are able to express values in lucid symbols and to place them in relation to each other . . . A game can originate, for example, from a given astronomical configuration, a theme from a Bach fugue, a phrase of Leibnitz or from the Upanishads, and the fundamental idea awakened can be built up and enriched through assonances to relative concepts. While a moderate beginner can, through these symbols, formulate parallels between a piece of classical music and the formula of a natural law, the adept and Master of the Game can lead the opening theme into the freedom of boundless combinations.

In this last sentence, Hesse describes the theory of digital computing. The wizard programmer can convert any idea, thought, or number into binary-number chains that can be sorted into all kinds of combinations. We reencounter here the age-long dream of philosophers, visionary poets, and linguists of a *universitas,* a synthesis of all knowledge, the ultimate data base of ideas, a global language of mathematical precision.

Hesse understood that a language based on mathematical elements need not be cold, impersonal, rote. Reading *The Glass Bead Game* we share the enthusiasm of today's hacker-visionaries who know that painting, composing, writing, designing, innovating with clusters of electrons (beads?) offers much more creative freedom than expressions limited to print on paper, chemical paints smeared on canvas, or acoustic (i.e., mechanical-unchangeable) sounds.

HESSE'S GOLDEN AGE OF MIND

In the Golden Age of Chemistry scholar-scientists learned how to dissolve molecules and to recombine the freed elements into endless new structures. Indeed, only by precise manipulation of the play of interacting elements could chemists fabricate the marvels that have so changed our world.

In the Golden Age of Physics, physicists, both theoretical and experimental, learned how to fission atoms and to recombine the freed particles into new elemental structures. In *The Glass Bead Game* Hesse portrays a Golden Age of Mind. The knowledge-information programmers of Castalia, like chemists and physicists, dissolve thought molecules into elements (beads) and weave them into new patterns.

In his poem, "The Last Glass Bead Game," Hesse's hero Joseph Knecht writes, "We draw upon the iconography . . . that sings like crystal constellations."

TECHNOLOGY INVENTS IDEOLOGY

Hesse apparently anticipated McLuhan's First Law of Communication: The medium is the message. The technology you use to package, store, communicate your thoughts defines the limits of your thinking. Your choice of thought tool determines the limitations of your thinking. If your thought technology is words-carved-into-marble, let's face it, you're not going to be a light-hearted flexible thinker. An oil painting or a wrinkled papyrus in a Damascus library cannot communicate the meaning of a moving-picture film. New thought technology creates new ideas. The printing press created national languages, the national state, literacy, the industrial age. Television, like it or not, has produced a global thought-processing very different from oral and literate cultures.

Understanding the power of technology, Hesse tells us that the new mind culture of Castalia was based on a tangible mental device, a thought machine, "a frame modeled on a child's abacus, a frame with several dozen wires on which could be strung glass beads of various sizes, shapes, and colours."

Please do not be faked out by the toy-like simplicity of this device. Hesse has changed the units of meaning, the vocabulary of thought. This is serious stuff. Once you have defined the units of thought in terms of mathematical elements you've introduced a major mutation in the intelligence of your culture.

THE EVOLUTION OF THE GAME

 The glass-bead appliance was first used by musicians: "The wires corresponded to the lines of the musical staff, the beads to the time values of the notes."

A bare two or three decades later the game was taken over by mathematicians. For a long while indeed, a characteristic feature of the game's history was that it was constantly preferred, used, and further elaborated by whatever branch of learning happened to be experiencing a period of high development or a renaissance.

At various times the game was taken up and imitated by nearly all the scientific and scholarly disciplines. The analytic study of musical values had led to the reduction of musical events to physical and mathematical formulae. Soon afterward, philology borrowed this method and began to measure linguistic configurations as physics measures processes in nature. The visual arts soon followed suit. Each discipline that seized upon the game created its own language of formulae, abbreviations, and possible combinations.

It would lead us too far afield to attempt to describe in detail how the world of mind, after its purification, won a place for itself in the state. Supervision of the things of the mind among the people and in government came to be consigned more and more to the intellectuals. This was especially the case with the educational system.

INTIMATIONS OF ARTIFICIAL INTELLIGENCE AND ALIENATED HACKERS

"The mathematicians brought the game to a high degree of flexibility and capacity for sublimation, so that it began to acquire *something of a consciousness of itself and its possibilities*" (emphasis mine).

In this last phrase, Hesse premonitors Arthur C. Clarke and Stanley Kubrick's nightmare about neurotic artificial intelligence:

"Open the pod doors, HAL."
"Sorry about that, Dave. This mission is too important to be threatened by human error."

Hesse tells us that the first generations of computer adepts created a "hacker culture," an elite sect of knowledge processors who lived within the constructions of their own minds, disdaining the outside society. Then Hesse, with uncanny insight, describes the emergence of a phenomenon that has now become the fad in the information sciences.

THE ARTIFICIAL-INTELLIGENCE CULT

By 1984 billions of dollars were being spent in Japan (the so-called Fifth Generation projects), in America, and in Europe to develop artificial-intelligence programs. Those nations that already suffer from a serious intelligence deficit—Soviet Eurasia and the third-world nations—seem to be left out of this significant development.

The aim of A.I. projects is to develop enormously complicated smart machines that can reason, deduce, and make decisions more efficiently than "human beings."

The megabuck funding comes from large bureaucracies, federal, corporate, the military, banks, insurance firms, oil companies, space agencies, medical-hospital networks. The mental tasks performed by the A.I. machineries include:

- **Expert systems that provide processed information and suggest decisions based on correlating enormous amounts of data. Here the computers perform, at almost the speed of light, the work of armies of clerks and technicians.**
- **Voice-recognition programs; the computer recognizes instructions given in spoken languages.**
- **Robotry.**

A.I. has become the buzzword among investors in the computer industry. There seems little doubt that reasoning programs and robots will play increasingly important roles in Western society, and, of course, Japan.

Just as the bead game became the target of outside criticism, so has there been much grumbling about the A.I. movement. Some have asserted that the very term "artificial intelligence" is an oxymoron; a contradiction in terms, like "military intelligence."

Other critics point out that A.I. programs have little to do with individual human beings. These megamillion-dollar machines cannot be applied to solve personal problems, to help Ashley get a date on Friday night, to help Dieadra's problem with self-esteem. A.I. systems are designed to think like super-committees of experts. Remember the decision that it was cheaper to pay off a few large injury/death claims than to change the position of the gas tank on the Ford? Recall those Pentagon figures about "tolerable loss of civilian lives in a nuclear war"? That's why many feel that these toys of top management are more artificial than intelligent.

As it turns out, our HAL paranoias are exaggerated.

Computers will not replace real people. They will replace middle- and low-level bureaucrats. They will replace you only to the extent that you use artificial (rather than natural) intelligence in your life and work. If you think like a bureaucrat, a functionary, a manager, an unquestioning member of a large organization, or a chess player, beware: You may soon be out-thought!

NATURAL INTELLIGENCE

Humanists in the computer culture claim that there is only one form of intelligence—natural intelligence, brain power which resides in the skulls of individual human beings. This wetware is genetically wired and experientially programmed to manage the personal affairs of one person, the owner, and to exchange thoughts with others.

All thought-processing tools—hand-operated pencils, printed books, electronic computers—can be used as extensions of natural intelligence. They are appliances for packaging, storing, communicating ideas: mirrors that reflect back what the user has thought. As Douglas Hofstadter put it in *Gödel, Escher, Bach:* "The self comes into being at the moment it has the power to reflect itself." And that power, Hesse and McLuhan, is determined by the thought tool used by the culture.

Individual human beings can be controlled, managed by thinking machines—computers or bead games—only to the extent that they voluntarily choose to censor their own independent thinking.

MAGISTER LUDI BEGINS TO QUESTION AUTHORITY

In the last chapters of *The Glass Bead Game* the hero, Joseph Knecht, has risen to the highest post in the Castalian order. He is "Magister Ludi, Master of the Glass Bead Game."

The game, by this time, has become a global artificial-intelligence system that runs the educational system, the military, science, engineering, mathematics, physics, linguistics, and above all, æsthetics. The great cultural ceremonies are public thought games watched with fascination by the populace.

At this moment of triumph the Mind Master begins to have doubts. He worries about the two-tier society in which the Castalian "computer" elite run the mind games of society, far removed from the realities of human life. The Castalians, we recall, have dedicated themselves totally to the life of the mind, renouncing power, money, family, individuality. A Castalian is the perfect "organization man," a monk of the new religion of artificial intelligence. Knecht is also concerned about the obedience, the loss of individual choice.

Hesse seems to be sending warning signals that are relevant to the situation in 1986. First, he suggests that human beings

Hesse seems to be sending warning signals that are relevant to the situation in 1986. First, he suggests that human beings tend to center their religions on the thought-processing device their culture uses. . . . Second, control of the thought-processing machinery means control of society. The underlying antiestablishment tone of **The Glass Bead Game** must surely have caught the attention of George Orwell, another prophet of the information society. . . . Third, Hesse suggests that the emergence of new intelligence machines will create new religions.

> Computers will not replace real people. They will replace middle- and low-level bureaucrats. They will replace you only to the extent that you use artificial (rather than natural) intelligence in your life and work. If you think like a bureaucrat, a functionary, a manager, an unquestioning member of a large organization, or a chess player, beware: You may soon be out-thought!

• •

tend to center their religions on the thought-processing device their culture uses. The word of God has to come though normal channels or it won't be understood, from the stone tablet of Moses to the mass-produced industrial product that is the "Good Book" of fundamentalist Christians and Moslems.

Second, control of the thought-processing machinery means control of society. The underlying antiestablishment tone of *The Glass Bead Game* must surely have caught the attention of George Orwell, another prophet of the information society. Like Joseph Knecht, Winston Smith, the hero of *1984*, works in the Ministry of Truth, reprogramming the master data base of history. Smith is enslaved by the information tyranny from which Hesse's hero tries to escape.

Third, Hesse suggests that the emergence of new intelligence machines will create new religions. The Castalian order is reminiscent of the mediæval monastic cults, communities of hackers with security clearances, who knew the machine language, Latin, and who created and guarded the big mainframe illuminated manuscripts located in the palaces of bishops and dukes.

Most important, Hesse indicated the appropriate response of the individual who cannot accept the obedience and self-renunciation demanded by the artificial-intelligence priesthood.

TO ACT AS MY HEART AND REASON COMMAND

After some hundred pages of weighty introspection and confessional conversation, Joseph Knecht resigns his post as the high priest of artificial intelligence and heads for a new life as an individual in the "real world."

He explains his "awakening" in a letter to the Order. After thirty years of major-league thought-processing, Knecht has come to the conclusion that organizations maintain themselves by rewarding obedience with privilege! With the blinding force of a

mystical experience Knecht suddenly sees that the Castalian A.I. community "had been infected by the characteristic disease of elitehood—hubris, conceit, class arrogance, self-righteousness, exploitiveness . . . "!

And, irony of all irony, the member of such a thought-processing bureaucracy "often suffers from a severe lack of insight into his place in the structure of the nation, his place in the world and world history." Before we in the sophisticated 1980s rush to smile at such platitudes about bureaucratic myopia and greed, we should remember that Hesse wrote this book during the decade when Hitler, Stalin, and Mussolini were terrorizing Europe with totalitarianism. The cliché Athenian–democratic maxim "think for yourself; question authority" was decidedly out of fashion, even in civilized countries like Switzerland.

Gentle consideration for the touchiness of the times was, we assume, the reason why Hesse, the master of parody, leads his timid readers with such a slow, formal tempo to the final confrontation between Alexander, the president of the Order, and the dissident game master. In his most courteous manner Knecht explains to Alexander that he will not accept obediently the "decision from above."

The president gasps in disbelief. And we can imagine most of the thought-processing elite of Europe, the professors, the intellectuals, the linguists, the literary critics, and news editors joining Alexander when he sputters, "not prepared to accept obediently . . . an unalterable decision from above? Have I heard you aright, Magister?"

Later, Alexander asks in a low voice, "And how do you act now?"

"As my heart and reason command," replies Joseph Knecht. ◎

II.3. OUR BRAIN

When you think of it, the ultimate wicked oxymoron is *organized religion.* Imagine a group of control-freak men getting together and saying, "We're going to impose our order on the fifteen-billion-year evolutionary chaotic process that's happening on this planet, and all over the galaxy. We're going to chisel out the rules of a bureaucracy to keep us in power."

The human brain—the most complex, infinitely and imaginatively complex knowledge system—has a hundred billion neurons, and each neuron has the knowledge-processing capacity of a powerful computer. The human brain has more connections than there are atoms in the universe. It has taken us thousands of years to even realize that we don't understand the chaotics of this complexity. The human brain can process more than a hundred million signals a second and counting.

The best way to understand the evolution of the human race is in terms of how well we have learned to operate our brain. If you think about it, we're basically brains. Our bodies are here to move our brains around. Our bodies are equipped with all these sensory inputs and output ports to bring information into the neurocomputer. In just the last ten years, our species has multiplied the ability to use our brains by a thousandfold.

The way to understand how efficiently you're using your brain is to clock it in rpm— realities per minute. Just on the basis of input/output, my brain is now operating at a hundred times more rpm than in 1960.

When we were back in the caves a million or so years ago, we were just learning to chip stones to begin making tools. We lived on a planet where everything was natural. There was almost nothing artificial or even handmade—but we had the same brains. Each of our ancient ancestors carried around an enormously complex brain that eventually fissioned the atom, sent human beings to the Moon, and created rock video. Long ago we had the same brains, but we weren't using the abilities. If the brain is like a computer, then the trick is to know how to format your brain—to set up operating systems to run your brain.

If you have a computer, you have choice. You can have word processing or not. If you have word processing, you have *WordStar* or *WordPerfect,* all these choices. Once you've formatted your brain, trained your brain with that method, you have to go through that program to use it. The process of formatting your brain is called imprinting.

Imprinting is a multimedia input of data. For a baby, it's the warmth of the mother, the softness, the sound, the taste of the breast. That's called booting up or formatting. Now baby's brain is hooked to Mama and then of course from Mama to Daddy, food, etc., but it's the Mama file that's the first imprint.

There is the ability to boot up or add new directories. To activate the brain is called yogic or psychedelic. To transmit what's in the brain is cybernetic. The brain, we are told by neurologists, has between seventy and a hundred buttons known as receptor sites that can imprint different circuits. Certain biochemical (usually botanical) products activate those particular parts of the brain.

In tribal times, before written language, communication was effected through the human voice, small groups, and body motion. Most pagan tribes had rituals that occurred at harvest time, in the springtime, or at the full Moon. The tribe came together and activated a collective boot-up system. They hooked all their computers to the same tribal language. This often involved the use of psychedelic plants or vegetables.

In terms of modern computers and electronic devices, this would be a multimedia imprinting ceremony. The fire was the center of light and heat. There were symbolic

> There is the ability to boot up or add new directories. To activate the brain is called yogic or psychedelic. ☞

vic keller

objects, such as feathers or bones. This experience booted up the brains of all present so they could share the basic tribal system. But each person could have his own vision quest. He could howl like a wolf, hoot like an owl, roll around like a snake. Each tribal member was learning how to activate, operate, boot up, and accept the uniqueness of his/her own brain.

A human being is basically a tribal person, most comfortable being together in small groups facilitating acceptance and understanding of each other as individuals. Later forms of civilization have discredited individualism. The history of the evolution of the human spirit has to do with new methods of media, communication, or language. About five thousand years ago, after the species got pretty good with tools and building, somewhere in the Middle East (possibly also in China) people began making marks on shells and on pieces of papyrus. This allowed for long-distance communication.

Handwriting, which linked up hundreds of thousands of people, gave total power to the people who knew how to control the writing. Marshall McLuhan reminded us that throughout human history, whoever controls the media controls the people. This is French semiotics. Literacy is used to control the poor. The educated use literacy to control the uneducated.

A typical feudal organization, such as the Catholic Church, restricted the power to send a message like this to a very special class of computer hacker-nerds called monks. Only *they* were authorized to touch the mainframe—the illuminated manuscripts up in the castle of the duke or cardinal. But to the others—no matter how important a person in the village or the city—the word *came down* from the Higher Ups.

Once people start organizing in large groups of thousands, or hundreds of thousands, the tribal situation could no longer be controlled. If a hundred thousand people are all hooked up, like a hive or termite colony, there has to be some central organization that keeps it going.

With thousands of people carrying rocks to build a pyramid, or thousands of people building the churches of the pope, a feudal society can't function if the workers are accessing their singular-brain programs. To illustrate the totalitarian power control of the feudal situation, consider the basic metaphor of the "shepherd" and the "sheep." "The Lord is my shepherd; I shall not want. He maketh me to lie down in green pastures." Now, if the Lord is your shepherd, who the fuck are you? Bah! Even today, when the pope flies around to third-world countries, they speak of "the pope and his flock."

Another example of brain control preventing the individual from accessing his or her own computer is the first chapter of the Bible. The opening text of Genesis lays it right out. God says, "I made the skies, I made the planets, I made the earth, I made the water, I made the land, I made the creepy-crawly things, and I made you, Adam, to be in my likeness, and I put you in the ultimate destination resort, which is the Garden of Eden. Boy, you can do anything you want. I'm going to pull out a rib and give you a help-mate like a little kitchen slave, named Eve. You can do whatever you want, Adam. This is paradise.

And a new philosophy emerged called quantum physics, which suggests that the individual's function is to inform and be informed. You really exist only when you're in a field sharing and exchanging information. You create the realities you inhabit.

"However, there are two Food and Drug regulations. See that tree over there? That's the Tree of Immortality. It offers cryonics and cloning. You shall not eat of the fruit of that lest you become a God like me and live forever. You see that tree over there? That's even more dangerous. You shall not eat of the fruit of that because that is the Tree of Knowledge. It offers expansions of consciousness."

Genesis makes it clear that the whole universe is owned, operated, controlled, and fabricated by one God—and he's a big, bad-tempered male. That's why we have a war on mind drugs. The one thing that no mass society can stand is individuals and small groups that go off to start learning how to program, reprogram, boot up, activate, and format their own brains.

There's a good reason for these taboos. The feudal and industrial stages of evolution are similar to the stages in the evolution of individuals. Young children are glad to have Daddy be shepherd, but after a while the child has to take responsibility.

Feudal societies imprinted millions to totally devote their lives to being herd-flock animals. Imagine living on a farm fifty miles from Chartres during the 15th Century. On Sundays you walked five miles to get to a little village. There the priest told you, "Listen, six months from now we're all going to Chartres. There's going to be a big ceremony because the archbishop will be there."

You spent a week to hike there. You walked into the central square of Chartres. You looked up and saw a cathedral taller than any trees, almost like a mountain, with its stained-glass windows and statues, and there were all those people the priest told you about. They're seven or ten feet tall. You walked in, looked up at the towering Gothic arches, the rose windows, heard the organ music and chanting, smelled the incense.

Talk about multisensory, multimedia imprinting! If you think that the Grateful Dead light show is something, for almost two thousand years the wizards of the Catholic Church have orchestrated one hell of a show. The smell of perfume, the candles, the chanting getting louder and louder, until suddenly the bishop appeared, bejeweled, carried in on a big golden throne. You'd never seen anything like that back on the farm.

**"All right, down on your knees. Say after me: 'Thine is the kingdom and power and glory.'
Now I want you all to go to the Middle East and kill heathens for Christ."**
"Sure, anything you say."

An earlier multimedia imprinting event took place near Athens before the birth of Christ. The Eleusinian mystery rite was an annual religious event that reoccurred for over a thousand years. The wisest people as well as ordinary folk came to the temple of Eleusis to participate in the secret ceremony. An LSD-type drink made from ergot of barley was drunk by all the initiates. An extravagant light show and a powerful dramatic reenactment was performed, resulting in a group experience of chaos and rebirth for the audience.

It's no accident that the Greek philosophers, dramatists, and poets left an incredible record of creative self-expression and polytheism. When Socrates said, "The function of human life is to know yourself; intelligence is virtue," he was invoking the Greek notion of humanism that was to later influence the Renaissance and the romantic periods.

Far more than by weapons, society is controlled by multimedia, neurological imprinting. Marshall McLuhan reminded us that the medium is the message.

When Gutenberg invented moveable type, it empowered dukes and cardinals to print and distribute thousands of Bibles and histories of the Crown. Within a few decades, many Europeans were learning how to do what only the monks could do. Gutenberg created the one device that was basic to the future industrial-factory civilization—mass production for consumers.

In the industrial age, the virtuous person was good, prompt, reliable, dependable, efficient, directed, and, of course, replaceable. There was not much need for the individual to operate his or her own brain in a factory civilization. The bosses can't have people on an assembly line becoming too creative, as in the Cheech and Chong movie where cars are coming down the line.

"Hey, Cheech, I'm gonna go eat now."
"You can't, not yet."
"Why not?"
"You can't eat until the bell rings."
"Okay, let's paint the next car rainbow."

You cannot operate industrial society with too much individuality and access to the multimedia capacities of the brain.

Around 1900 Einstein came up with the idea that space and time only exist in an interactive field, and Max Planck devised a theory that the basic elements of the universe are particles of information. Then came Heisenberg's proof that you create your own reality. And a new philosophy emerged called quantum physics, which suggests that the individual's function is to inform and be informed. You really exist only when you're in a field sharing and exchanging information. You create the realities you inhabit.

What's the brain for? Why do we have this incredible instrument? Our brains want to be hooked up with other brains. My brain is only in operation when she's slamming back and forth bytes and bits of information. Multimedia intercommunication.

The original basic dream of humanity is that the individual has divinity within. There is this enormous power within our bio-computer brains. We are going to have to learn how to use this power, how to boot it up. ◎

II.4. How to Boot Up Your Bio-Computer

The human brain, we are told, is a galaxy of over a hundred billion neurons, any two of which can organize and communicate as much complex information as a mainframe computer.

Many cognitive psychologists now see the brain as a universe of information processors. Our minds, according to this metaphor, serve as the software that programs the neural hardware (or wetware). Most of the classic psychological terms can now be redefined in terms of computer concepts. Cognitive functions like memory, forgetting, learning, creativity, and logical thinking are now studied as methods by which the mind forms "data bases" and stores, processes, shuffles, and retrieves information.

Noncognitive functions such as emotions, moods, sensory perceptions, hallucinations, obsessions, phobias, altered states, possession-trance experiences, glossolalias, intoxications, visionary images, and psychedelic perspectives can now be viewed in terms of ROM brain circuits or autonomous-sympathetic-midbrain sectors that are usually not accessed by left-brain or forebrain conscious decision. These nonlinear, unconscious areas can, as we well know, be activated intentionally or involuntarily by various means. The pop term "turn on" carries the fascinating cybernetic implication that one can selectively dial up or access brain sectors that process specific channels of information signals normally unavailable.

These concepts could emerge only in an electronic culture. The mystics and altered-state philosophers of the past, like the Buddha or St. John of the Cross or William James or Aldous Huxley, could not describe their visions and illuminations and ecstasies and enlightenments in terms of "turning on" electronic appliances.

There is no naïve assumption here that the brain is a computer. However, by using cybernetic terminology to describe mind and brain functions, we can add to our knowledge about the varieties of thought-processing experiences.

This use of a manufactured artifact like the computer to help us understand internal biological processes seems to be a normal stage in the growth of human knowledge. Harvey's notions about the heart as pump and the circulation of the blood obviously stemmed from hydraulic engineering. Our understanding of metabolism and nutrition inside the body had to await the science of thermodynamics and energy machines.

Two hundred years ago, before electrical appliances were commonplace, the brain was vaguely defined as an organ that secreted "thoughts" the way the heart processed blood and the lungs processed air. Forty-five years ago my Psychology 1-A professors described the brain in terms of the most advanced information system available—an enormous telephone exchange. This metaphor obviously did not lead to profitable experimentation; so the brain was generally ignored by psychology. The psychoanalytic theories of Freud were more useful and comprehensible, because they were based on familiar thermodynamic principles: Neurosis was caused by the blocking or repression of surging, steamy, over-heated dynamic instincts that exploded or leaked out in various symptomatic behavior.

During the early 1960s our Harvard Psychedelic Drug Research project studied the reactions of thousands of subjects during psilocybin and LSD sessions. We were able to recognize and classify the standard range of psychedelic-hallucinogenic experiences, and to distinguish them from the effects of other drugs like uppers, downers, booze, opiates, tran-

Those young, bright baby-boom Americans, who had been dialing and tuning television screens since infancy, and who had learned how to activate and turn on their brains using chaotic drugs in serious introspective experiments, were uniquely prepared to engineer the interface between the computer and the cybernetic organ known as the human brain.

quilizers. But we were able to categorize them only in terms of subjective reactions. There was simply no scientific language to communicate or model the wide range and "strange" effects of these chaotic phenomena. Psychiatrists, policemen, moralists, and people who did not use drugs accepted the notion of "psychotomimetic states." There was one normal way to see the world. Chaotic drugs caused all users to lose their grasp on the one-and-only authorized reality, thus mimicking insanity.

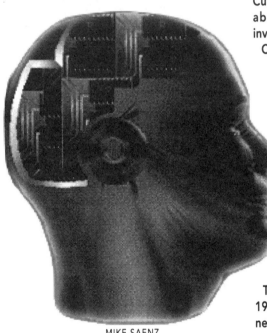

MIKE SAENZ

To talk and think about drug-induced experiences, the Harvard drug experimenters and other researchers were forced to fall back on the ancient literature of Christian mysticism and those oriental yogic disciplines that had studied visionary experiences for centuries. The scholars of mysticism and spiritual transcendence snobbishly tended to view "normal reality" as a web of socially induced illusions. They tended to define, as the philosophic-religious goal of life, the attainment of altered states.

Needless to say, enormous confusion was thus created. Most sensible, practical

Americans were puzzled and irritated by this mad attempt on the part of the mystical millions to enthusiastically embrace chemical insanity and self-induced chaotics. Epistemological debates about the definition of reality soon degenerated into hysterical social extremism on the part of almost all concerned, present company included. Arguments about the nature of reality are always heavy, often bitter and emotional. Cultural, moral, political, racial, and above all, generational issues were involved in the Drug Wars of the late 20th Century.

But the basic problem was semiotic. Debate collapsed into emotional babble because there was no language or conceptual model of what happened when you got "high," "stoned," "fucked up," "loaded," "wasted," "blissed," "spaced out," "illuminated," "satorized," "god-intoxicated," etc.

Here again, external technology can provide us with an updated model and language to understand inner neuro-function. Television became popularized in the 1950s. Many psychedelic trippers of the next decades tended to react like television viewers passively watching the pictures flashing on their mind-screens. The semantic level of the acid experimenters was defined by the word "Wow!" The research groups I worked with at Harvard, Millbrook, and Berkeley fell back on a gaseous, oriental, Ganges-enlightenment terminology for which I humbly apologize.

Then, in 1976, the Apple computer was introduced. At the same time video games provided young people with a

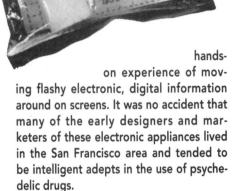

hands-on experience of moving flashy electronic, digital information around on screens. It was no accident that many of the early designers and marketers of these electronic appliances lived in the San Francisco area and tended to be intelligent adepts in the use of psychedelic drugs.

Those young, bright baby-boom Americans, who had been dialing and tuning television screens since infancy, and who had learned how to activate and turn on their brains using chaotic drugs in serious introspective experiments, were uniquely prepared to engineer the interface between the computer and the cybernetic organ known as the human brain. They could handle accelerated thought-processing, multilevel realities, instantaneous chains of digital logic much more comfortably than their less-playful, buttoned-up, conservative, MBA rivals at IBM. Much of Steve Jobs's astounding success in developing the Apple and the Mac was explicitly motivated by his crusade against IBM, seen as the archenemy of the 1960s counterculture.

By 1980 millions of young Americans had become facile in digital thought-processing using inexpensive home computers. Most of them intuitively understood that the best model for understanding

"If thou write stoned, edit straight. If thou write straight, edit stoned."

and operating the mind came from the mix of the psychedelic and cybernetic cultures.

Hundreds of New-Age pop psychologists, like Werner Erhard and Shirley MacLaine, taught folks how to re-program their minds, write the scripts of their lives, upgrade thought-processing. At the same time the new theories of imprinting, i.e., sudden programming of the brain, were popularized by ethologists and hip psychologists like Conrad Lorenz, Niko Tinbergen, and John Lilly.

Once again, external engineered tools helped us understand inner function. If the brain is viewed as bio-hardware, and psychedelic drugs become "neurotransmitters," and if you can reprogram your mind, for better or for worse, by "turning on," then new concepts and techniques of instantaneous psychological change become possible.

Another relevant question arises. Can the computer screen create altered states? Is there a digitally induced "high"? Can psyberdelic electrons be packaged like chemicals to strike terror into the heart of the Reagan White House? Do we need a Digital Enforcement Agency (DEA) to teach kids to say "No," or more politely, "No, thank you" to RAM pushers?

My opinion is in the negative. But what do I no? I am currently enjoying a mild digital dependence, but it seems manageable and socially useful. I follow the ancient Sufi–Pythagorean maxim regarding creative writing: "If thou write stoned, edit straight. If thou write straight, edit stoned."

And always with a team. ©

PERSONAL COMPUTERS,
PERSONAL FREEDOM

CYBERNAUT KNOW DIFFERENCE CYBERNOT

nce upon a time… knowledge-information was stored in extremely expensive mainframe systems called illuminated volumes, usually Bibles, carefully guarded in the palace of the duke or bishop, and accessible only to security-cleared, socially alienated hackers called monks. Then in 1456 Johannes Gutenberg invented a most important piece of hardware: the moveable-type printing press. This knowledge-information processing system could mass-produce inexpensive, portable software readily available for home use: the Personal Book.

Until recently, computers were in much the same sociopolitical situation as the pre-Gutenberg systems. The mainframe knowledge-processors that ran society were the monopoly of governments and large corporations. They were carefully guarded by priestly technicians with security clearances. The average person, suddenly thrust into electronic illiteracy and digital helplessness, was understandably threatened.

THE MAINFRAME MONOPOLY

My first contact with computers came in 1950, when I was director of a Kaiser Foundation psychological research project that developed mathematical profiles for the interpersonal assessment of personality. In line with the principles of humanistic psychology, the aim of this research was to free persons from dependency on doctors, professionals, institutions, and diagnostic-thematic interpretations. To this end, we elicited clusters of yes–no responses from subjects and fed back knowledge in the form of profiles and indices to the patients themselves.

Relying on dimensional information rather than interpretative categories, our research was ideally suited to computer analysis. Routinely we sent stacks of data to the Kaiser Foundation's computer room, where mysterious technicians converted our numbers into relevant indices. Computers were thus helpful, but distant and unapproachable. I distrusted the mainframes because I saw them as devices that would merely increase the dependence of individuals upon experts.

In 1960 I became a director of the Harvard Psychedelic Drug Research program. The aims of this project were also humanistic: to teach individuals how to self-administer psychoactive drugs in order to free their psyches without reliance upon doctors or institutions. Again we used mainframes to index responses to questionnaires about drug experiences, but I saw no way for this awesome knowledge-power to be put in the hands of individuals. I know now that our research with psychedelic drugs and, in fact, the drug culture itself was a forecast of, or preparation for, the personal-computer age. Indeed, it was a brilliant LSD researcher, John Lilly, who in 1972 wrote the seminal monograph on the brain as a knowledge-information processing system: *Programming and Meta-Programming in the Human Bio-Computer.* Psychedelic drugs expose one to the raw experience of chaotic brain function, with the protections of the mind temporarily suspended. We are talking here about the tremendous acceleration of images, the crumbling of analogic perceptions into vapor trails of neuron off–on flashes, the multiplication of disorderly mind programs slipping in and out of awareness like floppy disks.

The seven million Americans who experienced the awesome potentialities of the brain via LSD certainly paved the way for the computer society. It is no accident that the term "LSD" was used twice in *Time* magazine's cover story about Steve Jobs, for it was Jobs and his fellow Gutenberger, Stephen Wozniak, who hooked up the personal brain with the personal computer and thus made possible a new culture.

HANDS ON/TUNE IN

The development of the personal computer was a step of Gutenberg magnitude. Just as the Personal Book transformed human society from the muscular-feudal to the mechanical-industrial, so has the personal electronic-knowledge processor equipped the individual to survive and evolve in the age of information. To guide us in this confusing and scary transition, it is most useful to look back and see what happened during the

> **If we are to stay free, we must see to it that the right to own digital data processors becomes as inalienable as the constitutional guarantees of free speech and a free press.**

Gutenberg mutation. Religion was the unifying force that held feudal society together. It was natural, therefore, that the first Personal Books would be Bibles. When the religion market was satiated, many entrepreneurs wondered what other conceivable use could be made of this newfangled software. How-to-read books were the next phase. Then came game books. It is amusing to note that the second book printed in the English language was on chess—a game that became, with its knights and bishops and kings and queens, the Pac Man of late feudalism. We can see this same pattern repeating during the current transition. Since money/business is the unifying force of the industrial age, the first Wozniak bibles were, naturally enough, accounting spreadsheets. Then came word processors, and games.

The history of human evolution is the record of technological innovation. Expensive machinery requiring large group efforts for operation generally becomes a tool of social repression by the state. The tower clock. The galley ship. The cannon. The tank. Instruments that can be owned and operated by individuals inevitably produce democratic revolutions. The bronze dagger. The crossbow. The pocket watch. The automobile as self-mover. This is the liberating "hands-on" concept. "Power to the people" means personal technology available to the individual. D.I.Y. Do It Yourselves.

EVOLUTION/REVOLUTION

Digital-graphic appliances are developing a partnership between human brains and computers. In evolving to more physiological complexity, our bodies formed symbioses with armies of digestive bacteria necessary for survival. In similar fashion, our brains are forming neural-electronic symbiotic linkups with solid-state computers. It is useful to distinguish here between addictions and symbiotic partnerships. The body can become passively addicted to certain molecules, e.g., of heroin, and the brain can become passively addicted to electronic signals, e.g., from television. The human body, as we have noted, also requires symbiotic partnerships with certain unicellular organisms. At this point in human evolution, more and more people are developing mutually dependent, interactive relationships with their microsystems. When this happens, there comes a moment when the individual is "hooked" and cannot imagine living without the continual interchange of electronic signals between the personal brain and the personal computer. There are interesting political implications. In the near future, more than twenty million Americans will use computers to establish intense interactive partnerships with other inhabitants of cyberspace. These individuals will operate at a level of intelligence that is qualitatively different from those who use static forms of knowledge-information processing. In America, this difference is already producing a generation gap, i.e., a species gap. After Gutenberg, Personal Books created a new level of individual thinking that revolutionized society. An even more dramatic mutation in human intelligence will occur as the new digital-light appliances will permit individuals to communicate with individuals in other lands.

CHILDHOOD'S END?

It seems clear that we are facing one of those genetic crossroads that have occurred so frequently in the history of primates. The members of the human gene pool who form symbiotic links with solid-state computers will be characterized by extremely high individual intelligence and will settle in geographic niches that encourage individual access to knowledge-information–processing software.

New associations of individuals linked by computers will surely emerge. Information nets will encourage a swift, free interchange among individuals. Feedback peripherals will dramatically expand the mode of exchange from keyboard punching to neuro-physiological interaction. The key word is, of course, "interaction." The intoxicating power of interactive software is that it eliminates dependence on the enormous bureaucracy of knowledge professionals that flourished in the industrial age. In the factory culture, guilds and unions and associations of knowledge-workers jealously monopolized the flow of information. Educators, teachers, professors, consultants, psychotherapists, librarians, managers, journalists, editors, writers, labor unions, medical groups—all such roles are now threatened.

It is not an exaggeration to speculate about the development of very different postindustrial societies. Solid-state literacy will be almost universal in America and the other Western democracies. The rest of the world, especially the totalitarian countries, will be kept electronically illiterate by their rulers. At least half the United Nations's members now prohibit or limit personal possession. And, as the implications of home computers become more clearly understood, restrictive laws will become more apparent. If we are to stay free, we must see to it that the right to own digital data processors becomes as inalienable as the constitutional guarantees of free speech and a free press. ◉

... to teach individuals how to self-administer psychoactive drugs in order to free their psyches without reliance upon doctors or institutions. ... ◉ Psychedelic drugs expose one to the raw experience of chaotic brain function, with the protections of the mind temporarily suspended. We are talking here about the tremendous acceleration of images, the crumbling of analogic perceptions into vapor trails of neuron off–on flashes, the multiplication of disorderly mind programs slipping in and out of awareness like floppy disks.

II.6. QUANTUM JUMPS, YOUR MACINTOSH, AND YOU

Chalk: A soft, white, grey, or buff limestone composed chiefly of the shells of foraminifers.

Quantum: The quantity or amount of something; an indivisible unit of energy; the particle mediating a specific type of elemental interaction.

Quantum jump: Any abrupt change or step, especially in knowledge or information.

Chaos: The basic state of the universe and the human brain.

Personal computer: A philosophic digital appliance that allows the individual to operate and communicate in the quantum-information age.

A UNIVERSE OF USER-FRIENDLY BITS AND BYTES

The great philosophic achievement of the 20th Century was the discovery, made by nuclear and quantum physicists around 1900, that the visible-tangible reality is written in BASIC. We seem to inhabit a universe made up of a small number of elements-particles-bits that swirl in chaotic clouds, occasionally clustering together in geometrically logical temporary configurations.

The solid Newtonian universe involving such immutable concepts as mass, force, momentum, and inertia, all bound into a Manichæan drama involving equal reactions of good versus evil, gravity versus levity, and entropy versus evolution, produced such pious Bank-of-England notions as conservation of energy. This General Motors's universe, which was dependable, dull, and predictable, became transformed in the hands of Einstein/Planck into digitized, shimmering quantum screens of electronic probabilities.

In 1989 we navigate in a reality of which Niels Bohr and Werner Heisenberg could only dream, and which Marshall McLuhan predicted. It turns out that the universe described in their psychedelic equations is best understood as a super mainframe constellation of information processor with subprograms and temporary ROM states, macros called galaxies, stars; minis called planets; micros called organisms; metamicros known as molecules, atoms, particles; and, last, but not least, micros called Macintosh.

It seems to follow that the great technological challenge of the 20th Century was to produce an inexpensive appliance that would make the chaotic universe "user friendly," which would allow the individual human to digitize, store, process, and reflect the subprograms that make up his/her own personal realities.

Murmur the word "Einstein," put your hand reverently on your mouse, and give it an admiring pat. Your modest, faithful, devoted Mac is an evolutionary celebrity! It may be an

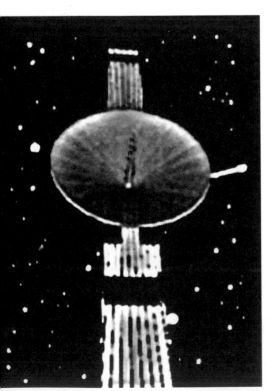

ANDY FRITH

advance as important as the opposable thumb, face-to-face lovemaking, the Model-T Ford, the printing press! Owning it defines you as member of a new breed—postindustrial, postbiological, post-human—because your humble VM (Volks–Mac) permits you to think and act in terms of clusters of electrons. It allows you to cruise around in the chaotic post-Newtonian information ocean, to think and communicate in the lingua franca of the universe, the binary dialect of galaxies and atoms. Light.

A PHILOSOPHIC APPLIANCE CONCEIVED BY QUANTUM PHYSICISTS

The chain of events that elevated us to this new genetic status, *Homo sapiens electronicus*, began around the turn of the century.

Physicists are traditionally assigned the task of sorting out the nature of reality. So it was Einstein, Planck, Heisenberg, Bohr, *et al.*, who figured out that the units of energy/matter were subatomic particles that zoom around in clouds of ever-changing, off–on, 0–1, yin–yang probabilities.

Einstein and the quantum physicists digitized our universe, reduced our solid realities into clusters of pixels, into recursive stairways of Gödel–Escher–Bach paradox. No one understood, at first, what they were talking about. They expressed their unsettling theories in complex equations written on blackboards with chalk. These great physicists thought and communicated with a neolithic tool: chalk marks on the blackboard of the cave. The paradox was this: Einstein and his brilliant colleagues could not experience or operate or communicate at a quantum-electronic level. In a sense they were idiot savants, able to produce equations about chaos and relativity without being able to maintain interpersonal cyberrelationships with others.

Is it not true that freedom in any country is measured perfectly by the percentage of Personal Computers in the hands of individuals?

Imagine if Max Planck, paddling around in his chalkboard skin-canoe, had access to a video-arcade game! He'd see right away that the blips on Centipede and the zaps of Space Invaders could represent the movement of the particles that he tried to describe in chalk-dust symbols on his blackboard.

Reflect on the head-aching adjustment required here. The universe described by Einstein and the nuclear physicists is alien and terrifying. Chaotic. Quantum physics is quite literally a wild acid trip! It postulates an hallucinatory Alice-in-Wonderland universe in which everything is changing. As Heisenberg and Jimi Hendrix said, "Nothing is certain except uncertainty." Matter is energy. Energy is matter at various forms of acceleration. Particles dissolve into waves. There is no up or down in a four-dimensional movie. It all depends on your attitude, i.e., your angle of approach to the real worlds of chaotics.

In 1910, the appliance we call the universe was not user friendly and there was no hands-on manual of operations. No wonder people felt helpless and superstitious. People living in the solid, mechanical world of 1910 could no more understand or experience an Einsteinian universe than Queen Victoria could levitate or fish could read and write English. Einstein was denounced as evil and immoral by Catholic bishops and sober theologians who sensed how unsettling and revolutionary these new ideas could be.

In retrospect we see that the first seventy-five years of the 20th Century were devoted to preparing, training, and initiating human beings to communicate in quantum-speak,

ANDY FRITH

i.e., to think and act at an entirely different level—in terms of digital clusters.

The task of preparing human culture for new realities has traditionally been performed by tribal communicators called artists, entertainers, performers. When Greek philosophers came up with notions of humanism, individuality, and liberty, it was the painters and sculptors of Athens who produced the commercial logos, the naked statues of curvy Venus and sleek Mercury and the other randy Olympian Gods.

When the feudal, anti-human monotheisms (Christian–Islamic) took over, it was the "nerdy" monks and painters who produced the commercial artwork of the Middle Ages. God as a bearded king swathed in robes. Madonna and Bleeding Saints and crucified Jesus, wall-to-wall anguished martyrs. These advertising logos were necessary, of course, to convince the serfs to submit to the All–Powerful Lord. You certainly can't run a kingdom or empire with bishops, popes, cardinals, abbots, and chancellors of the exchequer joyously running around bare-assed like Athenian pantheists.

The Renaissance was a humanist revival preparing Europeans for the industrial age. When Gutenberg invented the cheap, portable, rag-and-glue home computer known as the printing press, individuals had to be encouraged to read and write and "do it yourself!" Off came the clothes! Michelangelo erected a statue of David, naked as a jay bird, in the main square of Florence. Why David? He was the young, punk kid who stood up against Goliath, the hired Rambo hit man of the Philistine empire.

With this historical perspective we can see that the 20th Century (1900–1994) produced an avalanche of artistic, literary, musical, and entertainment movements, all of which shared the same goal: to strip off the robes and uniforms; to dissolve our blind faith in static structure; to loosen up the rigidities of the industrial culture; to prepare us to deal with paradox, with altered states of perception, with multidimensional definitions of nature; to make quantum reality comfortable, manageable, homey, livable; to get you to feel at home while bouncing electrons around your computer screen. Radio. Telegraph. Television. Computers.

DIGITAL ART! D.I.Y. (DO IT YOURSELF!)

 In modern art we saw the emergence of schools that dissolved reality representation into a variety of subjective, relativistic attitudes. Impressionists used random spots of color and brush strokes, converting matter to reflected light waves. Seurat and the Pointillists actually painted in pixels.

Expressionism offered a quantum reality that was almost totally spontaneous. Do it yourself! Cubism sought to portray common objects in planes and volumes reflecting the underlying geometric structure of matter, thus directly illustrating the new physics. The Dada and collage movements broke up material reality into diverse bits and bytes.

Surrealism produced a slick, smooth-plastic fake-reality that was later perfected by Sony. In Tokyo I have listened to electronic anthropologists argue that Dali's graphic "The Persistence of Memory" (featuring melting watches) created modern Japanese culture, which no one can deny is eminently surreal.

These avant-garde æsthetic D.I.Y. experiments were quickly incorporated into pop art, advertising, and industrial design. Society was learning to live with the shifting-screen perspectives and pixillated representations of the universe that had been predicted by the equations of the quantum physicists. When the Coca-Cola company uses the digitized face of Max Headroom as its current logo, then America is comfortably living in a quantum universe.

HACKING AWAY AT THE WORD LINE

 These same æsthetic trends appeared in English literature. Next time you boot up your Mac, breathe a word of gratitude to Emerson, Stein, Yeats, Pound, Huxley, Beckett, Orwell, Burroughs, Gysin—all of whom succeeded in loosening social, political, religious linearities, and encouraging subjectivity and innovative reprogramming of chaotic realities.

The most influential literary work of this period was produced by James Joyce. In *Ulysses* and *Finnegans Wake*, Joyce fissioned and sliced the grammatical structure of language into thought-bytes. Joyce was not only a writer, but also a word processor, a proto-hacker, reducing ideas to elemental units and endlessly recombining them at will. Joyce programmed reality using his own basic language, a quantum linguistic that allowed him to assemble and reassemble thoughts into fugal, repetitious, contrapuntal patterns. (It also helped that he was semi-blind and dyslexic.)

Imagine what James Joyce could have done with MS Word or a CD–ROM graphic system or a modern data base! Well, we don't have to imagine—he actually managed to do it using his own brainware.

JAZZ

The most effective pre-computer rendition of quantum-digital art was to be found in a certain low-life high-tech style of spontaneous, cool, subjective, improvisational sound waves produced by a small group of black audio engineers. Jazz suddenly popped up at the height of the industrial age, eroding its linear values and noninteractive styles. A factory society demands regularity, dependability, replicability, predictability, conformity. There is no room for improvisation or syncopated individuality on a Newtonian assembly line; so it was left to the African–Americans, who never really bought

Imagine what James Joyce could have done with MS Word or a CD–ROM graphic system or a modern data base! Well, we don't have to imagine—he actually managed to do it using his own brainware.

the factory culture, to get us boogying into the postindustrial quantum age. Needless to say, the moralists instinctively denounced jazz as chaotic, low-life, and vaguely sinful.

RADIO

The most important factor in preparing a society of assembly-line workers and factory managers for the quantum-information age was the invention of a user-friendly electronic appliance called radio.

Radio is the communication of audible signals, such as words or music, encoded in electromagnetic waves. Radio allows us to package and transmit ideas in digital patterns. The first use of "wireless" was by government, military, and business, but within one generation the home micro-radio allowed the individual to turn on and tune in a range of realities.

When Farmer Jones learned how to select stations by moving the dial, he had taken the first hands-on step toward the information age. By 1936 the comforting sounds of Amos 'n' Andy and swing music had prepared human beings for the magic of quantum-electronic communication, as well as the brainwashing powers of political leaders.

THE MOVIES PROJECTED REALITIES ONTO SCREENS

The next step in creating an electronic-computer culture was a big one. Light waves passed through celluloid frames projected life-like images on screens, producing new levels of reality that transformed human thought and communication.

It was a big step when computer designers decided to output data on screens instead of those old green-white Gutenberg printouts. The silent movies made this innovation possible. It is, perhaps, no accident that in the 1980s IBM used the lovable, irresistible icon of the Little Tramp in its commercials.

The next time you direct your hypnotized eyeballs toward your lit-up terminal, remember that it was cheerful Charlie Chaplin who first accustomed our species to accept the implausible quantum reality of electrical impulses flashing on a flat screen.

TELEVISION BROUGHT THE LANGUAGE OF ELECTRONS INTO OUR HOMES

World War II was the first high-tech war. It was fought on electronic screens: radar, sonar. The Allied victory was enormously aided by Alan Turing, the father of artificial intelligence, who used primitive computers to crack the German codes.

As soon as the war was over, these new technologies became available for civilian use. There is simply no way that a culture of television addicts can comprehend or appreciate the changes in human psychology brought about by the boob tube.

The average American spends more time per week watching television than in any other social activity. Pixels dancing on a screen are the central reality. People spend more time gazing at electrons than they do gazing into the eyes of their loved ones, looking into books, scanning other aspects of material reality. Talk about applied metaphysics! Electronic reality is more real than the physical world! This is a profound evolutionary leap. It can be compared to the jump from ocean to shoreline, when land and air suddenly become more real to the ex-fish than water!

TELEVISION PASSIVITY

The first generations of television watching produced a nation of "vidiots": passive amoeboids sprawled in front of the feeding-screen sucking up digital information. Giant networks controlled the airwaves, hawking commercial products

We seem to inhabit a universe made up of a small number of elements-particles-bits that swirl in chaotic clouds, occasionally clustering together in geometrically logical temporary configurations. . . .

and packaged politics like carnival snake-oil salesmen.

Perceptive observers realized that Orwell's nightmare of a Big-Brother society was too optimistic. In *1984* the authoritarian state used television to spy on citizens. The actuality is much worse: citizens docilely, voluntarily lining themselves up in front of the authority box, enjoying the lethal, neurological fast food dished out in technicolour by Newspeak.

Visionary prophets like Marshall McLuhan understood what was happening. He said, "The medium is the message." Never mind about the junk on the screen. That will change and improve. The point is that people are receiving signals on the screen. McLuhan knew that the new electronic technology would create the new global language when the time was ripe, i.e., when society had been prepared to take this quantum leap.

COMPUTER PASSIVITY

 The first generations of computer users similarly did not understand the nature of the quantum revolution. Top management saw computers as Invaluable Business Machines[TL]. Computers simply produced higher efficiency by replacing muscular-factory-clerical labor.

And the rest of us—recognizing in the 1960s that computers in the hands of the managers would increase their power to manipulate and control us—developed a fear and loathing of computers.

Some sociologists with paranoid-survival tendencies have speculated that this phobic revulsion against electronic communication shared by millions of college-educated, liberal book readers was deliberately created by Counter Intelligence Authorities[TL] whose control would be eroded by widespread electronic literacy.

The plot further thickened when countercultural code-cowgirls and code-cowboys, combining the insights and liberated attitudes of beats, hippies, acidheads, rock 'n' rollers, hackers, cyberpunks, and electronic visionaries, rode into Silicon Valley and foiled the great brain robbery by developing the great equalizer: the Personal Computer.

The birth of the information age occurred in 1976, not in a smoky industrial town like Bethlehem, PA, but in a humble manger (garage) in sunny, postindustrial Silicon Valley. The Personal Computer was invented by two bearded, long-haired guys, St. Stephen the Greater and St. Steven the Lesser. And to complete the biblical metaphor, the infant prodigy was named after the Fruit of the Tree of Knowledge: the Apple! The controlled substance with which Eve committed the first original sin: Thinking for Herself!

The Personal Computer triggered a new round of confrontation in the age-old social-political competition: control by the state and individual freedom of thought. Remember how the Athenian PCs, goaded by code-cowboys like Socrates and Plato, hurled back the mainframes of the Spartans and the Persians? Remember how the moveable-type press in private hands printed out the hard copy that overthrew theocratic control of the papacy and later disseminated the Declaration of Independence? Is it not true that freedom in any country is measured perfectly by the percentage of Personal Computers in the hands of individuals?

> It seems to follow that the great technological challenge of the 20th Century was to produce an inexpensive appliance that would make the chaotic universe "user friendly," which would allow the individual human to digitize, store, process, and reflect the subprograms that make up his/her own personal realities.

THE ROLE OF THE FREE AGENT IN THE COMPUTER CULTURE

 Those who like to think for themselves (let's call them free agents) tend to see computers as thought-appliances. "Appliance" defines a device that individuals use in the home for their own comfort, entertainment, or education.

What are the applications of a thought-appliance? Self-improvement? Self-educa-

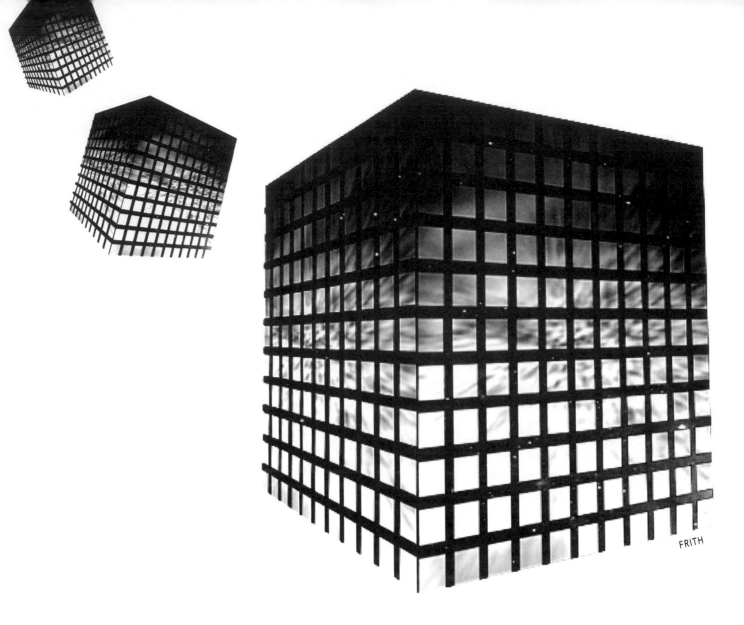

FRITH

tion? Home entertainment? Mind interplay with friends? Thought games? Mental fitness? Significant pursuits?

Free agents use their minds not to perform authorized duties for the soviet state or the International Bureaucracy Machine[TL] but for anything that damn well suits their fancies as Americans. In the old industrial civilization you called yourself a worker, but in the information age you're a free agent. As you develop your agency, you develop your skills in communication.

Personal Computer owners are discovering that the brain is:

- the ultimate organ for pleasure and awareness;
- an array of a hundred billion microcomputers waiting to be booted up, activated, stimulated, and programmed;
- waiting impatiently for software, headware, thoughtware that pays respect to its awesome potential and makes possible electronic internet linkage with other brains. ◎

III. COUNTERCULTURES

THE CITY OF SAN FRANCISCO
ORACLE

25¢

VOL. 1
NO 7

III.1. THE WOODSTOCK GENERATION

It was twenty years ago this summer that more than four hundred thousand young Americans spent three days and nights carousing spectacularly at the Woodstock rock festival. It was simply the biggest and wildest and most influential party in all of history! If not, please prove me wrong, so that we can learn how to improve.

The Woodstock festival was an all-star revival of the oldest and most basic religious ritual: a pagan celebration of life and raw nature, a classic group "possession ceremony" in which worshippers "go out of their minds" to recklessly confront the chaotic Higher Sources, protected by the power of group support.

Check the anthropology texts. Read Campbell, read Frazer, and you'll see that these rituals date way back before the upstart, aggressive, pushy, puritanical monotheistic (One Male God) religions. Pagan rites always celebrate the same natural, instinctive, guileless, eternal utopian values: Peace. Pure ecstatic sexuality. Equality in the eyes of the Higher Powers. Joy. Endemic rapture. Mirth. Tolerance. Affirmation of life, of the human spirit. The honest naked human body. Irreverence. And merry laughter.

It was twenty years ago today...

For one weekend this farm field became the third largest city in New York state. Almost half a million spoiled, affluent, educated young Americans crowded, jammed, squashed into a small cow pasture in upstate New York.

There was minimum sanitation. Minimum food (which was, of course, lovingly shared). Wall-to-wall mud. That's the down side.

On the up side these concert-goers experienced the greatest pagan, Dionysian rock 'n' roll musical event ever performed, with plenty of joyous nudity, and wall-to-wall psychedelic sacraments.

And click on this: not one act of recorded violence!

Such festivals reawaken the oldest and most utopian aspirations of the human brain.

However, be warned. If you stand up as an individual and declaim these goals, you are sure to be derided by the Rambo–Liddy–Ollie North steroid gang (and probably by most of the important adult authorities in your sector) as a hopeless, naïve idealist. "The world is a tough, mean neighborhood," you will be told by the conventional-wisdom experts.

But when four hundred thousand energetic, educated young people assembled, in August 1969, to proclaim these venerable pagan values in action, the effect was contagious. A fearless confidence flared up in young adults. You've seen the films of the 1960s. Sunny, impertinent smiles were infectious. A sense of undeniable togetherness. No secrecy. No shame for experiencing pagan moments. Psychedelic herbs proudly and openly exchanged. Can you imagine anyone sneaking off at Woodstock to shoot heroin behind a bush? Or surreptitiously tooting cocaine? Or sneakily dropping steroids—while listening to Jimi Hendrix and the Grateful Dead?

This "Woodstock experience" became the role model for the counterculture of that time. The Summer of Love kids went on to permanently change American culture with principles that the Soviets in 1989 called glasnost and perestroika.

Hippies started the ecology movement. They combated racism. They liberated sexual stereotypes, encouraged change, individual pride, and self-confidence. They questioned robot materialism. In four years they managed to stop the Vietnam War. They got

The War on Drugs made mellow marijuana prohibitively expensive. The DEA made sure that the peaceable, visionary elixirs like 'shrooms, mescaline, LSD, and MDMA became inaccessible. So good-bye to turn on, tune in, drop out . . . and hello to the motto of the 1980s: Hang on. Hang in. Hang over.

marijuana decriminalized in fourteen states during the Carter administration. Etc.

There was another by-product of the 'sixties generation so obvious that it is rarely considered. When more than four hundred thousand virile, nubile, horny young men and women assembled in the atmosphere of life affirmation there was, inevitably "a whole lotta shaking goin' on." It's possible that ten thousand babies were conceived that magical weekend in 1969.

Where are these "kids of the 'sixties kids" today? And who *are* they?

The babes of the Woodstock season are now, in 1989, twenty years old. In the next twelve years their younger cohort members will be swamping the college campuses.

Will these college kids of the 1990s, the grandchildren of Dr. Spock, be different from the conservative college kids of the 1980s?

If your Mom was running around bare-ass at Woodstock . . . if your Dad helped Abbie Hoffman levitate the Pentagon and helped end the Vietnam War . . . if your parents smoked dope during their formative years while listening to Dylan, the Rolling Stones, and the Beatles . . . if they wept at the fascist-assassination deaths of the Kennedys, Martin Luther King, Jr., and John Lennon . . . if your folks turned on, tuned in, dropped out . . . are you going to major in Business Administration and stampede to Wall Street to sell illegal junk bonds?

The poor, conservative, fearful, conforming college students of the Reagan years were stuck with Moms and Dads who grew up in the bland Eisenhower 1950s. The ghosts of that decade—Senator (Red-Scare) McCarthy and General Douglas ("nuke the slant-eyes") MacArthur and John Wayne and *Father Knows Best* came back to haunt the colleges in the 1980s.

THE REAGAN GENERATION

 The Woodstock revolution started in 1966, peaked in 1976, and hit the wall with a thud! in 1980 with the election of Nancy Reagan.

During the 1980s the gentle tolerance of Woodstock was replaced by a hard-line Marine Corps attitude. The pacifism of "Give Peace a Chance" gave way to a swaggering militarism. The conquest of Grenada. The glorious bombing of Qaddafi's tent. The covert war against Nicaragua. Star Trek gave way to Star Wars.

The War on Drugs made mellow marijuana prohibitively expensive. The DEA made sure that the peaceable, visionary elixirs like 'shrooms, mescaline, LSD, and MDMA became inaccessible. So good-bye to turn on, tune in, drop out . . . and hello to the motto of the 1980s: Hang on. Hang in. Hang over.

And what did the War on Drugs produce? A booze epidemic. Alcohol—the drug of choice of the NRA, the Bubba hunting crowd, the American Legion—is back in the saddle.

Turn down! Tune out!
Throw up!

And cocaine. An epidemic of toot, snort, snow, blow, base, crack has the inner cities wired and fired. Cocaine, the drug that fueled Hitler's SS and the Nazi Blitzkrieg suddenly is turning the inner cities of Reagan–Bush America into battlegrounds! Guns, rifles, automatic weapons conveniently supplied by the NRA and your government-licensed gun dealer. Just walk up and name your weapon, Bucko. No questions asked.

Turn out! Shoot up!
Drop dead!

And here's a pharmaceutical plus for the post–Woodstock America: what unique new Rambo drug did the stand-tall, muscle-bound Reagan–Bush regime give our youth to replace the wimpy Carter years?

Steroids!

Turn off! Tune out!
Pump up!

(Thanks a lot, Nancy.)

What about the college kids?

Remember, the 'sixties counterculture was centered on the campuses. Berkeley. Kent State. Columbia. Madison. Austin. Boulder. Seattle. In the 1980s, however, the colleges, the source of our future, have "seethed with rest." While brave students in South Korea, China, the Soviet Union were exhibiting the idealism they dutifully learned from Woodstock, back in America students have become conservative, materialistic, career-oriented, like the Japanese universities, and like the Russian colleges under Brezhnev.

In the last ten years there has been little campus concern for social issues. The Dan Quayle fraternity-sorority system flourished again. The ultimate college clowns, ROTC students, grown men and women dressed like Boy Scouts sporting Ollie North crewcuts, became, if not popular, at least acceptable.

The audible symbol of this change from the 1960s to the 1980s is the music. If you want to find the soul of a culture, listen to the lyrics that direct the sounds, the beats, the rhythms.

In the 1960s Dylan sang: "We ain't gonna work on Maggie's farm no more." Lennon sang: "Give Peace a Chance." In the somnambulant 1980s Michael Jackson, Prince, Madonna, George Michael kept us moving in the big auditorium-arenas under the

> The 1980s have given us a sequel to McCarthyism. The Civil War on Drugs has unleashed federal agents and hard-line police goons (led, believe it or not, by a "czar") to harass libertarians, intelligent hedonists, and thirty million marijuana fans who don't want the government telling them what to do with their minds.

watchful eyes of the security guards, but the lyrics are not high in socially redeeming value, while the anger of young activist musicians is limited to the denigrated punk-club scene.

Conservative politicians and fundamentalist preachers were delighted by the new conformity. College professors who were proud veterans of the 'sixties counterculture vainly expected the new students to carry on the individual-freedom tradition. The more thoughtful students sensed that they were somehow missing something. The sad nostalgia of tie-dye T-shirts couldn't revive the spirit.

THE SUMMER OF LOVE

How did the Summer of Love turn into the Winter of Irangate and drive-by shootings?

How long will this conservatism last? Will the 1960s renew? The answer is easily found in the demographics.

These conformist kids who were 20 years old in 1980 were raised by parents whose teenage social ideals emerged in the button-down 1950s. The replay is uncannily precise.

Back then we had a lovable old doddering president named Ike whose political tactics were a reassuring grin. There was a big Evil Empire Crusade that led to the pointless slaughter of the

 Korean War. And if your parents could tolerate Tricky Dick Nixon as vice president in 1959, then you are more able to swallow Dan Quayle as our second-in-command in 1989!

In the 1950s, the domestic cancer—the number-one peril that was threatening our nation from within—was subversive communism. Welcome to a thrilling Civil War that unleashed FBI agents and hard-line police goons to crack down and harass pinkos, communist sympathizers, traitorous peaceniks, and liberals who supported un-American plots to bring about racial and sexual equality.

The 1980s have given us a sequel to McCarthyism. The Civil War on Drugs has unleashed federal agents and hard-line police goons (led, believe it or not, by a "czar") to harass libertarians, intelligent hedonists, and thirty million marijuana fans who don't want the government telling them what to do with their minds.

RICK GRIFFIN

The 'eighties witch-hunt involves, not loyalty tests by the FBI, but mandatory urine tests by the DEA. The same inquisitional fanaticism is at work.

Careerism and unquestioning acceptance of authority were valued in the 1980s as then, in the 1950s. There was not a whimper in the 1950s when millions of youth were drafted and sent six thousand miles away to invade Korea. The most visible rowdy culture hero, Elvis Presley, reported dutifully to his local draft board, dressed up like a cute soldier boy, saluted smartly for the cameras, and coached by his father figure, Colonel Parker, proclaimed, "I'm looking forward to serving in the Army. I think it will be a great experience for me." (Sometime after his military service in Germany, Elvis wobbled into the office of J. Edgar Hoover while loaded on prescription drugs and volunteered to be a drug informant for the FBI. He boasted that his contacts with musicians would make him an ideal double agent. No John Lennon he.)

For an 'eighties college student whose parents' wildest moments of cultural individuality and social passion involved panty raids and fraternity-house telephone-booth pranks, is it surprising for them to appear apathetically cheerful in the Reagan–Bush period? Right-wingers and fundamentalists have exulted in the apathy and conformity of 'eighties campuses. "America," they exult, "has come to its senses. Father knows best!"

The ideals of the 1960s—of individuality, personal freedom, kick-out free expression—were written off as adolescent delinquency. American kids, thank God, have assumed the sober responsibilities of history—to wage the Cold War, to go to church and vote Republican (or Democratic, since it doesn't really matter), to dress and behave with decorum, to support the military and police who defend us against our deadly foes abroad and the enemies in our urban slums and ghettos.

By 1989, however, this right-wing fantasy was beginning to erode in the light of the new explosions of youthful idealism.

Twenty years after Woodstock, the national news once again is featuring hundreds of thousands of young people behind the Iron Curtain, their faces glowing with patriotic idealism, peaceably demonstrating to overthrow an aging federal bureaucracy. It's powerful *déjà vu* to witness long-haired German kids wearing headbands, flashing the universal peace sign, and putting their bodies and careers on the line for democracy and individual rights. Once again the confrontations with students peacefully defying the National Guard. Once again the daring yet playful tactics of television agit-prop theatre substituted for violence. Thousands of protesters riding bicycles (!) to the revolution! What would Karl Marx make of that maneuver?

Where did those Chinese students learn these clever methods of grabbing the news screens to express their ideals? Where did they learn the techniques of media savvy to counter the armed forces of the state? From the newsreel films of the American campus protests of the late 1960s, whose ideals are not dead. They were more powerful than ever in China's Tien An Men Square, as well as in the USSR, where glasnost and perestroika define freedom for the individual.

The youth in China, Russia, Czechoslovakia, South Korea are the kids of the 'sixties kids. Keep your eyes open, and you'll see a revival of this freedom movement coming soon to a college campus near you. ◉

III.2. FROM YIPPIES TO YUPPIES

Since my deportation from Harvard University many years ago, I have been, among other things, a free-lance college professor paid by students for one-night-stand lectures about topics too hot for salaried professors.

Back in the 1960s when I flew in for a lecture, the student committee showed up at the airport wearing long hair, sandals, blue jeans, and cheerful, impudent grins. The radio would be blasting out Mick Jagger and Jimi Hendrix as we drove to the campus. The students eagerly asked me about "high" technologies—methods of consciousness expansion, new brands of wonder drugs, new forms of dissident protest, up-to-date developments in the ever-changing metaphysical philosophies of rock stars: Yoko Ono's theory of astrology; Peter Townsend's devotion to Baba Ram Dass. I kept abreast of these subjects and tried to give responsive answers.

Today it's different. The lecture committee arrives at the airport wearing

CAROLYN FERRIS

This much we know: The yuppies are a new breed. They're the first members of the electronic society. They're the first crop of bewildered mutants climbing out of the muck of the industrial (late neolithic smokestack) age. ✍ ... These postwar kids were the first members of a new species, **Homo sapiens electronicus**.

> The phrase "young urban professionals" doesn't tell us much. I guess the implication is that they are not ORAs (old rural amateurs). But who are they?

three-piece suits, briefcases, clipboards with schedules. No music. No questions about Michael Jackson's theory of reincarnation or Sheena Easton's concept of sugar walls. The impudent grins are gone. The young people are cool, realistic, and corporate-minded. They question me about computer stocks, electronic books, and prospects for careers in software.

ANATOMY OF A YUPPIE

The phrase "young urban professionals" doesn't tell us much. I guess the implication is that they are not ORAs (old rural amateurs). But who are they?

The moralists of both left and right can froth with righteous indignation about this army of selfish, career-oriented, entrepreneurial individualists who apparently value money and their own interests more than the lofty causes of yesteryear. But behind the trendy hype, we sense that the twitchy media may be reflecting some authentic change in the public consciousness. The yuppie myth expresses a vague sense that something different, something not yet understood but possibly meaningful, is happening in the day-to-day lives and dreams of young people growing up in this very unsettling world.

Surely it's important to understand what's going on with this most influential group of human beings on the planet—the 76 million materialistic, educated or street-wise, performance-driven Americans between the ages of 22 and 40.

This much we know: The yuppies are a new breed. They're the first members of the electronic society. They're the first crop of bewildered mutants climbing out of the muck of the industrial (late neolithic smokestack) age. They showed up on the scene in 1946, a watershed year, marking the end of World War II—the war that induced the birth of electronic technology: radar, sonar, atomic fission, computers. In 1946, this incredible high-tech gear was

beginning to be available for civilian consumption.

Something else important happened in 1946. The birthrate in America unexpectedly doubled. Between 1946 and 1964, 76 million babies were born. That's 40 million more than demographers predicted. These postwar kids were the first members of a new species, *Homo sapiens electronicus.* From the time they could peer out of the crib, they were exposed to a constant shower of information beaming from screens.

They were, right from the start, treated like no other generation in human history. Their parents raised them according to Dr. Benjamin Spock's totally revolutionary theory of child care. "Treat your kids as individuals," said Spock. "Tell them that they are special! Tell them to think for themselves. Feed them, not according to some factory schedule. Feed them on gourmet demand, i.e., let 'em eat what they want when they are hungry."

This generation is the most intelligent group of human beings ever to inhabit the planet. The best educated. The most widely traveled. The most sophisticated. They have grown up adapting to an accelerated rate of change that is almost incomprehensible. They became highly selective consumers, expecting to be rewarded because they are the best.

Let's hasten to clear up one misconception here. This postwar generation of Spockies was not docilely manipulated by greedy admen or the cynical media. Nor was it the so-called imagemakers, the rock stars and television programmers and moviemakers, telling the kids what to do. Quite to the contrary. The Spockies themselves dictate to the imageers and marketeers about what they want.

BABY-BOOMERS GROW UP

The rapidly changing style and tone of American culture in the last four decades has reflected the elitist expectations of this Spock generation as it passed through the normal stages of maturation.

During the 1950s, kids were clean-cut and easygoing. The tumultuous 1960s marked the stormy adolescence of this astonishing generation and bore the hippies, bands of cheerful, muddling sensualists and self-proclaimed dropouts. By the 1970s, Spockies were busy stopping the Vietnam War, peaceably overthrowing the Nixon administration, and mainly trying to figure out what to do with their lives. The 1980s brought us a new breed of individualists turned professional.

The 1950s are fondly remembered as the child-centered, home-based decade. Popular music, being most free from parental control, provided the clearest expression of youthful mood. The first stirrings of adolescence changed the beat. Spockies wanted to wiggle their hips tentatively; so the hula-hoop craze swept the land. The music picked up the beat with rhythm 'n' blues, rockabilly, rock 'n' roll, the Surfer and the Motown sound. Just as cute, fuzzy caterpillars suddenly metamorphose into gaudy butterflies, so did the sweet, cuddly Mouseketeers moult into high-flying, highly visible, highly vulnerable hippies.

The Spockies emerging into teenage pubescence in the 1960s changed our traditional notions about sex, duty, work, conformity, and sacrifice. The postwar kids never really accepted the values of the industrial society or the æsthetics of the Depression era. They never bought the Protestant work ethic. After watching television six hours a day for fifteen years, would they settle docilely for a hard-hat job on the assembly line?

Bob Dylan set the tone for the adolescent rebellion: "Don't follow leaders/ watch your parking meters." The Beach Boys offered a California style of personal freedom. The Beatles picked up the theme of bouncy irreverence. It seemed so natural. All you need is love. Do your own thing.

The 1960s were unflurried, unworried, more erotic than neurotic. We're not gonna be wage slaves or fight the old men's wars. We're all gonna live in a yellow submarine!

It wasn't just middle-class white males calling for changes. The blacks were ready. They had been waiting four hundred years. The race riots and the civil-rights protests and the freedom marches were an unexpected fallout of Spockian philosophy. It is hard to overestimate the effect of the black culture on the Spockie generation. There was the music, of course. The style, the grace, the coolness, the cynical zen detachment from the system came from the blacks. No white professor had to tell the blacks to turn on, tune in, and drop out of conformity.

Then there was the women's liberation movement, perhaps the most significant change impulse of the century. This was the smartest, best-educated group of women in history, and they expected to be treated as individuals. And the gay-pride concept was stirring. Apparently their parents had read Spock, too. Not since the democratic, human-rights movements of the 18th Century had there been so much feverish hope for a fair and free social order.

But by the end of the decade it became apparent that utopia wasn't going to happen that easily, for three obvious reasons:

1. There were powerful forces dead-set against any change in American culture.
2. There were no practical blueprints or role models for harnessing a vague philosophy of individualism into a functioning social order.
3. Basically, we were not quite ready: The Spockies were still kids outnumbered demographically and unprepared psychologically to create the postindustrial phase of human culture.

The opposition to change had made itself very apparent in the cold-blooded assassinations of Jack Kennedy, brother Bobby, Malcolm X, and Martin Luther King, Jr. Lyndon Johnson, Richard Nixon, and the new cowboy governor of California, one

> Any predictions about the future that the yuppies are currently creating must be based on the fact that they are the first members of the information-communication culture. . . . Intelligence is their ethos and their model. They understand that the smart thing to do is to construct a peaceful, fair, just, compassionate social order.

Back in the 1960s when I flew in for a lecture, the student committee showed up at the airport wearing long hair, sandals, blue jeans, and cheerful, impudent grins. The radio would be blasting ... Today it's different. The lecture committee arrives at the airport wearing three-piece suits, briefcases, clipboards with schedules. No music.

R. Reagan, made it perfectly clear that they would happily use force to protect their system.

The social philosophy of the hippies was romantically impractical. Sure, they weren't gonna work on Maggie's farm no more, but what were they gonna do after balling all night long? Some retreated to gurus, others went back to a new form of antitechnological chic Amishness. Urban political activists parroted slogans of European or third-world socialism and made pop stars of totalitarian leaders like Che Guevara and Ho Chi Minh. The debacle at Altamont and the conjunction of overdose deaths of rock stars Joplin, Hendrix, and Morrison symbolized the end of the 1960s.

THE NEXT PHASE

By 1968, many young people had lost confidence in the old establishments. The phrase "Don't trust anyone over 30" reflected a disillusioned realism; you couldn't find answers in the grand ol' party of Nixon or the Democratic party of Hubert Humphrey. Big business and big labor were both unresponsive to the obvious need for change; the high ideals of socialism seemed to translate into just another word for police-state bureaucracy. By the end of the decade, it was also clear to any sensible young person that individualism and doing your own thing had a certain drawback. If you weren't gonna work for Maggie's pa no more, how were you gonna make out?

The obvious answer: You were

THE YUPPIES AS FREE AGENTS •

Before 1946, youngsters absorbed and joined their culture by means of personal observation of significant grown-ups. You watched the neighborhood doctor and the local carpenter and the nurse or the maiden aunt, and you drifted into a job. Books, sermons, magazine articles about heroic or antisocial figures also helped define the nature of the social game.

Television changed all that. The average American household watches television more than seven hours a day. This statistic means that yuppies learned about culture, absorbed the roles, rules, rituals, styles, and jargon of the game, not from personal observation but from television images. The cartoons, soap operas, prime-time dramas, and game shows tend to be escapist. The news broadcasts tend to feature victims and righteous whiners rather than successful role models. Politicians reciting rehearsed lies are not seen as credible heroes.

The only aspect of television that pre-

sents real people engaged in actions that are existentially true, credible, and scientifically objective are the sportscasts. This may explain the enormous media attention given to organized athletics. The average kid watches Fernando Valenzuela or Joe Montana or Kareem Abdul–Jabbar perform and is then exposed to endless interviews with and stories about these successful, self-made professionals. Their opinions, moods, physical ailments, philosophies, and lifestyles are presented in microscopic detail. People know more about Larry Bird as a "real person" than they do about Walter Mondale or George Bush or Dan Rather.

It can be argued that professional athletes were the first group to work out the tactics for surviving and excelling in a postindustrial world and have thus provided role models for the yuppies. Before the 1960s, professional athletic heroes were serfs indentured to baronial industrialists who literally owned them. The own-

gonna believe in yourself. That's what the 1970s were all about. More than 76 million Spockies reached the venerable age of 24 and faced a very practical challenge: Grow up!

The focus became self-improvement, EST, assertiveness training, personal excellence, career planning. Tom Wolfe, always the shrewd social critic, coined the term "the me-generation."

Then the recession hit. Arab-oil blackmail pushed up inflation rates. Adult society had no expansion-growth plans to harness the energies of 40 million extra people. Indeed, growing automation was reducing the work force. The Iran hostage crisis lowered morale. In the malaise of 1980, the voters chose the smiling Ronald Reagan over a frustrated Carter. Actually,

the Spockies boycotted the election; so the country went to an aging man who proceeded to heat up the threat of nuclear war and run up an enormous national deficit, a debt to be paid by future generations.

Most young Americans today don't want to be forced to work at jobs that can be done better by machines. They don't want to stand on assembly lines repeating mindless tasks. Robots work. Citizens in socialist workers' countries work. Grizzled veterans in the steel towns of Pennsylvania work. Third-world people have to work to survive.

What do self-respecting, intelligent, ambitious young Americans do? They perform. They master a craft. They learn to excel in a personal skill. They become entrepreneurs, i.e., people who organize,

operate, and assume risks. They employ themselves, they train themselves, they promote themselves, they transfer themselves, they reward themselves.

They perform exactly those functions that can't be done by CAD–CAM machines, however precisely programmed. They gravitate naturally to postindustrial fields—electronics, communication, education, merchandising, marketing, entertainment, skilled personal service, health and growth enterprises, leisure-time professions.

They are politically and psychologically independent. They do not identify with company or union or partisan party. They do not depend on organizational tenure. They are notoriously nonloyal to institutions. ☞

---

ers could trade them, fire them, pay them at whim. The rare athlete who "held out" was considered a troublemaker.

The first wave of athletes from the Spock generation hit the big leagues in the mid-1960s, and they immediately changed the rules of the game. In contrast to the older athletes, they were better educated, politically sophisticated, culturally hip individualists. In a curious way, young athletes accomplished the evolution in American society that the hippies were dreaming about. For starters, they eliminated their legal status as serfs. They became free agents, and hired their own lawyers and managers.

It was no accident that black athletes led this evolution. Wilt Chamberlain is credited as being the first super-pro to make gourmet demands on owners: first-class accommodations, hotel-room beds that fit his individual dimensions! Wilt was not a worker; he was a performer. He had figures to prove his worth. He understood

that, through the magic of television, he and his colleagues were providing America with a new, personal style that was making fortunes for the owners and the networks.

A basic concept here was attitude. The post-Chamberlain players realized long before the yuppies that free agents have to depend on themselves. The players even had to violate management regulations to conduct their own programs of physical fitness. The grizzled, potbellied coaches were convinced that weight-training and personal-exercise programs would hinder performance.

The blacks started it, and then the women caught on. Billie Jean King and Chris Evert and Martina Navratilova demanded to be treated as individuals. And to add to the singularity, they made the public accept the fact that they ran their personal and sex lives according to their own gourmet styles. All this made a lot of sense to the kids. There was no way

a 12-year-old could imitate Ronald Reagan, but every day in the playground, classroom, and video arcade, he could emulate the young professionals whom he saw performing on the screen.

The emergence of the electronic ministry and the television flock is pure 1980s. Preachers, like other professionals, are judged by their ratings.

Any predictions about the future that the yuppies are currently creating must be based on the fact that they are the first members of the information-communication culture. It is inevitable that they will become more realistic, more professional, more skilled. Intelligence is their ethos and their model. They understand that the smart thing to do is to construct a peaceful, fair, just, compassionate social order. ◎

III.3.
THE CYBERPUNK:
THE INDIVIDUAL AS REALITY PILOT

*Your true pilot cares nothing about anything on Earth but the river,
and his pride in his occupation surpasses the pride of kings.*
Mark Twain, *Life on the Mississippi*

"Cyber" means "pilot."

A **"cyberperson"** is one who pilots his/her own life. By definition, the cyberperson is
fascinated by navigational information—especially maps, charts, labels, guides,
manuals that help pilot one through life. The cyberperson continually searches for
theories, models, paradigms, metaphors, images, icons that help chart and define
the realities that we inhabit.

"Cybertech" refers to the tools, appliances, and methodologies of knowing and
communicating. Linguistics. Philosophy. Semantics. Semiotics. Practical
epistemologies. The ontologies of daily life. Words, icons, pencils, printing presses,
screens, keyboards, computers, disks.

"Cyberpolitics" introduces the Foucault notions of the use of language and linguistic-tech
by the ruling classes in feudal and industrial societies to control children, the
uneducated, and the under classes. The words "governor" or "steersman" or
"G-man" are used to describe those who manipulate words and communication
devices in order to control, to bolster authority—feudal, management,
government—and to discourage innovative thought and free exchange.

WHO IS THE CYBERPUNK?

Cyberpunks use all available data-input to think for themselves.
You know who they are.
Every stage of history has produced names and heroic legends for the strong,
stubborn, creative individuals who explore some future frontier, collect and bring back new
information, and offer to guide the human gene pool to the next stage. Typically, these time
mavericks combine bravery, and high curiosity, with super self-esteem. These three charac-

teristics are considered necessary for those engaged in the profession of genetic guide, *aka* counterculture philosopher.

The classical Olde Westworld model for the cyberpunk is Prometheus, a technological genius who "stole" fire from the Gods and gave it to humanity. Prometheus also taught his gene pool many useful arts and sciences. According to the official version of the legend, he/she was exiled from the gene pool and sentenced to the ultimate torture for these unauthorized transmissions of classified information. In another version of the myth (unauthorized), Prometheus (*aka* the Pied Piper) uses his/her skills to escape the sinking kinship, taking with him/her the cream of the gene pool.

The Newe World version of this ancient myth is Quetzalcoatl, God of civilization, high-tech wizard who introduced maize, the calendar, erotic sculpture, flute-playing, the arts, and the sciences. He was driven into exile by the G-man in power, who was called Tezcatlipoca.

Self-assured singularities of the cyberbreed have been called mavericks, ronin, free-lancers, independents, self-starters, nonconformists, oddballs, troublemakers, kooks, visionaries, iconoclasts, insurgents, blue-sky thinkers, loners, smart alecks. Before Gorbachev, the Soviets scornfully called them hooligans. Religious organizations have always called them heretics. Bureaucrats call them disloyal dissidents, traitors, or worse. In the old days, even sensible people called them mad.

They have been variously labeled clever, creative, entrepreneurial, imaginative, enterprising, fertile, ingenious, inventive, resourceful, talented, eccentric.

During the tribal, feudal, and industrial-literate phases of human evolution, the logical survival traits were conformity and dependability. The "good serf" or "vassal" was obedient. The "good worker" or "manager" was reliable. Maverick thinkers were tolerated only at moments when innovation and change were necessary, usually to deal with the local competition.

In the information-communication civilization of the 21st Century, creativity and mental excellence will become the ethical norm. The world will be too dynamic, complex, and diversified, too cross-linked by the global immediacies of modern (quantum) communication, for stability of thought or dependability of behaviour to be successful. The "good persons" in the cybernetic society are the intelligent ones who can think for themselves. The "problem person" in the cybernetic society of the 21st Century is the one who automatically obeys, who never questions authority, who acts to protect his/her official status, who placates and politics rather than thinks independently.

Thoughtful Japanese are worried about the need for ronin thinking in their obedient culture, the postwar generation now taking over.

THE CYBERPUNK COUNTERCULTURE IN THE SOVIET UNION

The new postwar generation of Soviets caught on that new role models are necessary to compete in the information age. Under Gorbachev, bureaucratic control is being softened, made elastic to encourage some modicum of innovative, dissident thought!

Aleksandr N. Yakovlev, Politburo member and key strategist of the glasnost policy, describes that reform: "Fundamentally, we are talking about self-government. We are moving toward a time when people will be able to govern themselves and control the activities of people that have been placed in the position of learning and governing them.

"It is not accidental that we are talking about *self*-government, or *self*-sufficiency and *self*-profitability of an enterprise, *self*-this and *self*-that. It all concerns the decentralization of power."

> The classical Olde Westworld model for the cyberpunk is Prometheus, a technological genius who "stole" fire from the Gods and gave it to humanity. Prometheus also taught his gene pool many useful arts and sciences.

The cyberpunk person, the pilot who thinks clearly and creatively, using quantum-electronic appliances and brain know-how, is the newest, updated, top-of-the-line model of the 21st Century: *Homo sapiens sapiens cyberneticus.*

THE GREEK WORD FOR "PILOT"

A great pilot can sail even when his canvas is rent.

Lucius Annæus Seneca

The term "cybernetics" comes from the Greek word *kubernetes,* "pilot."

The Hellenic origin of this word is important in that it reflects the Socratic–Platonic traditions of independence and individual self-reliance which, we are told, derived from geography. The proud little Greek city-states were perched on peninsular fingers wiggling down into the fertile Mediterranean Sea, protected by mountains from the land-mass armies of Asia.

Mariners of those ancient days had to be bold and resourceful. Sailing the seven seas without maps or navigational equipment, they were forced to develop independence of thought. The self-reliance that these Hellenic pilots developed in their voyages probably carried over to the democratic, inquiring, questioning nature of their land life.

The Athenian cyberpunks, the pilots, made their own navigational decisions.

These psychogeographical factors may have contributed to the humanism of the Hellenic religions that emphasized freedom, pagan joy, celebration of life, and speculative thought. The humanist and polytheistic religions of ancient Greece are often compared with the austere morality of monotheistic Judaism, the fierce, dogmatic polarities of Persian–Arab dogma, and the imperial authority of Roman (Christian) culture.

> In the information-communication civilization of the 21st Century, creativity and mental excellence will become the ethical norm. The world will be too dynamic, complex, and diversified, too cross-linked by the global immediacies of modern (quantum) communication, for stability of thought or dependability of behaviour to be successful.

THE ROMAN CONCEPT OF DIRECTOR, GOVERNOR, STEERSMAN

The Greek word *kubernetes,* when translated to Latin, comes out as *gubernetes.* This basic verb *gubernare* means to control the actions or behavior, to direct, to exercise sovereign authority, to regulate, to keep under, to restrain, to steer. This Roman concept is obviously very different from the Hellenic notion of "pilot."

It may be relevant that the Latin term "to steer" comes from the word *stare,* which means "to stand," with derivative meanings "place or thing which is standing." The past participle of the Latin word produces "status," "state," "institute," "statue," "static," "statistics," "prostitute," "restitute," "constitute."

CYBERPUNK PILOTS REPLACE GOVERNETICS-CONTROLLERS

*Society everywhere is in conspiracy against the self-hood of every one of
its members. The virtue in most request is conformity. Self-reliance is its
aversion. It loves not realities and creators, but names and customs.*

Ralph Waldo Emerson, Nature

Who so would be a man must be a nonconformist.

Emerson, op. cit.

The word "cybernetics" was coined in 1948 by Norbert Weiner, who wrote, "We have
decided to call the entire field of control and communication theory, whether in the machine
or in the animal, by the name of Cybernetics, which we form from the Greek for steersman.
[sic]"

The word "cyber" has been redefined (in the *American Heritage Dictionary*) as "the
theoretical study of control processes in electronic, mechanical, and biological systems, especially the flow of information in such systems." The derivative word "cybernate" means "to
control automatically by computer or to be so controlled."

An even more ominous interpretation defines cybernetics as "the study of human
control mechanisms and their replacement by mechanical or electronic systems."

Note how Weiner and the Romanesque engineers have corrupted the meaning of
"cyber." The Greek word "pilot" becomes "governor" or "director"; the term "to steer"
becomes "to control."

Now we are liberating the term, teasing it free from serfdom to represent the
autopoetic, self-directed principle of organization that arises in the universe in many systems
of widely varying sizes, in people, societies, and atoms.

OUR OPPRESSIVE BIRTHRIGHT: THE POLITICS OF LITERACY

The etymological distinctions between Greek and Roman terms are quite relevant to
the pragmatics of the culture surrounding their usage. French philosophy, for example, has
recently stressed the importance of language and semiotics in determining human behaviour and social structures. Michel Foucault's classic studies of linguistic politics and mind
control led him to believe that

> human consciousness—as expressed in speech and images, in self-definition and mutual designation . . .
> is the authentic locale of the determinant politics of being. . . . What men and women are born into is
> only superficially this or that social, legislative, and executive system. Their ambiguous, oppressive
> birthright is the language, the conceptual categories, the conventions of identification and perception
> which have evolved and, very largely, atrophied up to the time of their personal and social existence. It is
> the established but customarily subconscious, unargued constraints of awareness that enslave.

Orwell and Wittgenstein and McLuhan agree. To remove the means of expressing
dissent is to remove the possibility of dissent. "Whereof one cannot speak, thereof must one

remain silent." In this light the difference between the Greek word "pilot" and the Roman translation "governor" becomes a most significant semantic manipulation, and the flexibility granted to symbol systems of all kinds by their representation in digital computers becomes dramatically liberating.

Do we pride ourselves for becoming ingenious "pilots" or dutiful "controllers"?

WHO, WHAT, AND WHY IS GOVERNETICS

Damn the torpedoes, full speed ahead.
Captain David Glasgow Farragut's order to his steersman
at the Battle of Mobile Bay, August 5, 1864

Aye, aye, sir.
Unknown enlisted steersman
at the Battle of Mobile Bay, August 5, 1864

The word "governetics" refers to an attitude of obedience-control in relationship to self or others.

Pilots, those who navigate on the seven seas or in the sky, have to devise and execute course changes continually in response to the changing environment. They respond continually to feedback, information about the environment. Dynamic. Alert. Alive.

The Latinate "steersman," by contrast, is in the situation of following orders. The Romans, we recall, were great organizers, road-builders, administrators. The galleys, the chariots must be controlled. The legions of soldiers must be directed.

The Hellenic concept of the individual navigating his/her own course was an island of humanism in a raging sea of totalitarian empires. To the East (the past) were the centralized, authoritarian kingdoms. The governors of Iran, from Cyrus, the Persian emperor, to the recent shah and ayatollah, have exemplified the highest traditions of state control.

The Greeks were flanked on the other side, which we shall designate as the West (or future), by a certain heavy concept called Rome. The cæsars and popes of the Holy Roman Empire represented the next grand phase of institutional control. The governing hand on the wheel stands for stability, durability, continuity, permanence. Staying the course. Individual creativity, exploration, and change are usually not encouraged.

Cyber: The Greek word kubernetes, when translated to Latin, comes out as gubernetes. This basic verb gubernare means to control the actions or behavior, to direct, to exercise sovereign authority, to regulate, to keep under, to restrain, to steer. This Roman concept is obviously very different from the Hellenic notion of "pilot" [making their own navigational decisions]. . . . the meaning of "cyber" has been corrupted. The Greek word "pilot" becomes "governor" or "director"; the term "to steer" becomes "to control." . . . The terms "cybernetic person" or "cybernaut" return us to the original meaning of "pilot" and puts the self-reliant person back in the loop.

CYBERPUNKS: PILOTS OF THE SPECIES

"The winds and waves are always on the side of the ablest navigators."
Edward Gibbon

The terms "cybernetic person" or "cybernaut" return us to the original meaning of "pilot" and puts the self-reliant person back in the loop. These words (and the more pop term "cyberpunk") refer to the personalization (and thus the popularization) of knowledge-information technology, to innovative thinking on the part of the individual.

According to McLuhan and Foucault, if you change the language, you change the society. Following their lead, we suggest that the terms "cybernetic person, cybernaut" may describe a new species model of human being and a new social order. "Cyberpunk" is, admittedly, a risky term. Like all linguistic innovations, it must be used with a tolerant sense of high-tech humor. It's a stopgap, transitional meaning-grenade thrown over the language barricades to describe the resourceful, skillful individual who accesses and steers knowledge-communication technology toward his/her own private goals, for personal pleasure, profit, principle, or growth.

Cyberpunks are the inventors, innovative writers, technofrontier artists, risk-taking film directors, icon-shifting composers, stand-up comedians, expressionist artists, free-agent scientists, technocreatives, computer visionaries, elegant hackers, bit-blitting Prolog adepts, special-effectives, cognitive dissidents, video wizards, neurological test pilots, media explorers—all of those who boldly package and steer ideas out there where no thoughts have gone before.

Countercultures are sometimes tolerated by the governors. They can, with sweet cynicism and patient humor, interface their singularity with institutions. They often work within the "governing systems" on a temporary basis.

As often as not, they are unauthorized.

THE LEGEND OF THE RONIN

The ronin . . . has broken with the tradition of career feudalism.
Guided by a personally defined code of adaptability, autonomy,
and excellence, ronin are employing career strategies
grounded in a premise of rapid change.
Beverly Potter, *The Way of the Ronin*

Ronin is used as a metaphor based on a Japanese word for lordless samurai. As early as the 8th Century, ronin was translated literally as "wave people" and used in Japan to describe those who had left their allotted, caste-predetermined stations in life: samurai who left the service of their feudal lords to become masterless.

Ronin played a key role in Japan's abrupt transition from a feudal society to industrialism. Under feudal rule, warriors were not allowed to think freely, or act according to their will. On the other hand, having been forced by circumstances to develop independence, [ronin] took more readily to new ideas and technology and became increasingly influential in the independent schools.

Potter, op. cit.

The West has many historical parallels to the ronin archetype. The term "free lance" has its origin in the period after the Crusades, when a large number of knights were separated from their lords. Many lived by the code of chivalry and became "lances for hire."

The American frontier was fertile ground for the ronin archetype. "Maverick," derived from the Texan word for unbranded steer, was used to describe a free and self-directed individual.

Although many of the ronin's roots . . . are in the male culture, most career women are well acquainted with the way of the ronin. Career women left their traditional stations and battled their way into the recesses of the male-dominated workplaces . . . Like the ronin who had no clan, professional women often feel excluded from the corporate cliques' inside tracks, without ally or mentor.

Potter, op. cit.

SOME EXAMPLES OF CYBERPUNKS

Christopher Columbus (1451–1506) was born in Genoa. At age 25 he showed up in Lisbon and learned the craft of map-making. This was the golden era of Portuguese exploration. Many pilots and navigators were convinced that the Earth was round, and that the Indies and other unknown lands could be found by crossing the western seas. What was special about Columbus was his persistence and eloquence in support of the dream of discovery. For more than ten years he traveled the courts of Europe attempting to make "the deal"; to find backing for his "enterprise of the Indies."

According to the *Columbia Encyclopedia,* "Historians have disputed for centuries his skill as a navigator, but it has been recently proved that with only dead reckoning Columbus was unsurpassed in charting and finding his way about unknown seas."

Columbus was a most unsuccessful governor of the colonies he had discovered. He died in disgrace, his cyberskills almost forgotten. (At least that's what they tell us in the authorized history books.)

In 1992 the Political Correction Department dismissed Columbus as a racist colonialist.

Mark Twain. He purchased the Remington typewriter when it appeared in 1874 for $125. In 1875 he became the first author in history to submit a typewritten manuscript to a publisher. It was *The Adventures of Tom Sawyer.*

"This newfangled writing machine," Twain wrote, "has several virtues. It piles an awful stack of words on one page. It don't muss things or scatter ink blots around. Of course it saves paper."

Mathias (Rusty) Rust, a 19-year-old loner from Hamburg, Germany, attained all-star status as a cyberpunk when, on May 28, 1987, he flew a one-engine Cessna through the "impenetrable" Soviet air defenses and landed in Moscow's Red Square. There were no gubernal or organizational motives. The technological adventure was a personal mission. Rusty just wanted to talk to some Russians. German newspapers celebrated the event, calling it "the stuff of dreams," and comparing the youth to the Red Baron Manfred von Richthofen and Charles Augustus Lindbergh.

THE CYBERPUNK CODE: TFYQA

War Games is an electronic quantum signal, a movie about high-tech computers and human evolution that illustrates and condemns the use of quantum-electronic knowledge technology by governors to control. The film celebrates the independence and skill of cyberpunks who think for themselves and innovate from within the static system. The Captain and his wife use high-tech agriculture methods to enhance the potency of unauthorized botanical neuroactivators. The Captain makes an unauthorized decision to abort World War III. In both instances the Captain follows the cyberpunk code: *Think for yourself; question authority (TFYQA).*

The cyberkid Matthew Broderick is equally courageous, outrageous, creative, and bright. When the audience is introduced to the hero of *War Games,* he is in a video arcade playing a space-adventure game with poise and proficiency. An electron jock.

Late for school, he's pulled into the classic confrontation: the authoritarian teacher humiliates and punishes the Tom Sawyer kid, sends him to the principal's office. There he obtains the code for the school's computer system. Back home, he uses his PC to access the school records. He changes an unfair grade to a passing level. He thinks for himself and questions authority.

At the crucial moment he rushes to the library and researches the life of a physicist, scans scientific journals, scopes microfilm files—not to please the system, but in pursuit of his own personal grail.

Note that there is a new dimension of electronic ethics and quantum legality here. The Captain and Matthew perform no act of physical violence, no theft of material goods. The Captain processes some computer data and decides for himself. Matthew rearranges clusters of electrons stored on a chip. They seek independence, not control over others.

THE CYBERPUNK AS ROLE MODEL FOR THE 21ST CENTURY

The tradition of the "individual who thinks for him/herself" extends to the beginnings of recorded human history. Indeed, the very label of our species, *Homo sapiens,* defines us as the animals who think.

If our genetic function is *computare* ("to think"), then it follows that the ages and stages of human history, so far, have been larval or preparatory. After the insectoid phases of submission to gene pools, the mature stage of the human life cycle is the individual who thinks for him/herself. Now, at the beginnings of the information age, are we ready to assume our genetic function? ◎

> The "good persons" in the cybernetic society are the intelligent ones who can think for themselves. The "problem person" in the cybernetic society of the 21st Century is the one who automatically obeys, who never questions authority, who acts to protect his/her official status, who placates and politics rather than thinks independently.

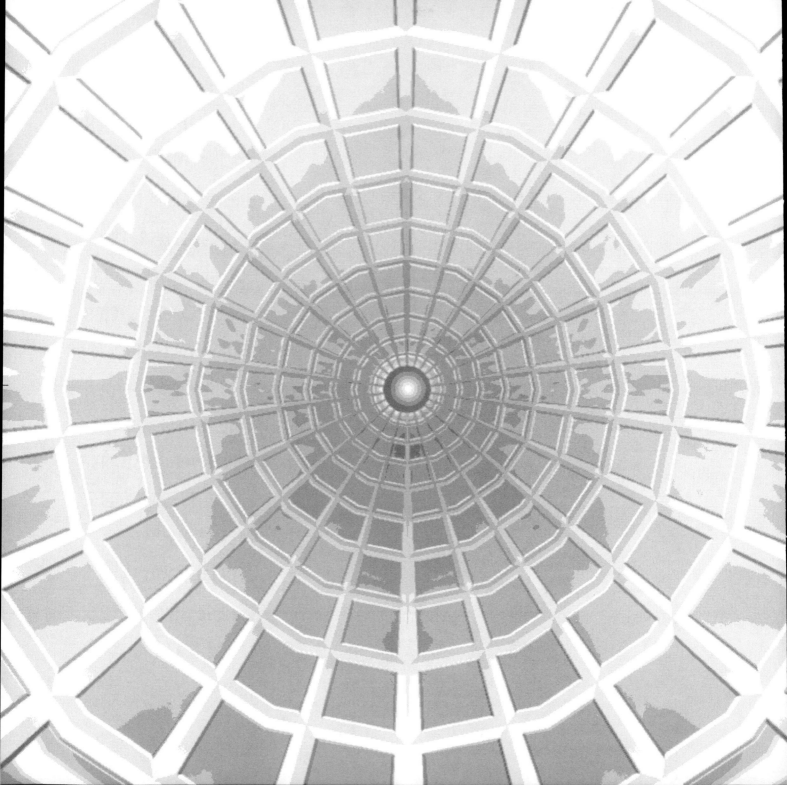

ANDY FRITH

III.4. THE NEW BREED

Memes: Self-replicating ideas that sweep across human populations, bringing about cultural mutations.

Neoteny: (1) attainment of improved functional maturity during the larval stage; (2) retention of survivally optimal larval or immature characters as adults, i.e., refusal to stop growing, extension of the developmental period.

● ● ● ● ● ● ● ● ● ● ● ● ● ● ● ●

November 9, 1989. None of us will forget those pictures of that menacing meme-icon, the Berlin Wall, crumbling in minds all over the world. We saw the faces of those young, upwardly mobile people in blue jeans and white running shoes who, for the first time in their lives, were experiencing self-navigation, free to choose their life options outside the control of the authorities.

November 24, 1989. The demonstrations in Prague led to a nationwide strike. Grizzled, hard-hat workers marched out of the factories shouting, "Long live the students!" The next day, the Czech hard-line regime resigned.

December 28, 1989. The repressive regime of Nikolae Ceausescu has fallen.

"It was a children's revolution," said an elderly woman to a reporter.

"Yes, the students," a young woman said.

"No, no, not students," a woman said. "The children. Our children saved us. They did this for us." (*Los Angeles Times, 12/29/89*).

It had finally happened: the inevitable and long-awaited climax of the youth revolutions. "They aren't going to work on Brezhnev's farm no more." The Dr. Spock-memes of self-direction had swept the world in less than three decades.

This is not a political revolution; it's more like a cultural evolution. A tsunami of electronic information. The emergence of a new breed. Young people all over the world are mutated, as Marshall McLuhan predicted, by highly communicable memes: documentary footage, rock 'n' roll music, MTV, pirate broadcasts, all coming to them through American–Japanese television screens. This new breed is centered on self-direction and individual choice, a genetic revulsion for partisan politics, a species horror of centralized governments.

This global youth movement cannot be discussed in the terms of politics or sociology or psychology. We are dealing with a new, post–Darwinian, genetic science.

This emergence of youth power has been called sociogenetics, cybernetic evolution, cultural genetics, memetics. It has to do with the communication and transmission of new ideas and attitudes. Dawkins has suggested the word "memes" to describe these self-replicating ideas that sweep across human populations, bringing about cultural mutations.

In the last thirty years, we have witnessed a new breed emerging during the juvenile stage of industrial-age society. (The key word here is juvenile, as opposed to adult. Adult is the past participle of the verb "to grow.") This new breed appeared when enormous numbers of individuals in the juvenile stage began intercommunicating some new memes, mutating together at the same time. The Japanese brand of this youth movement call themselves Ho Ko Ten, "the new society."

Biological evolution works through the competitive spread of genes. Logically, the mechanism of cultural change involves communication. Individuals are activated to change when they pick up new meme-signals from others of their cohort. The mode of communication determines not just the speed of the change, but the nature of the change.

THE MEDIUM IS THE MESSAGE
OF CULTURAL EVOLUTION

The Ten Commandments, chiseled on stone tablets, created a fundamentalist culture that discouraged change and democratic participation. There is one God, the author-creator, and his words are eternally true. This stone-tablet meme-carrier spawns a culture ruled by the inerrant "good book" and a priesthood of those who preserve, interpret, and enforce the commandments.

The printing press mass-disseminates memes that create a factory culture run by managers.

The electronic, McLuhanesque meme-signals that produced Woodstock nation and the Berlin Wall deconstruction are more a matter of attitude and style.

The television news has trained us to recognize "the robe-memes"—the feudal pope (or the Iranian mullah) and his solemn piety-reeking priests. We recognize "the suits," the adult politicians of the industrial age, with their no-nonsense sobriety. We observe "the uniforms," armed, booted, helmeted.

And since 1966, we have observed this new breed, "the students" who tend to wear blue jeans and running shoes. Their dress and gestural signals are as important as the identifying markings and scents of different species of mammals. Just like any new breed of mammals, these kids recognize each other across national boundaries. The faces of the Chinese youth shine with that same glow as the faces photographically captured in Berlin and Prague and—twenty years previously—in Woodstock.

IN A CYBERNETIC CULTURE, DEMOCRACY
BECOMES PRIME-TIME AUTHORITARIANISM

It is important to note that these students are not demonstrating for "socialist democracy" or "capitalist democracy." They are for "individual freedom." In the cybernetic age, "democracy" becomes majority-mob rule and the enemy of individual freedom.

Democracy works just fine in a preindustrial, oral society in which the men walk or ride horses to the village center and talk things over. Industrial societies produce a factory system of politics run by managers. Representative government involves full-time professional politicians and partisan parties. The dismal results are predictable.

As soon as cybernetic communication appliances emerged, political power was seized by those who control the airwaves. We've seen this since the rise of fascism and totalitarianism. American elections of 1980, 1984, 1988 produced an ominous demonstration of tele-democracy in a centralized country.

Less than 50 percent of the eligible voters bothered to register or vote in these three presidential elections. More than half of adult Americans were so disillusioned, apathetic, bored that they made the intelligent decision to vote, in absentia, for "none of the above." According to exit polls, more than half of voting Americans glumly admitted that they were choosing "the lesser of two evils."

Reagan and Bush were elected by around 25 percent of the citizenry. The only ones who really cared about these elections were those who stood to benefit financially from the results. The "apparatchiks" and government-payrolled "nomenclatura" of the two contending "parties" choose the "leaders" who would preside over division of the spoils.

History will note that the 1980s regimes of Reagan–Bush exquisitely mirrored the Brezhnevian anomie in the Soviet Union. It is now shockingly clear that the Republican party in this country plays the role of the Communist party in the pre–Gorbachev USSR: an entrenched, conservative, militaristic, unashamedly corrupt, secretive, belligerently nationalistic bureaucracy. It gave the country twelve years of stagnation, spiritless boredom, and cynical greed.

Meanwhile, the all-star huckster of freedom and decentralization, Mikhail Gorbachev, in five remarkable years persuaded an entire subcontinent to "drop out" of Stalinism.

In this climate it is obvious that the party apparatus with the biggest budget for television advertising and the marketing ability to focus on the most telegenic, shallow, flamboyantly lurid issues (abortion, drugs, pledge of allegiance, school prayer, no taxes, and jingoistic, bellicose nationalism) would sweep to a landslide win on the votes of the 25 percent majority.

It is ironic that in the oldest democracy, the U.S., partisan politics seems to have lost its touch with reality. In the elections of the 1980s, millions were expended on political advertising. Elections were won by paid-time commercials involving moralistic images, emotional theatrics, and malicious fabrications. Old-fashioned religious dæmonology and fake patriotism, skillfully splashed across the television screens, replaced rational discussion of issues.

> Gorbachev was dismayed to find that many Soviet youth, given freedom of the press, were more interested in UFOs, punk rock, astrology, and hashish than in political issues.

THE END OF MAJORITARIAN DEMOCRACY

In the feudal and industrial ages, majoritarian democracy was usually a powerful libertarian counterculture force defending the individual against regal tyranny and class slavery. In the early years of the electronic-information stage (1950–1990), the ability of the religious-industrial-military rulers to manipulate television converted town-hall democracy into majoritarian, prime-time, sit-com totalitarianism.

Cybernetic media in the hands of politicians with shockingly large advertising budgets plays to the dread LCD (lowest common denominator). The new fragile democracies in eastern Europe will probably have to pass through this phase of marketeer, televoid elections manipulated by "spin doctors" and dishonest advertising.

So much for the down side. The good news is that cybernetic media cannot be controlled. Electronic signals flashing around the atmosphere cannot be kept out by stone walls or border police dogs. Japanese tape-decks, ghetto-blasters, digital appliances in the hands of the individual empowers the HCD (highest common denominator).

THE SOCIOLOGY OF QUANTUM PHYSICS

The philosophy that predicted this movement is not capitalism or socialism. It is not industrial democracy (the tyranny of the 25 percent majority). Psychedelic concepts like glasnost and perestroika are based on the common-sense principles of quantum physics—relativity, flexibility, singularity.

Werner Heisenberg's equations described the fabrication of singular, personal realities based on free, open communication. Objective indeterminacy, that bane of the mechanical mind, means individual determinism and self-reliance—the mottoes of the new breed.

DR. SPOCK PERSONALIZES QUANTUM PSYCHOLOGY

In 1946, quantum physics was translated into common-sense, hands-on psychology by a pediatrician. The youth movement was generated by a genial child psychologist who taught two generations of postwar parents to feed their children on demand. "Treat your kids as individuals, as singularities." Here was the most radical, subversive social doctrine ever proposed, and it was directed to the only groups that can bring about enduring change: parents, pediatricians, teachers.

This postwar generation of indulged, "self-centered" individuals started to appear exactly when the new psychedelic-cybernetic brain-change technologies became available to individuals.

MARSHALL McLUHAN EMPOWERS QUANTUM PSYCHOLOGY

The baby-boomers were the first television species, the first human beings who used electronic digital appliances to turn on and tune in realities; the first to use neurotransmitting chemicals to

The postpolitical information society, which we are now developing, does not operate on the basis of obedience and conformity to dogma. It is based on individual thinking, scientific know-how, quick exchange of facts around feedback networks, high-tech ingenuity, and practical, front-line creativity. The society of the future no longer grudgingly tolerates a few open-minded innovators. The cybernetic society is totally dependent on a large pool of such people, communicating at light speed with each other across state lines and national boundaries.

change their own brains; the first members of this "global village" made possible by television.

The fall of the Berlin Wall was accomplished by youth seeking individual freedom. This student counterculture started in America in the 1960s, and it was spread via electronic media.

"Hongk is all the rage in the Mongolian People's Republic. It's a key part of the Shineshiel (perestroika) that has been sweeping the remote communist nation for weeks now . . . Hongk is the name of the rock 'n' roll band that has been playing its powerful, dissident songs to packed audiences in the state-owned auditoriums of Mongolia's capitol of Ulan Bator for months now. Its music has become the unchallenged anthem of the city's fledgling protest movement" (*Los Angeles Times*, 1/24/90).

THE FUNCTION OF POSTDEMOCRATIC GOVERNMENT

The primary function of a free society in the postdemocratic age is the protection of individual freedom from politicians who attempt to limit personal freedom.

This individual-freedom movement is new to human history, because it is not based on geography, politics, class, or religion. It has to do with changes, not in the power structure, not in who controls the police, but in the individual's mind. It is a "head" revolution: a consciousness-raising affair. It involves "thinking for yourself." This cultural meme involves intelligence, personal access to information, an anti-ideological reliance on common sense, mental proficiency, consciousness raising, street smarts, intelligent consumerism-hedonism, personal-communication skills. The meme-idea is not new. Countercultures go back at least as far as Hermes Trismegistus, and include Socrates, Paracelsus, the Renaissance, Voltaire, Emerson, Thoreau, Dada, Gurdjieff, and Crowley.

But the rapid spread of this mutational meme from 1960 to 1990 was due to the sudden, mass availability of neurochemical and electronic technology. Demand feeding. Chemicals and screens spraying electronic information into eyedrums and earballs, activating brains. Suddenly, youth all over the world are wearing jeans and listening to John Lennon's "Give Peace a Chance." The individuality meme that swept American youth during the 1960s has infected the world.

In the 1970s, the Spock–McLuhan epidemic spread around western Europe. The signs of this awakening are always the same. Young minds exposed to the free spray of electronic information suddenly blossom like flowers in the spring. The June 1989 demonstrations in Tien An Men square were a classic replay of Chicago 1968 and Kent State 1970.

Power, Mao said, comes from the barrel of a gun. That may have been true in the industrial past, but in cybernetic 1990, the very notion of political "power" seems anachronistic, kinky, sick. For the new breed the notion of "political power" is hateful, evil, ghastly. The idea that any group should want to grab domination, control, authority, supremacy, or jurisdiction over others is a primitive perversity—as loathsome and outdated as slavery or cannibalism.

It was not the Berlin Wall of concrete and guard houses that protected the "evil empire"; it was the electronic wall that was easily breached by MTV. McLuhan and Foucault have demonstrated that freedom depends upon who controls the technologies that reach your brain—telephones, the editing facility, the neurochemicals, the screen.

MASS INDIVIDUALISM IS NEW

This sudden emergence of humanism and open-mindedness on a mass scale is new.

In tribal societies the role of the individual is to be a submissive, obedient child. The tribal elders do the thinking. Survival pressures do not afford them the luxury of freedom.

In feudal societies the individual is a serf or vassal, peasant, chattel, peon, slave. The nobles and priests do the thinking. They are trained by tradition to abhor and anathematize open-mindedness and thinking for yourself.

After the tribal (familial) and feudal (childlike) stages of human evolution came the industrial (insectoid) society, where the individual is a worker or manager; in later stages, a worker-consumer.

In all these static, primitive societies, the thinking is done by the organizations who control the guns. The power of open-minded individuals to make and remake decisions about their own lives, to fabricate, concoct, invent, prevaricate their own lies is severely limited. Youth had no power, no voice, no choice.

The postpolitical information society, which we are now developing, does not operate on the basis of obedience and conformity to dogma. It is based on individual thinking, scientific know-how, quick exchange of facts around feedback networks, high-tech ingenuity, and practical, front-line creativity. The society of the future no longer grudgingly tolerates a few open-minded innovators. The cybernetic society is totally dependent on a large pool of such people, communicating at light speed with each other across state lines and national boundaries. Electrified thoughts invite fast feedback, creating new global societies that require a higher level of electronic know-how, psychological sophistication, and open-minded intelligence.

This cybercommunication process is accelerating so rapidly that to compete on the world information market of the 21st Century, nations, companies, even families must be composed of change-oriented, innovative individuals who are adepts in communicating via the new cyberelectronic technologies.

The new breeds are simply much smarter than the old guard. They inhale new information the way they breathe oxygen.

They stimulate each other to continually upgrade and reformat their minds. People who use cybertechnology to make fast decisions on their jobs are not going to go home and passively let aging, closed-minded white, male politicians make decisions about their lives.

The emergence of this new open-minded caste in different countries around the world is the central historical issue of the last forty years.

THE REVOLUTIONS OF 1989 BEGAN WITH THE BEATS

 In the 1950s in America, at the height of the television Cold War, there appeared a group of free people who created highly communicable counterculture memes that were to change history. The beats stood for the ecstatic vision and for individual freedom in revolt against all bureaucratic, closed-minded systems. They saw themselves as citizens of the world. They met with Russian poets to denounce the Cold War. They practiced oriental yoga. They experimented, as artists have for centuries, with mind-opening foods and drugs and sexual practices.

Most important, with their minds turning like satellite dishes to other cultures, they had an historical sense of what they were doing. They saw themselves as heirs to the long tradition of intellectual and artistic individualism that goes beyond national boundaries.

What made the beats more effective than any dissident-artist group in human history was the timing. Electronic technology made it possible for their bohemian memes, their images, and their sounds to be broadcast at almost the speed of light around the world. Just as soap companies were using television and radio to market their products, so the beats used the electronic media to advertise their ideas. The hippie culture of the 1960s and the current liberation movements in Eastern Europe are indebted to the libertarian dissenting of the 'fifties counterculture.

BRINGING THE 1960S TO CHINA

The original Be-In (San Francisco, January 1967) produced an ocean of youth who gathered to celebrate their be-ings and their solidarity. It turned out to be the dawning of the psychedelic-cybernetic age (or glasnost, as it is now called). This first San Francisco Be-In was not organized. The word got out via the underground press, progressive radio stations, word of mouth. Three months later the First (and only) International Monterey Pop festival harnessed the flourishing psychedelic spirit to electrically amplified music.

The symbol of the counterculture was the widely repeated image of a young man putting a flower in the gun barrel of the National Guardsman who was threatening him. The students in

The beats stood for the ecstatic vision and for individual freedom in revolt against all bureaucratic, closed-minded systems. They saw themselves as citizens of the world. They met with Russian poets to denounce the Cold War. They practiced oriental yoga. They experimented, as artists have for centuries, with mind-opening foods and drugs and sexual practices.

Most important, with their minds turning like satellite dishes to other cultures, they had an historical sense of what they were doing. They saw themselves as heirs to the long tradition of intellectual and artistic individualism that goes beyond national boundaries.

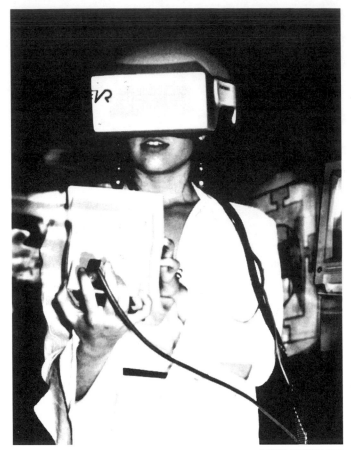

PETER BOOTH LEE

The social and political implications of this democratization of the screen are enormous. In the past, friendship and intimate exchange have been limited to local geography or occasional visits. Now you can play electronic tennis with a pro in Tokyo, interact with a classroom in Paris, cyberflirt with cute guys in any four cities of your choice. A global fast-feedback language of icons and memes, facilitated by instant translation devices, will smoothly eliminate the barriers of language that have been responsible for most of the war and conflict of the last centuries.

Tien An Men Square in June 1989 remembered. Their stated purpose was to bring the 1960s to China. The epidemic of freedom-memes in China caught the authorities totally off guard—just like the numbers at the Woodstock festival.

SELF-GOVERNMENT ENDS REPRESENTATIVE GOVERNMENT

Partisan politics is over. In the postpolitical age, people are catching on to the bottom-line fact: The only function of a political party is to keep itself in office.

This free-speech/free-thought movement emerges routinely when enough young people have access to electronic technology. When the rulers of China made telephones and television sets available to millions of people, the swarming of activated youth in Tien An Men Square was guaranteed. Many of the Chinese students had seen television coverage of student demonstrations in other countries. When East German television stations began transmitting programs from the West, the Berlin Wall was on its way down. In each nation, the free-thought movement of the 1980s was produced by students and intellectuals who learned how to use electronic appliances and digital computers to think for themselves, fabricate their personal mythologies, and communicate their irreverent aspirations.

THE POLITICS OF PRO-CHOICE:
THE RIGHT TO CHOOSE YOUR COLLEGE MAJOR

Freedom is an individual thing. It means something singular, unique, personal for each and every person. The Chinese students want something that is not mentioned by Marx or Margaret Thatcher. They want to say what's on their minds. The right to make their own career decisions. The right to choose their college major. The right to be silly and have fun. The right to kiss your boyfriend in public. The right to mug in front of a television camera. The right to flaunt their own personal lies, concoctions, invented truths in competition with the old official lies.

Gorbachev was dismayed to find that many Soviet youth, given freedom of the press, were more interested in UFOs, punk rock, astrology, and hashish than in political issues.

BLUE JEANS, RUNNING SHOES,
AND DESIGNER MEMES

 Most young people in the liberated lands want to depoliticize, demilitarize, decentralize, secularize, and globalize.

The new breed is jumping the gene pools, forming postindustrial, global meme-pools. They are the informates. From their earliest years, most of their defining memes have come flashing at light speed across borders in digital-electronic form, light signals received by screens and radios and record players. Their habitat is the electron-sphere, the environment of digital signals that is called the info-world. The global village.

They are the first generation of our species to discover and explore Cyberia. They are migrating not to a new place, but to a wide-open new time. The new breed will fashion, conceive, and design the realities they inhabit.

THE DESIGNER SOCIETIES OF THE 21ST CENTURY

Who controls the screen controls the mind of the screen watcher. The power-control struggles of the 1990s will occur on screens in the living rooms of individuals.

In nations where religious or partisan political groups control the screens to fabricate paranoias, the people will be incited to fear, anger, and moral outrage. In the last ten years, the Islamic states and the U.S. under Reagan–Bush have effectively made this point.

The manufacture and distribution of inexpensive communications appliances and software will be of enormous importance. Just as the USSR and the U.S. controlled the world for forty years by distributing weapons to every compliant dictatorship, now Japanese and Silicon Valley companies are liberating the world with an endless flood of electronic devices designed for individuals.

Inexpensive appliances will allow individuals to write on their screens the way Gutenberg hardware-software allowed individuals to write on pages five hundred years ago. These inexpensive digitizing and editing devices are already transforming the home into a cyberstudio in which individuals will design, edit, perform, and transmit memes on their screens.

Individuals clothed in cyberwear will be able to meet each other in virtual realities built for two. The world becomes a neighbourhood in which a person eight thousand miles away can be "right there in your windowpane."

The social and political implications of this democratization of the screen are enormous. In the past, friendship and intimate exchange have been limited to local geography or occasional visits. Now you can play electronic tennis with a pro in Tokyo, interact with a classroom in Paris, cyberflirt with cute guys in any four cities of your choice. A global fast-feedback language of icons and memes, facilitated by instant translation devices, will smoothly eliminate the barriers of language that have been responsible for most of the war and conflict of the last centuries. ◎

Who controls the screen controls the mind of the screen watcher. The power-control struggles of the 1990s will occur on screens in the living rooms of individuals. . . ⌸ The manufacture and distribution of inexpensive communications appliances and software will be of enormous importance. Just as the USSR and the U.S. controlled the world for forty years by distributing weapons to every compliant dictatorship, now Japanese and Silicon Valley companies are liberating the world with an endless flood of electronic devices designed for individuals.

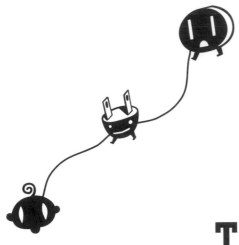

III.5. ELECTRONIC CULTURES

Let the word go out, to friend and foe alike,
that we are passing the torch to a new generation.

J.F.K., Inaugural Speech, 1960

This impassioned rhetoric was the first time that the leader of a superpower or empire had ever used the powerful meme: "generation." J.F.K. was a memetic agent, literally creating a new breed!

Did the speech writers who in 1960 passed along to Jack Kennedy that famous "torch" quote intuit what was going to happen? Did they foresee that the next two decades would produce, for the first time in human history, an economic, political power base called "the youth culture"?

In the 1950s, this new baby-boom generation was tuning in the dials of a new electronic-reality appliance called television to *Leave It to Beaver* and *American Bandstand*. And they were being lovingly guarded in maximum-security homes by devoted parents who had dutifully memorized Dr. Benjamin Spock's *Common-Sense Guide to Child Care*.

The basic theme of Spock's manual (we parents actually called it the Bible) is: Treat your children as individuals.

This innocent bombshell exploded at a pregnant moment of postwar national prosperity and global self-confidence. The Marshall Plan was pouring billions into the rehabilitation-recovery of former enemies. Instead of looting, raping, and occupying the defeated enemies, we treated them like errant offspring who had become delinquent gang members. We helped them get on their feet again and gain self-respect. We postwar Spock parents became the first generation to honour and respect our children and to support their independence from us.

The importance of this event is hard to overestimate. The baby-boomers became the first generation of electronic consumers. Before they were ten, their brains were processing more "realities per day" than their grandparents had confronted in a year.

THE IMPORTANCE OF PARENTAL HOME MEDIA

In 1950, the humble black-and-white television set marked the birth of the electronic culture. Suddenly, humans had developed electronic technology and the know-how to operate the brain and reprogram the mind.

The neurological situation is this: The language circuits of the brain are imprinted between ages three and eight. The media used in the home will format the brain of these children. Linguist-psychologists (Noam Chomsky, Piaget) have demonstrated that languages are imprinted during this brief window of imprint vulnerability. This means that the home media used by the family formats the thought-processing files (left-brain mind) of the children. Mind-change (reformatting) could occur only under conditions that duplicate "the home culture."

If the parents do not read and if there are no newspapers, magazines, or books in

> The neurological situation is this: The language circuits of the brain are imprinted between ages three and eight. The media used in the home will format the brain of these children. . . If the parents do not read and if there are no newspapers, magazines, or books in the house, the kids are at a tremendous disadvantage when they timidly walk (or swagger) into the scary, impersonal first-grade classroom.

the house, the kids are at a tremendous disadvantage when they timidly walk (or swagger) into the scary, impersonal first-grade classroom. (Most good teachers understand this principle, and convert the schoolroom into a homey, supportive environment.)

We also sense the implications for reformatting mind-files (formerly known as remedial reading). Cultures or individuals who wish to change must use different language media. For the illiterate, delinquent gang member, we offer a maximum-security, homelike environment jammed with media coaches. Malcolm X, for example, was taught to read by a stern, loving parent figure in a Massachusetts prison.

And the rest you oughta know!

THE STAGES OF HUMANIZATION

As I flash back on my seventy-plus years of service as Self-Appointed Change Agent and Evolutionary Scout, this viewpoint comes into focus. Our species has, in seven decades, surfed bigger, faster, more complex waves of brain change than our species experienced during the last 25,000 years.

Number of (tribal) generations from cave-wall painting to handwriting and large-scale, public Egyptian art (3200 B.C.)?
☞ About 1,500.

Number of (feudal) generations from the pyramids to Notre Dame Cathedral, oil painting, and book literacy?
☞ About 320.

Number of generations from first factory-printed book (the first home media) to the radios, telephones, record players, movies of A.D. 1950?
☞ About 23.

Number of generations from passive, black-and-white television (1950) to multichannel, multimedia, interactive digital home-screen design?
☞ 3.

ANDY FRITH

THE GENERATIONAL THING

Each generation since 1950 is the equivalent of an age or an epic or an era in past history. Each succeeding generation has accessed more-powerful electronic-language tools. For the first time, we can understand the mechanics of evolution—the language and technology. Finally, the evolution of human brain power is reaching the optimum mutation rate. Electronic brain tools change so rapidly that every fifteen to twenty years the new generation creates a new breed.

Each stage of human culture defines memetic evolution in terms of its media, its language. And the media and languages of cultures determine whether they actively evolve or if they remain passive and unchanging.

Static cultures have built-in, iron-clad linguistic protections against change. Their media-languages self-replicate via repetition, rote-learning, etc. Their reproductive media-languages glorify death as the step to eternal life in well-advertised, perfectly run retirement communities called Heaven, etc. Their media-languages prevent them from being exposed to, infected by, or fertilized by other languages.

To illustrate the importance of language in cultural solidarity, we cite the case of the Iranian Shi'ite ayatollahs who put a $5 million price "on the head" of author Salman Rushdie for a few taboo words in a novel published in far-away England. Or the case of militant Christians who try to force tax-supported schools to teach biblical creationism.

Cultures evolve only when their media-languages have built-in programs:

1. **To discourage rote self-replication;**
2. **To stimulate self-change via shock-humour, irreverent counterculture, chaotics, etc.;**
3. **To invite fusion with other cultures, and fusion with other media-languages.**

Feudal languages gave no words or graphics that encouraged, tolerated, or even mentioned the notion of evolution during earthly life. The almighty male God creates and controls. Heaven is the destination. Chaos, complexity, change are dæmonized, tabooed.

The tech-mech engineers of the industrial age (1500–1950) published texts, manuals, and handbooks defining evolution in terms of a Newtonian–Darwinian–Gordon Liddy competitive power struggle: survival of the most brutal, and by the book.

THE INFORMATION AGE (1950–2010)

In the information age, evolution is defined in terms of brain power.
- **The ability to operate the brain: activate, boot up, turn on, access neurochannels.**
- **The ability to reformat and re-edit mind-files.**
- **The ability to receive, process, send messages at light speed.**
- **The ability to communicate in the multimedia mode; to invent audiographic dictionaries and audiographic grammars.**

By 1995 the mainstream home-media array of inexpensive multimedia appliances will have combined the computer, television, video-cassette recorder, fax, compact-disc player, telephone, etc., into one personal home-digital system. During the feudal culture, brain power changed little from century to century. In the mechanical culture, media machines like telephone and radio reached Main Street homes a few decades after their invention. But the explosion of brain power in the electronic culture from 1950–1995 requires precise birthdates for each generation.

THE FOUR ELECTRONIC (LIGHT) CULTURES AND COUNTERCULTURES

As brain power accelerates exponentially, we can locate with precision the birthdates of the post-mech cultures.

Americans who were ages three to eight around 1950 became the first primitive electronic culture. As kids, they sat in front of the television and learned how to turn on, tune in, and turn off. Let us call them the "Ike-Knows-Best-Leave-It-to-Beavers," whose parents were sometimes known by the term "conformist."

They were happy. But they were not hip. Their bland passivity instigated the perfect antidote—the counterculture, which initially appears during the sociosexual imprint window known as adolescence.

The Beats! Hipsters! Rebels! They smoked weed and scored junk. They despised television. They were shockingly literate. They wrote breakthrough poetry and poetic prose, honored jazz by ultra-hip African–Americans. They were sexually experimental.

Our species has, in seven decades, surfed bigger, faster, more complex waves of brain change than our species experienced during the last 25,000 years.

EVOLUTION OF COUNTERCULTURES

BEATS
(1950–1965)

Mood:	Cool, laid back.
Aesthetic-Erotics:	Artistic, literate, hip. Interested in poetry, drugs, jazz.
Attitude:	Sarcastic, cynical.
Brain-Tech:	Low-tech, but early psychedelic explorers.
Intellectual Viewpoint:	Well-informed, skeptical, street-smart.
Humanist Quotient:	Tolerant of race and gay rights, but often male chauvinist.
Politics:	Bohemian, anti-Establishment.
Cosmic View:	Romantic pessimism, Buddhist cosmology.

HIPPIES
(1965–1975)

Mood:	Blissed out.
Aesthetic-Erotics:	Earthy, horny, free-love oriented. Pot, LSD, acid rock.
Attitude:	Peaceful, idealistic.
Brain-Tech:	Psychedelic, but anti-high-tech.
Intellectual Viewpoint:	Know-it-all, anti-intellectual.
Humanist Quotient:	Male chauvinist, sometimes sexist, but socially tolerant and global village visionary.
Politics:	Classless, irreverent, passivist, but occasionally activist.
Cosmic View:	Acceptance of chaotic nature of universe, but via Hindu passivity. Unscientific, occult minded, intuitive.

CYBERPUNKS
(1975–1990)

Mood:	Gloomy. Hip, but downbeat.
Aesthetic-Erotics:	Leather and grunge, tattoos, piercings. Hard drugs, psychedelics, smart drugs. Various forms of rock from metal to rap.
Attitude:	Angry, cynical, feel undervalued by elders.
Brain-Tech:	High-tech electronic.
Intellectual Viewpoint:	Informed, open-minded, irreverent. Inundated with electronic signals.
Humanist Quotient:	Non-sexist, ecological, global minded.
Politics:	Alienated, skeptical.
Cosmic View:	Pessimistic, but closet hope fiends.

NEW BREED
(1990–2005)

Mood:	Alert, cheerful.
Aesthetic-Erotics:	Invention of personal style. Eclectic. Prefer techno and ambient music.
Attitude:	Self-confident.
Brain-Tech:	Psychedelic, super high-tech. Smart drugs, brain machines, Internet.
Intellectual Viewpoint:	Informed, open-minded, irreverent.
Humanist Quotient:	Tolerant, non-sexist, ecological, global.
Politics:	Detached, individualistic. Zen opportunists.
Cosmic View:	Acceptance of complexity, willingness to be a "chaos designer."

The 21st Century will witness a new global culture, peopled by new breeds who honour human individuality, human complexity, and human potential, enlightened immortals who communicate at light speed and design the technologies for their scientific re-animation.

→

It is useful to see that the beats were older than the Beavers. In the 1940s, when the beats were three to eight years old, their home media were radio, films, records, books. The baby-boomers (76 million strong) were the television-watching Beavers of the 1950s and evolved into the hippies of the 1960s. Affluent, self-confident, spoiled consumers, ready to use their television-radio skills to be imprinted by turning on Bob Dylan, tuning in the Beatles, turning off parent songs, and fine-tuning colour screens.

The Nintendo generation of the 1980s became a pioneer group of cybernauts. They were the first humans to zap through the Alice Window and change electronic patterns on the other side of the screen. They will operate in cyberspace, the electronic environment of the 21st Century.

MILLENNIUM MADNESS (CHAOS COMING)

The next uncontrollable fifteen years (1995–2010) will accelerate this dizzy explosion of brain power. The fragmenting remnants of the old centralized social systems of the feudal and industrial civilizations are crumbling down.

The 21st Century will witness a new global culture, peopled by new breeds who honour human individuality, human complexity, and human potential, enlightened immortals who communicate at light speed and design the technologies for their scientific re-animation. ◎

III.6.

THE NEXT TWENTY YEARS

If one is asked to predict the next stage of human evolution, practical common sense suggests selecting the identifying survival characteristic of our species. What are our survival assets?

The instant glib answer would be that our species is defined by our enormous brains. Our survival asset is not hive intelligence, as in the social insects, but individual intelligence. Our species is classified as *Homo sapiens sapiens*. Victorian scholars apparently decided that we are the creatures who "think about thinking." Our growth as a species centers on our ability to think and communicate. Predictions about our future would focus on improvements in the way we think.

Our young, rookie species has recently passed through several stages of intelligence:

1. Tribal: For at least 22,000 years (approximately 25,000 to 3000 B.C.) the technologies for sapient thinking-communicating were those of a five-year-old child: bodily, i.e., oral-gestural.
2. Feudal: During an exciting period of approximately 3,350 years (3000 B.C. to A.D. 350) humans living north of the 35th-parallel latitude developed organized feudal-agricultural societies. The technologies for thinking–communicating were hand-tooled statues, temples, monuments. Their philosophy was enforced by emperors, caliphs, and kings.
3. It took approximately 1,250 years (A.D. 350 to 1600) to coopt the feu-

dal kings and to establish the mechanical assembly-line managerial society. In this age, the technologies of thought-communication were mechanical printing presses, typewriters, telephones, produced by efficient workers in highly organized factories, run by centralized bureaucracies.

By now, in 1988, most people in the industrial sectors are extremely dependent on digital thoughts and light images presented on screens. The average American household watches television 7.4 hours a day. Almost all business transactions are run by software programs communicated on screens. Without conscious choice or fanfare we have migrated from the "real worlds" of voice, hand, machine into the digitized info-worlds variously called hyperspace, cyberspace, or digital physics.

This migration across the screen into the digital info-world marks the first phase of the postindustrial society.

By 2008 most humans living in postindustrial habitats will be spending as much time "jacked in" to info-worlds on the other side of the screen as they spend in the material worlds. In twenty years we will spend seven hours a day actively navigating, exploring, colonizing, exploiting the oceans and continents of digital data. Interscreening—creating mutual digital-realities—will be the most popular and growthful form of human communication.

Interscreening does not imply a derogation or neglect of flesh interactions.

Psybernetic (management of the right brain). Mapping and colonizing the next frontier—one's own brain. Constructing info-environments in one's own neuroworld. Linking one's neurospace to others. Marketing, leasing, sharing one's brain power with others. Protecting one's brain from invasion and exploitation from without. 🔍

ANDY FRITH

Our genetic assignment is the receiving, processing, and producing of digital information.

Intimacy at the digital level programs and enriches exchanges in the warm levels. You do not lessen the richness of your murmur-touch-contact with your lover because you can also communicate by phone, fax, and hand-scrawled notes. Warm-breath interactions with your touch-friends will be more elegant and pleasant with the digital-reality option added.

Future global business will take two directions:

☞ **Cybernetic** (management of the left brain). Mapping and colonizing the digital data-worlds located on the other side of screens. Interpersonal computing. Interscreening with others. Building communal info-structures. Protecting cyber-spaces from invasion and exploitation by others.

☞ **Psybernetic** (management of the right brain). Mapping and colonizing the next frontier—one's own brain. Constructing info-environments in one's own neuroworld. Linking one's neurospace to others. Marketing, leasing, sharing one's brain power with others. Protecting one's brain from invasion and exploitation from without.

Digital business will be run by multinational corporations based in Japan and Switzerland. The "multinates" will use individual brains as tools. Just as slaves, serfs, and prostitutes were forced to lease their bodies during the three predigital stages, people in 2008 will be leasing their brains. Work will hardly exist. Most physical tasks will be performed by automated machines. Body work will be considered a primitive form of slavery. No human will be forced by economic-political pressure to perform muscular-mechanical tasks that can be done better by robots.

In the 21st Century, the old Judæo–Christian–Moslem sects will still be around, but they will have little power beyond entertainment and amusement. The future global religion will be intelligence increase. Upgrading rpms. The two main functions of a human being are consumption and production of thought. Our genetic assignment is the receiving, processing, and producing of digital information. ⑨

Themes Which Define Cultures

Culture   Theme   Counterculture

EMOTIONAL ATTITUDE

Based on Fear	**Based on Scientific Optimism**
Slow-steady or impulsive	Animated-radiant
Serious-solemn; worker	Happy; playful
Arrogant or self-effacing	Self-confident; candid
Tough-dangerous or meek-submissive	Friendly-sympathetic

MENTAL SKILLS

Mind Programmed by Obedience	**Mind Programmed by Self**
By the book	Curious-open-minded
Conservative thinker	Creative-original
Pious, reverent to organized religion	Cheerfully irreverent to organized religion
Loyal, unquestioning patriot	Irreverent to organized politics

NEUROLOGICAL REALITY

Passive Reality Consumer	**Electronic Reality Skills**
Conforms to culture's life style	Invents personal style
Conventionally moral & immoral	Sensual-sensitive
Avoids brain change; accepts cultural imprints	Operates own brain: psychedelic
Passive electronic consumer	Electronic communication skills: cybernetic

PHILOSOPHICAL APPROACH

Sin-Driven	**Pluralistic Viewpoint**
Deeply identified with own race, sex, age & nation	Humanist: respects all differences
Believes nature should be dominated	Ecological: earth conscious
Pessimistic about evolution	Optimistic about evolution
Order-control person	Chaos designer

HERB RITTS

III.**7**.
THE GODPARENT: CONVERSATION WITH
WINONA RYDER

In the old days there was less menu choice of one's life's decisions. Marriages were arranged by family and church to make sure that offspring would remain within the flock. Selection of one's religion was also prearranged. Soon after birth the newborn infant was rushed to church for baptism and enrollment in the familiar creed.

In our secular society the tradition of the godparent seemed to be fading away like the myth of Santa Claus or the Tooth Fairy or the Virgin Mother. Indeed, in the age of Coppola, the term godfather had taken on a sinister flavour. What reasonably good-natured adult would want to play the role of the dread Don Corleone in the overheated family drama?

These were my thoughts on the subject until a few years ago, when Winona Ryder made me an offer I couldn't refuse: She chose me to serve as her godfather.

So I am here to cheer this institution of godparent–godchild—when it is arranged by freely consenting people who have reached the age of reason.

It is the duty of parents and guardians to rush around acting like family therapist, FBI agent, Mother Teresa, Tommy Lasorda, and the neighbourhood savings-and-loan office. The duty of the teenager is precisely spelled out: to do everything conceivable to drive parents and guardians up the wall.

The godfather, however, has a role that is simple and simply divine: to be a friend and admiring student. The duty of the goddaughter is more complicated. It is her pleasure to entertain the godfather and to educate him diligently about current events, new developments, hot happenings, and thus prepare him to deal with the mysterious future. I now feel sorry for any adult who does not have a supportive, caring godchild to act as guide and role model.

Winona's parents, Michael and Cindy Horowitz, started the world's largest collection of books and materials about the use of psychoactive plants, foods, and drugs. Michael and I have worked together very closely for almost twenty years—he was my archivist and published a three-hundred-page bibliography of my writings. He came to visit me in 1972, while I was in exile in Switzerland. He had with him a photograph of Winona taken when she was about a week old; so I wrote an inscription on the picture welcoming a new Buddha to planet Earth.

The first time I met her she was perhaps seven years old. I visited her family's commune-estate in Mendocino county. We walked hand in hand, and Winona said that she had wanted to meet me because she had heard that I was a mad scientist. I thought that was a pretty good description; I marked her as a comer right there. We've seen each other regularly since then. We used to go to Dodger games together—she and her father are great fans.

Winona has so many talents that I hope to emulate. She is modest, changeable, solid, witty-wise, thoughtful, and full-tilt here and now: exuberant, intense, bouncy, passionate. Winona does her homework and comes fully prepared.

And so she arrived at my home for this interview. She helped me activate and test the tape recorder, and we began a typical godfather–goddaughter conversation.

TIMOTHY LEARY: You know, this is the twentieth anniversary of *Interview*, which of course started before you were born. This is the year of other anniversaries, too. We had the Chicago trials twenty years ago, and the Vietnam anti-war mobilization, the Weathermen—

WINONA RYDER: Woodstock.

TL: Woodstock—almost to the day. What do you make of it all?

WR: Well, it's weird . . . you know how I grew up. Even though I grew up in the 1970s and the 1980s, I could almost say that I grew up in the 1960s, because our house was like a library-museum of books and paraphernalia from the 1960s. All my life my dad has talked about that time, and I think he's still living in the 1960s in a way.

TL: Not to mention the cast of characters that came to visit your house.

WR: Yeah.

TL: Allen Ginsberg.

WR: Yeah, you! *[laughs]*

TL: And of course I was there as much as I could be.

WR: All the 'sixties and 'seventies fashion is interesting. You walk down Melrose Avenue now and you see platform shoes and all the psychedelic colours.

TL: Tie-dyes.

WR: Tie-dyes and all that. How does it feel to have your past become this trend now? The other day I was driving and I saw this group of girls who looked like they were right out of the 1960s. I started thinking: Here are these teenagers who are trying to be nostalgic about a generation they were never a part of.

TL: Well, it's the duty, the genetic responsibility, of every 16-year-old kid to do everything possible to drive their parents crazy. My stepson Zachary has done the one thing that could offend his mother,

> I think the great thing is that instead of watching TV we would make things up. We would use our imagination . . .

who loves him dearly, and that is, he's become a 'sixties freak *[laughs]*. He's a Deadhead, and he's letting his hair grow. And he's not looking fashionable. Bill Walton, the basketball player who was a hippie activist, is a longtime friend of mine, and he has taken Zach and me to Grateful Dead concerts. There's a feeling of communion there that you could cut with a knife. It's the revival of the ancient pagan festival: people getting together to have possession and trance experiences, and to share that communion.

I have been not surprised but offended by the way the media have trivialized Woodstock. All the interviews have been about the promoters. Who cares that the promoters lost money? There was an emphasis on the mud and the lack of housing. What interested me was that exactly the week of the twentieth anniversary of Woodstock, there was a rock concert in Moscow that over a hundred thousand Russian kids came to—with Ozzy Osbourne, of all people *[laughs]*. And they were wearing jeans and headbands, and talking about peace and love. In America you're not allowed to mention the fact that Woodstock was a kid caper. It was happening again that very weekend in Russia. It happened in May in China. You had a million kids. That was a Be-In. Nobody called it a Be-In. The connection between Woodstock and our 'sixties movement and the Chinese and the Soviets is never mentioned, because that would imply that the same thing is happening there that happened here.

One of my memories of you dates from the time that you were on the commune in Mendocino. Barbara—from the first time she met you—has raved about your style. And Barbara is, as you know, an obsessive perfectionist about such things. I was always amused by the fact that you used to send us letters and little style drawings and pictures every few weeks. And they were very avant-garde.

Maybe they were punk—they certainly were not braids and beads and barefoot stuff. Up on the commune you were probing, which I thought was charming. Do you remember that?

WR: Yeah. Very well *[laughs]*. I think that was all due to the fact that ever since I can remember I've been so obsessed with movies. And my mom ran a little movie house up in Elk, where we lived for a while, and she would show old movies. That's how I got introduced to the whole thing. It was like a warehouse. There were couches and beds, and people would pay fifty cents or a dollar to come in. And we'd all just sort of lie around and watch movies. That's where I first saw *A Face in the Crowd* and *East of Eden* and all these great movies. I think it was that that made me want to go home and start designing clothes for Patricia Neal or Lauren Bacall. I had no idea that they were older, or that they were retired, or they were dead, or whatever. I really thought that they were walking around like that.

TL: Some of your interviewers have commented that you seem more like a 'thirties or 'forties movie person than a Brat Packer. They were talking about your style, or your approach. Over and over again they say, "She's 16 going on 40," or "She's 17 going on 50" *[laughs]*. That's a wide span and scope of input there.

WR: Yeah. It's very flattering, but at the same time it's a little frightening, I think.

TL: *[with humour]* It's a hard job to live up to.

WR: Yeah! *[laughs]*

TL: You'll have to take it day by day here. Another thing that intrigued me about your past, Noni, is that there was not much television. There was no electricity for a while, and there was actually no television on the ranch.

WR: No, none.

TL: Now, that is a blessed and singular advantage you have. You're off to a fast start on a different track. Because most kids were watching television and didn't really get involved in movies.

WR: Yeah. There was no TV. One person, who lived on the next piece of land, had a TV, but they only got one channel. And so sometimes, if we were lucky *[TL laughs]*, if we wanted to we could see some fuzzy episode of, you know, *Starsky and Hutch* or whatever *[laughs]*. But it was never anything we really wanted to do. I think the great thing is that instead of watching TV we would make things up. We would use our imagination, and we would make up skits and perform them at the main house. Remember the main house?

TL: Sure do.

WR: Or we would make up different games and we would have contests. We would do stuff that exercised our mind much more than just sitting in front of a screen and staring at it. What's shocking, I think, about this day and age is how much television kids watch. I mean, I have friends back home who can't miss a show. They just can't do it. I'll go back to Petaluma and I think, "Oh, well, I'm here for a couple of days; I'll get to spend some time with my friends." And some people I know would actually love to see me, but they can't miss part two of *Family Ties*, or whatever they watch. I'm sure there's a lot of good TV, but, you know, television is just TV, as far as I'm concerned.

TL: Going back to that commune scene of a small group of young people with intelligent, college-educated parents—it's like a movie set. They're on a spaceship, or they're somehow isolated from the main currents of America, such as TV, so they begin making up their own minds. It's almost like an episode of *Star Trek*. Captain Kirk finds this Mendocino commu ...

WR: Yeah! *[both laugh]* What was also real neat about the land was that there were about three hundred acres. I forget how many people lived there, but every house had a name. We lived in "the Mansion." Then there was "the A-Frame," and then there was "the Cabin." Every little house had a name, and every time something was built, we would name it. Everything—even a field—was named.

TL: It was personalized.

WR: Exactly. There were so many opportunities to use our imagination. People always assume that I got frustrated and bored up there. But I was really blessed, because it taught me how much there is in here *[points to her head]* to use.

TL: Also, you grew up with a lot of books. After all, your father and mother had published three or four books. I've never seen a person more obsessed with books than your father.

WR: *[laughs]* I know.

TL: When he goes to a new town, he immediately heads for the secondhand bookstores.

WR: And he doesn't come back *[laughs]* for a long time! He literally moves in.

TL: Like "Daddy's down at the saloon. Let's get him home."

WR: Yeah!

TL: You were exposed to more books than most kids your age. That was part of the sea that you swam through.

WR: Absolutely. My dad would give me books at a really early age because he was so impatient. Some of the books I just was not old enough to understand. But he could never grasp that. So I'd end up having to read them once and then have to read them again about a year later and hope that I would get them. But both of my parents were so encouraging. I've been writing ever since I can remember. They really

worked with me.

TL: Now, wait a minute. You started writing at an early age?

WR: Yeah. I have been writing ever since I can remember, be it my journal or short stories or whatever. I actually wrote a short novel when I was 12, which was about *To Kill a Mockingbird*. I read it when I was about 10. It was one of my favorite books. So I told the same story—about Tom Robinson, the black guy who was convicted and killed—from his little sister's point of view. What really has influenced me with my writing is music. I wake up in the morning, and I put some tape or record on immediately, and that sort of determines how my day is going to be.

TL: You have to be pretty careful of that. It's like planning your wardrobe. You're planning your mood for the day. When was the first time that you ever heard of Andy Warhol?

WR: I first heard of him because I became fascinated with Edie Sedgwick when I was 11 or 12—I read that book about her.

TL: The one that George Plimpton and Jean Stein did. I knew Edie.

WR: Yeah. I read it driving with my dad to L.A. to visit you. It was about a nine-hour trip, and I remember I finished it just as we were pulling up your driveway.

TL: You've never been around New York that much.

WR: Well, I've been there a lot, but I basically went to Brooklyn to visit my grandparents. I wasn't in the Manhattan scene too much.

TL: During the late 1960s, as you know, my family and my friends were living in Millbrook, about an hour and a half north of New York City, which was ideal. We could be out all day hiking and playing around and just being with nature. At five o'clock, we'd take a shower and jump in the car, and by seven we could be at a cocktail party in New York. And then at two o'clock we'd get in the car and be home by three. So we had the best of both worlds there at Millbrook. It also meant that on weekends many of the New York people would come up. The Mellon family had this big house there. The Grateful Dead would be there a lot. At the same time we'd have the top artists and fashion people too. So I knew Andy very well during those days, and I used to go by the Factory and the loft. I think Andy has had a great effect on American culture. Andy used to take a Coca-Cola bottle and say, *[doing AW's voice]* "Isn't it wonderful? A peasant in Indochina can drink out of the same wonderful, shapely bottle that Liz Taylor can." That's Pop.

WR: Recently, you've been talking a lot about increasing your intelligence. How would you advise kids to become smarter? Navigate their own reality? Move things along? Is it possible to question authority and respect it at the same time?

TL: Well, my only advice and my only message is: Think for yourself and question authority. TFYQA. But "think for yourself" does not mean "think selfishly." It means "think independently." And questioning authority doesn't mean simply rejecting authority. Maybe you question authority, and 80 percent of what authority says, you buy. Good! I don't care what people think as long as they have thought for themselves. So if you end up a Republican, right wing, it's okay with me, as long as you have done it having had a gourmet, a connoisseur's selection of all the options. As long as you haven't done it out of fear or laziness.

WR: Yeah. I would like to ask you about literary heroes. I know that Huckleberry Finn is one of your literary heroes, and Holden Caulfield is definitely mine. And I found them a little bit similar. I read *Tom Sawyer*

and *Huckleberry Finn* long before I read *Catcher in the Rye*. But—

TL: Did they affect you?

WR: A great deal. I think it's safe to say that Holden changed my whole life as it did for so many young people. What was amazing about it was, I read it without knowing that it was a famous adolescent book, that everybody read it. I thought it was this sleeper or something. I didn't know. I guess everyone felt that way.

TL: You discovered it, huh? *[laughs]*

WR: Yeah. After I read it, from then on it was me and Holden—we were like this team. And then I found out that everybody had read it. What I loved about *Huckleberry Finn* was . . . well, obviously, that he did what he wanted to do, and was a freethinker. And I got a sense of that in Holden too. I think they would have probably been friends.

TL: They were both alienated in the best sense of the word. Holden was watching the craziness that was going on around him. I did that as a kid. And obviously Huck did that too.

WR: I think both Holden and Huck are the perfect role models. I guess I'm a little disappointed in the role models that kids are choosing now. You know, Axl Rose from Guns 'n' Roses.

TL: He gives some pretty raw interviews, doesn't he? Is he just being deliberately bad, or is he stupid?

WR: I think he's stupid, actually.

TL: I hate to hear you say that, because he claims to be a fan of mine. You know what he said to me? He said, *[doing Rose's voice]* "Man, I love yoah books, 'cause I just take yoah books and show 'em to girls, and I can get any girl I want."

WR: What a compliment! *[laughs]*

TL: Of course, it didn't imply that he'd read them.

WR: Just that he had them there on the nightstand . . . In *Rolling Stone*, maybe a month ago, right after they did a story on me, somebody wrote in and said, "Winona Ryder is my role model." I was really flattered. But then I got to thinking about it, and I started getting scared. I'm really going to have to watch what I do, watch what I say. I feel an instinctive responsibility.

TL: But your role is not to defend Christianity or the middle class. Your role is to be an independent, fresh, always-changing person. So they can never model themselves after anything you've said, because you've left it and gone.

WR: Yeah. *[laughs]*

TL: You've got to have that confidence, Noni. I've had that same problem. I've been in many great institutions where some of the leading figures come up and say, "Tim! You have always been my role model. Everything I have I owe to you." And of course they're prisoners at Folsom.

WR: Oh no! *[laughs]*

TL: Yeah. *[laughs]* But you can't worry about that. People say to me that they want to be followers. I say, "You can't follow me. I don't know where I'm going, for one thing. And number two, I'm gone by the time you get there."

WR: Kids today tend to think the ultimate thing is to be a movie star or a rock star. To be like Axl or like Madonna.

TL: Or an athlete . . . Well, there is a tremendous change happening in the world today, as we move from the industrial-factory society. In a factory society everybody wants to get to the top of that particular factory. You want to be the top movie star, or the top rock star, or the top

The great thing about being in movies is— and I think the movies and modern professional sports are the economic and cultural model of the future—that you're a free agent. And that's going to be typical of more and more people in the information age.

banker. That's the industrial age, which is a pyramid going up. In the information age it's all changed. Singularity, individuality—everyone is going to be a movie star within two or three years. I'm going to have you come and look at this little film in a minute, and show you how, for less than a hundred dollars, a kid at Christmas in 1990 will have lens goggles, a little cap, an electronic glove, and a bodysuit so that they can put themselves—and they can be dancing, walking, jumping—on the other side of the screen. Everyone is going to be directing and acting in their own movies.

WR: Well, that's wonderful! Because that's playing off yourself. And dealing with yourself.

TL: Think of how the Hollywood system and the music system have become like a factory. They even call it the movie industry. And they talk about this software industry, when it's not that at all. In the old days the studios would grind it out; it was like an assembly line for movies. And the stars were the com-

modities. But that's all going to change. Everyone will be making their own movies. And there are going to be networks set up so that every kid can be Marilyn Monroe, or can actually be like Jack Nicholson. You simply tape five minutes of Jack Nicholson and put it in your computer. And then you can be him walking around on the screen. The average kid will have access to film libraries and tapes. And even the news. Anything that's on your television you can tape, change it and put yourself in it. So that these monopolies, which are typical of the industrial age, are not going to be as powerful.

WR: *[laughs]* Well, that's a very reassuring thought.

TL: There's a new generation coming up. I'm sure you know this, but during the 1980s young people in this country became very conservative. For the next ten or fifteen years you're going to see the colleges filled with kids of flower kids. You were not a flower child, but you were the child of a flower child. And

you're Dr. Spock's grandkid. Your generation is simply hipper, more sophisticated, and less apt to become 'fifties-type stars. Isn't that being a good role model?

WR: *[embarrassed laughter]* I suppose. As I said before, my day is determined by what I put on in the morning.

TL: I hate to ask this question, Noni. What did you put on this morning?

WR: Oh, I put on *The Mission* sound track. It's my favorite thing now. It's really beautiful. But I don't know. I'm at that age where every day is different. One day I think to myself, I'm going to do this for the rest of my life. And the next day I think, I'm going to do that for the rest of my life. And one day I think I'm going to take everything light and life is great, and I'm just going to take things day by day, and I'm going to live in the moment and all that stuff. And then the next day I'm going to plan out everything. I'm going to have a map, and my road is paved. So I'm constantly changing, and I really do believe in living life in the moment. I think that that's important. I got a great piece of advice from Trey Wilson, who was in *Great Balls of Fire* and *Raising Arizona*. He said, "You always have to remember to have a good time. No matter what you're doing, just have a good time. Enjoy it. Because if you don't, then what are you doing it for?" Of course, I've gotten this advice before, but for some reason when he said it to me I really started to think about it.

TL: The great thing about being in movies is—and I think the movies and modern professional sports are the economic and cultural model of the future—that you're a free agent. And that's going to be typical of more and more people in the information age. I have a game I used to play at parties in Hollywood. I would ask people, "If you had to go to another planet and you could take ten movies with you, which ten would you take?" Which would you take, Noni?

WR: *A Face in the Crowd. To Kill a Mockingbird. Opening Night*, a John Cassavetes movie. *The Tempest* . . .

TL: Oh, the one that Susan Sarandon was in.

WR: Let me see . . . *Picnic at Hanging Rock*, probably. Maybe *Gallipoli. Don't Look Now*. Of course, that would be hard to watch in space *[laughs]*, because we'd probably get really scared. *Walkabout*. I love Nicolas Roeg. Then maybe *West Side Story*. And I really love the original *Something Wild*, with Carroll Baker and Ralph Meeker and Mildred Dunnock.

TL: When was that done?

WR: It was made in 1961, and it was based on a novel that was really big in the 1950s, called *Mary Ann*. It was one of those cheesy little novels, but it was a great movie. And *The Stripper*, with Joanne Woodward.

TL: Would you ever want to direct?

WR: Maybe. I've fantasized about it. I've done seven movies. And I've learned so much about good directing from bad directing. And I've learned from *bad* lighting how important good lighting is. In terms of working with actors, my favorite approach is when I'm directed without being intentionally directed. Michael Lehmann, the guy who directed *Heathers*, was amazing. We'd be setting up to do a scene and he would start to tell me a story, and I would have no idea that it had any relevance to the scene we were about to shoot. But before I knew it, we would have shot the scene. He would have maneuvered me into the scene and put me in the perfect state of mind just by telling me some weird little story. It gets really distracting when directors start saying *[in a "serious" voice]*, "Okay, this is what we're going to do." I hate it when they start out with that.

TL: So you'll have to learn how to tell stories to your actors. That's the tradition of the Zen person, or of the Sufi storyteller. You tell a funny story and then pretty soon it's all happened.

WR: Yeah. I usually get involved with whatever I'm doing and it becomes my life for those couple of months. Because I've immersed myself so many times, I know a lot about it, but it's all sort of in this hurricane in my head. It's not very clear yet. It's all *up* there, but not in any sort of order.

TL: That's the quantum-physics theory of the universe. It's up there, but it's out of order. You don't have to apologize for that. You're right on beam *[laughs]*. ◎

IV. INFO-CHEMICALS & DRUG WARS

CAROLYN FERRIS

IV.1.
CONVERSATION WITH
WILLIAM S. BURROUGHS

TIMOTHY LEARY: Do you want to do this, William?

WILLIAM S. BURROUGHS: Why not?

TL: The first topic is immortality. You know, I signed up for cryonics. Have you thought about cryonics?

WSB: Ah . . . I thought about it, but no, no, no. I feel that any sort of physical immortality is going in the wrong direction. It's a question of separating whatever you choose to call it—the soul—from the body, not perpetuating the body in any way. I think any perpetuation of the body is a step in the wrong direction. The Egyptians made their mummies, and preservation of the mummy was essential to their immortality. I think you want to get away from the body, not get into it.

TL: Why not have the option of readily jumping consciousness back into the body? You know, the Egyptians are really interesting. I see the tombs basically as re-animation capsules.

WSB: That's exactly . . .

TL: They used the highest science at the time. I've been working with some scientists in this new field called bio-anthropology. During twenty-five centuries there were four waves of tomb robbers. The first wave took the gold, the second wave took the art, and then came the British and the French. All these looters threw the wrappings—which were clotted with dried blood—into the corner. But now microbiologists can get DNA from the bio-remains. So the Egyptian plan has actually worked. Within ten years we'll be able to clone the pharaohs! Of course, the problem is, there would be no memories. But that's why they included their software in the form of the jewels and artifacts. I admire that.

Your book on *The Western Lands* fascinated me. I read it over and over again, and I quote you quite a bit in the stuff I write about cryonics.

How about postbiologic possibilities? Moravek—all of that. He says you can download the human brain and fit it in computers and build a new body with brush-like antenna software . . .

WSB: Certainly, certainly.

TL: How about language as a virus, Michel Foucault?

WSB: Language is obviously a virus, as it depends on replication. What other weighty topics do we have?

TL: Your paintings, shotgun and otherwise . . . of course, Brion Gysin was always the one doing the painting.

WSB: You see, I could never have started painting *really* until after Brion Gysin was dead. I could never have competed with him. But now I've made more money than he did his whole life.

TL: You've made probably more money from your paintings than your books, huh?

WSB: It's pulled me out of a financial hole. I can buy flintlock pistols.

TL: Good for you. It's an easier way to make money than running around giving lectures and debating G. Gordon Liddy.

WSB: Flintlock pistols are great.

TL: And what do you think about Liddy? You know Liddy's a big gun man.

WSB: Yes, I know. I know as much about guns as he does.

TL: Let's go on to the Drug-War hysteria.

WSB: Oh, now listen. Just a couple of tips, something that nobody has gone into, in this whole drug debate, is the simple fact that before the Harrison Narcotics Act in 1914, these drugs were sold across the counter.

TL: Opium, cocaine?

WSB: One-half the people—this is a sex survey—thought anal intercourse could result in AIDS even though neither one of the participants was infected with the AIDS virus. The Immaculate Conception!

TL: The Immaculate Infection!

... before the Harrison Narcotics Act in 1914, these drugs were sold across the counter.... Opium, cocaine, morphine, heroin. Sold over the counter. Well, these were in the days that the conservatives evoke as "the good old days." Was America floundering? Of course it wasn't. And how well the English system worked, until the American Brain Commission came over there and talked them out of it.

WSB: Opium, cocaine, morphine, heroin. Sold over the counter. Well, these were in the days that the conservatives evoke as "the good old days." Was America floundering? Of course it wasn't. And how well the English system worked, until the American Brain Commission came over there and talked them out of it. When I was there in 1967 and took the apomorphine cure with Dr. Dent, there were about six hundred addicts in the U.K., all registered and all known because they could obtain their heroin quite legally—cocaine and cannabis tincture, too. Now that they've made it impossible, and the doctors won't prescribe to addicts, God knows how many addicts we have. God knows how many narcotics *agents*.

TL: Once I took heroin in London with R. D. Laing. Ronnie sent out to the chemist. Ronnie Laing shot me up in the house of Alex Trocchi. Do you remember Trocchi?

WSB: Knew him well.

TL: Switzerland is interesting. They have parks in Zurich and other places where junkies can go. The attitude is humanistic. "We're one family; we're all Swiss. And if our junkies want to shoot up, we'll provide clean needles." There's no criminality involved.

WSB: I remember at one point I was at one of these Dutch places where they had needles and works—you put a coin in a thing and out came the needle.

TL: Works-o-matic.

WSB: Works-o-matic! Look at the history, the fact that for years there was no British heroin problem. The system worked very well.

TL: Well, the problem is the Puritan, Cromwellian moralists who have imposed their fucking neuroses on America and England for the last hundred years. Any sort of pleasure, or sort of idea that the individual has a right to pursue happiness, and they're after you. It's basically inquisitional . . . religiose. I blame the Puritans.

WSB: Well, perhaps, yes. But the thing is . . . I don't quite agree with that. The basic thing is how that creates a desire, a necessity in their minds to control the whole population. And the extent to which the general public has been stupidized is appalling. Have you heard these statistics? The polls show that one-half of the high-school graduates could not locate Vietnam on the map and did not know that we had fought and lost a war there? When you take WWII, forget it! They never heard of Churchill, couldn't locate France. The only one they knew about was Hitler.

TL: Costumes! He had the best wardrobe, that's why.

WSB: And 8 percent couldn't locate the United States on a map. It's absolutely appalling. Now listen to this one. One-half the people—this is a sex survey—thought anal intercourse could result in AIDS *even though neither one of the participants was infected with the AIDS virus.* The Immaculate Conception!

TL: The Immaculate Infection!

WSB: Can you imagine such nonsense? Such a complete lack of logic. One-half!

[James Grauerholtz announces it's time to go to the Leary–Liddy debate.]

TL: I want to say one more thing, William. You're with me every day. I talk about you all the time. I've learned so much from you, with you. And I'll be back.

WSB: And I think about you. ☺

IV.2. THE SOCIOLOGY OF LSD

n 1973 the federal drug agency estimated that more than seven million Americans had used LSD. When this number of young and/or influential people engages in an activity passionately denounced by every respectable organ of society as dangerous, chaotic, immoral, and illegal, we have a social phenomenon that is worthy of study. Here is a fascinating development: a new sin! A new counterculture. A new evil crime.

I hope the following observations will encourage anthropologists and sociologists to undertake more systematic analysis of the survival implications of this mass behavior. Even a Gallup poll in which users could describe the effect that LSD tripping had on their lives might produce provocative data—if we are ready to face the facts.

IT WAS JUST ONE OF THOSE TIMES

The postwar baby-boom generation that came into adolescence during the 1960s was probably the most affluent, confident, indulged crop in human history. Many social forces conspired to encourage this group to expect and demand more from life. The 'sixties kids were free from the economic fears that had dominated the lives of their depression-scarred parents. America was in a period of expansion and growth. Recruiters from large businesses used to line up on campuses to beg students to consider well-paying jobs! The nuclear fears that plagued the 1950s were quiescent. The new psychology of humanism and personal growth, developed by Carl Rogers, Abraham Maslow, encounter groups, and other developments of the human-potential movement reactivated the basic Emersonian values of self-exploration, self-reliance, transcendence of fear-inspired orthodoxies. The art world, always seminal in countercultural change, seethed with the effects of expressionism, improvisation, individualism. Chaos engineering. Even the staid physical sciences were exploding with theories of Einsteinian relativity, Heisenbergian alternate realities, expanding universes.

This had happened before. At similar moments in history when cultures reached similar states of national security, economic prosperity, and imperial confidence, the inevitable next step has been to look within. A counterculture encourages novel art forms and lifestyles, tolerates individual search for new meaning—self-indulgence, as opposed to survival drudgery and coerced indulgence of elite rulers. Exactly at these times when philosophy, science, art, religion vibrate with transcendent energies, two things often happen: external exploration into undiscovered geographical realms, and inner exploration using brain-change drugs.

The first book of the Vedas, the West's oldest extant spiritual text, emerging at the time of the Aryan conquest of India, defined the drug soma as the basic tool for philosophic inquiry.

The Athenians were pioneer navigators: self-reliant, empirical, antidogmatic people. The Greek mystery cult of Eleusis, which invigorated Mediterranean thought for many centuries, used an LSD-type substance (from ergot of barley) in its annual rebirth ceremonies.

> This had happened before. At similar moments in history when cultures reached similar states of national security, economic prosperity, and imperial confidence, the inevitable next step has been to look within.

The Renaissance eruption of individuality and free thought inspired great explorations, east and west, which brought back herbs, spices, unguents that added to the hedonic movements of the time.

R. Gordon Wasson, Richard Evans Schultes, Jonathan Ott, Terence McKenna, and other ethnobotanical scholars have argued that most of the great world religions were based on inner exploration employing brain-changing vegetables. The British Empire was supported for over a century by the opium trade, which was clearly related to the flowering of romantic, mystical, transcendental thought in England. Darwin, for example, was a chronic hypochondriac and a respectable opium addict.

THE SOUTH INVADES THE NORTH WITH BOTANICAL AGENTS

The acculturation of psychedelic drugs by Americans in the 1960s provides a powerful endorsement of religious rituals from the tropical latitudes. The psychedelic drugs are all derived from tropical plants. Psilocybin from mushrooms, mescaline from peyote, LSD from grain ergot, DMT and ayahuasca from tree bark and vines, and, of course, marijuana—the oldest cultivated plant on the planet. These are not the euphoriants, or energizers, or intoxicants favored by urban dwellers. Psychedelics produce states of possession, trance, delightful chaoticness, expanded consciousness, spiritual illumination, powerful, mystical empathies with natural forces. These experiences, which are the aim of the ancient humanist, pagan religions, are the worst nightmares of the organized religions.

The so-called 'sixties "drug culture" was not a campus fad; it was a world-wide renaissance of the oldest religions. The hippies intuitively sensed this as they proudly wandered around barefoot, playing flutes. Paganism 101 suddenly became the most popular campus elective.

Psychiatrists and law-enforcement officials and politicians automatically assumed that psychedelic experiences were self-induced bouts of mass insanity, i.e., hallucinatory psychosis. There were no terms or paradigms in the Western intellectual tradition to

MARK McCLOUD • PSYCHEDELIC SOLUTION

explain this bizarre chaotic desire to "go out of your mind."

It is of sociological interest that the drug culture in America and Western Europe (and more recently in segments of Eastern Europe) dutifully re-enacted the rituals of pre-Christian pagans and polytheists. In the 1960s and 1970s, millions living in industrial nations used psychedelics in the context of Hindu, Buddhist, and pagan practices. Psychedelic drugs were taken in groups and in public celebrations. The acid tests. The love-ins. The communes. The need for social bonding and tribal rituals was intuitively accepted by most psychedelic-drug users.

The importance of group support expressed in pagan-psychedelic experiences cannot be overestimated. The psychedelic culture proudly flaunted drug-taking because it was designed to produce nature-loving, tribe-solidarity, humanist experiences. The first San

Francisco Be-In was advertised as "A Gathering of the Tribes." This happens today at Grateful Dead concerts, when twenty thousand Deadheads routinely mingle together in dancing celebration.

INNER AND OUTER SPACE

Is it entirely accidental that our own space program, booming out to the stars, occurred exactly when our LSD-inspired inner-tripping was at its height? When the sense of national pride and confidence diminished during the Nixon years, both inner and outer exploration decreased. No surprise to any student of cultural evolution.

Can any acceptable history of our species fail to note the effects of drug countercultures and hedonic booms on the evolution of art and knowledge? Is it still too early for scholarly examination of our current drug culture, its antecedents and consequences? Well, let's make a small beginning.

WHY DID THE LSD BOOM DECLINE?

We have just considered some factors that lead to the emergence of an hedonic-philosophic drug culture. Conservatives are quick to point out that transcendental, self-indulgent movements usually lead to the fall of civilizations. Did not hot tubs, Eastern drugs, and mystical cults sap the martial vigor of Imperial Rome?

Probably. But we must hasten to add that it was natural and right that Rome fall. In the unbroken migration of intelligence and individual freedom from east to west, Rome had its day in the sun. But would you want to be ruled today from Italy? High civilizations do not fall; they blossom and send their seed pollens westward. Have not the descendants of the wily Sicilian Italians planted their roots today in Hollywood and Las Vegas? According to such observers as Kissinger, Herman Kahn, Reverend Falwell, and the Shah of Iran, our current hedonic drug culture represents a sophisticated corruption of the puritan American ethos. But in their self-serving zeal to restore the old morality, these imperialists fail to realize that hedonic movements go through predictable states of growth just like other social phenomena, and that the current American transcendentalism has hardly gotten started.

Hippies were the first naïve, innocent, idealistic babies of the new neurological-information society. Hippies were passive consumers of the new technology, childish utopians who believed that tie-dyed clothes, Grateful Dead concerts, and parroted love slogans were the ultimate flowers of evolution.

The hippie wave declined because its members were too passive, opting for enlightenment at the nearest dealer's pad. Advertising usually does get ahead of production in the development of new culture-changing technologies, and I am ready to accept responsibility for that. No blame, though. When a species wants an evolutionary tool, it will get it in a generation or two. By 1970 there were, apparently, some seven million lazy consumers expecting to be given the easy ticket to brain change. Meanwhile the feds had snuffed out the few reliable manufacturers. Predictably, the land was flooded with unreliable, low-quality acid. Good-hearted amateurs combined with unscrupulous scoundrels to distribute an inferior product.

Thus the wholesome decline in LSD use, which stimulated exactly what the drug culture needed. Smarten up, Sister. Smarten up, Brother! People were no longer so naïvely utopian. They warily thought twice before tripping. And the challenge, which no sophisticated chemist could resist, to produce high-quality LSD, was thrown down.

The last two decades have just whetted humanity's eternal appetite for technologies to activate and direct one's own brain function. The drug movement has just begun.

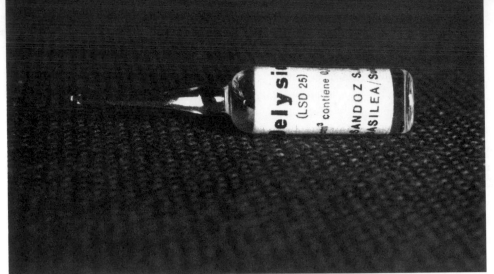

BIGWOOD

THE THIRD GENERATION OF BRAIN-CHANGE DRUGS

The first generation of psychedelic technology involved primitive preparation of botanicals: joint-rolling, hashish hookahs, bongs. The second generation of psychedelic technologies involved the synthesis of mescaline, psilocybin, LSD, DMT, STP, MDA—all crude, Wright brothers, Model-T stuff.

The third generation of brain-change drugs is now appearing in plentiful quantities. Designer drugs. Just as computers today are more efficient, cheaper, and more reliable than those thirty years ago, so are the new drugs. Home domestication of mushrooms is one charming example.

The time-consuming, complex, delicate, unwieldy procedures for synthesizing LSD have been streamlined so that, from police reports of arrests and sociological observations, we learn that more LSD is being used today than in the 1960s. There is almost no publicity, because drug usage is no longer a trendy topic for the media and politicians. We have new problems—oil, economics, crack, the new Cold War. There are almost no bad trips being reported, because the acid is pure and the users are sophisticated. The average suburban teenager today knows more about the varied effects of brain-change drugs than the most learned researchers twenty years ago. The proliferation of knowledge always works this way. The socialization of drugs has followed the same rhythm as the use and abuse of automobiles, airplanes, computers.

And the next decade will see the emergence of dozens of new, improved, stronger, safer psychoactive drugs. Any intelligent chemist knows it: There is an enormous market of some fifty million Americans today who would joyfully purchase a safe euphoriant, a precise psychedelic of short duration and predictable effect, an effective intelligence increaser, a harmless energizer, a secure sensual enhancer. An aphrodisiac! For millennia, intelligent persons undergoing the vicissitudes of aging have longed for an effective aphrodisiac. Only recently have we realized that the ultimate, indeed the only, pleasure organ is the brain, an enormous hundred-billion-cell hedonic system waiting to be activated.

The last two decades have just whetted humanity's eternal appetite for technologies to activate and direct one's own brain function. The drug movement has just begun.

THE RESURGENCE OF GOOD OLD LSD

The increased usage of acid is the forerunner of what is to come, and much can be learned from its resurgence. Now that the hysteria has died down, is it not obvious that LSD, pure LSD, is simply the best recreational/enlightenment drug around? A curious reversal of Gresham's law seems to operate. If good dope is available, it will be preferred. If good dope is in short supply, then bad drugs will be used. *Good dope drives out bad dope.*

During the recent LSD shortage did we not see a shocking emergence of teenage alcoholism? Don't you remember how drunks were scorned in the 1960s? The horrid PCP mania is directly caused by the acid drain. So is the cocaine mania, the post-Shah heroin epi-

Psychedelics produce states of possession, trance, delightful chaoticness, expanded consciousness, spiritual illumination, powerful, mystical empathies with natural forces.

demic. Looking at the shoddy replacements, is it not clear that psychedelic drugs are exactly what our Harvard research showed them to be in the 1960s? Wonderful gifts from the plant queendom to the animal kingdom; activators of those circuits of the brain that lead to philosophic inquiry, scientific curiosity, somatic awareness, hedonic lifestyle, humourous detachment, high-altitude tolerant perceptions, chaotic erotics, ecological sensitivity, utopian communality.

Weren't the 1960s, in retrospect, a decade of romance, splendor, optimism, idealism, individual courage, high aspirations, æsthetic innovation, spiritual wonder, exploration, and search? As President Reagan might have said, weren't we happier about each other and more optimistic when the high times were rolling?

In the Rambo 1980s, drugs were tooted, shot, free-based, cracked in secrecy. Often alone.

Drug-taking becomes drug abuse when practiced in narcissistic solitude. In 1988, thirty million Americans used illegal drugs safely, and fifty million used booze moderately. Indulgence in group rituals protects against abuse. Beer busts. Cocktail parties. Smoking grass or eating mushrooms with friends.

It is important to note that the only effective rehabilitation program for alcohol and drug abusers is A.A. The stated aims and tactic of A.A. are pagan-spiritual. Surrender to a higher power in an intense support-group setting. No churches. No government officials. No salaries. No funding. Just village-type group support.

THE WINTER OF FEAR AND DISCONTENT

Our psychedelic-drug research projects at Harvard and later Millbrook vigorously addressed the task of developing brain-change methods for eliminating human ignorance and suffering. We knew it could be done and that, eventually, it would be done. Biochemical knowledge will be applied to manage the synaptic patterns which keep people bogged down in repetitious helplessness. Self-managed brain control is in the future deck.

This seemed so commonsensical that it was hard for us to understand, in 1962, how any open-minded person could oppose the planful accessing of altered states of consciousness. Granted that the field was new and the avalanche of new data confusing, the parallels to the discovery of the microscope and telescope were so obvious that we were naïvely unprepared for the instinctive revulsion expressed by so many intelligent, distinguished scientists at the notion of brain change. Alan Watts, always the wry student of history, never tired of reminding us that Vatican astronomers consistently refused to look through Galileo's telescopes.

Our initial romantic idealism was soon sobered by the realization that there are powerful genetic mechanisms, reinforced by society, geared to react with fear at the approach of the new. This neophobia obviously has a survival value. At every stage of evolution each gene pool has been protected by those with nervous systems wired to cry *Danger! Caution!*

The evolutionist urging change says, "There is nothing to fear except fear itself." The survivalist replies, "There is everything to fear except fear itself." At most periods of human history those who promote fear have been in ascendance. When we examine every other form of life, we see that a nervous, jumpy animal alertness to danger is a constant preoccupation.

At certain times in the emergence of civilization, optimistic change-agents, believers in progress, manage to push our species into new adventures. Then, inevitably, the forces of

Since our research had demonstrated that set and setting determine the course of an altered-state experience, we consistently broadcast signals of intelligent reassurance: "Trust your nervous system, go with the flow, the universe is basically a beautiful and safe place."

caution, reason, tradition reimpose fear to preserve what the change-agents have created.

America has, since its conception, represented an optimistic, progressive future probe of the human race. Our country was founded by restless visionaries from the Olde World, who decided that anything new was better than the status quo. Such people are genetically wired to stir up excitement and adventure and unsettling discovery. This red-white-and-blue romantic pursuit of liberty and happiness, it seems to me, peaked in the 1960s. A generation of young Americans threw caution to the winds and recklessly rejected the fear-imposed systems that have kept human society surviving—the work ethic, male domination, racism, lifestyle conformity, inhibition of sensuality and self-indulgence, reliance on authority.

Fear, which has always been the glue that holds human hives together, was temporarily replaced by audacious, grinning confidence in a self-directed future.

Since our research had demonstrated that set and setting determine the course of an altered-state experience, we consistently broadcast signals of intelligent reassurance: "Trust your nervous system, go with the flow, the universe is basically a beautiful and safe place." We were amazed to witness otherwise intelligent and open-minded persons doing everything in their power to instill fear, to cry danger, to slander the brain with negativity. Do we recall the hoax perpetrated by the Pennsylvania Hospital director who invented the lie that eight patients were blinded by looking at the Sun while high on LSD? The chromosome-breaking prevarication? The armies of police officials visiting high schools to warn that smoking LSD would lead to rape and murder? We were forced to conclude at one point that LSD does indeed cause panic and temporary insanity—in bureaucrats who have never touched the stuff.

We were comforted by the history of science. Every new technology that compels change in lifestyle or in understanding of human nature has always taken one generation to be socialized and domesticated. The more furious and extravagant were the attacks on LSD, the more certain we became that an important mutational process was involved.

What was lost in the furor was any rational attempt to assay what was really happening. Few Americans realized, for example, that the drug culture was the purposeful creation of an extraordinary group of scholars and people-movers who worked in loose but conscious coordination to sponsor self-directed brain change: Aldous and Laura Huxley, Gerald Heard, R. D. Laing, Thelma Moss, Alan Watts, Adelle Davis, Gordon and Valentina Wasson, Stanislaus Grof, Joan Halifax, Ken Kesey, Allen Ginsberg, Paul Bowles, John and Louis Aiken, Huston Smith, Cary Grant, the brigades of philosopher-musicians who used lyrics to teach, the armies of writers and underground newspaper editors, the filmmakers, the chemists. Never, perhaps, since Athens and the Renaissance had so many culturally influential people been allied around a philosophic concept.

Also discarded in the controversy was any rational, scientific attempt to keep score. Granted, a lot of mentally disturbed persons took acid and then blamed the drug for their genetic instability, but there was never any comparative census count. Now that the smoke has cleared, we see that far from inducing window-jumping and self-destruction, the suicide rate for young people actually dropped during the LSD boom. Suicide is caused by boredom and hopelessness—and certainly these factors were lowered during the 1960s.

And surely it is obvious that psychedelic drugs, including cannabis, lower the violence indices. There are more alcohol-induced episodes of violence in one weekend these days than in the twenty years of psychedelic drug-taking. More kids are killed and crippled in any weekend by booze plus automobile-driving than during two decades of psychedelic consumption. There is no evidence to counter the claim that LSD drastically lowered the incidence of physical danger in those who tripped. It was Vietnam that killed more than fifty

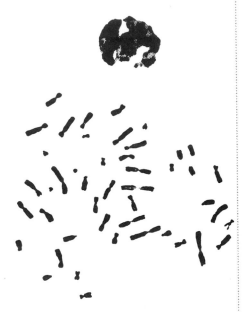

"Timothy Leary, much to our surprise, showed, in 200 cells, only two with chromosome aberrations, one in each cell. This finding is about as spectacular as must be the amount of LSD that he probably has taken in the past eight years. I am at a loss to understand or explain this negative finding."
—Hermann Lisco, M.D.
Cancer Research Institute
New England Deaconess Hospital
Boston, Mass.

thousand young Americans and several million Vietnamese. Acid is probably the healthiest recreational pursuit ever devised by humans. Jogging, tennis, and skiing are far more dangerous. If you disagree, show me your statistics.

This is not to say that the real dangers of LSD were exaggerated. Consciousness-altering drugs change minds and loosen attachments to old customs. Change triggers off intense fear reactions. Acid is a scary thing.

No one said it was going to be simple, and here is another complication. Acid should not be taken by scared persons or in a fearful setting. America is a spooked country these days. The genetic caste of danger-criers is operating in full voice. Never in our history has the national mood been so gloomy and spooky. The cause is obvious. Change causes fear, and the change rate is accelerating beyond comprehension and control. Chaotics! All the familiar comforts of yesterday are eroding with ominous rapidity. While the population rises, all the indices of intelligence, educational achievement, civility, and physical and economic security are plummeting. At the same time, paradoxically, the accomplishments of our scientific elite are eliminating the basic, eternal causes of human helplessness. Geneticists and immunologists predict enormous advances against illness, aging, and death. The space program has opened up a new frontier of unlimited energy, unlimited raw materials, unlimited room for migration. The new information society based on computers and home-communication centers is multiplying human intelligence to undreamed-of capacities. We are being flooded with new and better brain-change drugs.

The only way to understand and keep up with this acceleration of knowledge is to accelerate brain function. There are three suggested solutions to the seething, volatile situation that we now face.

> ☞ The religious answer is that since apocalypse is inevitable, the only thing to do is pray.

> ☞ The politicians assure us that the only thing to do is grab what you can and protect what you've got.

> ☞ The scientific answer is to increase intelligence, expand your consciousness, surf the waves of chaotic change planfully.

The future is going to spin faster and wilder, of that we can be sure. If you don't like acid, rest assured you're not going to like the future. Now, more than ever before, we need to gear our brains to multiplicity, complexity, relativity, change. Those who can handle acid will be able to deal more comfortably with what is to come.

A PERSONAL NOTE

People often ask me if, in hindsight, I would do it all over again. My answer, in foresight, is: Like it or not, we *are* doing it over again. And better. ◉

There are more alcohol-induced episodes of violence in one weekend these days than in the twenty years of psychedelic drug-taking.... 🦋 Acid is probably the healthiest recreational pursuit ever devised by humans. Jogging, tennis, and skiing are far more dangerous. If you disagree, show me your statistics.... 🗣 Now, more than ever before, we need to gear our brains to multiplicity, complexity, relativity, change. Those who can handle acid will be able to deal more comfortably with what is to come.... 🪑

Fascism: A philosophy or system of government that advocates or exercises an authoritarian rule of the extreme right, typically through the merging of state, military, religious, and industrial leadership, together with an ideology of belligerent nationalism. For synonym, see Communism.

IV.3. JUST SAY KNOW:

America, strangely enough, is becoming the global leader in developing new forms of fascist repression: mind control via control of brain-change medications.... The original model of a "people's democracy" (or a third reich or a dictatorship of the proles) was none other than the Republican party, USA. In 1866, while the European powers were struggling out of feudalism, our very own GOP produced the first, and most successful, fascist state.

The primitive mammalian emotions of fear and fight are mediated by the autonomic nervous system. When aroused, these reflexes produce in herd animals (including the most civilized human beings) the familiar, involuntary, irrational, pleasurable behavior called *tantrum*.

There is one strategy and four standard tactics used by certain male castes to maintain mastery over the herd, troop, flock, etc. These domination signals invoke this fear–fight reflex.

The strategy is to invent or provoke herd panic. This is variously called jihad, crusade, Holy War. The four classic control tactics are dæmonization, fanatic rage, sacrifice, and repression.

DÆMONIZATION:

To arouse the fear reflex one must convince the flock that it is menaced by a deadly evil. This peril must be more than a negotiable pressure from competitive neighbours. It must involve a moral difference. The alien enemy must be seen as a satanic threat to "our" way of life. To compromise in the slightest degree with this implacable foe would betray fatal weakness.

FANATIC RAGE:

Since this peril threatens our very way of life, a fever of national belligerence is clearly in order. War frenzy is mobilized via metaphor and symbol. The enemy is powerful. Everywhere. A cancer. An Evil Empire out to destroy us. A moral plague.

We all have, somewhere in our jittery midbrains, those ancient, down-home, turf-territory, snarling, racial programs which trigger off violent rage. Hey, anger can be a powerful kick! There's the paroxysmal convulsion that Dad uses to control the family. There's the cold, implacable, slit-eyed pressing of the Pentagon button. And then there's the impersonal, bureaucratic compulsion to humiliate those under your control, for example, by forcing them to urinate, on command, into a bottle.

Moral outrage allows one to perform extreme, genocidal cruelties upon the dæmonic enemy without guilt. The Holy War brings undeniable satisfaction to those trapped in any form of inhibited or frustrated boredom. When the mob or the electorate go crazy together, there's a certain blood-warm sense of secure togetherness, of hive or herd unity.

SACRIFICE:

To combat the deadly peril, great sacrifices must be made. Our defenders, the brave soldiers, the valiant policemen, the concerned politicians, must be given money, without stinting. What concerned citizen could be niggardly when our very moral existence is at stake? Who could oppose increasing taxes to fund this crusade?

is the number-one enemy to be eradicated totally by "final solutions" involving "zero-tolerance."

America, strangely enough, is becoming the global leader in developing new forms of fascist repression: mind control via control of brain-change medications.

It was not always this way in the United States. After its founding (1776) the fledgling American Republic presented,

THE ETERNAL ANTIDOTE TO FASCISM

REPRESSION:

During a crusade of this intensity, it is only logical that the normal, easygoing individual freedoms, the lax tolerance, the civil rights, the civilian protections of peacetime and logical debate must be suspended for the duration.

Party propaganda replaces truthful discourse. The "big lie" is eagerly accepted and repeated. The citizen's duty during an all-out war is unquestioning obedience, which is enforced by the no-nonsense police. Difference of opinion about the wisdom of the war is intolerable.

The existence of a strong, visible rival justifies the authoritarian control. The stronger and more menacing the enemy, the better. The basic threat to the authoritarian system is not the external enemy, but dissident citizens who question authority and think for themselves. The fascist-communist state is obsessively alert to detect and destroy self-reliance, self-confidence, self-discipline, self-respect, self-direction.

And now to eliminate the new and ultimately dangerous threat to an authoritarian system—*self-medication*. Self-management of one's own brain.

It is no accident, obviously, that in the year 1988, the ruling caste in America, the source nation of freedom and affluent consumerism, decided that self-medication

perhaps for the first time in human history (Australia and New Zealand came later), a most inhospitable habitat for the authoritarian-military impulse. The extraordinary isolation from external threat afforded by the almost empty new continent, the WASP homogeneity of the tiny population, the exciting challenges of building frontier settlements made it almost impossible to whip up a true Holy War.

Oh yes, there had been the Salem witch trials. The silly low-budget War of 1812, stirred up by the "Hawks," provided a few naval slogans. And the fortuitous presence of those pesky, omniscient heathen Indians produced a few pitiful national leaders like General Andrew Jackson and General (Tippecanoe) Harrison.

By 1860 the adolescent America was suffering from an acute "enemy deprivation." With the natives wiped out, there just wasn't any Evil Enemy on whom to commit belligerent nationalism. So the military Hawks, West Point trained, fell to quarreling amongst themselves. The War between the States (1861–65) was, at that time, the bloodiest conflict in history. All wars are convulsions of paroxysmal violence, but in retrospect, our Civil War has to be one of the most irrational: West Point classmates leading mechanically equipped armies against each other.

It is no accident, obviously, that in the year 1988, the ruling caste in America, the source nation of freedom and affluent consumerism, decided that self-medication is the number-one enemy to be eradicated totally by "final solutions" involving "zero-tolerance."

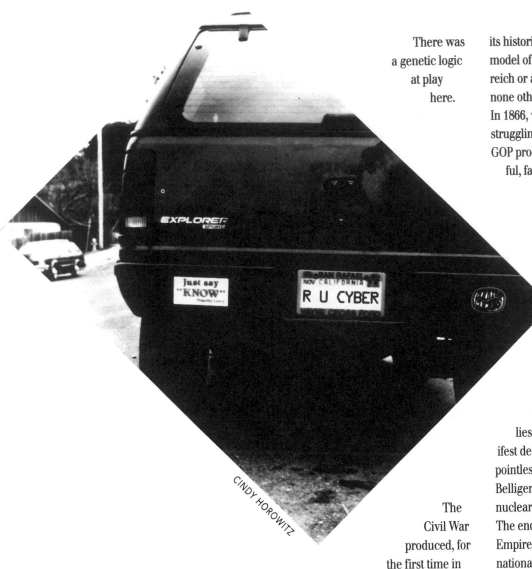

CINDY HOROWITZ

There was
a genetic logic
at play
here.

The
Civil War
produced, for
the first time in
human history, the
new update on the old
feudal-authoritarian program: the emergence of the industrial-military society.
Let's give credit where credit is due. Forget
that upstart Prince Otto Edward Leopold
von Bismarck. Forget the copy-cat Vladimir
Ilyich Lenin and the later impertinent mim-
icry of Stalin and Brezhnev. Forget even
Benito Mussolini. Credit our very own,
home-grown, WASP, Yankee-Doodle ingenuity. It was Honest Abe Lincoln who created the first and enduring model of a fascist
society—the authoritarian-military-indus-
trial complex controlled by an elite
"nomenclatura" known in every modern
state as "the grand old party."

The Heritage House think tank
(Edwin Meese *et al.*) that guides the party
today is understandably quite modest about

its historical importance. The original
model of a "people's democracy" (or a third
reich or a dictatorship of the proles) was
none other than the Republican party, USA.
In 1866, while the European powers were
struggling out of feudalism, our very own
GOP produced the first, and most successful, fascist state.

The ruling "industrial-military party" in America organized
during the Lincoln administration has managed to
keep one Holy War
after another
going for
more than a
hundred years. The
genocidal Indian Wars
gave us the final solution to
the redskin problem. The
Spanish War, sparked by the big
lies of Mr. Hearst, announced our man-
ifest destiny to become a superpower. Our
pointless participation in World War I?
Belligerent nationalism! World War II? The
nuclear holocausts of Hiroshima–Nagasaki?
The endless Cold War against the Evil
Empire? Korea? Vietnam? Belligerent
nationalism! In 1980 Americans elected as
president Ronald Reagan, a cheerful, mindless fanatic totally dedicated to the party's
authoritarian-military compulsions.

But a pesky problem emerged. The
fiasco of Vietnam had left the country in no
mood for a war binge. Rhetoric about
"standing tall against the Evil Empire"
could get record funding for the defense
industry, but there was no target-outlet for
the frustrations that had been building up
for decades. Grenada was a meaningless
twitch. The annoying little dictators in
Nicaragua, Libya, and later, Panama, could
hardly be taken seriously.

The Reagan Hawks were armed to
the teeth, all dressed up in uniforms, but
had nowhere to go. So, once again, the
"nomenclatura" fell back on the old stand-
by: a Civil War. A jihad against an insidious
domestic enemy corrupting us from within.

Once again, in the struggle for liberty, the motto becomes: JUST SAY KNOW.

The new scapegoat victims. The perverted smokers of the Assassin of Youth, the killer weed.

THE HOLY WAR ON SELF-MEDICATION

During the last Democratic administration (1976–80), fourteen states decriminalized marijuana, and President Carter announced his intention to do the same at the federal level. Carter was also active in promoting civil and human rights.

Shortly after the Grand Old Party assumed power in 1980, the standard belligerent nationalism ploy was dusted off. The Cold War against the Evil Empire was re-declared. Military budgets and the national deficits suddenly launched toward all-time peaks. But the Soviet Union under Gorbachev wouldn't play the game, and the threats from Iran–Qaddafi–Grenada–Central America were too feeble to justify a war economy.

So the Civil War card was played. A Holy War on Vegetables was declared. Illegal herbs were denounced as "cancers," moral plagues, lethal threats to national security. Politicians of both parties immediately fell into line, and the media, sensing circulation boosts and an audience hunger for moral outrage, scrambled to dramatize the menace.

There was no debate! No rational public discussion about the wisdom of waging a Civil War against some thirty million fellow-Americans who knew from experience that grass is less dangerous than booze. No questions about the common-sense practicality of violating that most basic frontier of liberty, the body and the brain.

Children were applauded for turning in their parents. Fill the prisons. Hang the peddlers. Urine tests for civilian workers. When marijuana arrests reached five hundred thousand a year, Nancy Reagan's Civil Warriors were far outstripping the Inquisition's witch-hunts.

And still no audible protests against this blatant fascism! Why were the ACLU and the civil-rights movement so silent? Where was Amnesty International? Where were the libertarian traditions of this land of freedom?

CRITICS OF THE WAR ON DRUGS

Three recently published books deal brilliantly with the evils and absurdities of the War on Drugs.

- *Dealing with Drugs, Consequences of Government Control,* ed. by Ronald Hanowy. Lexington Books, 1987.

- *Breaking the Impasse in the War on Drugs,* by Steven Wisotsky. Greenwood Press, 1986.

- *Why We Are Losing the Great War on Drugs and Radical Proposals That Could Make America Safe Again,* by Arnold Trebach. Macmillan, 1987.

Dealing with Drugs is a collection of essays by ten distinguished university scholars who demonstrate with fact and logic that the War on Drugs is futile, harmful, irrational, immoral, illegal.

Professor Hanowy's collection concludes with a magnificent essay, *The Morality of Drug Controls.* The author, psychiatrist Thomas Szasz, is one of the most important intellectuals of our times. For thirty years Szasz has brought to the dark, swampy field of psychiatry the same penetrating social logic and laser-sharp morality that Noam Chomsky has given to linguistics and politics. And more, because Dr. Szasz adds a certain down-to-earth, humanist common sense. He writes here, not about drugs, but about drug control as a moral issue, the "drug-user" as scapegoat.

A Holy War on Vegetables was declared. . . . 🔲 Children were applauded for turning in their parents. Fill the prisons. Hang the peddlers. Urine tests for civilian workers. When marijuana arrests reached five hundred thousand a year, Nancy Reagan's Civil Warriors were far outstripping the Inquisition's witch-hunts. And still no audible protests against this blatant fascism! Why were the ACLU and the civil-rights movement so silent? Where was Amnesty International? . . . 🔲 Once again, we are reminded that the only solution to human problems are intelligent thought and accurate, open communication.

I believe that just as we regard freedom of speech and religion as fundamental rights, so should we regard freedom of self-medication as a fundamental right; and that, instead of mendaciously opposing or mindlessly promoting illicit drugs, we should, paraphrasing Voltaire, make this maxim our rule: I disapprove of what you take, but I will defend to the death your right to take it.

Breaking the Impasse in the War On Drugs is a carefully researched, chilling account of the incalculable damages wrought upon our country and our southern neighbors by the Reagan regime's War on Cocaine. Long sections describe the assault on justice and civil liberties, the growth of big brotherism, the corrosion of the work ethic, the corruption of public officials, disrespect for the law, the international pathology of the War on Drugs, instability and narco-terrorism, the drug-problem problem.

Arnold Trebach, the author of *Why We Are Losing the Great War on Drugs and Radical Proposals That Could Make America Safe Again,* examines in scholarly fashion the failures, the hypocrisies, the corruptions, the repressive illegalities of the Holy War, and presents fourteen common-sense, practical, compassionate "peaceful compromises." Trebach goes behind the grim statistics to address the personal, human side of the conflict: interviews with and case histories of the victims—young people kidnapped by their own misguided parents; moderate, intelligent users harshly penalized; cancer, AIDS, and glaucoma patients prevented from using appropriate medication; street addicts caught in a system that treats them as criminals rather than as patients.

In the three books discussed, a total of twenty experts in the field agree that legal energy-mood-anæsthetic drugs (booze, nicotine, pills) are certainly as disabling and abusive as their illegal counterparts (heroin, marijuana, cocaine). They come to the common-sense conclusion that by decriminalizing and regulating the latter, we could reduce the "drug problem," in one day, from a fatal social cancer to a treatable health annoyance.

THE WAR ON PSYCHEDELICS

The most pernicious and hypocritical aspect of the current drug situation is the criminalizing of psychedelic drugs. Used with a minimum of common sense, marijuana, LSD, mescaline, and psilocybin are valuable tools for exploring the brain and changing the mind. "Psychedelic" means mind expanding. These vegetable products have almost no effect on mood or energy level. They are the very opposite of the "opiate anæsthetics," in that they produce hypersensitivity to external sensations and accelerated thought processing. They are not addictive. They have almost no effect on physiology. They change consciousness. They are information drugs. They have been used for millennia in religious ceremonies. Because they alter consciousness in such intense, individual ways, group rituals develop to support and protect the visionary trance. They are rarely used alone, because solitary visions create solipsistic "space-outs."

Psychedelic vegetables—when used with optimum regard for "set and setting"—are arguably the safest food substances that human beings can ingest. They obviously represent an ancient symbiosis between the sexual organs of flowering plants and the nervous systems of mammals to the mutual benefit of all concerned.

Since the dawning of the information age in 1946, these psychedelic plants have become extremely popular in regions where cybernetic-digital technologies (television, computers) have taken over. In the last twenty years the influence of psychedelic drugs on art, music, literature, fashion, language, electronic graphics, film, television commercials, holistic medicine, ecological awareness, and New-Age psychology has been so pervasive as to be invisible.

Psychedelic vegetables—when used with optimum regard for "set and setting"—are arguably the safest food substances that human beings can ingest. They obviously represent an ancient symbiosis between the sexual organs of flowering plants and the nervous systems of mammals to the mutual benefit of all concerned.

It is interesting that psychedelic substances are rarely mentioned by the Drug-War crusaders. Government experts and *Newsweek* editors rave and writhe about the dangerous pleasures of cocaine, the irresistible ecstasies of crack, the addictive seductions of heroin. One hit of these siren substances and you're a slave to their power. But they never discuss the reasons why millions of non-addicts prefer to use marijuana or LSD, or the benign and gentle MDMA. The law-enforcement doctors mumble about "gateway" drugs and let it go at that. That which you cannot possibly dæmonize ("killer weed") must be systematically ignored. The tactic is the familiar fear–fight line. Hey! This is no time for logical, academic discussions or treasonous undermining of the war effort! It's an all-out conflict between good and evil! The Dæmon Foe has our backs to the wall!

It is interesting that the authors of those three logical, scientific, libertarian books discussed above do not deal with the positive aspects of the psychedelic drugs, nor do they refer to the hundreds of scientific papers about the benefits, personal and cultural, which

can occur if these drugs are used with prudence and planning. They are not psychologists or humanist philosophers, after all. Thank God!

With calm unanimity these gentlemen come on as sober, rational academics. The attitude is magisterial, almost judicial. They express not one dot of approval for the use of mind-changing substances, legal or illegal. They condemn intoxication. They are opposed to the War on Vegetables only because it is futile and aggravates the problem.

Occasionally they sigh in regret for the human weaknesses that lead people to seek change and solace in drugs. (It appears unlikely that any of these prudent academics has ever been high.) Their prescription is simple: Substitute government regulation and education for repression.

I enthusiastically applaud this statesmanly approach. It could work in Belfast, in the Middle East, in Afghanistan, and here in our own Civil War on Drugs.

Once again, we are reminded that the only solution to human problems are intelligent thought and accurate, open communication.

Once again, in the struggle for liberty, the motto becomes:

JUST SAY KNOW. ©

IV.4.
CZAR BENNETT &
HIS HOLY WAR ON DRUGS

Czar: (1) a king or emperor. (2) a tyrant, autocrat.

Cossacks: D.E.A. agents.

Pogrom: (1) a domestic police action ordered by the Czar. (2) an organized and often officially encouraged persecution or massacre of people.

◆·····························▶

It is interesting to speculate why America is the only country in the world where self-medication has been decreed "Public Enemy Number One."

Since 1776, the U.S. has been engaged in a moralistic tug-of-war. On one hand, America sees itself as the guardian and inventor of individual liberty, tolerance, secular plurality, ethnic diversity, cultural idiosyncrasy, scientific inventiveness, free enterprise, and independent thinking. Much of our literature and mythology has taught us that it is the sacred duty of the patriotic American to maintain a healthy disrespect for authority and to resist every attempt on the part of religious or political officials to intrude into our private lives or to impose cultural or religious conformity. The mythic America is good natured, individualistic and creative: rowdy Ben Franklin; sturdy rebel David Thoreau; feisty, elegant Margaret Fuller; irreverent Mark Twain.

At the same time, there has been, from the beginning, a severe and moralistic Calvinist side to American culture that is antithetical to the "liberal society" described above. Like fundamentalist Islam, the American puritans believe that people are divided into the Select and the Damned, the chosen people and the satanic sin-

ners. Throughout history, this view has justified any number of crusades, morality crackdowns, witch-hunts, and Holy Wars.

Inflammatory Holy-War rhetoric, especially when spouted by politicians and governmental authorities, is the most dangerous drug of all. It arouses fear. It robs people of common sense and self-confidence.

Most recently, this view has fueled the Drug War, creating a social atmosphere that is violently impatient with hedonists of any kind. The War on Drugs is the quintessential American morality play. In it, we see clearly the distinctions between good and bad; insidious sinners and angry saints; outlaw gangs and the innocent, victimized majority. And this scenario is preached to us in easy to assess images in our newspapers and on our television screens.

The Drug War is fueled by the fact that at this historic moment, when American liberalism and free enterprise have "won" the Cold War, our politicians are suffering from enemy deprivation. Faced with the real problems of urban decay, slipping global competitiveness, and a deteriorating educational system, the government has decided instead to turn its energies toward the sixty million Americans who use illegal psychoactive drugs.

At the same time, there has been, from the beginning, a severe and moralistic Calvinist side to American culture . . . Like fundamentalist Islam, the American puritans believe that people are divided into the Select and the Damned, the chosen people and the satanic sinners.

CZAR BENNETT

 Czar: (1) a king or emperor. (2) a tyrant, autocrat.

The use of this pre-Soviet Russian term could be viewed only as comic in a rational atmosphere. The official use of this loaded term suggests that D.E.A. agents be called "cossacks." A domestic police action ordered by the Czar is usually called a "pogrom," defined as "an organized and often officially encouraged persecution or massacre of people."

Drug Czar William Bennett says that "with the weakening of political authority, the drug user, dealer, and trafficker believes that the laws forbidding their activities no longer have teeth, and they consequently feel free to violate those laws with impunity."

This is bombast. At least in the demoralized and impoverished inner city, the crack-cocaine trade will not be eliminated through beefed-up law enforcement, expanded prison facilities, or any other sort of strengthened political authority. Drug abuse in these geographic areas has fairly obvious causes: poverty, despair, and the enormous profits created by criminalization. But the prohibitionists, who have injected the debate with the hyperbolic language of sin and savagery, escape without having to address these complex social issues.

How should we deal with Americans who advocate this Rambo-concept "war" as a final solution to our inner-city problems? First offenders like Dan Rather should be sternly warned. Regular offenders should be banned from the Supreme Court, the NFL, the ABA, the ABC. Holy-War advocates should have their driver's licenses revoked and be sent to boot camp.

Multiple-offending adults like Nancy Reagan or Czar Bennett or Jesse Jackson, who hang around schools shamelessly dealing and advocating Holy War, should be committed to Abbie Hoffman De-Tox and Rehabilitation Centers.

DEFINITIONS AND CATEGORIES

DRUG:
1. a substance used as medicine in the treatment of disease; 2. a narcotic, especially one that is addictive.

LEGAL DRUGS:
Nicotine, alcohol, prescription tranquilizers, prescription sleepizers, prescription energizers.

ILLEGAL DRUGS:
Cocaine, heroin, marijuana, LSD, psilocybin mushrooms, peyote (except for Native American Church members), MDMA, etc.

DANGEROUS DRUGS:
(deaths per year) alcohol (60,000), prescription drugs (30,000), nicotine (25,000), cocaine (3,000), heroin (1,000).

SAFE DRUGS:
(deaths per year) marijuana (0), LSD (0), psilocybin mushrooms (0), peyote (0), MDMA (0).

MOOD-CHANGE FOOD & DRUGS:
are basically uppers or downers. Caffeine, heroin, cocaine, pills. Mood changers tend to be private, loner medicaments, thus leading to addiction and alienation. Alcohol, the most popular mood changer, has been acculturated in the industrial Western world and is used as a social-bonding, ceremonial, festival agent. Solitary use leads to abuse.

PSYCHEDELIC FOODS & DRUGS:
Marijuana, peyote, mushrooms, ergots (LSD), empathogens (MDMA) have been used throughout history in social-bonding ceremonials, festive celebrations, and shamanic rituals. They usually do not energize. They are not addictive. They are not injected. The rare cases of solitary ingestion are considered eccentric and alienated. Psychedelic drugs are usually freely shared. They are pacifistic, nonviolent, reflective, and, with appropriate set–setting, aphrodisiac.

Public officials of the prohibitionist persuasion who lump marijuana with cocaine and heroin are hypocritical, cynical, and, to borrow their term, "wicked."

USE AND ABUSE

Any rational solution to this situation requires the distinction between use and abuse.

Social use implies that the self-medicator knows what she/he is doing and weaves the ingestion into a planful, productive, rewarding lifestyle. Social drinking is a classic example. Reactions to psychoactive foods and drugs are strongly overdetermined by set and setting. In other words, mind state and environment determine what happens. In supportive, low-stress social settings, 90 percent of adults use normal doses of psychoactive substances with positive results. This is as true for illegal drugs as for legal drugs like alcohol. Common-sense education about set and setting eliminates 90 percent of the problems.

As wise societies throughout history have known, people have to be trained in the use of mind changers. "Safe drug use" is a common-sense truism now accepted by the alcohol industry. "Harm-reduction" is a current (1993) term for minimizing a drug's dangers by having knowledge of such things as purity and proper dosage level.

HI LEITZ

THE SOLUTION TO DRUG ABUSE

Drug addicts are a special category. About 10 percent of any population is physiologically unable to handle certain stimulants. Diabetics must say "know" to the ingestion of sugar or glucose substances, regardless of peer pressure.

Responsible education would prepare people to recognize the signs of addiction. Addicts are sick, bored people. Therapeutic intervention and immediate treatment are called for. Although counseling may comfort and rehabilitate, the specific treatment of addiction is chemical. Counseling does not prevent diabetes. Insulin does. Hospitals and clinics do not cure tuberculosis. Antibiotics do.

Researchers have located several promising compounds that inhibit addictive behavior. Addiction to cocaine and heroin could be cured in two years if normal medical research replaced the moralistic attitude of the government. In addition, private pharmaceutical firms should be encouraged to develop mood changers that are safe, nonaddictive, and precise in their effects.

Inner-city drug addiction and trafficking presents a catastrophic problem. There are two causes:

1. poverty and despair, and

2. the enormous profits created by criminalization. The solution is not to hire more "cossacks" and throw more youths in prison. The solution is to eliminate the poverty-despair, and to eliminate the profits.

Under no circumstances should drug use by minors be condoned; yet responsibility for their care and education should be undertaken by family members, peers, and honest educators—not by the government or the police, and not with propaganda and hypocritical pieties.

vic keller

The former will take years and much money. The latter can be accomplished in one week. Decriminalize, regulate, tax. With one stroke of the pen, President Clinton can put the cartel gangsters out of the picture, thus saving $8 billion in prosecution costs and diverting their $150 billion annual profits to legal enterprises that can be regulated, controlled, and supervised.

Under no circumstances should drug use by minors be condoned; yet responsibility for their care and education should be undertaken by family members, peers, and honest educators—not by the government or the police, and not with propaganda and hypocritical pieties.

America's love fest with drugs presents a tremendous chal-

DRUG WARS

The only catch is this. With the Cold War over and the War on Drugs peacefully ended, upon whom will the puritans wage their next Holy War?

lenge to liberal society. Essentially, we are engaged in a Civil War, testing whether our nation—conceived in liberty and dedicated to the ideals of civil society and individual rights—can endure. This is an uncivilized war, a test of whether common sense, compassion, civic understanding, and tolerance of difference can keep us from becoming a divided nation with one-quarter screaming "No!"; one-quarter fighting to keep their opinions heard at all; and half too stoned on narcotic prime-time TV to care what is happening in their own neighbourhood, much less in the neighbouring inner city.

The only catch is this. With the Cold War over and the War on Drugs peacefully ended, upon whom will the puritans wage their next Holy War? ◎

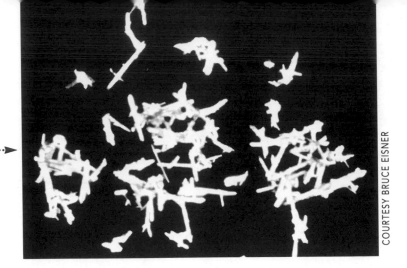

IV.5.
MDMA:
THE DRUG OF
THE 1980s

Let's face it, we're talking about an elitist experience. MDMA is a drug that is known by word of mouth to sophisticated people who sincerely want to attain a high level of self-understanding and empathy. We're talking about dedicated searchers who've earned a bit of Ecstasy...▶

Sociologists tell us that every stage of human culture produces its own art, its own music, its own literary mode, its own sexual style, its own unique slang, and its own ceremonial drug.

Take the 1980s, for example. The style of this decade comes from our leader, Ronald Reagan, who has given us an inhibited sexual style, a nostalgic 'fifties æsthetic, a series of Moral–Majority witch-hunts as public sport, a gloomy Cold–War paranoia, and an uncharitable ethic of corporate selfishness.

As an antidote, this decade of harsh rhetoric has witnessed a new type of drug called *empathogen*, referring to a state of clear empathy and compassionate understanding activated in the user's brain. [Later, the terms "entactogens" or "touching within" also came into favor—Ed.]

An earlier version of this drug was MDA—the "love drug" of the 1970s. The best-known current version is a rather more refined and shorter-acting analogue of the MDA family known as MDMA, Ecstasy, XTC, X, Adam, Venus, or Zen.

Dozens of researchers have described feelings of profound well-being, insight, understanding, empathy, and ease of communication that are activated by MDMA. Claudio Naranjo, the distinguished Chilean psychologist, has published this report on the very similar effects of MDA:

The MDA peak experience is typically one in which the moment that is being lived becomes intensely gratifying in all its circumstantial reality . . . The dominant feeling is of calm and serenity, love as it were, embedded in calm.

The perception of things and people is not altered; lives are held in abeyance and replaced by unconditional acceptance. This is much like Nietzsche's *amor fati*—love of fate, love of one's particular circumstances.—*The Healing Journey,* 1976.

A SENSUAL APHRODISIAC

The eminent Cornell psychopharmacologist Thomas Pynchon suggests that "the circuits of the brain which mediate alarm, fear, flight, fight, lust, and territorial paranoia are temporarily disconnected. You see everything with total clarity undistorted by animalistic urges. You have reached a state which the ancients have called Nirvana, all-seeing bliss."

The effects generally peak after a couple of hours and last around five hours; there is no distortion of reality, and you can—if you have to—perform normal functions. But you don't want to. Who'd want to play tennis or drive a car when you're sitting on the mountain of blissful wisdom?

THE DANGERS OF ECSTASY

The experienced person, hearing of a drug described with such pushing superlatives, is led to inquire: Come on, what are the drawbacks?

Clinical reports suggest that around 25 percent of first-time users experience a brief period of mild nausea, jaw-clenching, or eye wiggle, before passing Go and proceeding to Nirvana.

The experience is so powerful that everyone feels a bit drained the next day. Most users take the drug in the afternoon

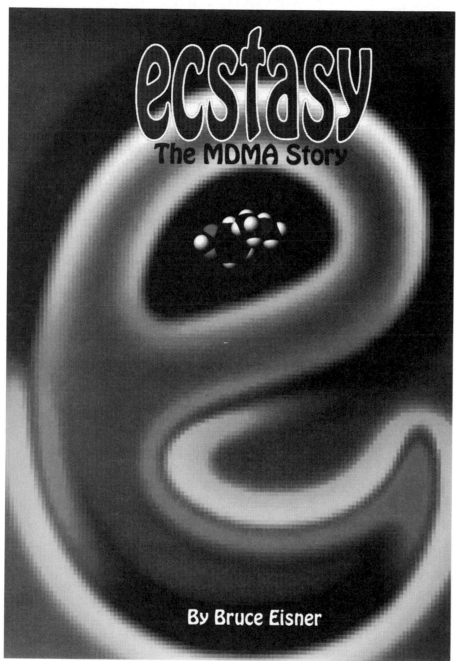

ecstasy
The MDMA Story

By Bruce Eisner

MARK FRANKLYN

...► If you want this experience, start hanging around smart, spiritually ambitious people who exhibit in their behavior the qualities that the drug promises. Even if you aren't interested in the MDMA, you could do worse than be on the lookout for people and places that give off that glow.

and by midnight are ready for a wonderful refreshing sleep, preferably in the arms of a loved one.

MDMA is not a genital aphrodisiac. The extraordinary sensuality of the experience is generalized over the body.

LEGALITY

At the present time, MDMA and similar drugs are legal. Why? Because there are no cases of abuse. The drug is not addictive; it doesn't distort reality or lead to antisocial or destructive behavior. There has never been a recorded case of a bad trip. *[By 1986, MDMA was classified as a Schedule I drug, and all research was halted, despite an enormous lobbying effort by therapists who had achieved good results with the substance, and against the recommendation of the federal judge who heard the voluminous testimony. By 1994, a small number of bad trips had been reported, usually resulting from excessive use, impurity of substance, or dehydration. —Ed.]*

One reason for the positive response to MDMA is consumer expectation. Its word-of-mouth reputation emphasizes love and peace. If you're a belligerent biker or a bar-room rowdy itching for a fight, the last drug you'd take is MDMA.

> And since our brain-marriage in 1978, we have watched dozens of our friends share the experience. It's a 90 percent success rate, if taken with the right motives in the right place. [MDMA] surely does help things along if you sincerely want to get there. And you must take it with someone you want to love.

A TYPICAL ECSTASY EXPERIENCE

In the fall of 1978 my wife Barbara and I were visiting New York City. We had cocktails one evening with a friend named Brian, who told us of this wonderful "love drug." He gave us a few tabs. Now I must add, Brian was not a dealer hanging around dark alleys pushing dope. He was a well-known psychologist using MDMA in his psychotherapy practice. He advised us to take the drug on an empty stomach and no alcohol.

Three hours later, Barbara and I had just tipsily finished a gourmet dinner at the 5-star restaurant, Chez Estuvay—cocktails, wine, brandy, cordon-bleu, and all. Feeling mellow, Barbara looked at me with that "let's do it, baby" twinkle in her eye. What could I do? The greatest successes in my life have come from saying yes to Barbara's invitations.

We each dropped one tab. About a half hour rolled by. Zap!

Barbara looked at me and laughed. "You're so lucky," she sighed. "It always hits you first."

Before long I was feeling better than I'd ever felt in my life (and I've had some pretty good times). Barbara was coming on to the same exquisite sensations. Without a second's delay we stripped off our clothes and hit the bed. I lay on my back. Barbara sat on top of me, her head and chest next to mine. Our bodies were glowing. A film of scented moisture, like the sheen of a lotus blossom, covered our skin.

We looked into each other's eyes and smiled. This was it. We both understood everything. All our defenses, protections, and emotional habits were suspended. We realized joyfully how perfect we were designed to be. Apparently the only thing to do was caress each other.

The experience went on and on. When we started to come down after three hours, we took another hit. Funny things happened. We chatted away like new-born Buddhas just down from heaven. The next day we flew back to Hollywood. Three days later we were married.

Here the cynical observer says, "So you had to take more Ecstasy to get back to that narcotic state of bliss."

Nope. That's not the way it works. The drug seems to activate the empathy-clarity circuit in the brain. Once it's turned on, it stays operative. It's like booting up your home computer.

Barbara and I have taken MDMA around twelve times in the past six years. We can return to that blessed state of fusion without the drug—by lying close to each other or by looking at each other in a serene environment.

And since our brain-marriage in 1978, we have watched dozens of our friends share the experience. It's a 90 percent success rate, if taken with the right motives in the right place. It surely does help things along if you sincerely want to get there. And you must take it with someone you want to love.

Ecstasy is not a party stimulant. It's not a recreational hit. It's not a street drug. *[Ecstasy became, in fact, all these things for a segment of users once it was outlawed and available only from underground chemists. It became a staple of rave culture by the late 1980s in Texas and the U.K., spreading soon after to Europe and the U.S.—Ed.]*

"INSTANT-MARRIAGE SYNDROME"

In the past six years we have heard many enthusiastic reports of MDMA experiences from high places around the country: Manhattan and Maui, San Francisco and Santa Fe, Austin and Ann Arbor, etc. Many New–Age psychologists use MDMA with their clients. After all, calm clarity is the aim of any program of self-improvement. The drug seems to especially benefit victims of trauma and people in relationship therapy.

One new "problem" has emerged: the Ecstasy instant-marriage syndrome.

Lots of people who didn't know each other very well have shared the experience, activated the love-empathy circuits, and rushed off the next day to get married. In some cases, after the rose-coloured smoke cleared, the couple realized that although they did, for a while, share the highest region of love, the practical aspects of their life were not in sync. You might say it's a cosmic summer romance.

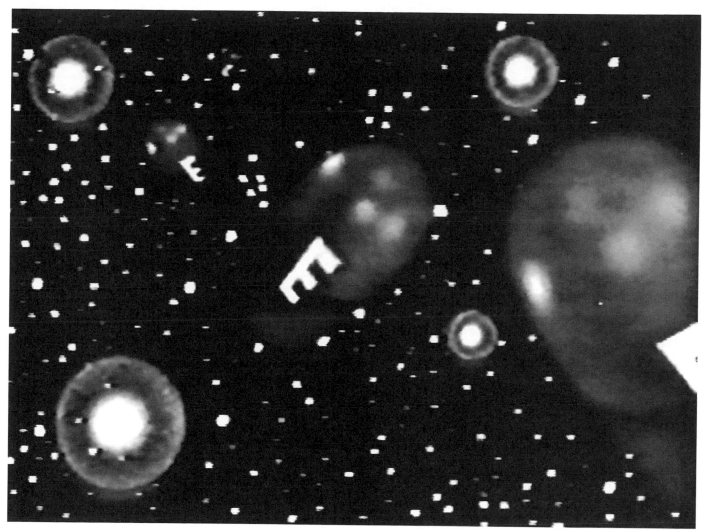

It got so bad in Boulder, Colorado, that bumper stickers and T-shirts were printed with the message:

"DON'T GET MARRIED FOR 6 WEEKS AFTER ECSTASY."

The basic rule of neurological common sense applies. Don't take any drug unless you know, trust, and admire the person providing it. There's little chance that you can get your hands on MDMA through the usual channels of drug distribution. Colombian gangsters and Mafia pushers aren't interested in selling a love-peace-wisdom drug.

Let's face it, we're talking about an elitist experience. MDMA is a drug that is known by word of mouth to sophisticated people who sincerely want to attain a high level of self-understanding and empathy. We're talking about dedicated searchers who've earned a bit of Ecstasy. If you want this experience, start hanging around smart, spiritually ambitious people who exhibit in their behavior the qualities that the drug promises. Even if you aren't interested in the MDMA, you could do worse than be on the lookout for people and places that give off that glow. ©

[Editor's Note: For a fuller description of MDMA and its subsequent history, see
- *Bruce Eisner, Ecstasy: The MDMA Story;*
- *Alexander and Ann Shulgin, PIHKAL (Phenethylamines I Have Known and Loved); or*
- *Nicolas Saunders, E for Ecstasy.]*

IV.6.

THE CASE FOR INTELLIGENT DRUG USE

MACLEAN'S: Why did LSD become so popular in the 1960s? Was it because of the times, or did the drug act as a catalyst to speed the process of cultural change and its own acceptance?

LEARY: The demographic situation was that you had 76 million baby-boomers in

The use of drugs, which are brain-change instruments, perfectly synchronized with home appliances like television, stereo players, and, later, computers. Drugs that alter states of consciousness are naturally going to be an integral part of an information-intelligence-knowledge society.

the U.S.A. who happened to be the first members of the information society. And you had Marshall McLuhan, television, and the beginning of computer technology. The use of drugs, which are brain-change instruments, perfectly synchronized with home appliances like television, stereo players, and, later, computers. McLuhan forecast this. Drugs that alter states of consciousness are naturally going to be an integral part of an information-intelligence-knowledge society.

The drugs did not cause the cultur-

al change but they were an inevitable by-product of it. And it is no accident that I am now inundated by requests from computer companies to act as a consultant. The younger generation involved in computer technologies recognizes the positive aspects of the consciousness movement of the 1960s and sees me sympathetically.

MACLEAN'S: How do you explain the decline in the use of LSD. Is it not a dead drug?

LEARY: Actually, police seizures of LSD have gone up 1,000 percent in Los Angeles County in the past year. But there had been a downward trend, and I applauded it. In the 1960s and 1970s there were seven million people taking it, but there was not always good LSD available, and bad LSD is a pharmaceutical disaster; so it was realistic to back away. The LSD that is around now is much purer and packaged in smaller doses.

MACLEAN'S: What do these changes indicate?

LEARY: That people are more concerned about the practicalities of their lives and less with philosophic meaning. There are times when it is good to scan and scope widely, and there are times when it is necessary and appropriate to fine-tune and become more practical. In pharmacology there has been a tremendous development of new drugs—MDMA, for example—that has enormous vogue in intelligence-increased circles.

vic keller

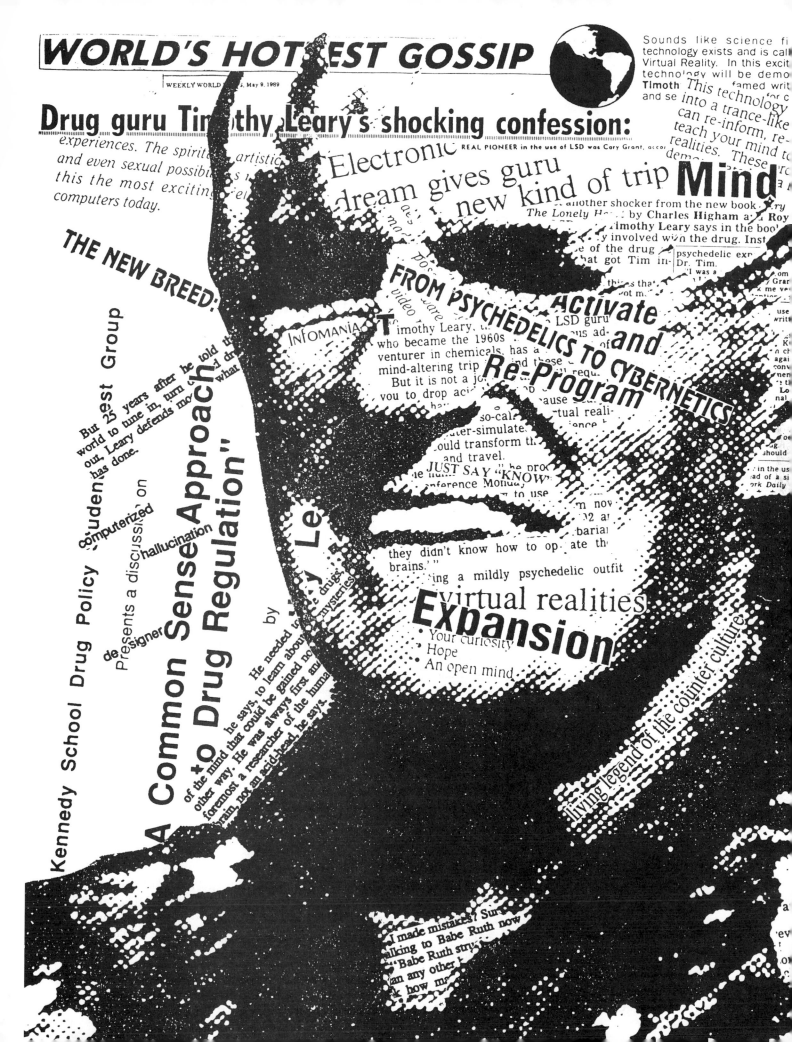

I am 100 percent in favor of the intelligent use of drugs, and 1,000 percent against the thoughtless use of them, whether caffeine or LSD. And drugs are not central to my life.

MACLEAN'S: How does MDMA affect a person?

LEARY: It does not provoke the quick reality change, the hallucinatory Niagara of perspectives of LSD. This drug and its analogues give a very clear, quite deeply affectionate experience.

MACLEAN'S: Does the renaissance of psychedelic drugs signal an eventual return to a time when people will become more inner-directed? Are we going in cycles?

LEARY: Not cycles, predictable stages. It is predictable that the first wave of baby-boomers is now getting into positions of responsibility in laboratories and research centers. It is inevitable that they would bring back research on improved psychoactive drugs. It is archaic and barbaric

to be limiting ourselves to alcohol and cocaine. We are going to have entirely new families of drugs, which will have the best aspects of the earlier generation but with improvements in safety and precision.

MACLEAN'S: With all the negative publicity on the use of drugs, have you changed your position on the use of any of them?

LEARY: I am continually experimenting. For example, I was off caffeine and now I use it selectively. The same with other drugs. I am much more selective and precise and intelligent in the timing of how, why, and when I use a drug. I am 100 percent in favor of the intelligent use of drugs, and 1,000 percent against the thoughtless use of them, whether caffeine or LSD. And drugs are not central to my life. ◎

V. CYBEROTICS

V.1. HORMONE HOLOCAUST

I recall eyeballing with dreamy lasciviousness a *Saturday Evening Post* (1936) illustration of a young woman swinging on a hammock, her head tossed back in a gesture of innocent merriment, her white dress and lace petticoat pulled up, revealing two inches of milky, white, soft, tender, moist, kissable inner thigh.

The year was 1938. Place: a small town in Western Massachusetts. Cultural background: Irish Catholic. Erotic climate: dry and frigid. Growing up in this chill environment I was taught there was virtue and mortal sin—nothing in between. Good was to think and act like the neighbours, to be proper and decent. Bad? The human body. Any passing reference to sexual functions was very bad. The mention of genital organs was taboo! Erotic feelings—bad. Sexual desire—beyond bad. It was evil!

In my family, morality was administered by my mother and her two spinster sisters. As a youth I became aware of their strange obsession with sexuality. I watched with fascination as they scanned every work of art, every movie, every song, for any signs of what they referred to as "funny business." And it soon occurred to me—with genetic dismay—that my family, dominated by such anti-sex fervor, was dying out! Of my generation I was the only one to carry the paternal name and one of only two survivors on the maternal side. This realization so disturbed me that I became determined to fight back. As the last remaining life form in my gene pool, I resolved that my family—and by extension, society's great Anti-Sex Gang—would not gain control over my precious bodily fluids. In short order, I managed to develop an equally sensitive counter-radar system that scanned every word and image in a fervent search for something—anything—mischievous, racy, erotic.

Sexual arousal is all in the mind.

My first experience with erotic literature was provided by the Bible. I would sit poring over Old Testament descriptions of lasciviousness, burningly aware of the fundamentalist erection bulging in my trousers while Mother and aunts beamed approval from the living room, sure that I would become a priest.

Soft-core porn abounded in the 1930s. Endlessly I eyeballed with dreamy lust the Montgomery Ward mail-order catalogue with its pictures of young trollops shamelessly modeling silken underwear. Pert wantons in nylon hose! Housewife harlots in steamy corsets. Voluptuous nymphomaniacs in one-piece bathing suits, crotch panels hugging tightly to the firm, labial curves. Sexual repression had created such a steamy hot-house atmosphere that the slightest spark could produce in me a pulsing flame.

This secret erotic library of my youth taught me a valuable lesson about the thermo-

vic keller

I have an innate, physical revulsion to violence. It disturbs me to look at films that involve fighting, gunfire, bloodshed. The Rambo type, to me, is a subhuman monstrosity. Written or graphic expressions that stimulate violent impulses—these are the true obscenities.

dynamics of sexual expression and repression. *Sexual arousal is all in the mind.* The human being comes equipped with sexual organs wired to the brain and booted up by hormones. The hardware is activated by various cues your brain has learned to associate with sexual invitations and availability. These cues, as shared by a particular society, become the pornography of that culture. Each society and each person develops unique trigger stimuli. The stimuli may change from person to culture to time frame. The girl in the hammock who was unbearably erotic to me in the 1930s would leave me yawning today. Even Jerry Falwell would rate the picture wholesome in the context of the 1980s.

But to someone else, in a personally or socially highly repressed environment, the innocent illustration may retain its tang of arousal. The sexual brain is wired to imprint as trigger stimuli any cue that turns you on. In this way, our brains always have the last laugh on the Anti-Sex Gang. The more that political or religious officials censor words and images about sex, the more suggestive and arousing becomes the lightest hint of double entendre, the slightest glimpse of a bodily part.

Or consider a photo of young men wrestling in Olympic competition, bodies locked and straining in muscular embrace. Such clean-cut, athletic activity could, for male homosexuals or certain horny, imaginative young women, became the porn trigger for hormone holocausts.

The prudish Arabs swathe their women in veils, and then writhe with lust at the sight of a bare ankle. Western feminists may wonder why their Islamic sisters put up with this male repression, but the veiled ladies are aware of the allure. I learned this in 1961 when Allen Ginsberg, William S. Burroughs, and I started flirting with a Moroccan singer in a Tangier café, and suddenly found ourselves being pulled into enormous, luscious nymphomaniac brown eyes as warm and melting as chocolate-pudding vaginas. I'm talking about two X-rated, hard-core eyeballs whose wet nakedness was demurely veiled by skillfully fluttering eyelids.

Those sexy Italians who grow and blossom in a Vatican-dominated black-robed repressive culture have developed an amazing shorthand for soft porn. Almost every fruit or vegetable, every household appliance—broom, rake, hammer, mop—is endowed with double meaning. Order a zucchini from the waiter in Naples, and a ripple of giggles goes 'round the table. Watch lusty Luigi hold a peach in his hot hand. Observe him slice it open, slowly, slowly. Watch him dreamily extract the stone, lovingly gaze into and then start to lick the pink-scarlet oval indentation! For Luigi, at that moment, no centerfold is as erotic as that hard-core, porno peach!

Pornography, then, is whatever turns you on. The dictionary agrees. Pornography is defined as written, graphic, or other forms of communication intended to excite sexual desires. What could be clearer? Or healthier? I happen to belong to that large percentage of human beings who believe that sexual desire, being the undeniable source of life, is sacred, and that when expressed by those whose motives are reasonably healthy and loving, it creates the highest form of human communication. And, to complete this confessional, I have an innate, physical revulsion to violence. It disturbs me to look at films that involve fighting, gunfire, bloodshed. The Rambo type, to me, is a subhuman monstrosity. Written or graphic expressions that stimulate violent impulses—these are the true obscenities. And yet these are the expressions that are of no concern to the anti-porn crusaders, the militaristic Hawks, the evangelical Rambos, the Thought Police, and the whole Anti-Sex Gang. It is no coincidence: The Anti-Sexers haven't the love or the tenderness or the horniness or the balls to appreciate pornography. Violence or sex—it's one or the other, it seems, and I know where I stand. As Mae West said to the guy with the bulge in his trousers, "Is that a gun in your pocket or are you glad to see me?" ◉

V.2. IN SEARCH OF THE TRUE APHRODISIAC

I want a new drug . . .

One that won't make me nervous, wonderin' what to do . . .

One that makes me feel like I feel when I'm with you.

Huey Lewis and the News

● ●

At a very early age, after comparing the rather routine existence of my family with the heroic adventures I read about in books, I concluded that the well-lived life would necessarily involve quests. Grail adventures for fabled goals to save the human race.

During these younger years I dreamed of becoming a warrior, an explorer, a great scientist, a wise sage. During adolescence a new noble challenge emerged.

Sex.

And here I encountered a great and enduring paradox of the human condition (male division). To wit: Although sex was obviously important to a happy life, I did not have perfect control over my erections. Apparently many other males shared this same inefficiency.

The first problem was that the erections came when I couldn't use them. The terrible embarrassment of the unexpected arousal in social situations. The inability to get up and walk across the room because of that mind-of-his-own down there.

Later came the nervousness of "making out." The wild excitement of foreplay. The unbuttoning of the bra. The removal of the panties. The wiggling into position in the front seat of the car. Would you believe a rumble seat? The zipper. The arrangement of the contraceptive. The heavy breathing. The anxieties. Do you hear someone coming? The maneuvering for penetration. Whew! What happened to my unit?

This interaction between the willing mind and the willful body suddenly became a most critical issue. And in puritanical 1936, there were no manuals on the care and use of this complex equipment.

I consulted the dictionary and discovered that something called an "aphrodisiac" increased sexual performance. I rushed to the library and consulted every encyclopædia available. Not a mention of aphrodisiac.

How curious that such an important topic was totally ignored.

Oh well, here was another unexplained, mysterious facet of adult life. Lindbergh could fly the Atlantic. We could put a man on the South Pole. But we couldn't get control of the most important part of our body. Maybe this was what philosophers meant by the "mind/body problem." I resolved to file this away for future study.

After I helped win World War II and then dutifully graduated from college, I decided to be a psychologist. This seemed to be the key profession. If you could understand your own mind, think clearly, and not be victimized by emotions, you could then master the other issues in life.

By 1950, sex was no problem. I was settled into the suburbs, happily married, and productively domesticated. My erections reported to duty promptly on schedule just as I did at the office.

THE QUEST FOR THE MAGIC POTION GOES TO HARVARD

In 1960, that magic year, I moved to Cambridge, Massachusetts, to join the Harvard faculty. My sexual situation was changed. I was a 40-year-old single person, facing, once again, the thrills, the chills, the spills of the mating ground. At this point I found that my sexuality (how shall I put this?) was very elitist and selective. I no longer felt that incessant, throbbing teenage desire to fuck any consenting warm body in the vicinity. A one-night stand could be a lust or a bust, depending on my feelings toward the woman, my emotional condition, my state of mind, and my period of heat.

> ## Sex means cheerfully giving up control to receive pleasure. The less sex, the more compulsion to control.

To find out more about these matters, I read extensively on the subject and talked to my friends in the psychiatric, clinical, and personality departments. I learned that male sexuality is not an automatic macho scene. The male erotic response turned out to be a most complex, delicate situation. More than two-thirds of the male population over the age of 35 reported less than perfect control over their desire. Adult males seemed to have cycles and rhythms and all sorts of fragile sensitivities that are usually attributed to the "weaker sex." Scientific observers agreed that most of the guys who claimed total virility were either lying or too primitive and callous to appreciate the exquisite complications of erotic interaction in the fast-moving, ever-changing, postindustrial, interactive civilization.

So here was an interesting social phenomenon. It was generally believed by psychologists back there in 1960 that much of the conflict, aggression, paranoia, and sadism that was plaguing society was due to sexual frustration. Freud started this line of thought. Wilhelm Reich carried it to its logical political conclusion. Sex means cheerfully giving up control to receive pleasure. The less sex, the more compulsion to control.

Take, for example, a control freak like J. Edgar Hoover. Here was a 70-year-old drag-queen who got his FBI kicks from collecting sexual dossiers on rival politicians.

Take, for example, Richard Nixon, whom no one ever accused of tender erotic feelings.

At this time, spring of 1960, I concluded that if a safe, dependable aphrodisiac were available, many of the psychological and social problems facing our species would instantly be ameliorated. So I descended on the Harvard Medical School library with a team of graduate assistants. We scoured the bibliographies and journal files for data about aphrodisiac drugs and discovered an enormous literature on the subject.

The mandrake root was apparently the first sex stimulus. It was mentioned twice in the Bible. Pythagoras "advocated" it. Machiavelli wrote a comedy about it.

The flesh and organs of horny animals had been used in almost every time and place. Hippomanes, flesh from the forehead of a colt, was mentioned in Virgil. Mediæval Europeans regularly used the penis of the stag, bull, ox, goat.

Ambergris, a jelly from the innards of the whale, was used by the royal mistress Madame du Barry and the insatiably curious James Boswell. Musk was a perennial favorite of erotic searchers; so was shellfish, of course, especially oysters and mussels. In Japan, the fugu fish, a form of puffer, is still used by hopeful lovers. Each year more than five hundred Japanese die while on this dangerous quest.

All the texts agreed that cantharides, Spanish Fly, is a "most certain and terrible aphrodisiac." An overdose causes unbearable itching and irritation to the genitals.

Over the centuries the plant kingdom has been ransacked by the sexually ambitious. Many believe that satyrian, a mythic herb mentioned by the Greeks and Romans, was nothing else than good old marijuana and hashish. Then there's truffles and mushrooms. The South American yage. The South Seas root kava kava. Damiana. The royal jelly and pollen from bees.

And, of course, the coca plant. Pre-Columbian Peruvian ceramics portrayed pornographic scenes on pots used to prepare the nose candy of the Andes. Is cocaine an aphrodisiac? "First you're hot and then you're not," reported most sophisticated researchers.

Casanova attributed his record-making lust to raw eggs.

The strong, hard, up-jutting horn of the rhino has caught the imagination of erection-seekers for centuries. You grind it up into powder and eat or toot it. In the Orient today, rhino dust goes for $2,000 an ounce. In Hong Kong restaurants they'll sprinkle some rhino-horn powder on your dinner for a hefty addition to your bill.

My research at the Harvard Medical School library thus demonstrated that my quest was not a lonely one. Throughout the ages, intelligent, affluent, ambitious, and just plain horny human beings have continually sought the alchemical grail—the true aphrodisiac.

So what does modern science have to contribute to this noble search? Nothing. Nada. Zilch.

Not only was there no proven aphrodisiac in the current medical literature, there was apparently no research being done on this most important topic. How curious. Here was a medicine that could cure many of our medical and psychological problems, and there seemed to be a veil of secrecy around the subject.

When I tried to talk to my friends on the medical faculty about this subject, they clammed up. Finally an endocrinologist pal explained it to me. "Listen, Timothy, the subject of aphrodisiacs is taboo. If any medical scientist or physiologist here, or in the Soviet

ANDY FRITH

Throughout the ages, intelligent, affluent, ambitious, and just plain horny human beings have continually sought the alchemical grail—the true aphrodisiac.

At this time, spring of 1960, I concluded that if a safe, dependable aphrodisiac were available, many of the psychological and social problems facing our species would instantly be ameliorated.

Union, were to apply for a grant to research this field, his reputation would be ruined. He'd be considered a flake."

"But it's a great research topic," I protested. "The first scientist who discovers an effective aphrodisiac will be a savior of mankind and make a bundle of money."

"No question of it," said the endocrinologist. "We all know that if a crack team of psychopharmacologists were to research this topic, they could come up with an aphrodisiac in a year. It will happen. Someday someone will win a Nobel prize and make a billion dollars marketing one. But this is only 1958. Eisenhower is president. Khrushchev is premier. There's an overpopulation problem. The culture isn't ready for a medicine that would have the male population running around with erect dicks bulging out of their pants. Jeez, we're just coming up with a polio vaccine. Come back in twenty years, and maybe we'll have an erection injection."

There was no doubt about it. There was a social taboo against the idea of a pill that would give man a calm, certain control over his precious equipment. I couldn't understand it. If your car decided to run when it wanted to, you'd have it adjusted right away. If your television set was temperamental and turned off at its own whim, you'd take steps to put you back in charge.

This resistance to self-improvement became really obvious when I was taken to see a sex show in the Reeperbahn of Hamburg, Germany. My guides were a very sophisticated editor of *Der Speigel* and a well-known psychiatrist. The show amazed me. Straight-out fucking on stage! I was most impressed by a big Swedish youth who bounded around the set with this enormous hard-on, fucking first this fiery red-head who wrapped her legs around him, and then a sultry brunette who lay on a couch holding up her arms invitingly, and then pleasuring the saucy blonde who bent over, leaning her head against the wall with her backsides wiggling.

vic keller

For twenty minutes this acrobatic young man pranced around with total self-mastery— in front of an audience of two hundred! We're talking Olympic gold-medal time!

"That guy's stamina is impressive," I said to my German hosts. They scoffed in that scornful, jaded Hamburg style.

"That's not the real thing," said the editor. "He's taken some drug."

The psychiatrist agreed, waving his hand in dismissal.

I leaped to my feet. "What drug!" I shouted. "What's it called? Where can you get it?"

No answer from my sophisticated friends. They just couldn't admit to being interested.

THE APHRODISIAC EFFECT OF PSYCHEDELIC DRUGS

 In August 1960, beside a swimming pool in Mexico, I ate psilocybin mushrooms and discovered the power of psychedelic drugs to reprogram the brain.

I rushed back to Harvard. Frank Barron and I started the Harvard Psychedelic Drug Research project. Aldous Huxley and Alan Watts and Allen Ginsberg were our advisors. We assembled thirty of the brightest young researchers in the area. We were on to something that could change human nature. We felt like Oppenheimer after his Almagordo bomb, except better, because psychedelic drugs allowed you to release the nuclear energies inside your own head.

In the next two years the Harvard Psychedelic Drug Research project studied the reactions of a thousand subjects to LSD. We discovered that the key to a psychedelic drug session is set and setting.

Set is your mind fix. Your psychological state. Be very careful what you want from a session, because you're likely to get it.

Setting is the environment. If your surroundings are scary, then you'll be scared. If your surroundings are beautiful, then you'll have a beautiful experience.

Our sessions at Harvard were designed for self-discovery. The sessions were held in groups. So neither the set nor the setting emphasized sex.

My colleague Richard Alpert, who later became the famous holy man Baba Ram Dass, was much more hip. He quickly discovered that if the set (and expectation) was erotic, and the setting was his bedroom, then psychedelic drugs were powerfully aphrodisiac. I give the wily Ram Dass a lot of credit for this breakthrough. He was

MANDRAKE ROOT · HIPPOMANES · STAG PENIS · AMBERGRIS · MUSK · OYSTERS · BULL PENIS · MUSSELS · FUGU FISH · CANTHARIDES · OX PENIS · SATYRIAN · MARIJUANA & HASHISH · HORSE PENIS · TRUFFLES

[Baba Ram Dass]: "All this inner exploration stuff is great. It's true you can access any circuit in your brain and change your mind. But it's time you faced the facts, Timothy. We're turning on the most powerful sexual organ in the universe! The brain."

certainly way ahead of me.

I remember the day he came to me and said, "All this inner exploration stuff is great. It's true you can access any circuit in your brain and change your mind. But it's time you faced the facts, Timothy. We're turning on the most powerful sexual organ in the universe! The brain."

Other sophisticated people came to Harvard and tipped us to the secret. The philosopher Gerald Heard. The beat poet Allen Ginsberg. The Buddhist sage Alan Watts. The western folk hero Neil Cassady. We were just rediscovering what philosophers and poets and mystics and musicians and hedonists had known for centuries. Marijuana, hashish, mushrooms, LSD were powerful sensory experiences.

For the next twenty years, like everyone else, I multiplied my sensory pleasure, learned the techniques of erotic engineering. Everything became a source of æsthetic-erotic pleasure, etc. The effect was in the head. If you knew how to dial and tune your brain, you could enrich your sex life beyond your wildest dreams.

But there was still that matter of controlling the rod of flesh. We could boogie around in our brains. Good! But why couldn't a man be able to operate his penis at will the way he moves the voluntary organs of his body?

A RISKY ENCOUNTER WITH MEDICAL SCIENCE

One night in 1983, I was having dinner with a friend who worked at the UCLA Neuropsychiatric Institute. During the evening, he mentioned that a breakthrough in the erection depart-

KAVA KAVA · COCA · GOAT PENIS · RAW EGGS · RHINO HORN · YOHIMBE · MANDRAKE ROOT · HIPPOMANES · STAG PENIS · AMBERGRIS · MUSK · OYSTERS · HORSE PENIS · MUSSELS · FUGU FISH · CANTHARIDES · OX PENIS · SATYRIAN · MARIJUANA & HASHISH · BULL PENIS · HASHISH · TRUFFLES · KAVA KAVA · COCA · GOAT PENIS · RAW EGGS · RHINO HORN · YOHIMBE · MANDRAKE ROOT · HIPPOMANES · STAG PENIS · AMBERGRIS · MUSK · OYSTERS · BULL PENIS · MUSSELS · FUGU FISH · CANTHARIDES · OX PENIS · SATYRIAN · MARIJUANA & HASHISH

ment was at hand. He said that a Stanford University research team was developing a pill that would give immediate control of your erections! The active ingredient was called yohimbe.

This was a discovery of historic importance! It could mean the end of male insecurity, cruelty, and war! This could break the wretched addiction to prime-time television!

My friend also said that a local group, the Southern California Sexual Dysfunction Clinic, was giving these new pills to research subjects. I phoned and made an appointment with the director. If the pill existed, I wanted to try it out, and help make it available to the public.

The clinic was in the Cedar Sinai Medical Center. There was a large waiting room. About eight very old men were sitting slumped over, staring glumly at the carpet. A couple had crutches.

Two old geezers were drooling.

The nurse greeted me cordially and asked me to fill out a form. I said, "I'm here to discuss research on aphrodisiacs with the

> Everything became a source of æsthetic-erotic pleasure, etc. The effect was in the head. If you knew how to dial and tune your brain, you could enrich your sex life beyond your wildest dreams.

doctor." She smiled compassionately and said she understood, but would I please fill out the forms. So I did.

After a while a male technician, about 40, with the graceful charm of a chic hair-dresser, asked me to come to a back room. I explained that I wanted to discuss research with the doctor. He smiled understandingly and asked me to take some tests. At this point I was about to say "forget it," but it occurred to me that this would be a great opportunity see what happens in these frontiers of medical science. And I realized that the doctor wasn't going to give me pills until I had taken the tests.

So I took the standard blood and urine tests.

Then came the mad-scientist stuff. The technician patiently explained that we had to find out if there was a strong and steady flow of blood to my unit. So he wired the tip of my module, the base of my module, and an artery in my leg to an amplifier and we sat back to listen. BOOM . . . BOOM . . . BOOM! My genital bloodstream filled the room with its strong stallion pulse! Sounded like the rhythm section of a heavy-metal rock group to me.

The technician nodded in approval.

Next he had me jog in place, my unit still wired for sound. The percussion section really took off. Boom . . . da . . . BOOM!

All the time I kept explaining that I had regular, if unpre-

dictable erections. I just wanted the pill! The technician was very understanding. "Tell it to the doctor," he said.

The doc was very cordial and understanding. He evaded my questions about the aphrodisiac. He explained how complicated this field was—the mind, the brain, the hormones, the circulatory system, phobias, repressions, venereal diseases, herpes, AIDS, alcohol and drug abuse, fatigue, overwork, marital discord, inherited dispositions, early traumas, fetishes, anxieties, menopausal life stages.

At this point it dawned on me that this clinic, supposedly set up to deal with sexual arousal, was the most antiseptic, mechanical, unerotic place I had ever encountered. I could feel my reservoir of sexual desire rapidly draining away. If I didn't have an erection problem before, I was very likely to catch one in here. This place could make Casanova take a vow of chastity.

I felt like the ambitious starlet who undressed for the producer, the casting director, the script writer, the director, the director's brother Max, and won a part in a safari movie that required her to live in a tent on the wind-swept, dismal Sahara desert. "Who do I have to fuck to get out of this sexual-dysfunction movie?" I thought to myself.

The doctor was relentless. He insisted that I take the erection-frequency test. You took the gadget home and wired up your module during sleep to measure the number and strength of nocturnal hard-ons. I explained that I had them all the time. "Listen, just phone my wife. She takes Richter-scale readings every night."

The male nurse outfitted me with the peter-meter, stored for travel in a large suitcase. All the old men in the waiting room looked up sadly as I bounced by with the case.

My wife was intrigued. She couldn't wait for me to try it. We rushed to the bedroom and set it up by the side of the bed. Velcro straps, wires hooked to dials, clocks, and meters. It was so science-fiction sexy that, in spite of myself, I got an erection. My wife applauded.

"That gadget is wonderful!" she marveled.

"Hey, look out," I shouted. "You'll ruin the experiment."

"Fabulous," murmured my wife.

"Hey," I worried, "everything we're doing is being recorded!"

"Three cheers for science," said my wife.

Well, we broke the machine. Wires pulled off. A cable apparently short-circuited. The clock motor heaved a buzzing sigh and stopped. All the meters went over the red, flickered, and came to a satiated rest.

"Fabulous," I said.

Next Monday I returned the destroyed gadget. I felt very guilty. I tried to explain what had happened to the technician. He gave me a stern look. When I asked about the aphrodisiac pill, he made an appointment for me to see the doctor.

That weekend my wife and I took some mushrooms and had a wonderful time. On Monday morning I reported for my interview with the doctor.

The old men were still in the waiting room. I raced back to see the male nurse and told him about the great sex party over the weekend. He looked at me coldly.

I told the doctor about the wonderful effects of the psychedelic. He seemed unimpressed. I asked him for the aphrodisiac pill once again. He flatly denied that such a potion existed. His position was clear. If you didn't have a circulatory problem that could be treated by normal medicine, your penile control and enhancement program was to be handled by a shrink, or your rabbi, priest, or minister.

A THRILLING BREAKTHROUGH IN MEDICAL SCIENCE

It was August 1984 when the news we had been awaiting for hit the wires. Physiologists at Stanford University made it official. They had developed a potent aphrodisiac. The potion was extracted from the bark of the yohimbe tree of tropical West Africa. Tests on laboratory rats proved "sensational." It seemed that the surprised and delighted rodents produced fifty erections an hour. Fifty times more than normal!

The researchers announced that they were ready to begin testing the drug on humans. The news flash stirred up the predictable enthusiastic response. A spokesperson at the Stanford Medical News Bureau reported that the item had "been accorded a good deal more space and time than most of the bureau's reports on medical progress."

The expected puritan reaction was not long in coming. One Daniel S. Greenberg, publisher of *Science and Government Report*, complained that "in terms of science's traditional quest for fundamental understanding, yohimbe research is pretty thin stuff." Mr. Greenberg prudishly asserted that this interest in happiness was a sign of passion, vanity, and self-indulgence—as opposed to a space shot to study the surface of Mars. The essay was widely reprinted—even in the staid *Los Angeles Times.* The purpose of the piece was to ridicule the research and discourage its continuation.

The politics of senility prevailed once again. If any scientific commission recommended funding for aphrodisiac research, it would be opposed by the Moral Majority and the right-wing politicians. If a large pharmaceutical house tried to market a sexual-enhancement drug—imagine the furor! The moralists would have another sin to denounce! Laws would be passed! The narcotic agencies would have another victimless crime to persecute.

Imagine the black market that will spring up. College campuses. Yuppie parties. Even the senior citizens' centers would be buzzing. A new drug underground? What normal, healthy person would not want to try a new love potion? ◎

I told the doctor about the wonderful effects of the psychedelic. He seemed unimpressed. I asked him for the aphrodisiac pill once again. He flatly denied that such a potion existed. His position was clear. If you didn't have a circulatory problem that could be treated by normal medicine, your penile control and enhancement program was to be handled by a shrink, or your rabbi, priest, or minister. . . . What normal, healthy person would not want to try a new love potion?

My wife was intrigued. She couldn't wait for me to try it.

We rushed to the bedroom and set it up by the side of the bed.

Velcro straps, wires hooked to dials, clocks, and meters.

It was so science-fiction sexy that, in spite of myself, I got an erection.

My wife applauded.

DANA GLUCKSTEIN

Do you want to be the center of attention at your next party—without disrobing or throwing up on the hostess? Here's a sure-fire tip. Turn to the person sitting next to you and ask this question: "Do you think America has undergone a change in sexual morals during the last five years?"

Almost everyone in a reasonable state of mental alertness will respond with some emotion. Most will say "Yes!" Some will say, "It depends." But everyone has an opinion. If you ask enough people, you'll get some thought-provoking answers.

WHAT HAPPENED TO THE GOOD OLD-FASHIONED SUBURBAN ORGY?

My ultra-jaded friend Larry Flynt, a one-time olympic erotic athlete, groaned when I popped him the "sex-change" question. "What happened to sexual freedom and the open marriage?" he complained. "I remember this party in Atlanta around 1972. I walked into this large house and there were like a hundred (!) men and women, ya know, all nude. Drinking! Talking! Smoking funny cigarettes! Dancing! Flirting!

"And ya know what? They were all there to fuck as many new and different people as the flesh could stand! Hey, I'm speaking about middle-class folks! Lawyers. Dentists. Accountants. And their ever-loving wives! Occasionally a couple or a trio heads for the heated pool or the hot tub or the rumpus room. In every bedroom you got two, three, four couples making out on big round beds. Hey, they're swapping partners back and forth like *elastic orgasms* had just come on the market! Jeez, you sure don't hear of those goings-on today!"

Larry had his own theory to explain the new celibacy.

"Jealousy. Yup! Plain, old-fashioned, male jealousy stopped all the swapping."

Larry smiled to himself, a real dirty grin, and rubbed his belly and shook his head. "Okay. Imagine Max the dentist. He's happy as a toothless oyster sucking away at that cute little Georgia Peach married to the insurance agent down the street. And then he looks over and ya know what! There's his own sweetie-pie wife, her legs planted firmly in the air, merrily boffing some total stranger, a TV weather reporter from Birmingham, Alabama, with a pot-belly and a twelve-inch erection! And what's worse, she's got this ecstatic, dazed look on her face!

"Well! Dentist Max freaks out. You gotta be very secure sexually to handle that sort of scene."

A CONCERN FOR THE PURITY OF OUR PRECIOUS BODILY FLUIDS

Maybe. But most people cite another obvious reason for the new morality. Fear of the new sex-related diseases.

According to Susan, an attractive (one might say voluptuous) psychologist in her thirties, "It started with herpes. Then AIDS put everyone into the diagnostic mode.

"There's another health-related sex inhibitor. Female contraceptives have been given a very bad press recently.

"Let's face it," said Susan, "it was the pill and the IUDs that kicked off the sexual liberation of the late 1960s. But now, many women are having second thoughts about the side effects. What can a horny young woman do? Barrier devices like diaphragms are undignified, and rubbers are crude."

Susan told a story about Fred, a doctor at her clinic. "He's a real cute guy. Cool, athletic, charming. Prides himself on being a playboy stud. Now, we've been eyeing each other for a long time, and one night after work Fred invites me to his place for a drink. I'm really turned on and thinking some steamy thoughts as we walk into his living room. Well, one thing leads to another—erotic music, drinking margaritas, candle light, smouldering glances, secret little smiles. Fred moves next to me on the deep, soft couch, and begins caressing my neck.

"Oooh! Delicious!

"I relax and shift my weight to be more comfortable. Fred puts his hand on my knee. I open my legs just a little. He slides his hand up my smooth thigh slowly, slowly. I'm about to go crazy, you understand. His hand moves up more and I'm opening my legs wider. One false move and I'm his!

"At this crucial moment Fred starts thinking about his precious bodily fluids. And mine. So he pulls back his hand and clears his throat and initiates the clinical interview. He says, 'I've been tested recently for herpes, AIDS, and VD. Including chlamydia. I'm clean as a bean, Susan. How about you?' "

Susan sighed and shook her head sadly. "Sorta puts a chill on the steamy tropical romantic climate, doesn't it!"

FRIGHTENING? FRUSTRATING? FADDISH? FRIENDLY?

I'm sitting in the Polo Lounge of the Beverly Hills Hotel, bored with movie talk. So I pop the sex-change question. Works like a charm. Everyone has an emotional reaction.

"It's frightening," said June, a liberal lawyer. "It's part of the Reagan conservatism. These right-wingers want to turn America into a prudish police state like Iran, with all the women in black veils and chastity belts."

"It's frustrating," said Charles, a sturdy, thoughtful aspiring screenwriter who had just moved to Hollywood. "I'm looking for a girlfriend out here, and I can't score a date. The women seem afraid of human contact. It's a lot easier to meet girls in Chicago."

"Shave your beard, sell a script, buy a Porsche. You'll have no trouble finding girls, believe me," purred June.

"This new puritanism is a fad," said Jon Bradshaw, a cynical journalist just in from the Tripoli front. "Morality fluctuates with the economy. When the stock market goes up, skirts rise. When people are worried about money, they fuck less. Period."

Bradshaw took a long sip from his scotch-rocks, unsheathed his war-correspondent leer, and scoped it in June's direction. "But I like that stuff about the Ayatollah's dancing girls with black veils and the belts. Sounds like fun."

"It's all about friendship," said Natalie, a producer's mistress. "People are definitely less promiscuous these days. Why? Because they want a relationship—not a one-night stand. And you're more likely to stay healthy and swing a movie deal if you make it with a pal."

A PASSIONATE ATTACK ON MALE DOMINATION

I continued my research at Oasis, the chic new restaurant in Dallas. Richard Chase, the suave owner, sat me next to Patricia, a beautiful brunette glowing with pregnancy. The sex-change question set her off!

According to Patricia, "Women are more self-confident and assertive these days. The male department just can't deal with it. I hear it all over Texas from intelligent, beautiful, successful women. It's these gun-slinging cowboys who are causing the new puritanism. Scared by the competition. Can't get it up for a self-confident Southern woman."

A LIMP DEFENSE OF MALE CHASTITY

The guy next to her, a young oil executive named Nick, reacted defensively to this notion. "Men I know are more interested in making money than making a woman. Playing around is high-school and college stuff. When you get out in the real world, you realize that you drill a gal, that's one-night crude. Make a deal for a pipeline and you got almost tax-free security, assuming you survive OPEC roller-coasters."

Patricia sniffed with impatience. "What is this grease-rigger talk about drilling a woman, Nick? How about a partnership with an equal?"

"No room on my busy schedule for merger propositions. Have your lawyer ring mine, and maybe we can set up a conference call," said Nick with a nervous laugh.

MEN WHO MAKE WAR, NOT LOVE— ARE THEY THE PROBLEM?

This really provoked Patricia. "For thousands of years power has been monopolized by men who hate women. These sexists can't stand the idea that women are smarter, nicer, more loving, more beautiful than men. So they form these men's-club religions that put women down. Judaism. Christianity. Islam. They all treat women as slaves, property, serfs, assistants to the boss. Women can't play any active role in the ceremonies or the politics.

"Boy, y'all get out there and lasso a purty gal and brand her and stick her in the breeding barn with a copy of the Bible to comfort her. You know how it says: The Lord is my shepherd! He maketh me lie down in green pastures! The Lord strokes mah big udders. Oh praise the Lord, cause he spraids mah laigs. He knocks me up. Glory be!

"Male monotheism! You know what that means? One God. Whose God? My God! And guess what! He's a man! A totalitarian, all-powerful, bad-tempered male. All the Bibles, Korans, Talmuds agree this big numero-uno God is of the male gender.

"And, let's face it. This big-shot Allah may own the oil fields of the Middle East, but he's a bad-ass Persian! The last guy you'd want to have a date with. I, for one, wouldn't go on that Mohammed's yacht, would you?

"And, to be fair about it, how about our pal Jehovah? Who in their right mind would want Him to move into the house next door, issuing commands and ruining property values by causing floods and turning people's wives to salt?"

At this point Nick wiped his brow with a napkin. I did too. Nick looked at his watch.

There was no stopping Patricia. She was on a roll. "Notice that in all these fundamentalist sects, the mullahs and the rabbis and the priests actually keep the women out of sight, behind veils, or barefoot in the kitchen, or in the balcony of the synagogue, or in the nunnery."

At this point Nick got up and tottered off from the table.

Patricia didn't miss a beat.

"These religious men are so threatened by women that they grab swords, flags, crosses, guns, power, uniforms, anything that will make them feel adequate. They make war because they're afraid to make love."

The two other Texas ladies at the table seemed fascinated by this stuff, their eyes bulging, their pretty heads nodding in agreement. Me, I'm listening and taking notes on an Oasis linen napkin.

"These religious men are so threatened by women that they grab swords, flags, crosses, guns, power, uniforms, anything that will make them feel adequate. They make war because they're afraid to make love."

WHAT ABOUT THE SEX CHANGES OF THE 1960S?

"But weren't things different ten years ago?" I inquired of Patricia.

"You better believe it, Doc," said Patricia. "There was that one amazing fourteen-year period between 1966 and 1980 when four thousand years of male domination were briefly overthrown. The key to this 'sixties cultural revolution was women's liberation! The hippies represented a feminization, a sensitization of consciousness, a gentle, erotic mellowing. The hippies totally ridiculed the male power structures just by grinning at the cops.

"Here, 1986, in Rambo–Reagan America, it's hard to remember that back there in 1972, Vietnam soldiers were ashamed to wear their uniforms in public. The Texas Rangers freaked out because their swaggering authority was being ignored. The draft and the drug laws were publicly defied. Male politicians and moralists went crazy, warning about Western civilization collapsing before this wave of paganism and hedonism and wild, bra-less feminism. It was a feisty woman, Martha Mitchell, who first blew the whistle on the Nixon Watergate cover-up.

"Remember long hair? Long hair on Texas dudes! That started the country-rock scene at the Armadillo in Austin, Texas. What did that long hair mean? Men accepting feminine erotic power. Remember that cop in Houston who requested permission to grow his hair long so that he could relate to members of the opposite sex—namely, his wife?

"It was the women who made all this 'sixties stuff happen. The sexual freedom was really women's freedom. God knows the men didn't need liberation. The Judæo–Christian–Moslem double standard always let Texan men do what they wanted.

"I don't know what it was like up North, honey, but down here in Texas 'round 1969, women suddenly understood that they were free to fuck whom-so-ever they wanted and how-some-ever they wanted. It was the women who learned about slow, serpentine, Hindu, fuck-me-Buddha sexuality.

"Yup, it was the cowgirls who demanded some variation on the missionary position. And gently pulled the heads of their astonished boyfriends down to the promised land and taught white lads how to make girls feel good.

"And it was the women who demanded the new aphrodisiac drugs from their guys. Don't you remember the motto of the Hippie Girl from Galveston? Keep me high, Long Horn, and I'll ball you all night long."

BUT WHAT HAPPENED TO THE SEXUAL LIBERATION OF THE 1960S?

Patricia looked at me, shook her head, and sighed. "Don't you get the point? It wasn't 'sexual liberation,' it was freedom for the two groups who were repressed by the male morality. First it was the women who took off their aprons and came out of the kitchens. Then it was the gays who came out of the closets, insisting that sex be beautiful and elegant and long and slow and graceful and funny. Mr. Redneck Macho from Fort Worth had to change his heavy-breathing, bar-room, slam-bam, steer-bull ways, and learn how to boogie and ball and fool around and be sweet and tender with his big red chap-stick.

"The Texas A&M co-ed looks at the guy and says, 'Is that a stupid jive-ass Colt 45 in your pocket, John Wayne, or have you suddenly learned how to express affection to a girl?' Hey, Buck, the penis is not a Bowie knife to be plunged into the gaping wounds of your prostrate victims! The penis is a shaft of pleasure and delightful fusion.

"What's changed from the 1960s is this: Smart, self-confident women, after listening to Mick Jagger and Jimi Hendrix and Willie Nelson, weren't gonna go back to lying down meekly, spreading their legs anytime some Rice University frat-kid

> The hippies represented a feminization, a sensitization of consciousness, a gentle, erotic mellowing.

> "That's what happening, by God! Monogamous relationships! People are staying home with their mates. Or if you don't have a steady, then you stay home alone and watch <u>Dynasty</u>."

decided he wanted to get his rocks off.

"No way, Don Jose. Smart women, like that lil' ole Jerry Hall, learned to be selective and more demanding. Today, women talk about the men they know and compare them for size and fit and performance and wit and charm. And wow! Does that threaten the SMU business-administration majors! No wonder poor Nick tottered off to the, excuse the expression, men's room a few minutes ago."

The three women at the table looked at each other and smiled in some sort of secret agreement.

SCIENTIFIC POLL REVEALS DIFFERENCE BETWEEN MEN AND WOMEN

My head spinning from Patricia's unorthodox theories, I phoned the research department and requested some hard data.

A diligent scan of the scientific literature revealed that in 1984, *Newsweek* polled students at ninety-eight campuses to find out if morals were changing. The major results: "Students are against casual sex; for fidelity in marriage, and split on the question of living together."

According to *Newsweek*, "The real legacy of the sexual revolution—and perhaps the women's movement as well—may lie in how men and women think about each other. Six out of ten say there are significant differences in the ways men and women think."

Confirming Patricia's cocky views, 24 percent of women believed that females are more intelligent than males! And only 6 percent thought men were smarter.

MACHO MEN LOSING OUT TO THE GAYS?

Patricia and other sophisticated women I interviewed kept making the point that today, during this confusing time of shifting sex roles, they feel more comfortable with gays.

I asked Julia Andrews, a successful geologist from Boulder, about this, and she came up with a word that I was to hear more and more as I researched the sex-change issue.

The word is *friendship*. Many women complain that it's almost impossible to maintain a friendship with a straight guy whom you don't want to fuck. Back in the 1950s men hung out with and enjoyed the company of other men, talking about sports, hunting, careers, entertainment, business, politics. And in the old days, women busied themselves with cooking, washing, æsthetics, fashion, families, and the softer human interests. Men and women lived in different worlds.

According to Julia, "All this has changed. Many intelligent, educated, alert women these days are equally interested in careers, political issues, IRAs, adult-education courses, and prime rates. Of course, they're still into fashion and elegance and high culture; so they're looking for wide-gauge men who can share their full-spectrum interests. And a lot of men just won't get hip.

"That's where the gays come in. As a group, homosexual men make more money, are better educated, are more sophisticated than straights. They are more open to make friendships with women. They're more sensitive. And to many of us, sensitive means smarter. Like there's this professor, Bruce, in my department. He's gay. I have great times with him. We can discuss our research projects. We can gossip about office politics. He knows more than I do about French and Japanese dress designers, and he's hip on the music and movie scene. He reads cookbooks and understands how erotic eating and food can be. But the main thing is, he's sensitive to my moods, my little double meanings, my funny little jokes. There's the added advantage that, with Bruce, there's no problem about exchanging contaminated metabolic liquids."

BUT HASN'T THE GAY SEX SCENE COOLED DOWN?

My next expert witness was a wise old closet homosexual. Jack Black is a 55-year-old ordained Episcopalian minister. As it happens, he doesn't practice his clerical calling. Sensibly enough, he's a full professor at an Ivy League divinity school. Jack is smart, scholarly, cynical, a skillful politician. He's got a satirical sense of humour—dry, desiccated, wizened as a vulture's claw. At the moment, Jack has mixed feelings about the New Morality.

On the down side, the AIDS epidemic had him crushed. "I can't believe it," he moaned. "After thirty years of hiding in the closet, I finally see this wonderful gay-pride thing emerging. Political strength, economic clout, gay churches, gay ministers preaching from pulpits! A real sense of gay power, and then . . ."

"Have gay morals changed?" I asked.

"Changed! Totally! Facts are, if you cruise the boulevard these days, the chances are 100 percent that you'll get the virus. Promiscuity is down 80 percent. The bath houses are all closed. The bar traffic is down 40 percent. And the sex practices have changed. Safe sex. People take precautions. No exchange of fluids."

On the up side, the new celibacy has done wonders for the tranquillity of Jack's relationship with his gorgeous, 23-year-old, live-in lover. Now that he has become an aging man of the cloth, Jack is vigorously preaching monogamy.

"That's what happening, by God! Monogamous relationships! People are staying home with their mates. Or if you don't have a steady, then you stay home alone and watch *Dynasty.*"

And here in this biblical context I heard again that label for the new sexuality. Friendship.

"Friendship. Agape. Monastic withdrawal from temptation. Male bonding in the spirit of the twelve apostles. Christian fellowship. Brotherly love. Yes," said Father

Jack quietly, "these days in the gay community you bugger your friend or you don't fuck at all."

FAREWELL SEXUAL FREEDOM?

Turning from the holy to the secular side of the debate, I found that *Futurist* magazine, true to its belief that our future lies ahead of us, has recently offered some sobering predictions about a "New Victorianism." Editor Edward Cornish expects that the uncontrollable hysteria about herpes and AIDS now sweeping the Midwest and South will lead to a return to romantic love. "Unable to realize their sexual longings, people will do a lot of pining and fantasizing. Popular music will move back to love themes."

- "Family life will seem safer."
- "Pornography will become less acceptable in polite society . . . but covert interest will intensify, as pornographic materials offer a substitute for risky live encounters."
- "Traditional religious practices may revive."

This is probably the only time, past, present, or future, when Jerry Falwell will find himself liking *Futurist.*

THE LAW-ENFORCEMENT VIEW ON THE NEW SEXUALITY

To resolve these wildly differing opinions, I went next door to get a more conservative slant on things.

My right-wing neighbour, Clyde, is an assistant district attorney. He awaited me at the door, escorted me to the study, and brought me a regulation Miller Lite. He drank standard-issue Perrier. Clyde wears a blue suit when he sweeps and dusts for footprints around his swimming pool.

> "... the uncontrollable hysteria about herpes and AIDS now sweeping the Midwest and South will lead to a return to romantic love."

> # "And too often all you can get your hands on is your own best friend, you know, yourself."
> # We both laughed.

When making social conversation, Clyde stands at attention like G. Gordon Liddy giving a lecture on the Red Menace.

I wasted no time in popping the sex-change question. You don't pull punches with Clyde.

"Sex practices depend on the ethnic and class demographics of the neighbourhood," said Clyde with that clipped, know-it-all, law-enforcement cadence. "In the poor neighbourhoods, it's low-life, misdemeanor mischief as usual. With those people, every man fornicates illegally and immorally with everyone. Lower-class individuals still coercively obtain the sexual favours of any helpless girl they can corner. Lower-class fathers still copulate with their daughters, cousins, you name it. They're animals, pure and simple." Clyde cleared his throat. I had a strong gut-feeling that he was enjoying this conversation, in some weird way.

"Middle-class people, as we well know, tend to restrict their immoral impulses and when they indulge, at least (here he coughed) they're discreet. Thank God.

"As for the kids! Nothing new there. Spank 'em or spoil 'em, rotten through and through. As usual they're in severe need of guidance, discipline, law and order."

At this point Clyde rested his case and was excused from the witness stand.

THE POLICEMAN'S SON'S OPINION OF THE 'EIGHTIES MORALITY

To check this out, I spent an hour talking to Clyde's son, Barry. He's a freshman at a small Eastern college. He said that there were nineteen kids in his dorm floor, and only two were virgins. They were both hopeless eggheads. Sexual activity tended to be located in your clique. The dopers, the jocks, the intellectuals fooled around with members of their own groups.

"You mean, friends do it with friends?" I asked.

"Yeah, for sure. Dumb kids make it with each other. Smart ones with their chums."

Basically Barry thought that all this talk about the new morality was just tired grown-ups talking wistfully about their own problems with waning sexual desire.

"Most kids think about sex all the time," said Barry with a shy smile. "At our parties, we get X-rated movies and they play all night. To give an atmosphere, you know?"

"Are you saying that teenage boys still want to fuck anyone they can get their hands on?"

Barry laughed sheepishly. "Yeah, something like that. And too often all you can get your hands on is your own best friend, you know, yourself." We both laughed.

"Haven't kids always been hung up on sex?" asked Barry. "Look at the Fort Lauderdale deal. In most Eastern schools, kids can't wait to cut loose. The weeks before spring break you can cut the tension with a knife. Girls can't wait to pile into a car and head south. Boys too. And you know they're not going to Florida to ski."

FAST TIMES AT THE LOCAL HIGH SCHOOL

To check this out I went right to the source. I interviewed Marilyn, a senior in a Seattle-area high school. I was impressed by her poise and wisdom. To every question she responded, "That depends."

"Are kids doing it as much as previous generations?" I asked.

"That depends. People fool around with the kids they hang out with. Like the jocks, they make it with the cheerleaders. The girls run around with bobby-sox and pom-poms screaming, 'All the way, Bears!' And the guys are always talking about getting their rocks off and crude stuff like that. These bonehead jocks go for that sloppy stuff. Crushing empty beer cans on their foreheads before they jump into the sack, you know.

"The fraternity-sorority kids act sedate, but don't be fooled. It's a scam on their parents. These kids get dressed up in 'fifties gowns and dinner jackets and dance the fox-trot in the gymnasium, and their parents are so pleased they're so conservative. Like little grown-ups. Well, hey! By midnight at the freeway motels, those lace dresses are being pulled off and hung neatly on chairs. And the yuppie drugs like cocaine and quaaludes are being passed around."

According to Marilyn, sexual activity among high-school kids also seems to depend on the family racial and religious beliefs. Oriental kids seemed more straight, prudish, and hardworking. Kids from born-again Christian families appear to be more conservative. Anti-abortion and stuff. They all love Reagan.

"It sorta depends," said Marilyn. "It depends on how good-looking they are. If the Christian girl is a real knock-out, she tends to forget Jerry Falwell when the glands start pumping. I remember one night this kid whose folks were away gave a party, and I walked into a bedroom, and there was this real hot-looking born-again Baptist girl on her knees in front of this football player. And she wasn't praying.

"Come to think of it," said Marilyn, "the most sincere Christian kids tend to be pimpled and chubby and running low on animal magnetism to begin with."

In general, Marilyn thought that kids today were pretty selective, and laid back. "They do it, but keep it quiet. It's kinda invisible. Friendship is important."

"Is there a different standard for boys and for girls?" I asked.

"For sure. Guys that screw around a lot are considered hot stuff. And girls who come on to a lot of guys are considered wild."

VOICES FROM THE 19TH CENTURY

My editor-archivist Michael and his wife/writing-partner Cindy came to visit me in Beverly Hills. In their research for *Shaman Woman, Mainline Lady*, an anthology of the drug experiences of famous women writers, they discovered that not only had many famous female authors experimented with the drugs of their time, quite a few of them had also linked drugs with sexual experimentation. Of course, these works were often published under pseudonyms and not discovered until much later.

One of their most interesting pieces of detective work concerned Louisa May Alcott, who, while writing *Little Women* and other books, secretly published "blood and thunder tales" under various pseudonyms. Among other things, she explored the link between drug use and sexual experimentation. Her most famous stories in this genre had the theme of seduction under the influence of hashish and opium.

She shared this interest with another great writer of that time, Mark Twain. Most people do not realize that the creator of Tom Sawyer and Huckleberry Finn wrote essays in praise of open sexuality. After his death his very proper wife burned most of his erotic works. At least *1601* survived—the American sexual classic of the period.

If these two icons of 19th-Century American literature could be teleported to the 1980s, they would probably be less shocked and more fascinated than most of their contemporaries by the cool hedonism flourishing today.

HOW COME KIDS DON'T KNOW WHERE BABIES COME FROM?

Next, I arranged a lunch with my friend Fred. He's a black counselor in an urban high school. As far as he was concerned, there had been no drop in sexual activity.

"What new puritanism? This country is floating in a sea of sexual stimulation. How about all these R-rated films on cable beaming into homes? Thirteen year olds watching naked bodies writhing away! In the past you could only see this stuff at American Legion smokers. Now, it's right there in the living room! How about the X-

> "They just won't take precautions. These kids apparently haven't figured out where babies come from! They cheerfully get themselves pregnant, not just once, but several times. These are not just unwanted pregnancies. They're unconscious pregnancies."

rated cassettes! Over a hundred porn movies a month coming on the market! Middle-class families screening hard-core on their home TV! And the Calvin Klein ads and the raunchy MTV clips! Madonna and Prince prancing around half bare-ass. Never before in history has an adolescent generation been exposed to such wall to wall sexuality. And it's all hooked up to advertising and merchandising."

Fred was worried. Not about immorality, but about the alarming jump in pregnancies. "I can't figure it out," he said. "They just won't take precautions. These kids apparently haven't figured out where babies come from! They cheerfully get themselves pregnant, not just once, but several times. These are not just unwanted pregnancies. They're unconscious pregnancies.

"I can't understand it. They have all this information about sex. Manuals and how-to books and magazine articles, and yet they're not using the data to manage

their lives."

Fred thought that television and films may have dulled consciousness and desensitized kids from the real, flesh-and-blood world. "You know, they watch Rambo in the theatres, bare chested, sweating, gunning down armies of gooks, and they watch Reagan smiling and waving while he's sending bombers over Grenada and Libya, and they don't realize the difference. They seem to think that sex is having aerobic fun rubbing body parts together like on the TV screen. They don't seem to connect sex with the deep significance of the procreative act. It's the yuppie-'eighties attitude. Sex is healthy exercise, good for your self-esteem. Like dancing and jogging and bowling.

"As I remember, it was different in the 1960s. It may sound naïve to say this today, but during the hippie years there was a big sense of the sacredness of life. Consciousness was the key. Everything was very important. Holy! They even called psychedelic drugs *sacraments*. Can you believe that!

"And sex was an act of yogic celebration. A resurrection of the body! Sounds corny to say this, but there was an undeniable reverence for life in the 1960s. Antiwar. Peace and love, baby! People talking about raising consciousness. Kids putting flowers in the barrels of National Guard rifles. Ecological concern for the oneness of life. Which led to vegetarianism. And goofy, pompous idealism. And gee-whiz spiritualism. But it's a statistical fact that the teenage suicide rates were way down in the 1960s and so were the unconscious pregnancies.

"In the 1960s there was almost no personal violence. People were blissed out, I guess. All the violence was governmental. Take Woodstock, for example. Can you imagine it? For three days five hundred thousand kids in gangs rolled around in the mud, listening to rock music, and apparently not one act of violence. Rape was unthinkable. Fighting was uncool, man.

"By contrast, during one week of spring break in 1986, seven college kids died in Fort Lauderdale, falling off hotel balconies, drunk. And in the Palm Springs Easter riots, kids roamed the streets, drunk, pulling bikinis off women in cars.

"Imagine the low state of consciousness of these kids when they get drunk and fuck. No wonder there are so many unconscious pregnancies.

"I'm talking about the coarseness, the meanness, the thoughtlessness, the materialism, the low consciousness of the Reagan years. Kids seem to be fucking more and enjoying it less, if you ask me."

So said Fred.

IS THERE A GENERATION SEX GAP?

 The bottom line to this discussion?

Well, based on more than a hundred interviews and an extensive review of the available scientific data, I conclude that the amount of sexual activity today, as always, depends on age. The older you are, the less you think about and indulge in sex. The wild gang of rock 'n' rollers who were our models in the past have unquestionably cooled down. I'm only talking about the living here, so to speak.

But look at those kids! If anything they're doing it more and earlier. The 1984 *Newsweek* poll revealed that, by the age of 23, only 10 percent of college kids were virgins. And adults, as always, are wringing their hands about youthful promiscuity.

There does, however, seem to be one consistent sex change in our American culture.

The quality and variety has improved. Especially for Americans in their twenties and thirties. They're more sophis-

ticated, and more selective about sex. Frenzied promiscuity is certainly out of fashion, especially among gays. The highly publicized orgies, the swinging, the swappings of the past turn out to be mainly media hype. It ain't happening at all now.

Everyone is talking about it less. The current attitude: Be cool, do it wisely, do it well, and don't flaunt it.

You won't find the New Women hanging around the 7-Eleven reading Jerry Falwell's biography. You'll locate New Women in that third of the population that is better educated, upwardly mobile, and more sophisticated.

The rise in teenage pregnancy is also for real, but mainly in urban ghettos and among the underclass.

YES, VIRGINIA, THERE IS NO NEW PURITANISM

What about that new conservatism that you've been reading about? It's a media hype. Network executives and magazine editors creating fads to boost newsstand circulation, reacting to the wishful thinking of vocal moral minorities.

Reformers and moralists come and go, but sexual attitudes today still reflect the basic, earthy American virtues of tolerance, good humour, common sense, and fair play. Sure, the right-wing fanatics continue to wring their hands at the idea that people are still pursuing life, liberty, and happiness. But rest assured; American women are not going to let themselves be put in veils and chastity belts. Despite Nancy Reagan, Americans still want to have fun and enjoy life.

There is no new sexual conservatism.

Nor is hedonism destroying our republic. Your daughters are safe, Archie Bunker. They are more realistic. They are smarter. They want to fuck friends, not strangers. And that has to be beneficial for the mind, for the body, for the soul, and for the American way of life. ☺

There is no new sexual conservatism. Nor is hedonism destroying our republic. Your daughters are safe, Archie Bunker. They are more realistic. They are smarter. They want to fuck friends, not strangers. And that has to be beneficial for the mind, for the body, for the soul, and for the American way of life.

CEREBRAL CORTEX

VISUAL CORTEX

CEREBELLUM

BRAIN STEM

BASAL FOREBRAIN

PONS

MEDULLA

vic keller

V.4.

DIGITAL ACTIVATION
OF THE EROTIC BRAIN

• •

A young woman named Vicki is alone in her bedroom. She sits on the edge of the chair with her legs spread wide. She is looking intently at a computer terminal on the desk in front of her.

Vicki is a novice cyberpunk. She is using an electronic-communication device for her own private pleasure, without institutional or government authorization.

At the moment, Vicki's eyes are fixated on letters that wiggle across her screen. Vicki blushes with excitement. She is breathing heavily. She squirms into a more comfortable position, not taking her optics off the letters squirting across the screen like spermatozoa.

Suddenly the words stop.

Vicki smiles. With her right hand she begins typing letters on the keyboard in front of her.

VICKI IN THE AROUSAL MODE

Vicki's words now appear on screen:

RECEIVE
OH RON . . . I FEEL SO BAUDY WHEN WE'RE ON LINE.
YOU'RE SUCH A GOOD TRANSMITTER!
AND YOU DOWNLOAD SOOOOO GOOD!
OOOH YOU'RE SO COMPATIBLE—LET'S INTERSCREEN . . .
I LIKE YOUR BIG, STRONG HARDWARE. (WHERE?)
I WANT TO PUT LOVE-BYTES ON YOUR KEYBOARD
AND SLIDE YOUR JOYSTICK INTO MY F-SLOT.
TELL ME HOW YOU WANT ME TO ACCESS YOU.
PRESS ENTER AND I'LL BOOT UP MY MALE-MERGE FUNCTION!
OOOH! DISK OVERLOAD! MY SYSTEMS ARE CRASHING!

CYBERNETWORKS

Vicki is using her Macintosh computer to boot up and artfully program the lust circuits in her brain. Her software is linked up, via telephone, to the Amiga of a man named Ron whom she has never met. Well, never seen in the flesh.

Vicki and Ron first interscreened in a computer network. They started off quite sedately, both contributing ideas to a public-access conference on "CIA Terrorism in Nicaragua." They came to like each other's ideas; so they agreed to chat on a private line—just the two of them exchanging electronic signals to each other through their computers.

Well, one thing led to another—as it often happens in male-female conversations. At

No one is implying that the basic skin-tissue hardware is in any way outmoded. Nothing can replace the kissing, cuddling, licking, nuzzling, nibbling, smelling, murmuring, sucking, joking, smoking, honey-moaning, fondling, biting, entering, and receiving the tender exchange of love's soft bruises.

But, however enjoyable, our bodily contacts exist for us only as registered in our brains. We sense the touch and taste and perfume and the membrane softness of our lovers only in clusters of electric signals picked up by our neurons and programmed by our mindware.

first they joked and flirted. Then they started having imaginary dates. First, they'd select a movie. Afterward they'd select a restaurant, then type in their wine and dinner orders. While waiting, they'd discuss their reactions to the movie.

Then, as the imaginary, transcontinental night-on-the-town started winding down,

RON TYPED:

VICKI, I THINK YOU'RE BEAUTIFUL.
I'D LIKE TO KISS YOU GOODNIGHT.

Vicki wasted no time typing her answer:

HER ANSWER:

WHY NOT COME IN FOR A NIGHTCAP. I'LL SHOW YOU MY DISPLAY MENU.

Well, the next steps were quite predictable. Both got slowly carried away. Vicki put a compact disc in the boom-box. Ron lit the fire. Slowly, timidly, they started typing out their sexual fantasies, step-by-step descriptions of foreplay, sly suggestions about what they would like to do to each other, and what each would like have done. Like most computer kids they are smart, inventive, and very shy, but just then, they were getting bolder and saucier.

Whew! After fifteen minutes of this cyberaphrodisia, they had constructed the most romantic, elegant, sophisticated, all-out, wanton, mutual sex affair imaginable. Prefrontal nudity, floppy disco, sloppy disco, hard disco, cyberporn.

Imagination, the creation of mental images in the brain, was realized in electronic form. The computer screen became the vehicle of their inner steamy, fantastic, cyberotic party.

THE ZEN OF CYBERFUCK

Ron and Vicki were using the power of modern electronics to brain-fuck, i.e., to link up their nervous systems by means of carefully selected signals transmitted between their computers by the phone lines. These lovers have thus become members of a fast-growing, erotic network—those who have discovered the intimate possibilities of cybersex. The secret is this: Computer screens have a powerful, hypnotic ability to create altered states in the brain. Two people communicating through their fast-feedback computers can access a range of brain circuits arguably wider than can be reached by bodily contact.

This is because the brain and the computer work the same way—in the language of electric impulses, of light.

THE BODY-BRAIN RELATIONSHIP

All of us, I am sure, want to improve the wondrous pleasures that come through the soft tissues and silky membranes. Tender hands. Soft, probing fingers. Wet lips. Soft, curving thighs. Sweet, satin mounds and bulging protuberances.

No one is implying that the basic skin-tissue hardware is in any way outmoded. Nothing can replace the kissing, cuddling, licking, nuzzling, nibbling, smelling, murmuring, sucking, joking, smoking, honey-moaning, fondling, biting, entering, and receiving the tender exchange of love's soft bruises.

But, however enjoyable, our bodily contacts exist for us only as registered in our brains. We sense the touch and taste and perfume and the membrane softness of our lovers only in clusters of electric signals picked up by our neurons and programmed by our mindware.

ANDY FRITH

QUANTUM SEX

People who use computer signals to arouse each others' sexual desires have stumbled onto the next evolutionary step in human interaction: quantum sex . . . cyberlust . . . multimate . . . infocum. Lotus 2–3–4. Electronic arts. Radio shacking? Broderbund? The Commodore, after all, is the commander of a fleet of pleasure craft!

It has been known for years that people who communicate via computer–phone link-ups can reach amazing levels of intimacy. This was a surprising development. Most respected newspaper columnists, pop psychologists, liberal ministers, and conservative moralists had been warning that computers will depersonalize humanity, alienate us more from each other.

These media experts made the classic, dreary conservative mistake: trying to understand and explain the future in terms of the past. Bureau-stats and managerials, their eyes firmly fixed on rear-view screens, think of the computer as a machine. A metal product of the industrial age. Sexless. Hard. No one, except certain decadent, black-leather, transvestite, hair-dyed, mechanico-freaks in the decaying slums of factory suburbs, fans of kinky, techno-punk musicians from Lou Reed, Talking Heads, and Devo, to Pornos for Pyros, Babes in Toyland, Pearl Jam, Ministry, and White Zombie, would think of using machines with ball bearings and transmissions and smoky, metal parts to enhance sexual and romantic experience.

THE BRAIN IS THE ULTIMATE ORGAN OF PLEASURE

But the computer is not a machine. It's a silicon subcircuit of an electronic brain. It's an interpersonal communication device, a cyberphone.

Now, think about it for a moment: The brain has no eyes, ears, full lips, strong thighs. The brain is a powerful knowledge processor packed away in, and protected by, the bony case of the skull. The same is true of the computer, a powerful thought-processor packed away in, and protected by, the metal case.

Both the brain and the computer receive, sort, and output "ideas" in clusters of electric on/off signals.

The brain, lest we forget, is the ultimate pleasure organ. And the personal computer, if we know how to use it, is a powerful organ for neurosexual intercourse.

When two people link up via computers, their "naked" brains are interscreening. Directly. All the complicated apparati of bodily contact—garter belts, bedrooms, zippers, bras, contraceptives, body parts—are bypassed. Your electronic tongue can slide along the Q-links into his soft pink receivers with no clumsy props to get in the way.

> It has been known for years that people who communicate via computer–phone link-ups can reach amazing levels of intimacy.

THE EMBARRASSING COMPLEXITIES OF THE TISSUEWARE

Suppose that Ron and Vicki had met at a discussion group and started dating. First at the coffee shop. Then maybe a cocktail lounge. Then dinners and movies. The first fumbling steps at intimacy—holding hands, knees rubbing under the table.

What to wear? The familiar mating-ground questions. My place or yours?

Then the complicated dance of mutual seduction. The nagging worries of the person with no more than average sexual competence.

He thinks: Shall I make my move now?
   She wonders: Will he think I'm a slut if I grab a handful?
Is she smart? Is she pretty enough? Can I get it up? Does she like to transmit head? Receive head?
   300, 1,200 or 2,400 baud?
32-bit clean?
   Is he hip enough? Too hip? Handsome enough? Can he get it up? Can he boot me up the way I want it?
   Who is this guy anyway?
Who is this dame anyway?
   Worry. Worry.

TELESEX ENCOURAGES BRAIN PLAY

Digital foreplay is a wonderfully natural way for two people to start their mating dance.

Why use the word "natural" to describe communication via phone-linked computers? Actually, almost every animal species has developed distance courting, tele-arousal signals to pave the way for the eventual sweaty, writhing contact of genital sex and the ejaculation of sperm.

Insects telecommunicate their sexual desires with amazing gusto. Every little cricket you hear scraping his violin-string wings on a hot summer night is telling the neighbourhood ladies exactly how he'd like to do it to them. The horny boy cicada is talking directly to the brain of the neighbourhood girls.

The chemical scents (pheromones) of the female dog in heat are like telephone messages telling every lusty male within miles how the horny young bitch smells, looks, and tastes.

THE BIRDS AND BEES DO IT

Bird songs are a compelling way for arousing sexual desire. At the right time of year, usually in the spring, the male songbird's body swells with testosterone—the male sex hormone. He bursts into song. He sends a long-distance, mating-dating message that is picked up by every female in the neighbourhood. The song boots up the sex circuits in the female's brain and she suddenly starts thinking how nice it would be to have a lusty guy around to nibble her willing neck and stroke her soft, feathered body with his wings and climb on top with his wiry, strong, warm body and open her up with his straining hard modem and make her feel just the way her brain tells her a young bird should feel in the springtime.

ASTONISHING EVIDENCE ABOUT NEUROTUMESCENCE

Fernando Nottebohm and his colleagues at Rockefeller University have recently announced a discovery that "shakes the conventional wisdom of brain science ... Nerve cells in birds go through giant cycles of birth and death ... At the time of hormonal changes, the

ANDY FRITH

brain anatomies change. The specific portion of the forebrain responsible for singing, which is large in the spring, becomes half as large in the fall . . . Furthermore, talented canary singers have larger specialized regions than those deemed less talented."

In other words, the brain is a sexual organ that can swell and subside like the pink membranes of penis and vagina. And the steamy brain gets turned on by compatible signals. And the songbirds who can give "good phone" grow bigger brains! What an advertisement for quantum sex!

TELEPHONE SEX

Telecommunicated sexual messages have become a standard courting technique in industrial-urban societies where boys and girls don't get to meet and look each other over around the village square.

How do city kids get to know each other, test each other out as mating partners? The use of the telephone by courting adolescents is an inevitable step in human evolution. Q-sex is just adding a new dimension to the conversation of good, honest boy-girl lust. Appletalk is a direct way of turning on the teenage circuits of our brains.

THE CYBERNETICS OF THE ADOLESCENT BRAIN

At the onset of puberty, new circuits of our brains activate. The human body under-goes a sudden change, almost as dramatic as the metamorphosis from caterpillar to butter-fly.

All sorts of new bumps and protuberances emerge on the nubile body. Breasts begin to swell and strain to be caressed. The little worm-penis of the school boy grows into a swelling, red tube of incorrigible desire. New circuits of the brain suddenly turn on, flooding the body with impetuous hormones and hot mating juices. The teenager becomes obsessed with sex.

Psychologists tell us that the teenager thinks of sex several times an hour. Involuntary erections strain the jeans of the embarrassed lad. Hot steamy currents of desire lash the body of the perturbed young lady—she screams at rock stars and swoons over the pinups of handsome movie stars.

Let's face it, teenagers are often coarse, crude, and insensitive to the delicate needs of others. In the desperate grip of passion, they trip over themselves and hurt each others' feelings.

That's where electronic foreplay comes in.

CYBERFUCKING AND ELECTRONIC FOREPLAY

Teenagers use any means possible to turn on and channel their sexual drives. Boys study magazines like *Hustler*, letting the pictures and the text trigger off their imaginations. Girls devour magazines about rock stars and movie actors. The pictures activate the swelling "sex areas" of the brain. Remember the horny songbirds?

Moralists condemn solitary sex and try to suppress erotic-æsthetic publications that people use to trigger off their imaginations and boot up the "sex areas" in their brain. The Moral Majority gets convenience stores to ban *Penthouse, Playboy*, and *Hustler*.

EAR SEX IN THE CONFESSIONAL BOX

When I was a teenager in the dark ages of the 1930s, we were warned in the sex manuals that masturbation caused nervousness, mental breakdown, and eventual brain damage. The Catholic Church was pursuing its insane policy of stamping out genital pleasure and preventing the "sex areas" of my brain from swelling. I remember the kinky conversations in the confessional box.

I would kneel in the dark booth and whisper through the screen into the invisible ear:

"Forgive me, Father, I am guilty of impure thoughts."

"Which impure thoughts, my son?"

"I thought about making love to my cousin Margaret because of her dimpled knees, to Dr. O'Brien's wife because she is blonde and has big boobs, to Clara Bow, to all the members of the chorus line of the Radio City Rockettes, to a girl I saw on the bus . . ."

"That's enough, son," Father Cavenaugh sighed. "Have you used any sinful books or magazines?"

"Yes, Father." *Spicy Detective. Spicy Adventure. Spicy Western. Film Fun. Captain Billy's Whiz Bang Joke Book. Atlantic City Bathing Beauties. Hollywood Starlets.*

"Enough, enough!" cried the flustered priest. "Such books and magazines are occasions of sin. You must destroy them."

"Yes, Father."

"Now, say a heartfelt Act of Contrition. And as your penance, say five Our Fathers and five Hail Marys."

This whispered "tell and listen" ritual did little to prevent the "sex areas" of my brain from growing. Might as well try to stop the testosterone-drenched songbirds from singing!

Telecommunicated sexual messages have become a standard courting technique in industrial-urban societies where boys and girls don't get to meet and look each other over around the village square.

Confessions were heard by bored or sex-tortured priests because it was their only erotic contact. They obviously got off on it. In a way we sinners were giving the good Fathers aural sex by kneeling there in the dark box, whispering our sweet little dirty secrets into the warm, open, trembling ear of the priest.

Teenagers today spend hours on the phone joking and flirting because it's a safe and calm way to explore erotic interests without being swirled into grappling scenes. They stimulate each other's imaginations, exploring and experimenting with erotic signals.

CYBERVAMPS: TELEPHONE CALL GIRLS

The telephone-sex call services advertised in the back of magazines like *Hustler* are another step forward in the art and science of brain sex.

Sandi's phone-sex ad invites you to "Talk dirty to me! I'll rub my nipples hard. I want to cum with your phone fantasies."

Anal Annabelle promises, "I'll spread myself wide open and give you all of me, Big Boy."

"Beg for it!" says Mistress Kate. "I know what you deserve."

"Climax with me! I'm hot, wet, and waiting!" murmurs Lisa.

IMMORAL EXCHANGE OF ELECTRONS?

Maybe you've felt that this stuff is a bit kinky. Perhaps you felt that telephone call-girl sex is a masturbation aid for lonely people with low self-esteem.

Maybe not. The moralists and spoilsports want us to feel guilty about phone sex. Bureaucratic cyborgs are automatically offended by any frivolous, hedonic, dilettante use of technology for personal delight. Phones are leased to us by Ma Bell to help us become better citizens and to call home at holidays.

Actually, neurophone sex link, if employed with a light touch-tone, can be a wonderful way to learn how to become skilled at telefucking.

TAPPING THE EROTIC MEMORY BANKS

The archives of our brains carry electric memories of our earliest teenage passions. So why not retrieve them, turn them on, and enjoy them at will?

The trick is this: You learn how to format your brain to receive the cues, the sensory signals that activate your horniest 16-year-old memories. You can use a telephone call service or do it with a friend. Ask her or him to whisper to you the coded names and phrases of your first crushes. The songs of your heated season of rut. You'll find yourself booting up your adolescent circuits with the teenage access codes. You are performing a neurolinguistic experiment. You are executing a self-hypnotic age regression. You are "commanding" your own brain to expand the "sex areas."

Now here is some good news: Your brain is apparently eager to oblige. Your brain wants to be stimulated, opened up, caressed, jacked into by a sure mind.

Your brain hates boredom. If you keep your brain repeating the same old reality tape, month after month, your brain will sigh and give up on you, just like a neglected lover.

For many people, cybersex—using the telephone or computer to arouse the brain— is easier than running around like a horny robot, pulling clothes off and on, jumping in and out of sacks with strangers. Unless you are incredibly cool and poised, it's difficult on a first

Confessions were heard by bored or sex-tortured priests because it was their only erotic contact. They obviously got off on it. In a way we sinners were giving the good Fathers aural sex by kneeling there in the dark box, whispering our sweet little dirty secrets into the warm, open, trembling ear of the priest.

For many people, cybersex—using the telephone or computer to arouse the brain—is easier than running around like a horny robot, pulling clothes off and on, jumping in and out of sacks with strangers.

date to teach a new partner how to turn on your imagination and then start acting it out, while at the same time trying to master the private signals that turn his or her brain on.

COMPUTER SIMULATIONS

Cybersex is a relaxed way of learning how to explore this brand-new frontier of cybercourse. The computer is a wonderful appliance for simulations and "as if" experiments. The hottest selling software in the hobbyist market is simulation games. Flight simulation: practice takeoffs and landings. Submarine commander: act out the Battle of the North Atlantic. Wall Street simulations: pretend you're a hot-shot broker.

Now, if it's all right to use software to simulate war, why is it not okay to simulate the most important game of all?

Why not get on line and link up with the brain of your partner? Murmur teenage sweet nothings into her brain-ROM? Stick your floppy disk in his cerebral software and whisper exactly the things he wants to hear?

Simulation: You are back again in your parent's house flirting with your high-school crush! And while you are taking advantage of your parent's absence by disporting naked in the rumpus room of your cerebellum, give yourself some credit. You are a neurosexual pioneer! You belong to the first generation of your species to use your magnificent brain as a sexual organ. Without guilt. With healthy curiosity. And a desire to please your cybermate.

Cybersex uses the powerful instruments of knowledge processing and communication to perform the most important task of this stage of human evolution.

You are learning how to use your head, to take over the programming of your bored brain. Surfing your own brain waves.

Cybersex and brain-fucking could be a key to freedom and growth. If you don't use your head for your own pleasure, entertainment, education, and growth, who will? ◉

VI. GUERILLA ART

VI.1.

PRANKS: AN INTERVIEW*

ANDREA JUNO: V. Vale and I are doing a book on pranks, but not just run-of-the-mill college pranks. We're interested in pranks as they reveal linguistic and behavioural insights—

TIMOTHY LEARY: Performance art, in a way . . .

AJ: In a way. We interviewed Paul Krassner and Abbie Hoffman because their activities stand outlined against a whole social and historical milieu of spontaneous pranksterish comments on politics and society. Just as in a sense the whole history of LSD was a prank. You helped shape a key period of history.

TL: I like the idea of "prank" in the sense of *play*. What does a prank do? It's spontaneous, a little shocking, a little mischievous, a little jab in the ribs, or a push toward something different. In a general sense I think the entire consciousness movement was dedicated to a playful rather than a serious approach, and certainly levity rather than gravity. Following great psychological teachers as Alan Watts, for example, who described everything as a play of energy or Goddess playing hide-and-seek with herself, things like that.

To me the essence of consciousness change is *humour and gentle satire.* It actually gets quite theological. One of my ten favorite movies is Monty Python's *The Meaning of Life.* What is the meaning of life—is it all just a joke? So many theories of God have God as a very worried, compulsive, power-oriented person trying to keep everything in order. A theology just as plausible to me is the notion of chaotics of play and delight . . .

innovation. There's something exploratory about pranks—shaking things up, which, of course, is the basic technique of evolution. Chaos engineering.

AJ: Can you recall the early days of LSD research at Harvard and Millbrook?

TL: When we were at Harvard we were fortunate enough to have wonderful coaches, people like Aldous Huxley and Alan Watts. There was a wonderful Englishman named Michael Hollingshead who had a very mischievous sense of humour. His brain was so addled with mystical experiences that he saw everything as a prank. He was my assistant at one time; we were trying to test the ability of psychedelic drugs to change people's behaviour. So we went to a prison, because that's the obvious place where you

> I have always seen evolutionary steps, or psychedelic drugs, or tremendously life-changing events as being basically joyous, in the sense that you're liberating yourself and empowering yourself to change. You're recognizing the basic fun of the life adventure.

can measure change: whether they go back and commit more crimes, or whether they stay out of prison.

So we were taking LSD and similar drugs with maximum-security prisoners who were all volunteers. We explained what we were doing. We weren't doing anything *to* them; we were doing it *with* them. We would take LSD with them in the prison. The first time we did it, it seemed

CAROLYN FERRIS

RE/Search #11: Pranks!

> I think the philosophic prank, the intelligent prank, the life-affirming prank, is one that gives people a broader perspective or a new insight, so that they're not taking themselves so solemnly, and realize that life is basically supposed to be joyous and merry.

like the most scary, reckless, insane thing we could do: to be going out of our minds in a maximum-security prison with the most dangerous, evil, homicidal people in the world!

We got to a moment in one of the first sessions when we were all looking at each other. We psychologists were afraid of the prisoners because obviously they were dangerous maniacs, and they were afraid of us because we were crazy scientists. Suddenly we were looking at each other, and they said, "What's happening?" and I said, "Well, I'm afraid of you," and they all laughed, "Well, we're afraid of you," so then we just broke up in laughter.

For the next two years the entire prison experiment continued (which was very scientific; we had personality tests, controls, and the usual procedures), but basically everyone who was involved in it knew it was a big escape plot. We were trying to help them get out of prison—we would get them paroles, and in general help them get going in life. The whole thing was a big joke in the sense that it seemed so simple to rehabilitate prisoners and make it into a *prank*, rather than make it into a crime-and-punishment saga of grand-opera criminality. That was an experiment which did in fact cut down the prisoners' recidivism rate in Concord, Massachusetts, about 75 percent.

Another prank that we performed at Harvard was for the Divinity School. We worked with about thirty Divinity students. We had several professors from the Harvard Divinity School, famous ministers, and the dean of the Boston University Chapel involved. It was on a Good Friday, and we gave half of the Divinity students psilocybin mushrooms (the other half didn't take them) to see if they indeed had mystical experiences. It developed into an incredibly wonderful, warm, funny mystical experience in which in the most lighthearted way we were helping people get beyond the confines of the church and the ritual.

When we would come back to our homes after working in the prison, we were exultant: *What a prank!* Here we were, taking these wild drugs inside a prison, while the criminal-justice officials were all cheering us on! Meanwhile we were seeing the comedy of life and the foolishness of repetitious behaviour and having a good chuckle. The same thing was true after the Divinity School project. It started out so solemn and so serious with the hymn singing and the dean of the chapel giving sermons, and it ended with a tremendously life-affirming sense of joyous laughter. We got back to my house and were drinking beer afterward, feeling that we had tested ourselves, and tested human nature, and tested the extreme limits of the nervous system in a way that would seem almost unbelievable. We were taking "dangerous" drugs in a prison or giving "dangerous" drugs to Divinity Students with the top professors from Harvard, the Newton Seminary, and Boston University—and it all turned out to be a human coming-together!

AJ: How did they react afterward?

TL: They laughed their heads off with relieved joy.

AJ: And what about even later? Do you think these people made profound changes in their lives?

TL: Well, that's something else. Having a revelatory experience or a deep mystical experience is one thing. *What you do about it* depends on an enormous number of factors. Everyone's lives were *changed* by these in one way or another, but as for their behaviour—well, some would leave their wives, and some would get married. We had three ministers quit the church, for example, to go out and make an honest living!

I think the philosophic prank, the intelligent prank, the life-affirming prank, is one that gives people a broader perspective or a new insight, so that they're not taking themselves so solemnly, and realize that life is basically supposed to be joyous

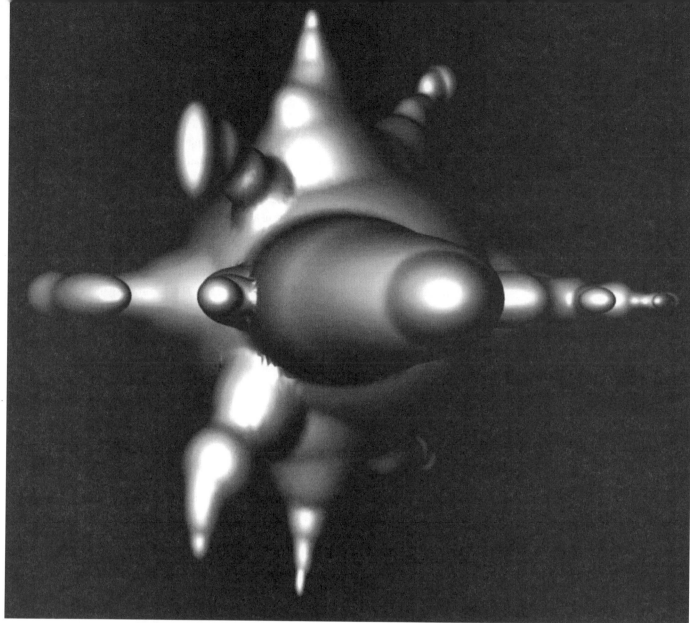

ANDY FRITH

and merry.

One of the problems with the 'sixties consciousness movement was: some people's pranks are other people's hurt feelings. So there's an *aesthetic courtesy* about pranks. Forcing your sense of humour on somebody else, or disrupting people in a way that makes them angry, is not a productive prank. A productive prank is one in which you're not doing something to somebody, but there's some invitation for it, and there's some openness to it.

AJ: Your work with LSD opening up consciousness did make some people fearful, resulting in your being fired from Harvard. A lot of people stop opening up, because it's scary to start evolving your consciousness.

TL: But I have always seen evolutionary steps, or psychedelic drugs, or tremendously life-changing events as being basically joyous, in the sense that you're liberating yourself and empowering yourself to change. You're recognizing the *basic fun of the life adventure.*

Looking back, you could say that everything we were doing over a period of ten years was basically a prank. Ken Kesey, of course, called his group the Merry Pranksters.

AJ: Tell us about Millbrook.

> There's something exploratory about pranks—shaking things up, which, of course, is the basic technique of evolution. Chaos engineering.

Well . . . this mad Englishman, Michael Hollingshead, had a typical prank. . . . he would solemnly tell everyone that there was a mysterious cave or tunnel under the castle where you could confront "the wisest person in the world." ....➤

TL: Millbrook was a very special moment in modern history, I think. We had 3,200 acres on an incredible estate where a mad Bavarian millionaire had built castles, drawbridges, gatehouses, and extraordinarily architected forests, shrines, hidden lakes, and secret groves. It was like a Tolkienian situation where we were almost totally protected, being in the middle of a 3,200–acre realm. It was very difficult for law enforcement, or anyone, to get to us.

We were on our own property minding our own business; yet the whole adventure was so mind-boggling and scary to those people who wanted to see it that way. For about five years we used this wonderful geographic base station as a place to explore human consciousness and the far antipodes of the human brain.

Basically, we'd keep changing the script. I've talked to many people who were there for a week or a month and they would say it was like *this*. But actually it would change each month. A teacher of Gurdjieff would come along and for many weeks we would study and live out and try to imprint the ceremonies and the notions of that particular approach. The next week some crazy vegetarians would come and we'd all go on nonprotein diets for awhile. There was an openness to change, and to experiment, and to innovate. Usually once a week there would be a psychedelic experience; someone would guide it. That person could design it: choosing the music, the rituals, the æsthetics, the schedule . . . taking people basically on *trips*.

There was a sense of adventure and a sense of excursion. There was always a sense of prankiness because we felt that what we were doing was the most innocent and the most idealistic—ultraromantic in a way—based on books like Hesse's *Journey to the East* and *Mount Analogue* by René Daumal: the classic stories of the epic adventures of the mind.

So on the outside what we were doing might seem very dangerous to society and threatening to the police, but it was a very innocent sort of adventuring.

AJ: Can you recall any peak moments?

TL: There were an *endless* number of peak moments—it's hard to pick out one, because there was such a rich texture of events flowing one into another.

Okay—I'll tell you a prank. There was a professor from Princeton who was a lifetime student of Persian mystical poetry. He had done a great deal of translating. He wrote us, and then came up and visited. He said, "Obviously, most of the translations into English are wrong, e.g., that famous line from the *Rubaiyat*, 'a loaf of bread, a jug of wine, and thou.' The Islamic people don't drink wine. The original Persian signified hashish." But this word was not in the vocabulary of people like Edward Fitzgerald and other Oxford dons who were translating Persian poetry into some kind of Scoutmaster Upper High Anglican prose. Having dedicated his life to the study of this mystical state, yet never having *experienced it*, this Princeton professor was very eager to have us provide an "initiation" for him.

So we set up an LSD experience for him in the enormous baronial "living room" of this castle we lived in, which boasted high arched ceilings and a fireplace that could hold twenty people. We transformed this room into the motif of a Persian paradise, bringing in mattresses that we covered with silken tapestries. On the walls we hung Sufi paintings and embroidered wall hangings, and scattered Persian artifacts about. The whole room was lit with Aladdin's lamps. The music playing was Persian music and Sufi chants, some of which he had provided.

The professor was having the time of his life—his eyes were closed, and he was chanting along, and so forth. Then three of the young women of the staff came dancing into the room wearing belly-dance costumes. They were carrying trays of fruit, fine wine, and beautiful cutlery. It was the most elegant kind of presentation—not bawdy in any sense; it was just as though they had walked right out of the canvas of that famous Haroun al Raschid painting. I know that when I looked up, I couldn't believe it either—but the amazed professor from Princeton felt he had definitely gone into Allah's realm!

Incidentally, apparently there are some sections in the Koran that describe heaven where Allah lives as being this kind of situation; so we were literally making heaven come true! At first the professor was quite stunned, but he transitioned smoothly into the program, and enjoyed it. But do you think that was a prank?

AJ: Of course!

TL: Well . . . this mad Englishman, Michael Hollingshead, had a typical prank. During the heightened suggestibility of an LSD experience, he would solemnly tell everyone that there was a mysterious cave or tunnel under the castle where you could confront "the wisest person in the world."

He would have everyone hold burning candles. With dilated eyes and spinning heads, people would follow him down into the basement, which was kind of old and dark. And then, with the torches burning, he'd lead you down into a tunnel where you'd have to start crawling under the foundation of the house, holding your candle. You'd crawl through various passageways, then suddenly come around a corner where the mischievous prankster Hollingshead had put a mirror! That was the ultimate confrontation with the wisest person in the world! Some people got freaked out by that, but . . .

Most of the time at Millbrook, after sorting through all the Buddhist and Hindu philosophies (some of which can get pretty tedious, pretty solemn, and pretty moralistic), we tended to end up with a Sufi approach, in which there was that light touch, and a sense that if you take enlightenment too seriously, then you've pulled it *down*—it's got to have a bounce or a joyous movement and a smile on it.

AJ: Please tell more!

TL: Well, I'll give you another example of a prank. Richard Alpert was my partner at Harvard. He came from a wealthy New England family; his father was the president of the New York/New Haven/Hartford railroad. Richard had his own private plane.

We would fly around the country in his Cessna, basically dosing people. One morning we left New York and flew down to Duke University in North Carolina, where Dr. Joseph B. Rhine, the world's leading authority on extrasensory perception, had kept his parapsychology laboratory going for years.

Rhine was a Harvard graduate. His main problem was: He was so intent on proving that it was scientific that it was impossible for anything telepathic to happen! He was using cards, and sorting, and using the rituals of highly experimental contrived psychology. But at least he was still gung ho. He'd been studying parapsychology for twenty years, and nothing much had happened; he needed all the help he could get.

I'd originally met Rhine a bit earlier, when he came to Harvard and gave a lecture. It was the first time he'd been back in twenty years, because he'd been kicked out for parapsychology. No one on the faculty would introduce him. I did; so there was a bond of affection between us, besides the Harvard connection.

Richard and I flew down to Durham; we taxied over to the Duke University laboratory. Rhine had assembled about eight or ten of his staff to take psilocybin or mescaline or something. We sat around the laboratory where he had all these experimental devices set up. You'd be working cards or be predicting movements on graphs—these were highly structured experiments.

People took the psychedelic drug he gave, and after about a half hour he said, "Everybody line up for their assignment." It was hard to keep people disciplined—I remember that one Indian gentleman, a famous Hindu professor from Benares, a

. . .▶ **With dilated eyes and spinning heads, people would follow him down into the basement, which was kind of old and dark. And then, . . . he'd lead you down into a tunnel where you'd have to start crawling under the foundation of the house, holding your candle. . . . then suddenly come around a corner where the mischievous prankster Hollingshead had put a mirror! That was the ultimate confrontation with the wisest person in the world!**

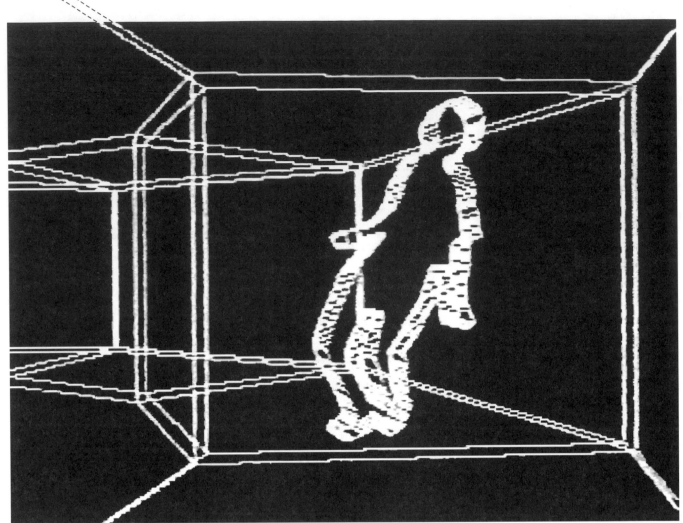

ANDY FRITH

very *serious*, nontrivial student of parapsychology, just wandered off. Someone went with him, because we didn't want people just wandering around the Duke campus.

He wandered outside and picked a rose and came back. He handed it to Professor Rhine, and said, "This represents the ultimate in parapsychology." That's an old Hindu trick. Somehow this seemed very profound and impressive.

Soon Rhine "got the message" and called us all into his office. He sat down on the floor with his shoes off. It was the first time anyone had seen him with his shoes off—he was a "dignified professor gentlemen."

He was sitting there leaning against the wall; then he said, "Well, let's figure out where we're going to take this thing. I'm beginning to understand why

we're not getting more results. We've been too . . ." Then he led a free-form discussion of changes in their plans that went on for about two or three hours. Then people brought in fruit juice and fruit and cheese and crackers. Richard and I saw that everyone had been brought back to planet Earth; so we looked at our watches and said, "See you around!" Then we grabbed a cab and drove to the airport.

We jumped into the plane and flew back to New York. We landed at La Guardia at Butler Aviation and took a cab into New York. The New York/New Haven/Hartford railroad had a suite at the Waldorf–Astoria that Richard could use; so we walked into the hotel, ordered champagne, and laughed our heads off at the implausibility of flying down to North Carolina, turning on ten or twelve very prominent and serious-minded academicians, leaving them in a wonderful kind of creative shambles, and then jumping on the plane and coming back!

That was an example of the way Richard and I looked at each other. There was a sense of real basic healthiness and openness about what we were doing. We simply *couldn't* make any mistakes, because our hearts were in the right places. And we were watching carefully, and we would not let anybody go off on their own. There was just such an aura of youthful innocence (although we were in our forties) and a confidence in the goodness of human nature that during those days bad trips were almost *impossible.*

Richard in particular always had that mischievous sense. For a while he became a holy man—Baba Ram Dass—and got a little preachy; a little too holy for me. He'd say, "God, I'm a Jewish boy from Newton, Massachusetts, and now I'm a holy man!" But Richard always had that twinkle in his eye and that saving grace of Jewish humour that could always bring you down to earth.

I've often compared Richard Alpert and me to Huckleberry Finn and Tom Sawyer. We were going down that river having these adventures with, I must say, quite pure motives. We were not out to win the Nobel prize or to make money.

Mark Twain is one of my favorite authors of the 19th Century. There is such a prankish quality to his wisdom. He was a very, very powerful philosopher. *A Connecticut Yankee in King Arthur's Court* and *Puddin' Head Wilson* with all those little twists. There is a sense of pranksterism that runs all through his writings that influenced us and guided us.

AJ: Can you describe that event when people tried to levitate the Pentagon?

TL: I was never very involved in mass meetings like that, although I think they were useful in the sense of a demographic show of strength. One reason things could be done by the young people in the 1960s was because demographically there were twice as many of them. It was the baby boom. Instead of 36 million, there were 76 million. So they could just call a mobilization, or call a celebration, or call a Be-In, and plenty of people would show up.

And 5,000 people smoking marijuana at a Be-In, or 14,000 at a mobilization against the war, or 300,000 at the Pentagon, was a show of presence that was very similar to the flocking of birds at twilight. There's a certain survival tendency on the part of the gene pool—and I'm talking generational genetics here—for groups to check each other out to see who are we, and what are we doing, and how healthy and big are we.

I respect and honour that aspect of the big mobilizations. But basically I thought it was silly to try to levitate the Pentagon. I remember we didn't go; I think we had something going on at Millbrook. I thought they were positive, but I was never involved in them. There were many groups zooming around the country in those days: the Psychedelic Rangers, the Diggers from San Francisco, and Emmett Grogan, who was a great, mischievous, and somewhat hard-minded prankster. There were a lot of pranks going on. Ken Kesey is, of course, the number-one prankster.

AJ: Are there any more anecdotes from that period before we jump ahead?

TL: I'll give you one more example. Allen Ginsberg came to Harvard when we were very square professors, and he just laid down the whole trip to us and said, "This has been going on for centuries." He knew a lot about Buddhism, Hinduism, the beats, dharma, Kerouac, and all that; so he became our "coach." Allen and I had a deal that we were going to turn on the most influential people in New York. Allen had this thick address book, and he'd peer at it with his thick lenses and say, "Come down next weekend. I'll call Robert Lowell. Or Charles Mingus."

One afternoon I flew down to New

> There was a sense of real basic healthiness and openness about what we were doing. We simply **couldn't** make any mistakes, because our hearts were in the right places. And we were watching carefully, and we would not let anybody go off on their own. There was just such an aura of youthful innocence (although we were in our forties) and a confidence in the goodness of human nature that during those days bad trips were almost **impossible.**

------·----·---·----·---·----·----

------·----·---·----·---·----·

------·----·----·----·---·----·---·

------·----·---·----·---·----·----·

------·----·---·----·---·----·----·

------·----·----·----·---·----·---·

------·----·---·----·---·----·----·

------·----·----·----·---·----·----

------·----·----·----·---·----·---·

------·----·---·----·---·----·----·

------·----·----·----·---·----·---·

------·----·----·----·---·----·---

------·----·---·----·---·----·----·

York and got to Allen's tremendous, flamboyantly impoverished, filthy apartment. There was something so emblematic about his disdain for middle-class values, which was very interesting for me. We took psilocybin or something with Jack Kerouac and others. The next morning, without any sleep and with Peter Orlovsky, we took the subway and went uptown to the Hudson River westside-view apartment of Robert Lowell, the great Pulitzer Prize-winning poet, and we turned him on—very cautiously, because he'd had a long history of psychotic episodes and manic-depressive flights. But anyway, Allen sat with him while Peter and I hung out with his wife. And we finished that and got him safely landed back onto planet Earth.

Then we jumped into a cab and went over to the house of Barney Rosset, who at that time had Grove Press and *Evergreen Review*. Here's a classic New York neurotic intellectual with five psychiatrists and worry, worry, worry, and with a wonderful, extremely elegant, and æsthetic apartment in Greenwich Village. And we took extremely powerful mescaline . . . it was a very memorable, æsthetic experience. Most of the time Barney was in his study worrying and complaining to Allen Ginsberg that he paid psychiatrists $70 an hour to keep him from having visions like that! Anyway, it all worked out.

Then it was dawn the next morning and there was snow all over New York. We left Barney Rosset's apartment. The snow had fallen on the garbage cans, everything was glistening, and the sun was coming up, and it was almost impossible to tear your eyes away from this blanket of magic that covered the squalor of New York.

Finally we got back to Allen's apartment and had another one of those philosophic laughs, just thinking of what we'd done in twenty-four hours. We had turned on Jack Kerouac, and then Robert Lowell, and then the top publisher in New York. It took courage and it took confidence in our-

selves and knowledge of the yogic process to do this. And when it was all over, we looked back at what we had done, and could hardly believe we had performed these implausible acts.

AJ: I assume that you're against spiking people—giving them LSD without their knowledge?

TL: Oh, yeah! That's very unethical: to use something as powerful as that involuntarily. That's what the CIA was doing. There's a new book out called *Acid Dreams*, by Marty Lee, which is an annotated story of the CIA experiments. There were hundreds of experiments in which they would dose unwitting people.

We had one involuntary dosing at Millbrook. Someone had been keeping LSD in a sherry bottle—I forget what the exact rationale was. No; it was a bottle, and we put sherry in it—that was it—but we had had some LSD in it before, and we thought that we'd washed it out.

Apparently what happened was: A very famous Canadian television journalist with a crew had come down to film us. He was a very large gentleman; he must have weighed two hundred pounds and was about 6′2″. My wife and I were sitting around in our living room with a bunch of people watching the fire. I'd had the sherry and my wife had had some sherry too, and after about ten minutes we looked at each other and realized, Wow! This sherry was loaded.

And just at that minute the Canadian producer came barreling up and said, "Boy, this is wonderful sherry!" And we looked at each other and said, "Well, sit down because—sorry about that, but we just found out ourselves." And that guy had a real wing-ding of an experience.

AJ: Did he relax into it at all? What was his reaction when you told him?

TL: He was pretty scared, because he assumed that he had been deliberately dosed. He was trying to call Pierre Trudeau and have the Mounties sent down to protect him! For several hours we hung in with him and saw him through it. And the next day he slept well, got up, took a shower, got out and took a walk, and was feeling fine. And this was an experience he'd never forget.

For him it was a very powerful experience, because at that time Allen Ginsberg was there, chanting and playing drums, and there were a bunch of Hindus wandering around the house as well; so the whole thing was like the worst nightmare for an uptight Canadian to be suddenly in this weird situation.

But the next day I went out for a walk with him, and he was fine. We came back up to our living room and sat down. My wife said to him, "Would you like a drink?" and he turned white and said, "No, thanks!"

That was not a prank, and I would consider that an unfortunate event. But it turned out all right. I was reacting to your question about dosing people.

AJ: What did he think about it later? Did he have a beneficial experience? Do you think he was glad afterward?

TL: Well, yes. He felt he'd gone through an ordeal, and was proud to have survived it. In general, Canadians have a lot of ballast and solidity!

AJ: You used to put on these huge multimedia shows; you pioneered these spectacles and extravaganzas that almost simulated an LSD experience.

TL: Well, we had been working for several years at Harvard and Millbrook to develop a language to express the so-called "visionary" experience. So we were experimenting with slides, anatomical designs, and cellular programs that then developed into what was called "psychedelic art," like the slide shows at rock concerts.

We were developing libraries of sounds and of mythic icons and so forth; developing a language of the ineffable. One summer, hanging around Millbrook, we decided to have a summer school. We were not allowed to use drugs (although people did on their own, I'm sure). The summer school ended with a pageant in which we used Hermann Hesse's *Steppenwolf.* The last chapter is the Magic Theatre of the Mind—Price of Admission Is Your Mind. Harry Haller, the uptight, worried European intellectual, is guided by Pablo, and he has some kind of psychedelic experience. He runs through all these incredible hallucinations and inner trips.

So we acted them out, and there were about two hundred people attending a masquerade party. You'd wander from one part of the castle to another, and be "set up" as you went; people would be acting out sections of Steppenwolf. It all ended up in the bottom of a big basement where we acted out the last scene where the hero tries to hang himself—he's gonna go through the Judæo–Christian guilt trip, and at the end the young woman says, "Take off the noose." It was all done in silhouette and pantomime with the rope and the noose, and 90 percent of the people there were probably pretty loaded.

Some producers who were present were so impressed by it that they said, "Let's put it on Broadway!" We brought it down to the East Village and then started doing psychedelic celebrations. They were multimedia events with a tremendous amount of script and sound and lighting. This was a very innovative art form that in essence led to a lot of special effects. A lot of people from Hollywood came and saw it. It was in the air at that time.

AJ: One more question about your debates with G. Gordon Liddy. It almost seems like a weird prank for you to be on the same stage with him. How did those shows come about?

TL: We had the same agent. You see, Gordon got to the White House because he was the assistant prosecutor in Duchess County, near where we were living in Millbrook, and he was raiding us all the time. He *did* drive us out of the county. Although he never got us for any drugs, he took credit for our leaving. As a result of his midnight raids on us he was brought to Washington, and this led to the midnight raids on Watergate.

I would say, as a finale to this funny conversation, that one of the greatest pranks that I enjoyed was escaping from prison. I had to take a lot of psychological tests during the classification period, and many of the tests I had designed myself; so I took the tests in such a way that I was profiled as a very conforming, conventional person who would not possibly escape, and who had a great interest in gardening and forestry.

So they put me on as a gardener in a prison where it was easier to escape. It was a very acrobatic and dangerous escape, because it was under the lights of sharpshooters and so forth. I hit the ground and ran out and got picked up by the escape car. I wanted to be able to get out at least to the highway. If they caught me after that, at least I had made it that far.

The feeling that I had made a nonviolent escape was a sense of tremendous exaltation and humour and joy. I laughed and laughed and laughed, thinking about what the guards were doing now. They were going to discover my absence, and then they'd phone Sacramento. Heads would be rolling. The bureaucracy would be in a stew. This kept me laughing for two or three weeks. I felt it had been a very successful piece of performance art. Providing an example, a model of how to deal with the criminal-justice system and the police bureaucracies. Nonviolent theatre. That was a good prank . . . which was never appreciated by the law-enforcement people. . . . ◎

VI.2.

KEITH HARING:
FUTURE PRIMEVAL

Keith Haring was life embodied. He glowed, sparkled, danced through our visibilities; splashed living colours across our pop-eyes.

Was he not our graceful blonde Greek god Pan in track shoes spraying retinal trails of rainbow rods and technicoloured cones behind him as he buzzed our minds, zooming by at ninety smiles-an-hour, revving up his rpms (realities per minute) to record speeds?

Keith Haring played a vital role at a crucial time in world history. He accomplished his mission during the 1980s, a turbulent scary decade of negative pandemonium. At this time of cultural collapse and social chaos, Keith took up the traditional role of performing philosopher—humanizing, popularizing, personalizing, illustrating the great pagan insights of our race. He celebrated life, intoxicated dance, the jumping-jack-jill-joy of wise children, erotic energy, dæmonic confrontations.

Barry Blinderman has described the nature of Keith's play as "the hallucinatory interface of biology and technology in our increasingly cybernetic society." *Future Primeval,* Barry's title for the Keith Haring Exhibition, really gets it right. Keith's art spanned the history of the human spirit. Keith could have jumped out of a time capsule in the paleolithic age and started drawing on cave walls, and those people would have understood and laughed—particularly the kids. I showed his drawings to the Australian aborigines who initiated me, and they grinned and nodded their heads. Keith communicated in the basic global icons of our race.

And here we see another awesome dimension of Haring's genius. As we move into the information age of the 21st Century, it is clear that a global language will develop. Literacy—the use of let-

ters to communicate—is the major barrier between classes, races, nations. This new language will be iconic. It will be communicated in digital patterns through fiber-optic lines flashed on screens and virtual-reality eye-phone receivers. Graphics is the key to the information world of the future. Television passivity will be replaced by personal expression. Just as everyone was expected to "read and write" in the factory society, everyone will be expected to "receive and graphicize" in the future. Everyone will use digital appliances to become a graphic artist. The graffiti impulse seen now in our inner cities is an interesting forecast. And whose art has most inspired this future?

There is one final point to be made about the Dionysian power of Keith Haring. In his last years he confronted, wrestled with, and triumphed over the ultimate-major dæmon of the human existence. Death.

In his legendary 1989 *Rolling Stone* interview, David Sheff asked Keith how having AIDS changed his life.

KEITH HARING

"When you are getting close to the end of the story, you have to start pointing all the things to one thing. That's the point that I am at now, not knowing where it stops but knowing how important it is to do it now."

Keith responded: "The hardest thing is just knowing that there's so much more still to do. I'm a complete workaholic. I'm so scared that some day I'll wake up and I won't be able to do it."

David Sheff: "Do you make time for life outside of work?"

Keith: "You force yourself to. Otherwise I would just work. I spend enough time enjoying, too. I have no complaints at all. Zero. In a way, it's almost a privilege. To know. When I was a little kid I always felt that I was going to die very young, in my twenties or something. So in a way I always lived my life as if I expected it. I did everything I wanted to. I'm still doing whatever I want."

Here are Keith's final words in the Sheff interview: "When you are getting close to the end of the story, you have to start pointing all the things to one thing. That's the point that I am at now, not knowing where it stops but knowing how important it is to do it now. The whole thing is getting much more articulate. In a way it's really liberating."

Literacy—the use of letters to communicate—is the major barrier between classes, races, nations. This new language will be iconic. It will be communicated in digital patterns through fiber-optic lines flashed on screens and virtual-reality eye-phone receivers. Graphics is the key to the information world of the future. Television passivity will be replaced by personal expression. Just as everyone was expected to "read and write" in the factory society, everyone will be expected to "receive and graphicize" in the future.

● ●

Now these are words. Strong words. Wise words. But still words.

Keith was repeating the wisdom of the Buddhist mystics who wrote *The Tibetan Book of the Dying.* There they listed the stages experienced as people face the ultimate event in their lives. Modern psychologists agree. First there is denial, then total anguish, and then, hopefully, the liberating acceptance. What is so moving is that Keith lived out, acted out, realized these powerful emotions in his last works.

In 1987, at the time he learned he was HIV–positive, he produced an astonishing drawing titled *Weeping Woman.* This work is shockingly different from Keith's usual expressions. It conveys the anguish, the terror, that he felt and that we all felt when we learned of Keith's condition.

A year later he was producing the most radiant paintings of birth and life celebrations.

And two years later Keith, in collaboration with his idol and mentor, William S. Burroughs, produced the monumental piece, *Apocalypse,* consisting of twenty silk-screens of poetry and inspired drawings celebrating the end of the Christian millennium and the beginning of the new paganism.

In the elegantly rendered introduction to *Apocalypse,* Burroughs precisely outlines the virtual-reality art of the future:

When art leaves the frame and when the written word leaves the page—not merely the physical frame and page, but the frames and pages of assigned categories—a basic description of reality itself occurs; the liberal realization of art. . . . Each dedicated artist attempts the impossible. Success will write *Apocalypse* across the sky. The artist aims for a miracle, the painter wills his pictures to move off the canvas outside of the picture, and one rent in the fabric is all it takes for pandemonium to sluice through. ☺

Material matters—from flashy atoms to clunky planets—are frozen clumps of electrons continually and rapidly melting, thawing, dissolving, fusing into what humans experience as chaos.

Speaking of "chaotics" always reminds me of Robert Williams, because his optical wizardry and his retinal philosophy-lyrics and his elegant eye-catching scholarisms are the clearest, most brilliant, down-for-real, flesh and bone expositions of quantum dynamics, quantum neurology, and chaos theory herself. The chromatic chaos disseminated by Williams is as masterful as it gets in the wood-pulp trade.

Einstein eliminated space-time. So does Robert Williams.

VI.3. ROBERT WILLIAMS: POWER TO THE PUPIL

ROBERT WILLIAMS AND THE ROARING 20TH CENTURY

It was the historic function of the information-wizards of the 20th Century (artists, poets, psychologists, philosophers, musicians, linguists) to popularize, personalize, publicize, realize, actualize, visualize, and animate the scary, shocking, paradoxical implications and applications of quantum dynamics, such as:

1. The human brain is a network of a hundred billion neurons (each more complex than a mainframe computer). The brain is formatted and programmed by visual icons that attract our sluttish eyeballs, and imprint on our lazy, curious minds, determining the realities which we inhabit and maintain with others with similar visual addictions.

2. Those who control the illumination and sound, those who control what ripples our eyeballs and earbells, are those who program the "authorized realities" of the culture. Here is Robert Williams on the power of the pupil:

"Retinal supremacy" and "dictatorial power of vision" and "sight as domineering instruments of input" and "evolution . . . is greatly dictated by appearance" and "mystery is the eyeball's food and it will eat a trillionfold its weight a day! The Peeping Toms are given the keys to the observatory."

3. Perceptions of the solid so-called "normal" external worlds of rationalities are local, consensual. They are authorized hallucinations that are jealously guarded by the custodians of our eyeballs.

4. Marshall McLuhan taught us that to change the culture, you must change the media, the modes of communication. The mindscapes of "authorized reality" images can be deconstructed, jiggled, defocused, scrambled into chaotic fragments, and creatively recombined by a special breed of humanity: wizards, chaos engineers, designers of "unauthorized realities."

Williams combines the mechanical with the bodily. The most banal, ordinary familiar objects merge, morph, blend, melt into disordered heaps of garish, technicoloured garage-sale piles of thoughts, icons, images.

Speaking of "chaotics" always reminds me of Robert Williams, because his optical wizardry and his retinal philosophy-lyrics and his elegant eye-catching scholarisms are the clearest, most brilliant, down-for-real, flesh and bone expositions of quantum dynamics, quantum neurology, and chaos theory herself.

THE COMICS

In the decades before television, comics—for obvious neurological reasons—were a most influential media for expressing "unauthorized" thoughts. Comics are visual, colourful, nonverbal, unreal, fantastic, nonserious, irreverent. They appeal to juveniles and adults seeking escape from serious, respectable, authorized realities.

I BLAME IT ALL ON FELIX THE CAT

Looking back, at the age of 72, I am embarrassed to discover that my basic bio-script, down to the smallest details, was based on a cartoon hero who was born, like me, in 1920.

Felix the Cat was this cheerful, bouncy, black-on-white figure whose mouth emitted musical notes. He whistled through life.

In his hand he often carried a cigarette and a champagne glass. This was during Prohibition—so Happy the Cat was publicly indulging in an illegal drug.

Felix was continually getting into scrapes, running up against "authorized realities" headlined in the other grey-print pages of the newspaper. At these moments, an electric bulb would light up over the cat's head, and he would "think" himself out of the scrape.

COMICS AND OIL PAINTING

Although his work emerged in the counterculture underground press in the 1960s and 1970s, Williams considers himself a painter rather than a cartoonist. I do 2.

Please do not be confused by the appearance of comic-book, kid-stuff prank-ishness. Williams typically wraps his paintings with precise, sophisticated, scientific explanations.

He has not been accepted by the serious East-coast art establishment for obvious reasons. Oil paintings from Titian to Warhol have traditionally been used to program the eyeballs and brains of the "general public" to create "authorized realities." Oil, canvas, and written word are the sacred tools, monopolized for centuries by popes, kings, authorities, to program authorized realities. Now here comes Robert Williams, scrawling graffiti on the Vatican Ceilings and the Oval Offices of our minds.

Williams's paintings disturb the "general public"—but they delight and inspire the "specific public," those millions who enjoy right-brain fuzzy chaotics and hunger for "unauthorized realities."

His prefaces to *Low Brow Art* and *Visual Addiction* are brilliant literary events. Like his paintings, Williams's writings are multileveled. He blends biting satire, comic wit, blazing libertarian bravado with a profound understanding of the psychology of visual-optical perception.

CHAOS ENGINEER AND UNAUTHORIZED REALITY DESIGNER

Like Geiger, the spooky Swiss wizard, Williams combines the mechanical with the bodily. The most banal, ordinary familiar objects merge, morph, blend, melt into disordered heaps of garish, technicoloured garage-sale piles of thoughts, icons, images.

Williams has mastered the jumpy, mind-jamming art of mixing left-brain-focused realisms with the jumbled, unfocused phantasms of the right brain. He overwhelms us, dizzies us by jumping our focus from figure to ground.

A Robert Williams canvas explodes with dozens of eye-grabbing images, objects, events rendered in irresistible screams of colour.

Any comments about Robert should pay tribute to his wife, Suzanne, who is beautiful, elegant, witty, and a brilliant designer of chromatic geometric paintings.

I consider him to be one the best informed, effective communicators around. ◎

ROBERT WILLIAMS

A Robert Williams canvas explodes
with dozens of eye-grabbing images,
objects, events rendered in
irresistible screams of colour.

VI.4.

ON WILLIAM S. BURROUGHS'S INTERZONE

Burroughs paints with words. He slashes at the page with expressionist, surrealistic word-strokes and verbal shotgun blasts.

William S. Burroughs is one of three 20th-Century literary giants who fissioned, dissolved, transformed, and digitized the English language; who beamed it and strobed it in holographic images into the 21st Century.

The American William S. Burroughs, his compatriot Thomas Pynchon, and the Irishman James Joyce are the alchemists who applied quantum dynamics and chaos theory to linguistics. These three wizards are not writers as much as they are "word procesors."

Just as the equations of the three great German philosophers Einstein, Heisenberg, and Planck reduced Newton's laws to local ordinances and dissolved solid, molecular-atomic matter into clusters-waves of electronic information, so did Joyce and Pynchon and Burroughs fission, with laser precision, the grammatical structures and semantic machinery of the old, classic language of Shakespeare.

It is no accident that physicist Murray Gell-Mann, who discovered the basic elemental unit of information, named it "quark," a term borrowed from Joyce's epic *Finnegans Wake*.

And it was Burroughs, with his partner Brion Gysin, who invented the "cut-up" method of wordmanship, slicing paragraphs from different writings—news clips, novels, instructional manuals, pornographic scenes—and splicing them together in random order.

In the words of Burroughs's friend and editor James Grauerholz, "This repetition lends a kaleidoscopic quality to the writing—and what is a kaleidoscope but a device to reassemble endlessly the same particles? As if anticipating modern quantum physics, his world model is that of an indeterminate universe of endless permutation and recombination."

Burroughs was born in 1914 in St. Louis. His grandfather, for whom he was named, made important contributions to the development of a computer-like machine that was marketed in America as "The Burroughs Calculator." After a modestly affluent childhood, Burroughs attended Harvard University, where his intelligence, homosexuality, literary sophistication, and wide-band drug addiction launched a lifelong odyssey into altered states and neurological realms which have

been charted by mystics throughout history.

Since 1938 Burroughs has operated as a visionary archæologist; as an alienated, deep-cover espionage agent reporting about the human condition as observed from the seamy, gritty, sordid underworld of port towns, exile colonies, border crossings, and cultural black-market interzones. Tangier. Times Square. Mexico City. Panama City. The Left Bank. The Amazon jungle. Etc.

Burroughs describes the visionary landscapes, the detailed sociologies of imaginary tribes, hallucinatory cities, science-phantasy showers of steaming hot silver sperm sprayed by Venusian transvestites with platinum skin. While "the Jordanian soldier, convicted of selling a map of the barracks privy to Jewish agents, hanged in the marketplace of Amman, crawls up onto the gallows poop-deck to hoist the Black Wind Sock of the Insect Trust."

And so forth.

Bill Burroughs is a master journalist because he describes what is really happening in personal terms about specific people. Danny the junkie car wiper. The pimps and hustlers in the Socco Chico. Heroin cures at Benchimal Hospital. The Interzone Café, reeking of rotting, aborted, larval archetypes. Etc.

The book titles tell the story— *Junkie, Queer, Naked Lunch, Soft Machine, The Ticket That Exploded, Nova Express, The Wild Boys, Blade Runner.* And the magnificent final trilogy about apocalypse-death-immortality: *Cities of the Red Night, The Place of Dead Roads, The Western Lands.*

Interzone is a collection of dusty fragments and lost manuscripts that were rediscovered in the archives of Allen Ginsberg in 1984. It has been beautifully edited and introduced by James Grauerholz. The story? A savage satire. A dour, sour, grim, cynical exposure of official hypocrisy, puritanical repression, religious authoritarianism. *Interzone* provides a cool, dry, jaded, semi-tender glance at the social rejects, the dispossessed, the outcasts of the underworlds. A weary cheer for humanity in all its messy forms.

Burroughs has invented a postliterate language, a new medium in which words become clouds or clumps or clusters of meaning sprayed relentlessly at the reader like the explosive technicolour jungle of neon signs in Tokyo's Roppongi district. Burroughs paints with words. He slashes at the page with expressionist, surrealistic word-strokes and verbal shotgun blasts. Like pictures in a gallery, Burroughs's paragraphs need not be scanned in linear order. His work has been called "hologramic" or "fractal," in that any paragraph might contain compressed sequences that unfold and recycle in later versions.

Above all, Burroughs's work is humourous. He sees through the tinsel jumble of raw sweat details to the eternal comic strips of life. If any.

Bill Burroughs is a very funny man, and one of America's greatest artists. ☺

Just as the equations of the three great German philosophers Einstein, Heisenberg, and Planck reduced Newton's laws to local ordinances and dissolved solid, molecular-atomic matter into clusters-waves of electronic information, so did Joyce and Pynchon and Burroughs fission, with laser precision, the grammatical structures and semantic machinery of the old, classic language of Shakespeare.

Since 1984 William Gibson has splashed across our screens with four flashy, sexy, 21st-Century cybertexts.

Gibson's first novel, *Neuromancer,* swept the science-fiction awards and defined the cyberspace game. He imagined digital cycology and gave names, roles, rules, rituals, and geographical labels to those big, new, scary, abstract algorithms that are changing our virtual realities. The name was "cyberpunk." The role was quark. The new digital terrain the "matrix," *aka* cyberspace, *aka* Cyberia.

Gibson writes like a cyber-reggae musician, translating implausible, impersonal, unpopular, indecipherable equations into hip human terms. He turns quantum physics into Electric Ladyland!

VI.5.
WILLIAM GIBSON:
QUARK OF THE DECADE

PERFORMING PHILOSOPHY

The literature and art of any culture performs (popularizes) the science and philosophy of that epoch. For one example: The science of feudalism is theology. Therefore the art, literature, architecture, and music of the Cat Stevens cross-and-crescent crowd celebrates the religious myths and the luxurious lifestyle of the nobility, and the stern sword-and-dagger symbols wielded by the self-appointed special agents of God.

PERFORMING INDUSTRIAL SCIENTOLOGY

A second example: The science of the industrial age involves Newtonian law and order and the equally dogmatic, macho injunctions of genetic competition (unnatural selection) hallucinated by Darwin. The art/literature/music of this factory culture is institutionalized, socialized, formalized. Like contemporary science, it is obsessed with size, quantity, and replicability.

Please meet the cast of characters: orchestra directors, art gallery owners, officials and members of the Writers Guild who typi-

cally stake out, colonize, and exploit a class or region or genre. The mystery story. The romance. The biography. The historical novel. The Southern novel. Poetry. The Jewish novel. Science fiction.

Literary factory assembly lines. The highly profitable Book-of-the-Month currently owned by Time–Life, Inc. best-seller lists. Crown and Waldenbook chains. The Pulitzer Prize! The Nobel Prize! Newton, Darwin, and the engineer scientologists of the 19th Century sought to impose law and order upon a chaotic universe. So did the authoring world.

PERFORMING PSYCHOLOGY

And here comes the postindustrial-electronic age. Quantum linguistics. Einstein, Heisenberg, Planck, Bohr, Fredkin faxed us the scary news. Who among us could handle it? It seems that the universe, from galaxy to atom, is made up of bits of very highly miniaturized units of data. These singular bit-izens of the galaxy are called quarks. This fifteen-billion-year-old information array is literally an electronic telecommunication show. The universe is a bunch of digital programs running, running, running. There are no "laws." And no "orders." Evolution is programmed by algorithms that use the adjacent geometry of cellular automata recursion. The universe is evolving every second with or without you or me.

Here come the quarks!

There goes the von Neumann neighbourhood!

It gets worse! Realities are determined by whoever determines them. The elements of the universe are digital, electronic, linguistic. Matter and energy are transitory hardware constructions. (Plato and Buddha, it turns out, were early cyberpunks.)

The human brain is hereby and henceforth owned and operated by an individual. It is equipped with a hundred billion micro-info-centers called neurons, and is a miniaturized digital representation of the galaxy, which is equipped with a hundred billion mini-info-centers called stars. The universe is equipped with (naturally) a hundred billion mega-info-centers called galaxies.

Let us not be confused by outmoded tech-mech, latch-jockey, engineer-hardware Newtonian bullshit. In the feudal and industrial ages, size was everything. Bigger was better. Darwin was all about big numbers. Viral genetics. Spread that sperm, Mr. Macho

Male! Infect every dumb egg you can bang your penetration stinger into. Replicate yourself. More is better.

Good news, Ladies! In the info-world, smaller is beautiful. *Smaller is more.* Because it means singularity. Selectivity. Miniaturization-compaction means "power to the individual." That noisy, polluting, factory-made mass-matter-energy-momentum that the male-order crowd enjoys? It works off static hardware constructed by robotic Newtonian laws governing gravity (!), matter lumbering along at a snail pace of c, the speed of light. Matter is frozen boulders of information. Matter is thinking by committee. Start dissolving matter, and you free individual intelligence. "Individual intelligence" is a redundancy, just like "Harvard Square." Artificial intelligence is an oxymoron. The alchemists knew this. *Solve et coagulare.* Warm it up. Loosen it up, and you free the units of intelligence (quarks). Quarks are programmed to link up with other individual data-pax. This is called "jacking in."

Digital-information cloud constellations are what count in the info-economics of nature. A quark is almost pure information. It has only one hardware function: "off-on." A quark probably has as much cyberpower as an atom. Don't be so impressed by the gigantic atom, spinning around with heavy nucleus and myriads of planetary electrons and space debris. The average atom is the vehicle navigated and programmed by quarks. This is not to depreciate the atom, an info-center that has as much cyberpower as a neuron, which, in turn, has as much cyberpower as a galaxy.

$E = mc^2$ is an engineering blueprint. The basic equation is $I = mc^2$, where "I" am information. Grammatically speaking, the quark should be thought of as first person singular. A single neuron has more information power than a sun! The exploding star is just noisy hardware! Your brain has more information crammed into it than all the stars in the galaxy. A brick-size cram of digital information is more powerful than Mount Everest.

Here's a pop version of this principle: an invisible packet of DNA has enough algorithms to grow you an Amazon rain forest!

This quantum reality is unbearably light stuff for a culture of God-fearing, up-tight farmers and factory engineers. This simple minimalist *mathematique* of apparent disorder seems to offer no mercy to the unprepared. None!

Well, fuck it! What self-respecting singularity, quark, or neuron wants mercy, anyway? And, for that matter, who are these self-appointed feudal judges and industrial managers who want to convict a brain-carrying human, at birth, of indescribable sins/crimes and claim for themselves the power to give mercy? Give mercy to a quark? To a brain? To a galaxy? To a strand of DNA?

We are stuck with these jolly Sartrean, Foucault, Fredkin algorithms that have been churning out radio and television signals for fifteen billion years and the meter still running. The realities include Koran, Bible, Talmud, in addition to peacock feathers, passionflowers, aphrodisiac resins of certain æsthetic vegetables, Jimi Hendrix tapes, interpersonal computers, and the enigmatic smile on your lover's face at the moment of orgasm.

Q. Who can explain these mysterious digital programs? Who can read us young, wanna-be quarks nice bedtime stories to make us feel secure about loosening up? Who can make us feel comfortable with the chaotic science of our wild times? Who can make us laugh at the structures crumbling before our eyes in Einstein smiles because relativity and the fractal natures of the running programs are always funny? (Why? Because they surprise us.) Who will get us giggling like shocked schoolkids at the facts of life? Who will tickle us with accurate disorder?

A. The artists-poets-musicians-storytellers. The popularizers of quantum linguistics.

James Joyce (who coined the word "quark") taught us elementary word processing and demonstrated how to atomize the molecules of grammar. Think of Joyce as a primitive, predigital visionary like Alan Turing. William S. Burroughs was the next alchemical writer to slash the word line, dissolve the chains of static grammatical form, cut up pages of prose, free the squirming atomic words, and let them reassemble in random disorder.

....

Gibson writes like a cyber-reggae musician, translating implausible, impersonal, unpopular, indecipherable equations into hip human terms.

....

Burroughs and his pal Brion Gysin knew how the algorithms unfolded. IF you free the individual info-units, THEN they will combine in the natural way (i.e., as programmed). Burroughs was the first author to use scientific concepts in his art—no accident, perhaps, since his grandfather and namesake invented the first successfully marketed mechanical computer.

Thomas Pynchon was the greatest and last of the "quantum linguists." (We do not use the nervous term "science fiction" to describe the quantum-science writers.) Classical science fiction was tech-mech fantasy, a serious attempt to impose engineering law and order on the future. Asimov, Heinlein, Lucas, and their ilk were loyal company men using art in a last attempt to impose mechanical order on the postmechanical future. The ultimate writer of the

Gibson has produced nothing less than the underlying myth, the core legend, of the next stage of human evolution. He is performing the philosophic function that Dante did for feudalism and that Melville, Tolstoy, Mann, and Lawrence did for the industrial age.

industrial age was L. Ron Hubbard. His factory-writ tin-can books, engineered by "Hubbard, Inc.," still sell millions of copies.

Timing is everything in the info-world. After fifteen billion years of evolution, Gibson hit that small window, born between 1946–64 in North America, right on target! As a member of the first cybernetic (television) generation, he was not the only available brain-carrying info-unit programmed to "flip on." The program had readied a million or so baby-boom quarks with the same if/then algorithms.

Let me suggest some of the techniques used by William Gibson to illustrate/personalize quantum psychology (cycology).

First we note that all of Gibson's writings, like those of Pynchon and Burroughs, humanize high technology. His cybertech characters are street-smart inhabitants of countercultures. Digital appliances and space-tech gadgets jam the landscapes through which his characters move.

His anti-heroes—Case, Bobby Newmark [sic], Bobby Quines, Johnny Mnemonic, Fox's partner in *New Rose Hotel,* are "cyberpunks." They are human versions of the basic element of the quantum universe. They are quarks. Prime numbers—divided by themselves and 1.

Quarks are loners. Free agents. Quarks have minimal hardware power in the material world. They have little interest in, and no loyalty to, institutions. They are alien-ates. Outsiders. Dropouts. Their function is to activate themselves by "turning on" to psyberspace within and to be ready to "tune in" (jack in) to cyberspace on the other side of the screen.

Quarks are free-radical individuals who flip "in" to receive the algorithmic instruction from their neurons and then flip "out" to cybertown. When they are operating "in" psyberspace or operating "out" in cyberspace, they are pilots navigating the oceans of digital information.

Cyberpunks are bored with "hard reality." They are happiest when operating in the inner or outer matrix.

Dixie Flatline is the code-cowboy whose wetware-brain was scrubbed and whose ROM version coached Case through his epic adventures. As his reward, he wished only to be left alone in the matrix with no involvement in the hard world.

Gibson's definition of women in the cybernetic age also deserves admiring scrutiny. Unlike his males, his female characters are strong, independent, effective, heroic, and powerfully attractive. They are shaman ladies, sophisticated wizards, playful, humorous, hip diviners. Gibson's women have more material power, worldly know-how, political juice, although they rarely "jack in" with "trodes." They seem more at home in the matrix. It's as though the women are out there in Cyberia already, watching—with patronizing fondness—the klutzy guys scrambling around in both the material and the digital worlds.

Nor can we ignore the global, international interracial nature of his casting. We note his slick mixture of voodoo power, oriental wit, and American innocence. He wisely bases his 21st-Century cyberculture on pre-Christian, preindustrial pagan, feminine, trance cultures. His use of voodoo foundations is inspired.

Gibson has produced nothing less than the underlying myth, the core legend, of the next stage of human evolution. He is performing the philosophic function that Dante did for feudalism and that Melville, Tolstoy, Mann, and Lawrence did for the industrial age.

Gibson gives us the cast of characters and the landscapes of the immediate future. Other, more influential performing Homeric philosophers may come along to script, direct, and screen our futures, but they will consciously and gratefully build on the foundations given us by Bill Gibson. ◉

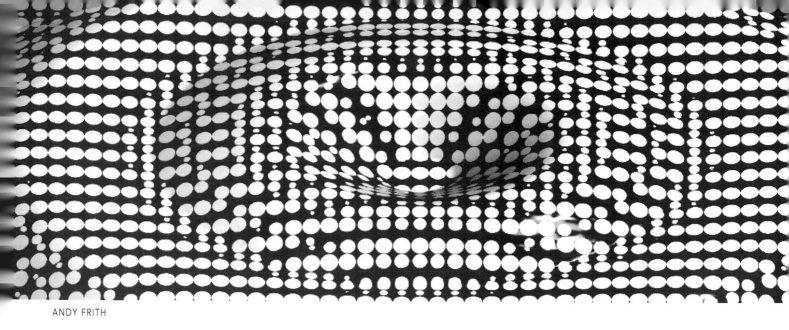

ANDY FRITH

VI.6.

HOW TO PUBLISH HERESY IN MAINLINE PUBLICATIONS

The French *semiotix*, Michel Foucault, has demonstrated that those who control the thought-engines (i.e., the mass media) control the minds of the people. The Tien An Men students in China learned how to use television to create history from American dissidents of the 1960s. The geriatric Deng clique learned to deal with student revolts by watching Nixon's Kent State massacre on television.

Like many outsiders, I have become fascinated by the manufacture of "news" by those who control our press and television. Therefore, for the last few years I have experimented with methods by which the lone individual can insert irreverent, dissident, and libertarian perspectives into the information assembly lines.

For example, the editorial pages of newspapers publish opinion pieces by well-known columnists. These syndicated pundits are selected to give the illusion of a variety of viewpoints, but in reality such columns cover only a narrow spectrum between the extreme right wing of the CIA–Pentagon fan club (Safire, Will Buckley, etc.) and the bland, tame platitudes of the loyal "liberal" opposition. If somebody like me—or Alexander Cockburn or Noam Chomsky or even Gore Vidal—were to submit a truly dissident essay to the mainstream press, no matter how convincing the facts and witheringly brilliant the logic, there is little chance that it would be published.

"Letters to the Editor" is the only section of the paper where far-out opinions are expressed. The publicity wings of the various political and religious groups know this, and tend to flood the editorial offices with their boiler-plate propaganda.

> **I have a high rate of success when I write under pen names, particularly if the social-ethnic flavor of the name fits the content.**

The most effective info-raid technique is to avoid stating dissident opinions openly. Simply adopt the current establishment line. Select the most outrageous, flamboyant aspect of the hard-line position. Exaggerate it a bit (in the manner of Voltaire), and "defend" it in the passionate jargon of the true believer. Satire teaches those deaf to logic and evidence.

Extreme fascist opinions, which "respectable" columnists dare not mention, can be published this way; and sometimes even libertarian or truly heretical views can also creep into print this way.

In the last ten years I have written hundreds of letters to the *Los Angeles Times*, the *Los Angeles Herald Examiner*, and *Los Angeles Weekly*. Letters signed with my own name usually vanish down the memory hole and do not appear in print. However, I have a high rate of success when I write under pen names, particularly if the social-ethnic flavor of the name fits the content. For example, I invented the name of Mary Agnes O'Brien, to question the position of Mother Teresa and the pope on birth control. I invented I. J. Katz, a

retired rabbi, to criticize Zionist extremism. Zachary Chase was a junior-high-school student who was disturbed by the blood-bath mentality revealed in the many quotes from President Reagan.

The most effective info-raid technique is to avoid stating dissident opinions openly. Simply adopt the current establishment line. Select the most outrageous, flamboyant aspect of the hard-line position. Exaggerate it a bit (in the manner of Voltaire), and "defend" it in the passionate jargon of the true believer. Satire teaches those deaf to logic and evidence.

Here, for example, is a letter that addresses the recent Bush-generated hysteria about the American flag-burning episode.

Dear Editor,

Even flaming liberals agree that scrawling anti–American or anti-religious graffiti on the Washington Monument should not be constitutionally protected. Nonetheless, some card-carrying ACLU lawyers apparently convinced the Supreme Court that a flag bought and paid for by some individual mental patient is not a national monument.

Surely, now other self-appointed civil-liberties lawyers will defend the more insidious case of "closet creeps" who will undoubtedly continue to burn flags in the privacy of their own homes, thus evading detection and prosecution even if Bush's proposed amendment is passed. Can not our schools and police educate children to turn in such parents?

In this current climate of global disrespect for authority and for sacred symbols, should not the right to possess, transport, and sell sacred symbols like the flag, the Blessed Sacrament, guns, and Bibles be restricted to patriotic and God-fearing citizens whose loyalties are beyond suspicion and who can be counted on not to desecrate in public or in private?

For example, suppose you saw a Jesse Jackson follower like Willie Horton swaggering down the street with an American flag in his hand, or a Dukakis follower with a Bible in his hand. Wouldn't this make you wonder uneasily what people like that might do with these sacred relics when nobody is watching?

Mary Agnes O'Brien

Readers are encouraged to experiment with this American method of samizdat, info-guerilla tactics. ⊚

Reproduce: to generate offspring by sexual or asexual union; to produce again or renew; to recreate.

Authentic: Entitled to acceptance because of agreement with known fact or experience, reliable, trustworthy. For example, an *authentic* portrayal of the past, present, or future.

VI.7. REPRODUCED AUTHENTIC: THE WIZARDRY OF DAVID BYRNE

Reproduced Authentic is a magnificently bound art book containing five paintings by David Byrne and four other artists that were converted to 8¹/₂ x 11" images transmitted from New York to Tokyo via telephone line by facsimile. They were exhibited at Galerie Via Eight, a show curated by Joseph Kusuth.

I consider this apparent oxymoron, "Reproduced Authentic," to be the most fascinating issue confronting us as we move from the solid, possessive materialism of the feudal-industrial societies to the relativity-recreativity of the electronic stage.

Now that Newton's laws have become local ordinances, clunky, static art treasures of wood, marble, canvas, and steel become crumbling curiosities, their value insanely inflated by well-marketed "rarity." These archæological antiques are huckstered at Sotheby auctions, guarded by armed guards in vault-like galleries, or in the mansions of wealthy collectors.

Thus the wretched caste-class possessiveness of feudal and industrial cultures that prized "rarity." Thus the $80 million market for canvases that the unauthentic painter Van Gogh could not "transmit" for a 5-franc meal at the local bistro.

To the feudal aristocrat as well as the Manhattan art critic, "authentic" means a "rare original": a commodity traded by gallery merchants and monopolized by owners. The politics of solid-state æsthetics is authoritarian and one way. There are the owner-producers. And there are the gawkers.

TRANSMISSIBILITY REPLACES RARITY

According to the German philosopher, Walter Benjamin, "The authenticity of a thing is the essence of all that is transmissible from its beginning ranging from its substantive duration . . . to the history which it has experienced. Rarity . . . now is a . . . mask of art's potential for meaning . . . and no longer constitutes the criterion of authenticity . . . Art's meaning then becomes socially (and politically) formed by the living."

These liberating, egalitarian notions of "reproduced authentic" and transmissibility are the application of quantum-field dynamics and Einsteinian relativity and interpersonal psychology to humanist electronic communication.

The implications are profound and timely. The politics are interactive. The

David Byrne is a member of a small group of illuminati who perform the important role of navigating our future. Multimedia wizards who experiment with new forms of reproducing and transmitting. People who *perform philosophy*, if you will.

What is "authentic" is not the possessed object but the ever-changing network, the entangled field of electronic interactions through which the essence-icon is continually re-created and re-animated.

passive consumers become active agents who receive electronic patterns on their screens, disks, fax machines, and then transform . . . transmit . . . re-create . . . re-animate.

What is "authentic" is not the possessed object but the ever-changing network, the entangled field of electronic interactions through which the essence-icon is continually re-created and re-animated.

The 12-year-old kid in the inner city slides the disk containing the Mona Lisa into her Macintosh, colours the eyes green, modems it to her pal in Paris, who adds purple lipstick and runs it through a laser copier; it is then faxed to Joseph Kusuth for the next Galerie Via Eight show in Tokyo.

It is this transmissibility, this global interactivity that David Byrne authenticates so gracefully.

David Byrne is a member of a small group of illuminati who perform the important role of navigating our future. Multimedia wizards who experiment with new forms of reproducing and transmit-

ting. People who *perform philosophy*, if you will.

For starters, David helped found The Talking Heads, arguably one of the ten most important rock bands of all time. He directed two innovative films—*True Stories* and *Ile Aiyé*, a haunting documentary about Brazilian religious festivals. He won an Oscar for scoring *The Last Emperor*.

His publishing house, Luaka Bop, transmits global sound. His album *Uh Oh* fuses the best of Byrne: biting hard rock, pulsing Latin drive, 21st-Century flair, Talking Head sass.

David Byrne transmits the message of the new breed, the Mondo 2000 spirit. Human. Funny. Global. Passionate. Laid back. Friendly. Ironic. Wise.

And, oh, yeah . . .
Reproduced.
Re-creational.
Authentic. ©

CAROLYN FERRIS

VI.8. CONVERSATION WITH
DAVID BYRNE

> With television and movies and records being disseminated all over the globe, you have instant access to almost anything, anywhere. But it's out of context—free-floating. People in other parts of the world—India, South America, Russia—have access to whatever we're doing. They can play around with it, misinterpret it, or reinterpret it, and we're free to do the same. It's a part of the age we live in. There's that kind of communication—even though it's not always direct.

TIMOTHY LEARY: I mention you in every lecture I give, because you represent the 21st-Century concept of international-global coming together through electronics. How did you get into that?

DAVID BYRNE: With television and movies and records being disseminated all over the globe, you have instant access to almost anything, anywhere. But it's out of context—free-floating. People in other parts of the world—India, South America, Russia—have access to whatever we're doing. They can play around with it, misinterpret it, or reinterpret it, and we're free to do the same. It's a part of the age we live in. There's that kind of communication—even though it's not always direct.

TL: The young Japanese particularly. Read those Tokyo youth magazines! They pick up on everything. *Rolling Stone* is like a little village publication compared to Japanese mags.

DB: They're very catholic in that sense.

TL: What's your image in the global new-breed culture? How are you seen in Brazil, for instance?

DB: I'm seen as a musician whom some people have heard of—not a lot—who has an appreciation of what Brazilians are doing. Sometimes it's confusing for them, because some of the things I like are not always what their critics like.

For instance, some of the records on Luaka Bop—like music from the Northeast, and even some of the Samba stuff—is considered by the middle and upper class and intelligentsia to be lower-class music. Like listening to country and western or rap here. They're surprised that this "sophisticated" guy from New York likes lower-class music instead of their fine-art music.

But sometimes it makes them look again at their own culture and appreciate what they'd ignored. Much in the same way that the Beatles, Rolling Stones, and Eric Clapton made young Americans look at Muddy Waters and Howling Wolf. I'm not doing it intentionally, but it has that effect.

TL: What music do you listen to? Who are your favorite musicians now?

DB: The last Public Enemy record was just amazing—a dense collage with a lot of real philosophy. I listened to the last Neil Young record. I have some records from Japanese groups, and Brazilian and Cuban stuff—all the stuff we've been putting out on the label.

TL: Tell us about Luaka Bop.

DB: I put together a compilation of songs by important Brazilian artists a couple of years ago, and afterward I thought it could be an ongoing thing. I figured that I might as well have an umbrella mechanism so that people might see the label and check it out. It was a practical thing in that way. We're now slowly getting into a greater range of things. In the future we're going to release soundtracks for Indian movies, an Okinawan pop group, and a duo from England. That will be one of our few releases in English.

TL: Marshall McLuhan would be very happy with that—globalization. What about your symphony, *The Forest?*

DB: It was originally done for a Robert Wilson piece. The idea was that we'd take the same story—the Gilgamesh legend. He'd interpret it for stage and I'd do it as a film. We'd use my music. The hope was that we'd present them in the same city at the same time. So you could see two vastly different interpretations of a reinterpreted ancient legend. I found it's the oldest story we know. We updated it to the industrial revolution in Europe.

TL: Cosmology and immortality.

DB: It was written in the first cities ever built. Oddly enough, it deals with the same questions that came up during the industrial revolution and persist today—when cities and industry expand at a phenomenal rate.

It deals with what it means to be civilized versus natural. So it has a current resonance, although it's as old as you can get.

TL: The older I get, the more I see everything in stages. I start with the tribe and move through the feudal, Gilgamesh, the industrial . . . But what's impressed me about your music is that regardless of the setting, there's always the African body beat.

DB: It's part of our culture now. It's something we've been inundated with. The Africans who were forcibly brought here have colonized us with their music, with their sensibility and rhythm. They've colonized their oppressors.

TL: Michael Ventura, who explains how Voudoun came from Africa, says the same thing. I wrote an article about Southern vegetables—we colonials going into Southern cultures and grabbing their sugar, coffee, and bananas. The industrial people arrive, build factories, and then they become countercolonized by the music, the food, and the psychoactive vegetables. It happened to the British in India.

DB: In a subtle way it changes people's ways of thinking; it increases the possibilities for what they could think and feel. And they're not always aware of what's happening to them.

TL: I see the industrial age as a stage—a very tacky, messy, awkward stage of human evolution. We *had* to have the smoky factories, and we must mature beyond them. I was very touched by your comments about *The Forest*. You were trying to acknowledge the romance and the grandeur of the factory civilization even though it was fucking everything up.

DB: My instinctual reaction is that this stuff sucks. It's created the mess that we're in. But you're never going to find your way out of the mess unless you can somehow, like

the samurai, identify with your enemy. Become one with your enemy, understand it, or you won't be able to find your way out of the maze.

TL: The Soviet Union is a great teacher about the horrors of fire power and machine tech. You see the smog and those grizzled old miners coming out of the deep, sooty mines with their faces black. On the other hand, there was a grandeur to it, and you can't cut out the industrial side of our nature, because it has brought us to this room where we can use machines to record our conversation. That's something that I find interesting in Japan, which is the perfect machine society. There's not much pollution there—you never see any filth on the street.

DB: No, it's cleaned up pretty quickly. You get scolded for tossing a can out your car window. I've seen people get scolded for not washing their car! It's a matter of face.

TL: And nothing is old there. I didn't see one car that was more than four years old or with a dent in it.

DB: That's taking L.A. one step further.

TL: I spent some time today watching your video *Ile Ayié.*

DB: It's about an Afro–Brazilian religion called Candomblé. "Ile Ayié" in Yoruba, an African language, roughly translates as the *house of life* or *the realm that we live in.*

TL: The biosphere I . . .

DB: Yeah, the dimension that we live in rather than other existing dimensions. It was done in Bahia, in the city of Salvador, on the coast of northeastern Brazil. It's

about an African religion that's been there since slavery times. It's mutated and evolved over the years to the extent that now it could be called an Afro–Brazilian religion—there's a lot of African elements. The ceremonies, the rituals consist of a lot of drumming, people occasionally go into trance, offerings are made, altars are made . . . the occasional sacrifice . . . It's an ecstatic religion—it feels good.

TL: I've never seen so many dignified, happy human beings in any place at any time. For over ninety minutes the screen is filled with these stately older black women . . .

DB: It's very joyous and regal. When the drums and dancing kick in, it's like a really hot rock or rhythm-and-blues show. When the music hits that level where everybody tunes into it, it's the same kind of feeling.

TL: That's what religion should be. But it's not all joyous. At times there's a sternness—a sphinx-like trance to it.

DB: It deals with acknowledging and paying homage to the natural forces. Some of those are deadly, some are joyous, some are dangerous, and some are life giving. That's the flux of nature, and Candomblé acknowledges the entire dynamic.

TL: You also said that the aim of these ceremonies is to bring the Orixás—deities who serve as intermediaries between mortals and the supreme force of nature. Tell us about that.

DB: When the vibe is right somebody gets possessed by one of the Gods. There's a pantheon of Gods like in ancient Greece or Rome. The God is said to be there in the room, in the body, so you can have a conversation with him, or dance with him. God isn't up there unreachable, untouchable. It's something that can come right down into the room with you. You can dance with God or ask direct questions.

TL: The great thing about the Greek Gods was that they had human qualities.

But you're never going to find your way out of the mess unless you can somehow, like the samurai, identify with your enemy. Become one with your enemy, understand it, or you won't be able to find your way out of the maze.

DB: These as well. They can be sexy, jealous, vain, loving, whatever—all the attributes of people.

TL: William Gibson has written about Voudoun. Many of his Voudoun people talk about the human being as a horse, and how the God comes down and rides the human being.

DB: That's the Haitian metaphor—the horse. It's the same idea.

TL: The healer, the warrior, the mother bubbling—one after another these archetypes of characters or natural forces—basic human situations, roles . . .

DB: The nurturing mother or the warrior man or woman, the sexy coquette . . .

TL: The seductive female warrior—that's Yarzan. I became confused when that man dressed as a Catholic priest ranted about false prophets.

DB: The African religion is periodically being persecuted by the Catholic Church, by the Protestant Church, by the government. They go through waves of being recognized and persecuted and going underground and coming back up again and being recognized and pushed down again.

TL: I know the cycle well.

DB: So that was a scene from a fictional film there dramatizing persecution by orthodox religion.

TL: You wrote it in . . .

DB: It was something I found in a Brazilian film. It was an example of recent persecution; so I threw it in.

TL: That's a very powerful moment, because it wasn't orchestrated. It was *authentic,* as your friend here would say. *[Points to a copy of* Reproduced Authentic.*]* Would you comment on this book?

DB: An artist named Joseph Kusuth organized it. He's most well-known for art that looks like your shirt.

TL: *[Displays shirt.]* It's designed by

Anarchic Adjustments. The front reads "Ecstasy," and on one arm it reads "Egos In, Egos Out."

DB: Joseph Kusuth would have a definition of a word and just frame that. He invited me to be part of this exhibition in Japan where the idea was to create art with a fax machine. I did something equivalent to the seven deadly sins. It didn't exist—I collaged it, sandwiched it in the fax machine, and it came out the other end. They took the fax and blew it up to the size of a painting. When it was transmitted, rather than receiving it on paper, they received it on acetate. The acetate became a photo negative. They have fax machines that can receive other materials, and then they can blow it up to any size.

TL: You say you didn't want to be a scientist because you liked the graffiti in the art department better. If you *had* been a scientist what would you have been?

DB: At the time I was attracted to pure science—physics—where you could speculate and be creative. It's equivalent to being an artist. If you get the chance, and the cards fall right, there's no difference. The intellectual play and spirit are the same.

TL: Nature is that way—it's basically playful. Murray Gell-Mann, who is one of America's greatest quantum physicists, used the word "quark" to describe the basic element from a funny line from James Joyce, "three quarks from Muster Mark."

DB: I had a math teacher in high school who included Lewis Carroll and *Alice in Wonderland* in his higher math studies. I thought, "This guy knows what he's doing."

TL: Dodgson, the fellow who wrote it, knew what he was doing. That metaphor of *through the looking glass* on the other side of the screen. Talk about your Yoruba Gods and Goddesses. Talk about Yarzan and Shango. Alice is the Goddess of the electronic age. ◎

VII. DE-ANIMATION/RE-ANIMATION

1. COMMON-SENSE ALTERNATIVES TO INVOLUNTARY DEATH

2. HYBERNATING ANDY

VII.1.

COMMON-SENSE ALTERNATIVES TO INVOLUNTARY DEATH

CO-WRITTEN WITH ERIC GULLICHSEN

> Death is the ultimate negative patient health outcome.
> —William L. Roper, Director,
> Health Care Financing Administration
> (which administers Medicare)

Most human beings face death with an "attitude" of helplessness, either resigned or fearful. Neither of these submissive, uninformed "angles of approach" to the most crucial event of one's life can be ennobling.

Today, there are many practical options and methods available for navigating the dying process. Passivity, failure to learn about them, might be the ultimate irretrievable blunder. Pascal's famous no-lose wager about the existence of God translates into modern life as a no-risk gamble on the prowess of technology.

For millennia the fear of death has depreciated individual confidence and increased dependence on authority.

True, the loyal members of a familial or racial gene pool can take pride in the successes and survival tenacity of their kinship. For example, around the year 1600, at the height of the obedient, feudal stage, the Chinese philosopher, Li Zhi, wrote a revealing essay outlining "the five ways to die":

1. death for a worthy cause,
2. death in battle,
3. death as a martyr,
4. death as a loyal minister, unjustly attacked,
5. premature death after finishing some good piece of work.

Thus we see that the aim of the "good (G. Gordon Liddy) life" was one of submission to authority. If your life was dedicated to serving the gene pool, then, logically, your death is the final, crowning sacrifice of your individuality.

But for the humanist who believes in the sanctity of the individual, these traditional prospects are less than exalted. Let's be honest here. How can you be proud of your past achievements, walk tall in the present, or zap enthusiastically into the future if, awaiting you implacably around some future corner, is Old Mr. D, the Grim Reaper?

What a PR job the wordmakers did to build this death concept into a prime-time horror show! The Grave. Mortification. Extinction. Breakdown. Catastrophe. Doom. Finish. Fatality. Malignancy. Necrology. Obituary. The End. Note the calculated negativity. To die is to croak, to give up the ghost, to bite the dust, to kick the bucket, to perish. To become inanimate, lifeless, defunct, extinct, moribund, cadaverous, necrotic. A corpse, a stiff, a cadaver, a relic, food for worms, a *corpus delecti*, a carcass. What a miserable ending to the game of life!

Note the calculated negativity. To die is to croak, to give up the ghost, to bite the dust, to kick the bucket, to perish. To become inanimate, lifeless, defunct, extinct, moribund, cadaverous, necrotic. A corpse, a stiff, a cadaver, a relic, food for worms, a **corpus delecti**, a carcass. What a miserable ending to the game of life!

In the past, the reflexive genetic duty of top management (those in social control of the various gene pools) has been to make humans feel weak, helpless, and dependent in the face of death. The good of the race or nation was ensured at the cost of the sacrifice of the individual. Obedience and submission were rewarded on a time-payment plan. For his/her devotion, the individual was promised immortality in the postmortem hive center variously known as heaven, paradise, or the Kingdom of the Lord.

FEAR OF DEATH WAS AN EVOLUTIONARY NECESSITY IN THE PAST

 In the past, the reflexive genetic duty of top management (those in social control of the various gene pools) has been to make humans feel weak, helpless, and dependent in the face of death. The good of the race or nation was ensured at the cost of the sacrifice of the individual.

Obedience and submission were rewarded on a time-payment plan. For his/her devotion, the individual was promised immortality in the postmortem hive center variously known as heaven, paradise, or the Kingdom of the Lord. In order to maintain the attitude of dedication, the gene-pool managers had to control the "dying reflexes," orchestrate the trigger-stimuli that activate the "death circuits" of the brain. This was accomplished through rituals that imprint dependence and docility when the "dying alarm bells" go off in the brain.

Perhaps we can better understand this imprinting mechanism by considering another set of "rituals," those by which human hives manage the conception-reproduction reflexes, the fertilization rituals. A discussion of these is less likely to alarm you.

The mechanisms of control imposed by the operation of social machinery are similar in the two cases. Let us "step outside the system" for a moment, to see vividly what is ordinarily invisible because it is so entrenched in our expectation.

At adolescence each kinship group provides morals, rules, taboos, ethical prescriptions to guide the all-important sperm-egg situation.

Management by the individual of the horny DNA machinery is always a threat to hive inbreeding. Dress, grooming, dating, courtship, contraception, abortion patterns are fanatically conventionalized in

tribal and feudal societies. Personal innovation is sternly condemned and ostracized. Industrial democracies vary in the sexual freedom allowed individuals, but in totalitarian states, China and Iran, for example, rigid prudish morality controls the mating reflexes and governs boy-girl relations. Under the Chinese dictator Mao, "romance" was forbidden because it weakened dedication to the state, i.e., the local gene pool. If teenagers pilot and select their own mating, then they will be more likely to fertilize outside the hive, more likely to insist on directing their own lives, and, worst of all, less likely to rear their offspring with blind gene-pool loyalty.

Even more rigid social-imprinting rituals guard the "dying reflexes." Hive control of "death" responses is taken for granted in all precybernetic cultures.

In the past, this conservative degradation of individuality was an evolutionary virtue. During epochs of species stability, when the tribal, feudal, and industrial technologies were being mastered and fine-tuned, wisdom was centered in the gene pool, stored in the collective linguistic consciousness, the racial data base of the hive.

Since individual life was short, brutish, aimless, what a singular learned was nearly irrelevant. The world was changing so slowly that knowledge could be embodied only in the breed-culture. Lacking technologies for the personal mastery of transmission and storage of information, the individual was simply too slow and too small to matter. Loyalty to the racial collective was the virtue. Creativity, premature individuation was anti-evolutionary; a weirdo, mutant distraction. Only village idiots would try to commit independent, chaotic, unauthorized thought.

In the feudal and industrial eras, management used the fear of death to motivate and control individuals. Today, politicians use the death-dealing military, the police, and capital punishment to protect the social order. Organized religion maintains its power and wealth by orches-

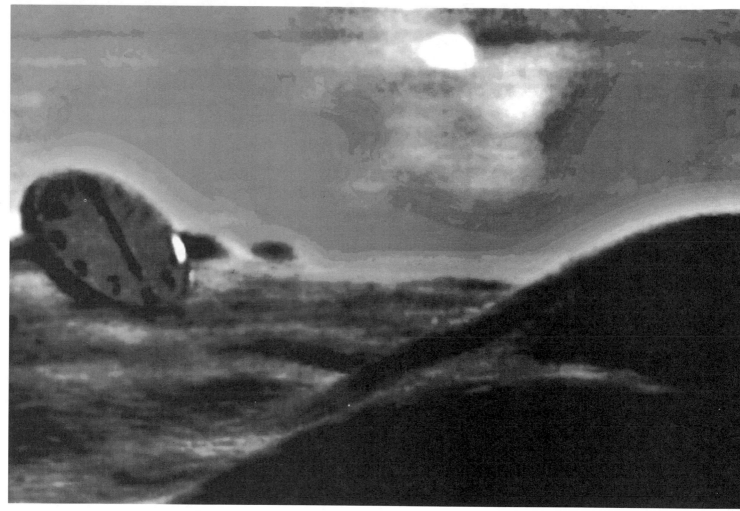

trating and exaggerating the fear of death.

Among the many things that the pope, the ayatollah, and fundamentalist Protestants agree on is that confident understanding and self-directed mastery of the dying process is the last thing to be allowed to the individual. The very notion of cybernetic postbiologic intelligence or consumer immortality options is taboo, sinful, for formerly valid reasons of gene-pool protection.

Religions have cleverly monopolized the rituals of dying to increase control over the superstitious. Throughout history the priests and mullahs and medical experts have swarmed around the expiring human like black vultures. Death belonged to them.

As we grew up in the 20th Century, we were systematically programmed about how to die. Hospitals are staffed with priests/ministers/rabbis ready to perform the "last rites." Every army unit has its Catholic chaplain to administer the Sacrament of Extreme Unction (what a phrase, really!) to the expiring soldier. The ayatollah, chief mullah of the Islamic death cult, sends his teen-aged soldiers into the Iraq minefields with dog-tags guaranteeing immediate transfer to the Allah's destination resort, Koranic Heaven. A terrible auto crash? Call the medics! Call the priest! Call the reverend!

In the industrial society, everything becomes part of big business. Dying involves Blue Cross, Medicare, health-care delivery systems, the Health Care Financing Administration (HCFA), terminal patient wards. Undertakers. Cemeteries. The funeral rituals. The monopolies of religion and the assembly lines of top management control the dying and the dead even more efficiently than the living.

We recall that knowledge and

For millennia the fear of death has depreciated individual confidence and increased dependence on authority.

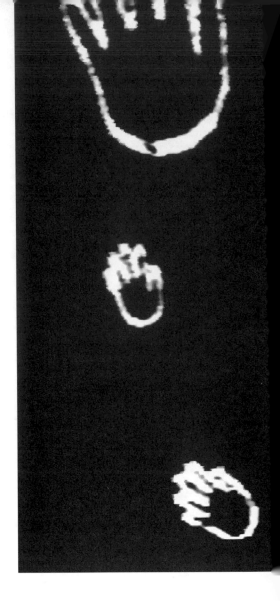

The cybernetic age we are entering could mark the beginning of a period of enlightened and intelligent individualism, a time unique in history when technology is available to individuals to support a huge diversity of personalized lifestyles and cultures, a world of diverse, interacting, small social groups whose initial-founding membership number is one.

selective choice about such gene-pool issues as conception, test-tube fertilization, pregnancy, abortion are dangerous enough to the church fathers.

But suicide, right-to-die concepts, euthanasia, life-extension, out-of-body experiences, occult experimentation, astral-travel scenarios, death/rebirth reports, extraterrestrial speculation, cryogenics, sperm banks, egg banks, DNA banks, artificial-intelligence technology—anything that encourages the individual to engage in personal speculation and experimentation with immortality—is anathema to the orthodox seed-shepherds of the feudal and industrial ages.

Why? Because if the flock doesn't fear death, then the grip of religious and political management is broken. The power of the gene pool is threatened. And when control loosens in the gene pool, dangerous genetic innovations and mutational visions tend to emerge.

THE AGE OF INDIVIDUAL RESPONSIBILITY AND SELF-CONTROL

The cybernetic age we are entering could mark the beginning of a period of enlightened and intelligent individualism, a time unique in history when technology is available to individuals to support a huge diversity of personalized lifestyles and cultures, a world of diverse, interacting, small social groups whose initial-founding membership number is one.

The exploding technology of light-speed and multimedia communication lays a delicious feast of knowledge and personal choice within our easy grasp. Under such conditions, the operating wisdom and control naturally passes from æons-old power of gene pools, and locates in the rapidly self-modifying brains of individuals capable of dealing with an ever-accelerating rate of change.

Aided by customized, personally programmed, quantum-linguistic appliances, individuals can choose their own social and genetic future, and perhaps choose not to "die."

THE WAVE THEORY OF EVOLUTION

Current theories of genetics suggest that evolution, like everything else in the universe, comes in waves.

At times of "punctuated evolution," collective metamorphoses, when many things are mutating at the same time, the ten commandments of the "old ones" become ten suggestions. At such times of rapid innovation and collective mutation, conservative hive dogma can be dangerous, suicidal. Individual experimentation and exploration, the thoughtful methodical sci-

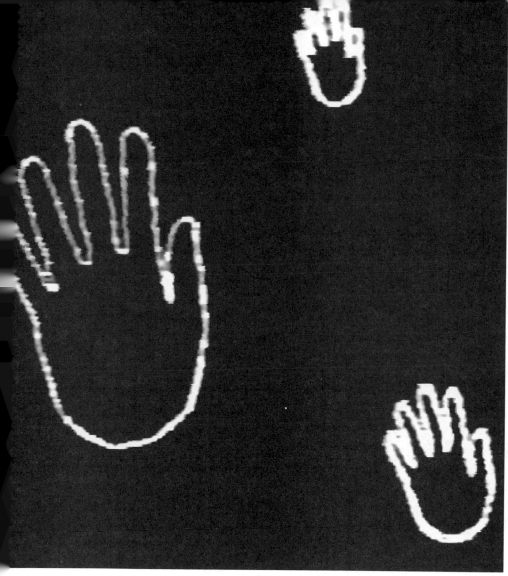

ANDY FRITH

It is beginning to look as though, in the information society, individual human beings can script, produce, direct their own hybernation and re-animation. Dying becomes a "team sport."

entific challenging of taboos, becomes the key to the survival of the gene school.

As we enter the cybernetic age, we arrive at a new wisdom that broadens our definition of personal immortality and gene-pool survival: the postbiologic options of the information species. A fascinating set of gourmet consumer choices suddenly appear on the pop-up menu of The Evolutionary Café.

It is beginning to look as though, in the information society, individual human beings can script, produce, direct their own hybernation and re-animation. Dying becomes a "team sport."

Here we face mutation shock in its most panicky form. As we have done in understanding earlier mutations, the first step is to develop a new language. We

should not impose the values or vocabulary of the past species on the new cybernetic culture.

Would you let the buzzwords of a preliterate, paleolithic cult control your life? Will you let the superstitions of a tribal-village culture (now represented by the pope and the ayatollah) shuffle you off the scene? Will you let the mechanical, planned-obsolescence tactics of the factory, Blue Cross culture manage your existence?

RE-CREATIONAL DYING

Let us have no more pious, wimpy talk about death. The time has come to talk cheerfully and joke sassily about personal responsibility for managing the dying process. For starters, let's demystify dying and develop alternative metaphors for con-

ANDY FRITH

We recognize that the dying process, which for millennia has been blanketed by taboo and primitive superstition, has suddenly become accessible to human intelligence.

sciousness leaving the body. Let us speculate good-naturedly about postbiologic options. Let's be bold about opening up a broad spectrum of Club–Med postbiologic possibilities. Let us explore the option of re-creational dying.

For starters, let's replace the word death with the more neutral, precise, scientific term: metabolic coma. And then let's go on to suggest that this temporary state of coma might be replaced by auto-metamorphosis, a self-controlled change in bodily form, where the individual chooses to change his or her vehicle of existence without loss of consciousness.

Then, let's distinguish between involuntary and voluntary metabolic coma. Reversible and irreversible dying.

Let's explore those fascinating borderlands—the periods between body dying and neurological dying and DNA dying in terms of the knowledge-information pro-

cessing involved.

Let's collect some data about that even more intriguing zone now beginning to be researched in the cross-disciplinary field of scientific study known as artificial life. What knowledge-information–processing capacities can be preserved after both body death and brain cessation? What natural and artificial systems, from the growth of mineral structures to the self-reproduction of formal mathematical automata, are promising alternative candidates to biology for the support of life?

And then let us perform the ultimate act of human intelligence. Let's venture with calm, open-minded tolerance and scientific rigor into that perennially mysterious *terra incognita* and ask the final question: What knowledge-information–processing possibilities can remain after the cessation of all bio-logical life: somatic, neurological, and genetic?

How can human consciousness be supported in digital, light-wave, zero–one wafers outside the moist envelope of graceful, attractive, pleasure-filled meat we now inhabit? How can the organic, carbon-constructed caterpillar become the silicon butterfly?

POSTBIOLOGICAL RE-CREATIONAL AWARENESS

We recognize that the dying process, which for millennia has been blanketed by taboo and primitive superstition, has suddenly become accessible to human intelligence.

Here we experience the sudden insights that we need not "go quietly" and passively into the dark night or the neon-lit, Muzak-enhanced Disney–Heaven of the Jesus Corporation. We realize that the concept of involuntary, irreversible metabolic coma known as "death" is a lethal, feudal superstition, a cruel marketing tactic of industrial society. We understand that one can discover dozens of active, creative alternatives to going belly-up clutching the company logo of the Christian Cross, Blue Cross, or Crescent Cross, or the eligibility cards of the Veterans Administration.

Recognition is always the beginning of the possibility for change. Once we comprehend that "death" can be defined as a problem of knowledge-information memory processing, solutions to this age-long "problem" can emerge. We realize that the intelligent thing to do is to try to keep one's knowledge-processing capacities around as long as possible. In bodily form. In neural form. In DNA form. In the silicon circuitry and magnetic storage media of today's computers. In molecular form, through the atom-stacking of nanotechnology in tomorrow's computers. In cryogenic form. In the form of stored data, legend, myth. In the form of offspring who are cybernetically trained to use postbiologic intelligence. In the form of postbiological gene pools, info-

pools, advanced viral forms resident in world computer networks and cyberspace matrices of the sort described in the "sprawl novels" of William Gibson.

The second step in attaining postbiologic, re-creational awareness is to shift from the passive to the active mode. Industrial-age humans were trained to await docilely the onset of termination, and then to turn over their body for disposal to the priests and the factory (hospital) technicians.

Our species is now developing the cybernetic information skills and the activists' confidence to plan ahead, to make one's will and testament prevail. The smart thing to do is to see dying as a change in the implementation of information processing: to orchestrate it, manage it, anticipate and exercise the many available options.

We consider here twenty-three distinct methods of avoiding a submissive or fearful dying.

POSTBIOLOGICAL RE-CREATIONAL PROGRAMMING INTELLIGENCE

In previous writings the authors have defined eight stages of intelligence: biological, emotional, mental-symbolic, social, æsthetic, neurological-cybernetic, genetic, atomic-nanotech. At each of these stages there is an input recognition stage, followed by a programming-reprogramming stage, and an output communication stage.

In order to reprogram, we must activate the circuits in the brain which mediate that particular dimension of intelligence. Once this circuit is "turned on," we can re-imprint or reprogram.

Cognitive neurology suggests that the most direct way to reprogram emotional responses is to reactivate the emotional stage and reprogram, replace fear with laughter. To reprogram sexual responses, it is logical to reactivate and re-experience the original teenage imprints and to re-

The time has come to talk cheerfully and joke sassily about personal responsibility for managing the dying process. For starters, let's demystify dying and develop alternative metaphors for consciousness leaving the body. Let us speculate good-naturedly about postbiologic options. Let's be bold about opening up a broad spectrum of Club–Med postbiologic possibilities. Let us explore the option of re-creational dying.

We realize that the intelligent thing to do is to try to keep one's knowledge-processing capacities around as long as possible. In bodily form. In neural form. In DNA form. In the silicon circuitry and magnetic storage media of today's computers. In molecular form, through the atom-stacking of nanotechnology in tomorrow's computers. In cryogenic form. In the form of stored data, legend, myth. In the form of offspring who are cybernetically trained to use postbiologic intelligence. In the form of postbiological gene pools, info-pools, advanced viral forms resident in world computer networks and cyberspace matrices of the sort described in the "sprawl novels" of William Gibson.

imprint new erotic stimuli and new sexual responses.

The circuits of the brain which mediate the "dying" process are routinely experienced during "near-death" crises. For centuries people have reported: "My entire life flashed before my eyes as I sank into the water."

This "near-death, out-of-the-body" experience can be turned on via certain anæsthetic drugs. Ketamine, for example. Or by learning enough about the effects of out-of-the-body drugs so that one can use hypnotic techniques to activate the desired circuits without using external chemical stimuli.

We see immediately that the rituals intuitively developed by religious groups are designed to induce hypnotic-trance states related to "dying." The child growing up in a Catholic culture is deeply imprinted (programmed) by funeral rites. The arrival of the solemn priest to administer extreme unction becomes access codes for the pre-mortem state. Other cultures have different rituals for activating and then controlling (programming) the death circuits of the brain. Until recently, very few have permitted personal control or customized consumer choice.

Almost every animal species manifests "dying reflexes." Some animals leave the herd to die alone. Others stand with legs apart, stolidly postponing the last moment. Some species eject the dying organism from the social group.

To gain navigational control of one's dying processes, three steps suggest themselves:

1. **Activate the death reflexes imprinted by your culture, experience them. Imagine** dressing up like a priest, rabbi, minister, and mimic their solemn, hypnotic rituals. Visualize. Recite the prayers for the dying. Do these things in the virtual reality of your mind. Officiate at your own platonic funeral.

2. Trace their origins; then

3. Reprogram, install your own pre-mortem plan for immortality.

BRUMMBAER

The aim is to develop a scientific model of the chain of cybernetic (knowledge-information) processes that occur as one approaches this metamorphic stage—and to intentionally develop options for taking active responsibility for these events.

ACHIEVING IMMORTALITY

Since the dawn of human history, philosophers and theologians have speculated about immortality. Uneasy, aging kings have commanded methods for extending the life span.

A most dramatic example of this age-long impulse is ancient Egypt, which produced mummification, the pyramids, and manuals like the *Book of the Dying*.

The Tibetan Book of the Dying presents a masterful (Buddhist) model of post-mortem stages and techniques for guiding the student to a state of immortality which is neurologically "real" and suggests scientific techniques for reversing the dying process.

The new field of molecular engineering is producing techniques within the framework of current consensus Western science to implement auto-metamorphosis. The aim of the game is to defeat death—to give the individual mastery of this, the final stupidity.

We do not endorse any particular technique of achieving immortality. Our aim is to review all options and encourage creative thinking about new possibilities.

We do not endorse any particular technique of achieving immortality. Our aim is to review all options and encourage creative thinking about new possibilities.

It seems likely that, by the year 2000, ceremonial, dignified celebration of one's own transition will be considered a basic human ritual.

PSYCHOLOGICAL-BEHAVIORAL TRAINING TECHNIQUES

The techniques in this category do not assist in attaining personal immortality per se, but are useful in acquiring the experience of "experimental dying," reversible-voluntary exploration of the territory between body coma and brain death, sometimes called out-of-body experiences; or near-dying experiences. Others have termed these experiences astral travel or reincarnation memories.

1. Meditation, hypnosis.

The classic yogic routes to exploration of nonordinary states of consciousness, well-known to be labor and time-intensive. The aim is to attain an out-of-body experience.

2. Psychedelic drug experiences.

The use of re-creational (psychedelic) drugs to access information and operational programs stored in the brain of the individual. In normal states of consciousness, these states are not available for voluntary access.

3. Re-creational anæsthetics.

Carefully designed for experimental out-of-body experiences. John Lilly has written extensively about his experiences with small dosages of anæsthetics such as Ketamine. It is possible that the out-of-body subjective effects of such substances are interpretations of proprioceptive disruption. Nevertheless, information is available through these investigative routes.

4. Sensory deprivation.

Primarily accomplished in isolation-tank immersions, a method most comprehensively investigated by John Lilly.

5. Reprogramming exercises.

Suspending and replacing socially imprinted "death" imprints.

6. Development of new rituals to guide the post-body transition.

Our cultural taboos have prohibited the development of much detailed work in this area, but some important research has been done by E. J. Gold and others.

7. Pre-incarnation exercises.

Using the preferred altered-state method (drugs, hypnosis, shamanic trance, voodoo ritual, born-again frenzies) to create future scripts for oneself.

8. Voluntary dying.

This procedure is called "suicide," i.e., "self-murder," by officials who wish to control the mortem process. Until recently, self-induced death has been considered a cowardly or insane attempt to interfere with the natural order. Anyone who wished to manage and direct their own dying was condemned by law and custom.

In a pagan or nature-attuned tribal culture, there is a common-sense genetic wisdom implied in this passive acceptance of one's termination. The brain continually

monitors the vital functions of the body, and as the body starts failing, terminal programs take over. The brain quietly shuts down the body and during the few minutes between body death and neurological death, the brain's hundred billion neurons probably enjoy an astonishing "timeless" review of all and everything.

In the late 20th Century, however, mechanical medical science started "interfering" quite dramatically with the "natural" order. Tubes and machines are now used to keep patients "alive" long after the cessation of consciousness. A stroke victim who twenty years ago might have died in an hour can now be revived, only to spend years in machine-induced coma.

Most people are shocked and outraged by mechanical-medical methods that strip dignity and human consciousness from the terminal-coma patient. The American Medical Association has supported the right of the family to remove medical treatment from terminally ill comatose patients.

Then there is the problem of intractable pain suffered by patients terminally ill from "artificial" diseases caused by industrial pollution like cancer, which cause agonizing pain. The brain housed in the body of a person living in the industrial low-rent, tacky culture of the late 20th Century is not programmed to handle these new diseases. The brain is capable of producing endorphin pain-killers naturally. The brain is beautifully geared to slowly, gracefully turn out the lights for humans— as they do for other animals. Our sisters and brothers, the other pack animals like wolves and dogs and cats (for example), manage to die in dignity without screaming to veterinarians for sedation or priests for extreme unction.

But the factory-hospital environment, run efficiently by factory managers (doctors and nurses), is a very strange environment for any normal hundred-billion-neuron brain. Hospitalized patients whose brains are imprinted to perform as factory

units when terminally ill and in great pain passionately beg to be put out of their hopeless misery.

Fundamentalist religious groups and neofeudal officials oppose any "pro-choice" initiative that allows individuals to manage their own lives. These groups also are actively opposed to "euthanasia."

[By 1990 a growing movement had developed in California to allow terminally ill patients to arrange for their own dying: Americans Against Human Suffering (Freedom of Choice for Physician Aid-in-Dying). In Holland, "euthanasia on request" is made available after a prudent, suitable period of review. Since 1992 Michigan doctor Jack Kevorkian has repeatedly tested the law by helping his terminally ill patients exercise their right to choose the time and manner of their death.]

It seems likely that, by the year 2000, ceremonial, dignified celebration of one's own transition will be considered a basic human ritual.

9. Pre-mortem hybernation.

In the last section we have considered active management of one's own dying: voluntary irreversible metabolic coma. This planful procedure takes on a different meaning when the person does not "die," but slides into cryonic or brain-bank hybernation. This option is called "pre-mortem suspension." It has been ruled legal in California, in a case brought by the Alcor Foundation.

SOMATIC TECHNIQUES FOR LIFE EXTENSION

Techniques to inhibit the process of aging comprise the classic approach to immortality. In the present state of science, these serve to buy time.

10. Diet.

The classic research on diet and longevity has been done by Roe L. Walford,

> The brain is beautifully geared to slowly, gracefully turn out the lights for humans—as they do for other animals. . . . wolves and dogs and cats (for example), manage to die in dignity without screaming to veterinarians for sedation or priests for extreme unction.

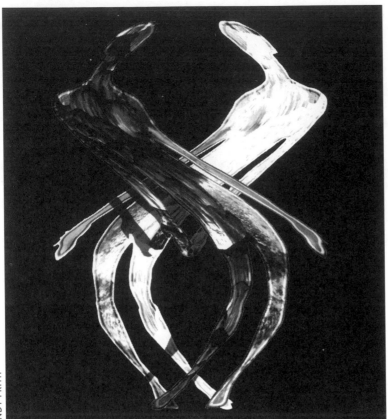

ANDY FRITH

coma. They are alternatives for preserving the structure of tissues until a time of more advanced medical knowledge.

16. Cryonics or vacuum-pack body "pickling."

Letting one's body and brain rot seems to imply no possibility at all for your future. Why let the carefully arranged tangle of dendritic growths in your nervous system which store all your memories get eaten by fungus? Perpetual preservation of your tissues by freezing is available today at moderate cost.

17. Cryonic preservation of neural tissue or DNA.

Those not particularly attached to their bodies can opt for preservation of the essentials: their brains and the instructional codes capable of regrowing something genetically identical to their present biomachinery.

Techniques are now emerging to permit a much more vivid guarantee of personal persistence, a smooth metamorphic transformation into a different form of substrate on which the computer program of consciousness runs.

M.D. *(The 120–Year Diet; Maximum Life Span)*. The bottom line: gluttony and greed are the killer addictions. Skinny folks live much longer.

11. Life-extension drugs.

Anti-oxidants, etc. A comprehensive reference is Sandy Shaw and Durk Pearson's *Life Extension.*

12. Exercise regimens.

13. Temperature variation. Heat kills.

14. Sleep treatments (hybernation).

15. Immunization to counter aging process.

SOMATIC-NEURAL-GENETIC PRESERVATION

Techniques in this class do not ensure continuous operation of consciousness. They produce reversible metabolic

BIOGENETIC METHODS FOR LIFE EXTENSION

Is there any need to experience metabolic coma? We have mentioned ways to gain personal control of the experience, to stave it off by "conventional" longevity techniques, to avoid irreversible dissolution of the systemic substrate. Techniques are now emerging to permit a much more vivid guarantee of personal persistence, a smooth metamorphic transformation into a different form of substrate on which the computer program of consciousness runs.

18. Cellular/DNA repair.

Nanotechnology is the science and engineering of mechanical and electronic systems built to atomic specifications. Nanotechnology has a potential for production of self-replicating nanomachines living within individual biological cells. These artificial enzymes will effect cellular repair, as damage occurs from mechanical causes, radiation, or other aging effects. Repair of DNA ensures genetic stability.

19. Cloning.

Biologically based replication of genetically identical personal copies of yourself, at any time desired, is approaching the possible. Sex is fun, but sexual reproduction is biologically inefficient, suited mainly for inducing genetic variation in species that still advance through the accidents of luck in random combination. The idea is to reserve sex as a means of communication and to reproduce asexually!

CYBERNETIC METHODS FOR ATTAINING IMMORTALITY
(ARTIFICIAL LIFE "IN SILICO"), BY ERIC GULLICHSEN

Some silicon visionaries believe that natural evolution of the human species (or at least their branch of it) is near completion. They are no longer interested in merely procreating, but in designing their successors. Carnegie–Mellon robotics scientist Hans Moravec writes,

> We owe our existence to organic evolution. But we owe it little loyalty. We are on the threshold of a change in the universe comparable to the transition from nonlife to life.

Human society has now reached a turning point in the operation of the process of evolution at which the next evolutionary step of the species is under our control. Or, more correctly, the next steps, occurring in parallel, and resulting in an explosion of diversity of the human species. We are no longer dependent on fitness in any physical sense for survival. Our quantum appliances and older mechanical devices provide the requisite means in all circumstances. In the near future, the (now merging) methods of computer and biological technology will make the human form a matter totally determined by individual choice.

As a flesh-and-blood species we are moribund, stuck at "a local optimum," to borrow a term from mathematical optimization theory. Beyond this horizon, which humankind has reached, lies the unknown, the scarcely imagined. We will design our children, and co-evolve intentionally with the cultural artifacts that are our progeny.

Humans already come in some variety of races and sizes. In comparison to what "human" will mean within the next century, we humans are at present as indistinguishable from one another as are hydrogen molecules. Our anthropocentrism will decrease.

Consider two principle categorizations of the form of the human of the future, one more biological-like: a bio/machine hybrid of any desired form; and one not biological at all: an "electronic life" on the computer networks. Human *as* machine, and human *in* machine.

Human *as* machine is perhaps more easily conceived. We already have crude prosthetic implants, artificial limbs, valves, and entire organs. The continuing improvements in the old-style mechanical technology slowly increase the thoroughness of human-machine integration.

The electronic life form of human *in* machine is even more alien to our current conceptions of humanity. Through

From this viewpoint, the immortality options become cybernetic methods of preserving one's unique signal capacity. There are as many souls as there are ways of storing and communicating data.

storage of one's belief systems as on-line data structures, driven by selected control structures (the electronic analog to will?), one's neuronal apparatus will operate in silicon as it did on the wetware of the brain, although faster, more accurately, more self-mutably, and, if desired, immortally.

[end of Eric Gullichsen]

20. Archival-informational.

One standard way of becoming "immortal" is by leaving a trail of archives, biographies, tapes, films, computer files, and publicized noble deeds. The increasing presence of stable knowledge media in our cybernetic society make this a more rigorous platform for persistent existence. The knowledge possessed by an individual is captured in expert systems and world-scale hypertext systems, thus ensuring the longevity and accessibility of textual and graphical memes.

Viewed from outside the self, death is not a binary phenomena, but a continuously varying function. How alive are you in Paris at this moment? In the city in which you live? In the room in which you are reading this?

21. Personality data-base transmission.

"Head Coach" is a system developed by Futique, Inc., one of the first examples of a new generation of psychoactive computer software. The program allows the user (performer) to digitize and store thoughts on a routine daily basis. If one leaves, let us say, twenty years of daily computer-stored records of thought-performance, one's grandchildren, a century down the line, can "know" and replay your information habits and mental performances. They will be able to "share and relive experiences" in considerable detail. To take a mundane example, if an individual's moves in a chess game are stored, the descendants can relive, move by move, a game played by Great-Great-Grandmother in the past century.

As passive reading is replaced by "active rewriting," later generations will be able to relive how we performed the great stories of our time.

Yet more intriguing is the possibility of implementing the knowledge extracted over time from a person: their beliefs, preferences, and tendencies, as a set of algorithms guiding a program capable of acting in a manner functionally identical to the person. Advances in robotics technology will take these "Turing creatures" away from being mere "brains in bottles" to hybrids capable of interacting sensorily with the physical world.

22. Nanotech information storage: direct brain-computer transfer.

When a computer becomes obsolete, one does not discard the data it contains. The hardware is merely a temporary vehicle of implementation for structures of information. The data gets transferred to new systems for continued use. Decreasing costs of computer storage, CD–ROM and WORM memory systems mean that no information generated today ever need be lost.

We can consider building an artificial computational substrate both functionally and structurally identical to the brain (and perhaps the body) of a person. This can be achieved with predicted future capabilities of nanotechnology. Communicating nanomachines that per-

BRUMMBAER

vade the organism may analyze the neural and cellular structure and transfer the information obtained to machinery capable of growing, atom by atom, an identical copy.

According to the *American Heritage Dictionary,* "soul" is "the animating and vital principle in man credited with the faculties of thought, action, and emotion, and conceived as forming an immaterial entity distinguishable from but temporarily coexistent with his body." From the perspective of information theory, "immaterial" can be understood as "invisible to the naked eye, i.e., atomic-molecular-electronic," and "soul" refers to information processed and stored in microscopic-cellular, molecular, atomic packages. "Soul" becomes any

information that "lives," i.e., that is capable of being retrieved and communicated.

All tests for "death" at every level of measurement (nuclear, neural, bodily, galactic) involve signal unresponsiveness. From this viewpoint, the immortality options become cybernetic methods of preserving one's unique signal capacity. There are as many souls as there are ways of storing and communicating data. Tribal lore defines the racial soul. The DNA is a molecular soul. The brain is a neurological soul. Electron storage creates the silicon soul. Nanotechnology makes possible the atomic soul.

23. Computer viral existence in the cyberspace matrix.

The previous option permitted personal survival through isomorphic mapping of neural structure to silicon (or some other arbitrary medium of implementation). It also suggests the possibility of survival as an entity in what amounts to a reification of Jung's collective unconscious: the global information network.

In the 21st Century imagined by novelist William Gibson, wily cybernauts will not only store themselves electronically, but do so in the form of a "computer virus," capable of traversing computer networks and of self-replication as a guard against accidental or malicious erasure by others or other programs.

Given the ease of copying computer-stored information, one could exist

In the 21st Century imagined by novelist William Gibson, wily cybernauts will not only store themselves electronically, but do so in the form of a "computer virus," capable of traversing computer networks and of self-replication as a guard against accidental or malicious erasure by others or other programs.

ANDY FRITH

simultaneously in many forms. Where the "I" is in this situation is a matter for philosophy. We believe that consciousness would persist in each form, running independently (and ignorant of each other's self-manifestation unless in communication with it) and cloned at each branch point.

[Note: The above options for voluntary reversible metabolic coma and auto-metamorphosis are not mutually exclusive. The intelligent person needs little encouragement to explore all these possibilities, and to design many new other alternatives to going belly-up in line with management memos.]

KON-TIKI OF THE FLESH

In the near future, what is now taken for granted as the perishable human creature will be a mere historical curiosity, one point amidst unimaginable, multidimensional diversity of form. Individuals, or groups of adventurers, will be free to choose to reassume flesh-and-blood form, constructed for the occasion by the appropriate science.

Preserve your body—

preserve your brain—

preserve your DNA.

To immortalize: digitize!

VII.2.

HYBERNATING ANDY

This is an excerpt from a forthcoming novel about high-tech decadence in the film, computer, and art-fashion-literary worlds, as they interface the frontiers of pop science.

The narrator, Dani Mellon du Pont, is currently on assignment as publicity director of the Alcor Foundation, Riverside, California, to popularize the cryonic-hybernation re-animation option.

TRANSFER

atdt17147361703
connect 14,400

OKay. Let's get organized here.

I am on American Airlines flight 103 from J. Fitz. K. to Miami, Florida, my flop-top computer lapping-flapping away, writing to the Alcor Foundation to report on how the cryonic suspension (hybernation) of Andy Warhol's body and soul was accomplished.

ANDY WARHOL'S SECRET DESIRE TO REJOIN HIS IDOL, WALT DISNEY

Andy became interested in cryonic immortality (as he so quaintly called it) when he learned that Walt Disney's soul (brain) and flesh is being hybernetically frozen and preserved until Eric Drexler's M.I.T. nanotechnology (atom stacking) has mastered the logical steps to re-animate and restore him, i.e., Walt Disney.

Andy shared the almost universal belief that Walt Disney was one of the most important members of the 20th Century. You see, Walt Disney created "screen-iconic" entities of such global-mythic attraction that they are immediately recognized and loved by almost every quark on this globe. Andy told me over and over again that Walt Disney created pop culture. By pop, Andy means the popularization, humanization of ideas.

Andy was well aware of my assignment as publicity director of the Alcor Foundation to personalize, popularize, humanize, Disneyize the cryonic-hybernation re-animation option.

Andy shared with us the reasonable aversion to having his body and soul (i.e., brain) eaten by maggots or burned in an oven. For this reason (and others) he had discussed with me the procedures involved and shyly, as was his wont, wrung from me a promise that I would arrange for his "hybernation re-animation" at

that moment when his body had been "flat-lined," i.e., when he was being evicted from his current (and let's face it) tacky, mittel-European, washed-out, low-energy, unstylish, albino meat vehicle.

I "undertake" (ha ha) this assignment because the funereal dread I sense in American culture, the very concepts of cemeteries, undertakers, tombs, burials, crematoriums, obituaries, and life-insurance policies (which are, when you think about it, death assurance policies), have become a nightmare of insanity.

May I put it bluntly in four-letter words? I did not want worms to eat Andy Warhol.

And neither did he!

THE LEGAL AUTHORIZATION FOR LIBERATING ANDY WARHOL'S BODY AND SOUL (BRAIN)

The first logical question in anyone's mind is: Did Andy choose neurological (head-soul) freezing? Or total body cryonic hybernation?

At first he was undecided. Andy could, of course, afford total body ($100,000), but he seemed more interested in the neurological option ($35,000). Andy liked the idea that, when his meat functions flat-lined, his brain (soul) could be preserved, awaiting the kinky moment when an attractive young person of either or both sexes would—as the tragic result of some car accident after the Junior Prom or a crack-house shoot-out—be lying comatose in the emergency ward, a brain-dead neo-mort, available for a transplant from a super-attractive brain.

I promised Andy, on three occasions, that I would do everything necessary to prevent him from being buried by the MOMA or

Andy Warhol is not dead. He hybernates, a regal Ice Queen in cool serendipity.

His new life cycle has begun!

No thanks to medical silence (and given a little bit of luck),

Andy will return to paint and paradox again!

---

the equally insidious Valerie Solanis/Saint Patrick Cathedral gang, or turned over to the M&O (maggot and oven) crowd, i.e., destroyed by legally sanctioned DNA-killers. In return for this promise, Andy gave me his power of eternity, which I transmitted by American Express.

On these three occasions, Andy begged me, "Please don't let my body be exhibited publicly in the Museum of Modern Art or Saint Patrick's Cathedral."

The documents signed by Andy authorizing his hybernation–re-animation have been properly affidavitted. Andy's plans will remain, as per his wishes, secret.

There were several witnesses: Ultra Violet, who still wants to rock 'n' roll like days of old despite the fact that she's become a Mormon or a Christian Scientist. I have witnesses! Viva, two. These were two, fine pioneer women that Andy signed up in his weirdo wagon train. Edie Sedgwick, three.

Andy, by the way, recorded these conversations and shot Polaroid pix of all present.

A DISTRESSING PHONE CALL TO GRACE JONES

At 6:00 A.M. PST on Hybernation–Day-minus-1, I was notified that Andy's meat vehicle was deteriorating sharply and that cardiac arrest was, at most, two days away. I reserved space on the noon flight to New York. My cover for this mission was to model a Guess gene commercial shoot by Helmut Newton. My true mission was:

1. to assist in the removal of Andy's body from the hospital to our mortuary on West 91st Street;

2. to assist in the cryonic freezing of Andy;

3. to ship the cryonic patient (Andy) to the California depository;

4. to attend the Andy Warhol funeral at Saint Patrick's Cathedral and the subsequent ghoulish body-destruction festivities to see if there were any signs that anyone was aware that Andy's body had been liberated from Christian neuro-terrorists who were so enthusiastically driven to consign all of Warhol's organic tissue-information banks to the ever-hungry worms.

My flight was delayed; so I called Grace Jones from the airport to tell her I'd be late.

Grace was not part of the freezing operation, although she played major roles in some of Andy's last public triumphs. Andy symbolically married Grace in public shortly before his hybernation. His very last video performance occurred on Grace's MTV production of "I'm Not Perfect, But I'm Perfect for You." Andy, a Cabalist and numerologist (to put it mildly), knew at the time that his nights were numbered.

I suggest you play this MTV tape and observe Andy's comatic state. How well he concealed his 1968 illness!

Andy's chronic impression was contagious. It nibbled at my brain like worms. These are certainly strange daze!

Writing becomes difficult, and I have to be careful not to let my imagery become too disteanciated. My writing is nothing if not

... all this for a barbaric tissue-destruction ceremony. I can no longer remain silent when the people I love wind up in squirm holes and cremation barbecues.

the history of my illness. The entire staff of *Interview* magazine is in danger of suffering from the same chronic impression.

The role of the Museum of Modern Art in this matter is not exemplary. They showed no great enthusiasm for Andy during his long, long period of dying (1968–87). And then they go after him *con brio* as soon as they think (erroneously) that he is dead. The bake-meats are barely frozen cold upon the funeral table when MOMA announces the palladium of a full-scale retrospective!

Well, the joke's on they who are marketing Andy like a combination of Jesus Christ and Donald Duck, and don't realize that Andy is not dead, but sleeping. Next to . . . guess who?

WHY I RAN UP A $3,500 PHONE BILL WHILE ALOFT

I was, at this point in time, fucking 35,000 feet high, a nervous wreck, suffering mental fatigue with the portable phone linked to my Toshiba laptop, jacking into certain counterculture sectors of cyberspace, of which there are literally infinite numbers. I was not phoning my bookmaker, undertaker, pimp, wall-street pallbearer. I was not ordering call girls or fast pizza delivery.

I spent a most pleasant hour on "interscreen" digitizing with the Chaos Hacker group in Germany, who are very well known to Interpol and the KGB. We have developed these hilarious, international, digital intersex romances. I tell you, you can learn a lot about human nature quarking around in Cyberia! Digital intercourse is the best way to prepare for the juicy, sweaty, warm-flash transaction of "hard reality."

At last, my touchdown in Eastern Metropolis! Am I happy? No way! My bumper sticker reads: I ♣ N.Y.

THE SWITCHING OF THE BODIES; THE RAPID COOLING OF ANDY'S

Within an hour, Couri Hay from Team B knocks on my hotel-room door and murmurs the password. We drive in Couri's limo to the hospital. Our people—nurses, ward physician, attendants, security guards—are in total control of the ward. I wait down the hall with the perfusion team. And the substitute corpse, whom we Andy fans remember from the hoax in Salt Lake City.

At 3:45 A.M. EST we were notified that Andy was experiencing final, agonal respirations. At 3:59 A.M. our man, Dr. Mellon Hitchcock, pronounced Andy legally dead.

The switching of corpses was performed swiftly. We immediately started cardiopulmonary support using a heart-lung resuscitator. We employed an esophageal gastric tube airway to secure Andy's airway against stomach secretions and ventilate him. Andy quickly regained colour and showed good chest expansion. He looked better, in fact, than he had since 1968, the year he was shot by Kynaston McShine, one of the hangers-on at his studio at MOMA.

Andy was then packed in ice and wheeled to the back elevator. We arrived at our mortuary on West 91st Street at approximately

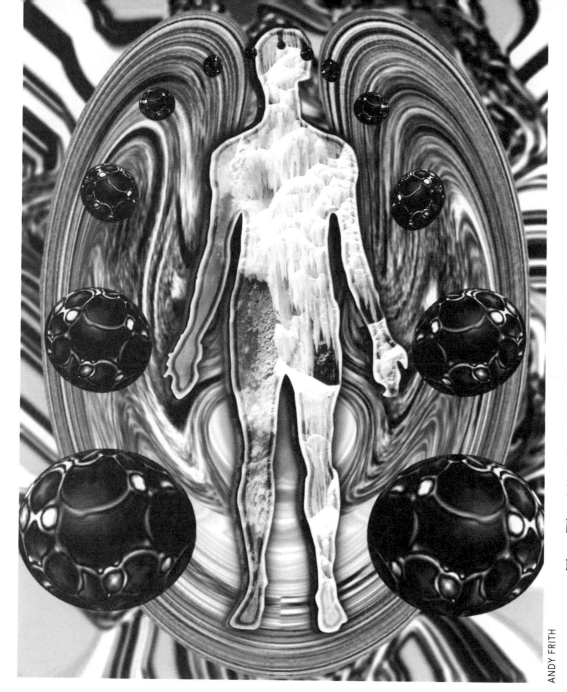

This weird ritual demonstrates that We cannot escape Their mortal coil. The semiotic message is clear. Everything in this mediæval stone castle warns us it is folly for individuals to seek immortality except through faith in one of the three Mediterranean monotheistic mafias.

ANDY FRITH

4:30 A.M. and began administration of transport medications at 4:40 A.M. By 5:25 A.M. Andy was positioned on the mobile advanced life-support system, and surgery was underway to raise his femoral artery. In addition to his continuing good skin color, Andy's arterial blood was bright tomato red (indicating good oxygenation), and he had bright red capillary bleeding into the wound during surgery—all good signs. The coy blandness, pervasive and teasing in its appeal to the media, was gone! The deathless, albino pallor was gone!

I know, I think, how Andy felt at this moment.

Andy often experienced the stigmata of the insane science-fiction artist: alienation, blurred reality, despair. And here he lies, on the hibernation table, no longer looking like the last dandy. Flushing with cool blood, he is no longer the figure of the Artist as Nobody, but the Romantic Stereotype of the Artist—pinkish, involved, grappling with fate and transcendence.

He had already cooled to 29.3°C by the time bypass was started, and he rapidly cooled to a rectal temperature of 9°C over the next forty-five minutes. Imagine that!

A REGAL ICE QUEEN AWAITING THE KISS OF RE-ANIMATION

After supervising this delicate business, I am, understandably, thoroughly descoobied. So I went out to an Eighth Avenue bar, which was noisy with kinky sexual innuendoes. My whole head

They were lined up behind police fences, gaping at celebrities talking and grinning at the wide-eyed cameras celebrating the destruction of Andy's precious tissues. (Or so they hoped!)

revolved around laughter and crying, as my life turns down.

By the time I returned, blood washout and cryoprotective perfusion had progressed nicely. At 8:43 A.M. I approved the decision to discontinue perfusion. Was this fair to Warhol? No, if you are among those who think he had about five remarkable years (1962–67) followed by a long down-slope decline into money-making banality with his silk-screen editions of dogs, famous Jews of the 20th Century, and Mercedes Benzos. Yes, if you think that Andy was the most important American artist since Jackson Pollack. In any case, following the closure of the scalp and chest incisions, Andy was placed inside two heavy plastic bags and submerged in a silicone oil (Silcool) bath that had been precooled to –17°C.

Warhol's life force, uneven as it was, lay in an emotional fiction that contradicted the cold, fixed, iconic surface, lowered at a rate of approximately 1°C per hour to –17°C by gradual addition of dry ice to the artificial (fake?) calm. My sense of Jamais Vue could hardly be blamed on the MOMA curator who selected these icons. A high-capacity pump was used to circulate the oil through a spray-bar assembly positioned over the patient. This technique completely eliminated the "hot spots" and "cold spots" that have plagued other artist's careers.

At 19:42 EST, the dewar was completely filled with nitrogen, and Andy Warhol had entered long-time hybernation! With him was put to rest gloomy images of foreboding and death, like the skulls that plagued the last years of his first, brief life.

That night, at the Gramercy Park Hotel, how I envied Andy's cool tranquillity as the hot fevered hand of sleep sucked me down into the grave-ity of that dark ground.

Andy Warhol is not dead. He hybernates, a regal Ice Queen in cool serendipity.

His new life cycle has begun!

No thanks to medical silence (and given a little bit of luck), Andy will return to paint and paradox again!

THE PUBLIC CELEBRATION OF ANDY'S DESTRUCTION
Dateline: April 1, 1987.

Fifth Avenue in front of Saint Patrick's Cathedral was teeming with spectators and photographers and these last survivors of the human race who live in giant time-warp bubbles that they leave only to go to funerals, cremations, autopsies, and airplane crashes. They were lined up behind police fences, gaping at celebrities talking and grinning at the wide-eyed cameras celebrating the destruction of Andy's precious tissues. (Or so they hoped!)

The large doors of Saint Patrick's Cathedral opened this time portal into the Muddle Ages, high Gothic arches designed to

dwarf the spirit of us individual quarks. Inside, this organist is playing, not Lower Eastside punk rock, not Velvet Underground, but
fucking Bach!

People file in with unhappy expressions. Young men with
rainbow-dyed hair looking uncomfortable in suits and ties. And all
this for a barbaric tissue-destruction ceremony. I can no longer
remain silent when the people I love wind up in squirm holes and
cremation barbecues.

HOMAGE TO THE MAGGOTS. THE DREAD SIGN OF CRUCIFICTION. THE CLOWN OF THORNS.

The orthodox Catholic witchcraft rituals begin predictably.
The dread Sign of the Cross! The ominous kneeling in submission.
Meanwhile, the clerical aliens quietly observing the humans,
unsmiling in black-cloth (!) garments, family and friends sitting in
peaceful twisted apathetic conformity. Don't be fooled by them,
these Catholic–Jewish–Islamaniacs who sit brooding silently in
darkened stone buildings. Behind their frozen faces they are thinking about their loved ones in the grave. Don't be fooled by this fake
Bible–Talmud–Koran piety. Their Holy Books are male-order cata-
logues of death worship. Their minds are busy thinking about the
maggots eating the flesh and brains (souls) of their presumed loved
ones. Or about the cruel oven flames (dials turned to roast!) crackling the skins of their dearly departed. Do you seriously think that
they can repress, just ignore the culinary facts? Not hear the squish-
ing noises of the maggots breeding cheerily in the tissues of their
sincerely departeds? The more honest of these mourners are probably pondering their own fate that awaits them in the fire and worms
departments.

The grisly papist plot crumbles to Gothic horror! To put it
charitably, Andy's funeral in Saint Patrick's Cathedral is not an
immortalist commercial. This weird ritual demonstrates that We
cannot escape Their mortal coil. The semiotic message is clear.
Everything in this mediæval stone castle warns us it is folly for individuals to seek immortality except through faith in one of the three
Mediterranean monotheistic mafias.

WOULD ANDY LET ALIEN PRIESTS SEND HIM PACKING, SOUL AND BONES, TO THE MAGGOT FARM?

Our little, silver-haired pal, the solemn, socially insecure,
East European waif from Pittsburgh got the point. Andy understood
the cold, mechanical impersonality of the industrial culture. Didn't
he just blow into the Big Applesauce factory from Pittsburgh, PA,
and call himself the Pope of Pop? Call his studio the Factory? Send a
reasonable facsimile, silver-wigged model of himself around to give
Warhol lectures at colleges? Enter the Campbell Soup contest? Paint
reasonable facsimiles of soup-can labels and Marilyn Monroes to
win gigantic cash prizes? And admission to correspondence art
schools?

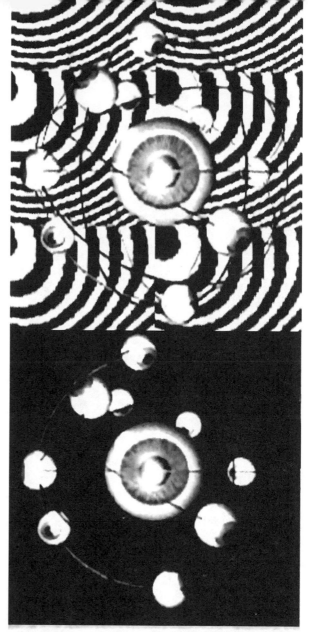

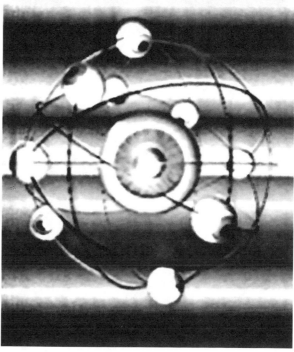

ANDY FRITH

You think this crafty fox would let them pack him, brain and bones, in a factory carton for easy delivery to the maggot farm? Can you possibly think that Andy Warhol would allow this public snuffing of his essence by black-garbed minions of the cardinal? Who, come to think of it, never tended to hang out at the Factory and the office of *Interview* magazine.

ANDY INVITES YOU TO HIS RE-BIRTHDAY PARTY

I understand that members of the Alcor Cryonics Foundation and thoughtful people around the four worlds who know about the hybernation of Walt Disney and Andy Warhol are celebrating and drinking toasts to the brave team who snatched Andy, literally, from the mouths of the maggots.

I also understand that some members of the Alcor Foundation, being of the very sincere, sober, scientific extraction, are concerned that a person of my colourful reputation could undermine Alcor's respectability and credibility. Particularly since disrespectability and incredibility are my predestined career goals in life.

I worry, myself, that since Alcor's important work is the ultimate threat to religious and political control, the last thing needed is to take on the negative public baggage of a notorious jet-set victim of the *National Enquirer* mentality.

Then I remember that to be a member of Alcor is to elect oneself as part of a noble band of heroes who are about to save humanity from the horror of involuntary, irreversible, metabolic coma. And therefore Alcor members are tolerant of my eccentricity, knowing it is a hard job, in this weirdo, death-worshipping culture, to be continually recast in these "Oscar Wilde" sequels.

By the way! Andy asked me to especially invite all of you to his re-animation party.

Andy was very insistent that, at the glorious moment of re-animation, when his friends gather around his hybernation crystal, that you be there. Either in the ice tray or on the hoof. Write the Alcor Foundation if you have any questions about transportation to the party. "PLAN A HEAD" is our motto!

The grey-haired black man warned Andy, as he did me and Bill Burroughs: Stay out of prisons and hospitals, son. Avoid ministers, priests, and rabbis. All they got is the key to the shit house. And promise me, boy, you will never wear the badge of a lawman. And if you do end up serving time in the white man's body factories (complete service from womb to tomb), join a gang of friends that will cover for you. And if you have to be admitted to the disposal room (planned obsolescence is their marketing strategy), just be sure you've got friends hanging around, watching over you day and night, lest someone make off with your beloved albino animal skin. And contents thereof. ◎

By the way!
Andy asked me
to especially
invite all of
you to his
re-animation party.

VIII. MILLENNIUM MADNESS

1. BACKWARD CHRISTIAN SOLDIERS: A BRIEF HISTORY OF THE WARRIOR CASTE IN AMERICA

2. GOD RUNS FOR PRESIDENT ON THE REPUBLICAN TICKET

3. WHO OWNS THE JESUS PROPERTY?

4. HIGH-TECH PAGANISM

VIII.[1].
BACKWARD CHRISTIAN SOLDIERS:
A BRIEF HISTORY OF THE WARRIOR CASTE IN AMERICA

Legionnaires' disease: so called from its first recognized occurrence
during the 1976 American Legion convention: a lobar
pneumonia caused by a bacterium *(Legionella pneumophila).*

squire magazine says war is the secret love of a white man's life. The cover of its November 1984 issue shows a gorgeous young white woman wearing a Marine helmet and torn brown GI T-shirt.

The effect was sexually ambiguous, but steamy!

Great cover lines: "War! It is a sexual turn-on. . . . It is a brutal, deadly game, but the best game there is. It is for men what childbirth is for women. It is like lifting the corner of the universe and looking at what is underneath."

At the halfway point of the Brezhnev–Reagan era, *Esquire's* motto is, "Man at His Best." The title of the cover story: "Why Men Love War." The subhead is lyrical: "The Awesome Beauty, the Haunting Romance, of the Timeless Nightmare." The piece was written by William Broyles, Jr., a white Protestant ex-Marine from Texas, who made a good living in the 1980s refighting the Vietnam War in magazines and glorifying the enduring addiction of the American warrior caste and its sponsor, the Republican party, to killing coloured people with high-technology weapons.

The *Esquire* piece appeared just when Reagan was lobbying to bully our Latin neighbours—once again. It's a recurrence of that old Caribbean fever, a paroxysmal virus that plagues the White House. Apparently the Oval Office can't be disinfected. President after president keeps coming down with the Latin-basher Legionnaires' disease.

When Ronald Reagan was elected president in 1980, everyone knew he was itching and feverish to send American troops into action. Somewhere. He just had to stand tall and bully some third-world country to regain the American manhood that General William Westmoreland and Rambo say we lost in Vietnam.

But where to conduct a nice, little, easy to win, ego-massaging war?

The Russkis? Too mean.

Asians? The slopes proved too tough for MacArthur in Korea and for Westmoreland in 'Nam.

The Middle East? Much too volatile. Ronnie blustered a bit in Lebanon, but pulled out quickly after frivolously, whimsically wasting the lives of hundreds of U.S. military personnel.

Oh well, back to the old, familiar playground for the Republican party and the warrior caste. Let's snuff some Latins for God and manhood.

Cuba? Too risky.

Grenada was fun for a warm-up, but short and limited and easy.

> . . . Reagan was lobbying to bully our Latin neighbours— once again. It's a recurrence of that old Caribbean fever, a paroxysmal virus that plagues the White House. Apparently the Oval Office can't be disinfected. President after president keeps coming down with the Latin-basher Legionnaires' disease.

CAROLYN FERRIS

Hmmm . . . Well, there's always good old Nicaragua. Since the 1890s, the American military has occupied or controlled this least-populated nation in Central America. And for almost a century, guerrilla forces there have opposed American intervention. In 1933, we pulled out our occupation troops and set up a puppet dictatorship run by the Somoza family. The younger Somozas were protégés of the American warrior caste. Anastasio Somoza Debayle, for example, graduated from the U.S. Military Academy, returned home, and, at age 21, took command of the National Guard. Because of the brutality of this regime, all democratic elements of the Latin World despised America. In 1979, the Sandinistas overthrew the Somozas, to the dismay of the West Point Academy classmates of Somoza.

> Lincoln, as would Lenin sixty years later, created a centralized, industrial, militaristic, expansionist government. Just as the Communist party has managed the USSR since 1921, so has the Republican party, USA, controlled the police, the military, the banks, the manufacturing plants, the organs of information.

IT STARTED WITH THE SPANISH CONQUISTADORES

The first Europeans to subdue Cuban, Nicaraguan, and South American natives for Christ and Plunder were the Spanish. In 1493, Christopher (Christ–Carrier) Columbus returned to the Newe World with a disorderly rabble of male buccaneer thugs seeking gold. It was hard going. No quick payoff. So, to man his third expedition in 1498, Columbus was forced to impress hooligans, convicts, rapists, and thieves. An ominous precedent for Ollie North.

The next centuries of Spanish intervention were not designed to raise the morale of Caribbean natives, who were immediately looted, raped, baptized, and reduced to serfdom by hoodlums representing Crown and Church. The Spanish settlements were rigidly controlled by Madrid. The colonists were the scum of Europe—soldiers, priests, and plunderers. Black Africans were kidnapped to work as slaves.

Few Spanish women were involved in the first expeditions; so there was much forcible interbreeding with Indian and African slave women. This ancient custom produced the rich mestizo races, which now people these fertile lands. On the up side, Latin America was at least spared the shameful genocidal policies that characterized the North American colonization. Better to use the Catholic plan, to rape 'em and enslave 'em, than use the Cromwell–Protestant–Puritan tactic of spermless genocide.

When the South American countries gained independence from Spain, the feudal-military-Catholic traditions remained. Thus was created the unstable, volatile, romantic cultural environment that has left Latin America masochistically vulnerable to enduring and relentless Protestant, Yankee adventuring.

THE REPUBLICAN PARTY AND THE WARRIOR CASTE LOVE WAR

Esquire's ex-Lieutenant Broyles tells us that he and his Marine Corps buddies adored Vietnam because war "offers a sanction to play boys' games."

- ... Because "war replaces the difficult grey areas of daily life with an eerie, serene clarity."

- ... Because "war is the best game there is."

- ... Because "no sport I had ever played brought me to such deep awareness of my physical and emotional limits."

- ... Because the "love of war stems from the union, deep in the core of our being, between sex and destruction, beauty and horror, love and death."

- ... Because some youths "who never suspected the presence of such an impulse in themselves have learned in military life the mad excitement of destroying."

- ... Because war is funny. "After one ambush my men [sic] brought back the body of a North Vietnam soldier. I later found the dead man propped against some C–ration boxes. He had on sunglasses, and a *Playboy* magazine lay open in his lap; a cigarette dangled jauntily from his mouth; and on his head was perched a large and perfectly formed piece of shit. I pretended to be outraged, since desecrating bodies was frowned on as un-American and counterproductive. But it wasn't outrage I felt. I kept my officer's face on, but inside I was . . . laughing."

Believe me, ex-Lieutenant Broyles, the people who founded our country—thoughtful men such as Thomas Jefferson and Ben Franklin—would not have considered this funny. Nor would three billion non-Caucasians with whom we share the planet. Including Yours Truly.

HOW AN INDIAN CHIEFTAIN'S HEAD ENDED UP ON A POLE IN MASSACHUSETTS

In the early 17th Century, New England was controlled by a wise and benevolent leader. His friends called him Massasoit. In 1620, the first wave of immigrants from Europe started arriving in the lands of Massasoit. The original Plymouth colony was dominated by a Moral Minority, a small sect of fanatic fundamentalist Cromwellian Protestants. These Puritans were regenerate (born-again) Christians who held a strict Calvinist belief in "the Elect versus the Damned," and who publicly confessed their conversion experiences. These militant, fanatic Protestants doggedly believed that human nature was inherently sinful and evil.

Over the decades the actions of the Republican party (exactly like the Nazi party in Germany and the Communist party in Russia) can be understood only if we recall that they were bred to the terrible notion of being the Elect of God. Ronald Reagan deeply believes that there can be no mercy for nonbelievers. Those who are not "one of us" deserve no pity. Remember how Ronnie called the Democrats "immoral" when they didn't vote for his military budget? Recall how he gave bloodcurdling sermons about the need to destroy Godless communism? That's not election rhetoric. The guy believes it. He really feels that he and his military friends are agents of the totalitarian God. Brezhnev and his friends believed that they were agents of their own weird totalitarian prophet, Karl Marx.

Believe me, ex-Lieutenant Broyles, the people who founded our country— thoughtful men such as Thomas Jefferson and Ben Franklin—would not have considered this funny. Nor would three billion non-Caucasians with whom we share the planet. Including Yours Truly.

When the Puritans showed up in Plymouth, they considered it their right and religious duty to plunder the land of the heathen Pequot Indians. Poor King Massasoit wasn't ready for a Jesse Helms approach. In all good faith he had signed a peace treaty in 1621, to which he and his son, King Philip, faithfully adhered for many years in spite of continued land-grabbing by the white settlers.

In 1675, a typical colonial-liberation war broke out. King Philip's forces successfully avoided pitched battles and kept the conflict going until the European invaders, using "search and destroy" methods, and with the help of local contras, overthrew the native government. Philip, betrayed by a Christian convert, was drawn and quartered, and his head stuck on a pole in front of the church in Plymouth. This was known as the final solution.

It was all right, you understand, because these heathens were already damned. In the 365 years since the Pilgrims landed at Plymouth Rock, the holy-war faction of the white, spiritual fathers of the Republican party has kept up a continual series of expansionist crusades against people with darker skins.

Indeed, for the born-again militants, it has become a tradition, a rite of passage, a religious ritual. This is not just my opinion; Mr. Broyles agrees.

A RELIGIOUS KICK

In *Esquire*, William Broyles tells us that war provides æsthetic and religious ecstasies. He recounts the case of a "sensitive" Marine officer who watched enemy bodies being disposed of "like so much garbage" with a "look of creative contentment on his face that I had not seen except in charismatic churches. It was the look of a person transported into ecstasy."

"War is beautiful," Broyles gushes. "There is something about a fire fight at night . . . brilliant patterns that seem, given their great speeds, oddly timeless, as if they had been etched in the night." Here Broyles soars into elegant gourmet connoisseurship. "Many men loved napalm . . . I preferred white phosphorous."

Intoxicated by this toot of white phosphorous, ex-Lieutenant Broyles invokes his white Calvinist divinity. "And then perhaps the gunships called Spooky come in and fire their incredible guns like huge hoses washing down from the sky, like something God would do when He was really ticked off."

Here we have the official Republican-warrior-caste version of the Christian God: a vengeful colonial deity casually wasting third-world peasants who irritate Him.

THE ELECT AND THE DAMNED

The Republican party is the warrior caste. The Republican party, white and very Protestant, has always represented the militarist tradition in America.

The Democratic party, by and large, represents the anti-warrior constituency. During this century Democrats have been the party of progressives, Catholics, passivists, scientists, gays, intellectuals, ecologists, agnostics, Jews, blacks, Latins—minority groups that have always been barred from the highest ranks of the military.

In the 1985 budget fight, it was the Republicans who wanted to cut social-educational programs and the Democrats who wanted to trim the military funds.

The warrior caste in America—the generals, the admirals, the cops—is overwhelmingly Republican. This is ominous. George Marshall, the only famous Democratic general of this century, is most renowned for his plans to wage peace.

This linkage of the GOP and the warrior caste is not new. From the Civil War through Eisenhower, seven out of twelve Republican presidents have been ex-generals or glamourous warriors.

I'm a total, all-out 101 percent patriot, Jack. I yield to no one in my contempt for socialism, communism, or any enemy of freedom. I also believe in a strong, intelligent, effective military to defend our beloved land.

That's exactly why I oppose the Christian fanatics and the war wing of the Republican party.

That's why I write about the con job that they have pulled off for the past hundred years.

This tradition of the warrior president goes back to the beginning. George Washington, the Father of our Country, won his first fame in the Indian Wars.

It is important to note that the other "Father of Our Country," Thomas Jefferson, the spiritual founder of the Democratic party, was an antimilitarist. It was Jefferson who framed the philosophic and legal documents that led to the Revolution and who wrote the Declaration of Independence. Their Constitution was exquisitely designed to protect states' rights and individual rights against a centralized federal authority.

A JEFFERSONIAN PRESIDENT MAKES A SENSIBLE PROPOSAL TO AVOID WAR WITH EUROPE

President James Monroe, a disciple of Jefferson, is known for the treaties and diplomatic accords with England, France, and Spain that managed to expand American interests without war. The Monroe Doctrine is his most famous achievement. There were two important and interdependent clauses in this manifesto. The first was a formal restatement of the Washingtonian America–first neutrality. Beware of foreign entanglements! America promised not to intervene in European and (implicitly) Asian politics. In return, America declared the Newe World off limits for European intervention.

> It is important to note that the other "Father of Our Country," Thomas Jefferson, the spiritual founder of the Democratic party, was an antimilitarist. It was Jefferson who framed the philosophic and legal documents that led to the Revolution and who wrote the Declaration of Independence. Their Constitution was exquisitely designed to protect states' rights and individual rights against a centralized federal authority.

Modern American presidents such as Kennedy and Reagan are on solid historical and common-sense ground when they object to Russian meddling in Cuba and Central America. We all want to ban Soviet weapons from the Newe World. But Reagan is in direct violation of the Monroe Doctrine when he turns around and meddles in conflicts of the Olde World. Arms to Pakistan and Turkey. More than two hundred thousand U.S. troops in Germany. Forty thousand in Korea. Marines landing in Lebanon to protect our oil interests.

THE FILIBUSTER PRESIDENT

Filibuster: . . . An adventurer who engages in a private military action in a foreign country . . . (originally freebooter . . . from Dutch *vrijbuiter*, pirate, "one who plunders freely").

The classic device of using a foreign adventure (the filibuster) as a stepping-stone to the presidency was invented by Andrew Jackson. In 1818, Jackson, then a major general, was sent off to Florida to campaign against the Seminole Indians. These natives, employing standard liberation tactics, fled across the border to Spanish Florida. Disregarding his orders and violating international laws, Jackson invaded Spanish territory and wasted various natives. He also executed two British subjects. Jackson's own private war created an interna-

tional crisis. Responsible American officials denounced the action, but Jackson's illegal wog-bashing won support from populists, expansionists, ultranationalists, imperialists, and Calvinist Protestants looking for a crusade against the heathen.

Jackson rode a wave of personal popularity that almost won him the presidency in 1824. In 1828, he swept into office, and for two terms was able to use his populist Western support to protect Eastern financial interests. Sound familiar, Ronnie?

IS IT A CONDITION OF MANHOOD TO LOVE WAR?

In his *Esquire* piece, which passionately glorifies the mechanized mass murder of Orientals, ex-Marine William Broyles, Jr., is less than scientific. He writes, "Most men who have been to war would have to admit, if they are honest, that somewhere inside themselves they loved it . . . loved it as much as anything that happened to them before or since."

But wait a minute. Isn't ex-Lieutenant Broyles describing a well-known altered state of consciousness that can be and usually is attained by many other less-violent means?

The scientific situation seems to be something like this. There are circuits in the human brain that when activated produce heightened states of awareness. Among these are certain neural tracts, mainly centered in the midbrain, which mediate convulsive survival behavior. These ancient primitive circuits are involved in height, flight, territorial defense, and male dominance. When a guy engages in violence, he falls into a trancelike state that produces an incredible adrenaline rush. Some call this the mad-dog reflex, or going berserk.

This sympathetic-nervous-system hit is necessary for our survival repertoire. It's like the endorphin-opiate rush that protects us from pain. Useful for desperate survival, but dangerously addictive.

At this point we must remind ex-Lieutenant Broyles that the destructive paroxysmal state (DPS), which he glamourizes and politicizes, is not restricted to war.

We have all felt on occasions this seductive invitation to "flip out" in wild destructiveness. You don't have to ship eight million young Americans eight thousand miles across the Pacific to waste a small Asian country. Just go downtown, Broyles, and catch a barroom brawl in a Burt Reynolds–Clint Eastwood movie. Tune into a prime-time television show like *The A–Team.*

Alcohol trips off the DPS. Drop into any redneck saloon in Texas, Broyles. Visit a clinic for battered wives, ex-Lieutenant Broyles, and you'll get a glimpse of your favorite "corner of the universe." Put on some black leather and join a bikers' club. Bullies love to express their manhood by riding in male-bonded packs. Join the Mexican Mafia, an inner-city gang. Cops and Bloods in the ghetto feel it. The Waffen SS felt it. It's called "warrior love."

FROM THE HALLS OF MONTEZUMA TO THE SHORES OF TRIPOLI

The Mexican War (1846–48) is another good example of the fun-fame-fortune rewards of Latin-bashing. After this conflict Mexico conceded two-fifths of its land to America. Are you listening, Adolf?

There are circuits in the human brain that when activated produce heightened states of awareness. Among these are certain neural tracts, mainly centered in the midbrain, which mediate convulsive survival behavior. These ancient primitive circuits are involved in height, flight, territorial defense, and male dominance. When a guy engages in violence, he falls into a trancelike state that produces an incredible adrenaline rush. Some call this the mad-dog reflex, or going berserk.

The Mexican War was a bonanza for the warrior caste and for ambitious Republican politicians. Take Zachary Taylor. For starters, Zach earned his general's stars by snuffing Sac, Fox, and Seminole Indians, for which he won the label "Old Rough and Ready." His Mexican War triumphs assured him the presidency at the age of 65.

General Winfield Scott had good wog-busting credentials. He fought the Creeks and the Seminoles and supervised the removal of the Cherokee to the Southwest. Scott won the battle of Mexico City and proceeded to defy the U.S. envoy during the peace negotiations, causing considerable embarrassment in Washington. Agents of God shouldn't have to obey diplomatic rules; Reagan and Ollie North understand that. So did Adolf and Brezhnev!

THE RECENT REHABILITATION OF THE FREEBOOTER ETHIC

How, we wonder, can a presumably respectable journalist like William Broyles, Jr., get away with a cover story in *Esquire* celebrating the wanton, lustful Nazi–Stalinist–Marxist Pol–Pot slaying of millions of Asians in the name of self-fulfillment? Well, it turns out that Broyles, for self-esteem and profit, was shrewdly surfing the wave of neomilitarism generated by the Reagan regime.

During the humanist "give peace a chance" antiwar movement of the 1960s, and the human-rights moments of the Carter period, the Puritan-killer ethic got pushed around a bit, but it never disappeared. The Schwarzenegger–Stallone hero figures were still packing them into the theatres. The Reagan administration brilliantly rehabilitated militarism. Ronald was a film star. He knew how to put the adventurist hero back in the saddle! Wog-bashing was back in style. It was the triumphant return of the Wild West, John Wayne–Ollie North pirate who scornfully ignores the legalities of effete politicians and takes the law into his own hands.

Lieutenant Calley, you're forgiven. The heroes of My Lai are marching down Fifth Avenue in a ticker-tape parade. Crank up Ollie North.

This Christian-soldier stuff is not limited to the redneck South and Southwest. It plays well all around white, Calvinist America. The American Legion, the National Rifle Association, the Hell's Angels, the Marine Corps Association, the survivalists, the G. Gordon Liddy crowd, and *Soldier of Fortune* readers are visible tips of a profoundly deep, white American need to get kicks from wasting coloured people.

A STRANGE LITTLE EPISODE IN NICARAGUA

William Walker (1824–60) merits a footnote in history as a classic case of an Ollie North American warrior compulsively involved in private, illegal plundering raids of Caribbean countries. In 1853, Walker led a group of frontier hoodlums in quest of Latin American plunder. First these white, American thugs tried Sonora, Mexico. The freebooting mission failed miserably. Walker was arrested for violation of neutrality laws. An understanding frontier American jury acquitted him. He was apparently a charismatic, John Wayne kind of thug. A good communicator, you might say. And after all, it was only Mexicans he had wasted.

In 1855, Walker joined a group of contra terrorist revolutionaries in Nicaragua. After overthrowing the government, Walker obtained recognition from the U.S. State Department and set himself up as dictator of Nicaragua. But the real power in Nicaragua those days was American tycoon Cornelius Vanderbilt, whose Accessory Transit Company monopolized

This Christian-soldier stuff is not limited to the redneck South and Southwest. It plays well all around white, Calvinist America. The American Legion, the National Rifle Association, the Hell's Angels, the Marine Corps Association, the survivalists, the G. Gordon Liddy crowd, and <u>Soldier of Fortune</u> readers are visible tips of a profoundly deep, white American need to get kicks from wasting coloured people.

Onward Christian Soldiers! It's another crusade against Satan. It's jihad time. 💣 Blow it all up for Allah! Kill for Qaddafi! 🔫 Praise the Lord and pass the ammunition! Hand me that red phone, boy. Howdy there, God. Time to drop the Big One on the Godless heathens like the Good Book says! 👆

trade in that inviting land. When Walker's operation became competitive, Vanderbilt ran him out.

But Walker still suffered from that old Caribbean Freebooter Legionnaires' disease, as recurrent as malaria. In 1860, based now in Honduras, he led still another pirate attempt to take over Central America. It failed, and Latin-basher William Walker was finally done in by a Honduran government firing squad, leaving behind a book that has some relevance today. It's called *War in Nicaragua!*

THE COMMUNIST PARTY TAKES OVER AMERICA

The American Civil War (1861–65), one of the bloodiest conflicts in history, was provoked when a manic-depressive, psychotic, Christian bully strongman, Abraham Lincoln, used federal troops to ruthlessly suppress the independence of the southern states and force them unwillingly into the American Union. Before this "Brezhnev maneuver," the United States of America was a loose confederation of small sovereign, agricultural states. Lincoln, as would Lenin sixty years later, created a centralized, industrial, militaristic, expansionist government. Just as the Communist party has managed the USSR since 1921, so has the Republican party, USA, controlled the police, the military, the banks, the manufacturing plants, the organs of information.

This change from small, feudal, independent-interdependent agricultural states to a highly organized, mechanistic, imperialistic, monolithic, state-centered society is an inevitable stage in human evolution. Let us not dæmonize Abraham Lincoln. The time had come for the industrialization stage. In the eighty years after Lincoln and the "party" seized control of America, other smokestack countries—Japan, Germany, Italy, Russia—set up similar centralized military-industrial systems controlled by a "party."

After the Civil War the party leadership in the American Union automatically went to military men. U. S. Grant was succeeded by Major General Rutherford B. Hayes. Then Major General James Garfield, a lay preacher in the Disciples of Christ, was succeeded by Quartermaster General Chester A. Arthur. President Benjamin Harrison was a brigadier general. All, of course, were party members.

It was during this stage of industrial-military growth that the glorification of the warrior caste hit its peak. Statues were raised in the center of every town and city: a general (and party leader) on a bronze horse, riding off to war. With the Cross of Jesus going on before!

THE RELIGIOUS ISSUE JUST WON'T QUIT

Now comes *Esquire* magazine, publishing an inflammatory moral justification of warfare at a spooky moment in history when nuclear conflagration threatens and when the religious right wing in this country and in several Islamic theocracies speaks approvingly of Holy Wars, Evil Empires, and Armageddons. Onward Christian Soldiers! It's another crusade against Satan. It's jihad time. Blow it all up for Allah! Kill for Qaddafi! Praise the Lord and pass the ammunition! Hand me that red phone, boy. Howdy there, God. Time to drop the Big One on the Godless heathens like the Good Book says!

Reflect for a moment on the quotes from the Broyles article. Glazed-eye babble about brotherly love among the napalm, and God as the gunner in a helicopter gunship, and blissed-out looks on the faces of charismatic Protestants, and the psychotic Marine assassin with "Just You and Me, Lord" tattooed on his shoulder.

My wife is worried about this article.

She thinks that I've gone too far. She fears that this exposé of the warrior caste is going

to sound unpatriotic. "America is a young country without traditions," she explains.

"We need heroes and a glorious history."

CARIBBEAN FEVER STRIKES AGAIN

The war for Southern independence ended in 1865. Between 1869 and 1878, more than two hundred pitched battles were fought against a newly invented enemy: the Plains Indians. The Massacre of Wounded Knee was the final solution for this overpopulation problem. More than two hundred unarmed men, women, and children were killed. "The soldiers later claimed that it was difficult to distinguish the Sioux women from the men," a complaint to be heard again in later wars against coloured people.

By 1898, the expansionists and war lovers and heretic-bashers had simply run out of poor neighbours to invade. A new generation of young men hungered for the "awesome beauty, the haunting romance, the timeless nightmare" of a colonial war. Well, how about a little rumble in Cuba?

It so happened that there were heavy American investments to protect on the island. The military, with its eye on Panama and Nicaragua for a canal, stressed the strategic position of the island. It was easy for the press to whip up support for the contras fighting against Spain.

Cuba was a media war. William Randolph Hearst broadcast fake propaganda. There was a Gulf of Tonkin–Korean Air Lines Flight 007 faked incident involving the American battleship USS Maine.

The war itself was a pushover. The Spanish put up token resistance. The biggest winner was a wealthy politician named Teddy Roosevelt, who organized his own semiprivate regiment (Western cowboys and "adventurous blue bloods from Eastern universities") and whose routine exploits were highly publicized. Quick results: Within three years Roosevelt—a swashbuckling, militaristic, Reagan-type—was in the White House. Roosevelt's regime was continually involved in Latin-bashing, dollar diplomacy, Venezuela, and the Philippines. He infuriated all of Latin America by placing, in the Dominican Republic, U.S. customs officers who stole revenues for the benefit of American business. He backed a group of contras who hijacked Panama from Colombia. Just eight years ago, when Jimmy Carter returned the canal to Panama, the Republicans screamed, "Treason! We stole that canal fair and square!"

Teddy Roosevelt's jingoistic imperialism made him the scourge of Democrats, progressives, and Jeffersonian Americans. And in 1906, Teddy, the ultimate war freak and ultra-imperialist, won the Nobel Peace Prize. Shades of Henry Kissinger!

A BUSY TIME FOR THE WARRIOR CASTE

During the 20th Century, every generation of young Americans has been offered a foreign expeditionary war. World War I against the Huns. World War II against the Nazis and Japanese. To prop up the unspeakably fascist regime of South Korea, our generals sacrificed more than fifty thousand American lives. General Douglas MacArthur, the ultimate freeboot-

er, started to wage his own little psychotic war against a billion "slant-eyed" Chinese until he was forcibly removed by President Truman. "Dugout" Doug returned as a hero and announced his candidacy for the presidency. On the Republican ticket, of course.

Then came Vietnam. And Cambodia.

More explosives were dropped on Vietnam than during all of our two hundred years of warfare. Not to mention a small sea of Agent Orange, which has left much of that unfortunate land blighted for years to come. We have listened recently to a deafening chorus of aggrieved-victim complaints from Vietnam vets who feel unrewarded; we hear very little about the punishing casualties we inflicted upon the peoples of Vietnam and Cambodia. We won the Body Count War! We wasted 'em—soldiers, civilians, women, and children.

Esquire is off to a good start. Let's encourage these psycho vets to tell their stories about the fun of body desecration, and the "perfectly formed piece of shit" on the non-Caucasian's head, and "the mad excitement of destroying." And about how impossible it is to talk about it unless you were there. It's good Freudian catharsis. And let's build them a monument where they can weep, not for Vietnam and Cambodia wasted, not for America rent by conflict, not for Jeffersonian ideals lost, but in pity for themselves.

But the ticker-tape parade led by General Westmoreland isn't enough. Even cover stories in national magazines can't heal the scar of ex-Lieutenant Broyles. Even a full-page picture of him in natty suit and tie, looking very serious-grim like a young Dallas stockbroker, standing in front of a war memorial with his blonde kid (a boy, of course) in his arms, holding (no shit) the American flag in front of an enormous bronze statue of three real young, clean-cut, good-looking white soldiers—Texas A&M types—raising still another American flag over Iwo Jima, Managua, or even Havana?

PATRIOTISM AND THE CHRISTIAN SOLDIERS

My wife is worried about this article.

She thinks that I've gone too far. She fears that this exposé of the warrior caste is going to sound unpatriotic. "America is a young country without traditions," she explains. "We need heroes and a glorious history."

Her warning is well taken; so let me explain. I'm a total, all-out 101 percent patriot, Jack. I yield to no one in my contempt for socialism, communism, or any enemy of freedom. I also believe in a strong, intelligent, effective military to defend our beloved land.

That's exactly why I oppose the Christian fanatics and the war wing of the Republican party. That's why I write about the con job that they have pulled off for the past

> common sense, optimism, and good-natured skepticism of bureaucracy and authority. People who believe in fair play and who dislike armed bullies running around in uniforms.

hundred years.

As I review American history, I see a large glorious company of heroic men and women who represent our red-white-and-blue ideals of initiative, intelligence, tolerance, humour, compassion, common sense, optimism, and good-natured skepticism of bureaucracy and authority. People who believe in fair play and who dislike armed bullies running around in uniforms.

Let's list a few examples of true American heroes—gentle William Penn, founder of Philadelphia, city of brotherly love; Henry David Thoreau, the Concord libertarian; Edgar Allan Poe, a West Pointer who became a literary star; inventors such as Eli Whitney, Robert Fulton, and Thomas Edison; Ralph Waldo Emerson, philosopher of self-reliance; Walt Whitman and Mark Twain.

Let's recall the long line of blacks who have provided us models of noble humanity, creatively waging peace, not war—George Washington Carver, Ralph Bunche, and Dr. Martin Luther King, Jr., among others.

THE CIVILIZED AMERICAN HERO

What, indeed, is any thoughtful American going to feel when exposed to this American Legion, born-again fake patriotism?

Most of us—Catholics, Jews, Latins, women, and men—are descendants of those who came to the United States of America to escape militarism and to create a better social order. Basically, most of us don't want to stir up foreign adventures and turn our country into a Christian empire. We've got enough real problems here at home—the complicated transition from an industrialized economy; the agonizing racial tensions; the collapse of our education system. There is a need for heroes, not to lead religious crusades, but to apply goodwill, tolerance, and intelligence to make the American Dream come true.

So let's issue some patriotic American commands to ex-Lieutenant Broyles and his comrades.

ABOUT FACE! ORDER ARMS! AT EASE!

Hear this, lads: We have called off the Christian crusade. You don't have to bully others to prove your manhood! ☺

So let's issue some patriotic

American commands to

ex-Lieutenant Broyles

and his comrades.

ABOUT FACE! ORDER ARMS!

AT EASE!

Hear this, lads: We have

called off the Christian

crusade. You don't have

to bully others to prove

your manhood!

Brace yourselves, folks. The Roaring 20th Century is boiling up to a Chaos Climax.

In the next few years Millennium Madness is gonna inundate this planet!

VIII.2. GOD RUNS FOR PRESIDENT ON THE REPUBLICAN TICKET

Check out the history books and read about the years 987 to 1000. In those days a lot of fruit loops were running around stirring up trouble. Exactly one thousand years ago Grand Prince Vladimir of Russia started a religious Cold War by joining the Eastern Orthodox Catholic Church. The Persians and Arabs and Christians were waging a Holy War. People were scared and confused back then—just as they are today.

And in the next few years, I believe we will see similar irrational kookiness, messianic megalomanias, mass insanities, apocalyptic paranoias, end-of-world prophecies; demented demagogues, Holy Wars, crazy crusades, lunatic leaders, disharmonic divergences, and thousands of just plain old four-square evangelical bad trips. Ollie North, Jim Bakker, Muammar Qaddafi, Shirley MacLaine, the Ayatollah Khomeini, Oral Roberts, and, yes, Pat Robertson—they're just warm-ups for the eccentricities and terror-activated manias to come.

No question about it, most of the violence and angry politics that are apparent these days pit one biblical God against another. The Cold War has taken a back seat. It's as if America and Russia have become mere pawns on God's chessboard. It's the Roaring 9th Century all over again! Feudal Super Bowl crusader time! My God versus your Great Satan! Israel versus Rome versus Byzantium. Shi'ites versus Sunnis. Hindus versus Buddhists. Hindus versus Sikhs. Bosnia, Croatia, Serbia. Jehovah versus Allah for the world championship.

And now, with the emergence of the militant evangelicals and the candidacy of Reverend Pat Robertson, the angry, jealous, fundamentalist God has thrown his bellicose hat into the American political ring.

I have studied the skillfully written press releases of the Christian Broadcasting Network, a monstrously successful media empire that had a take of $182 million in 1987. I have pored over stacks of lavishly adulatory columns on Robertson from small-town newspapers and unashamedly adoring articles in mainline publications. I was stunned, for example, to read this *Chicago Tribune*

headline: **The $70 Million Miracle Named CBN.** It was subtitled: *"With the Lord's Grace, Pat Robertson Builds a Cable Empire."*

Huh? A presumably rational, mainstream newspaper invokes the Deity in its discussion of a political candidate? What is Chicago coming to?

Robertson's platform is not surprising. It's your standard right-wing, strident, millenarian kook show. Predestination, here we come. The familiar Jimmy Swaggart, Oral Roberts, Pat Buchanan, Ronnie Reagan platform. An appeal to the chosen people. An expectation of the imminent and miraculous intervention of God or his messianic prophet. A belief in the total transformation to the perfect kingdom. An eternal struggle against the Evil Empire.

Fiercely ascetic white-bread puritanism. Anti-abortion, anti-gay witch-hunting. Pro-school prayer, pro-creationist "science." What most astonishes and disturbs, however, is the shamanic power of Robertson's evangelical television show. The "700 Club" is designed to produce an altered state of consciousness, a classic voodoo hypnotic trance.

To begin with, the show's production is that of state-of-the-art prime-time television, using the same slick, commercial techniques that seduce us into buying Coors beer and Extra-Strength Tylenol. The actors who appear on the show look like local news anchors. Dignified Ben Kinchlow with his white trimmed mustache looks like a Supreme Court justice. The lovely assistant, Danuta Soderman, looks like a model for some sensible home product such as Drano or Roach Motel.

The program builds efficiently toward its climax, namely the invocation of the Deity. Buckle your seat belts, trippers, while Shaman Pat leans over, his eyes clenched in painful concentration. Hey, the guy's possessed! When the audience is whipped into a classic trance state and is neurologically vulnerable, Robertson starts to imprint the commercials. He dials up the sponsor and starts to discuss God's agenda—namely His impatience with what's happening on the planet. Both Robertson and the Almighty Lord are "sick and tired" (the candidate's favorite buzz phrase) of God's country being taken over by sinners, homosexuals, Democrats, secular humanists, atheistic scientists, communist dupes, pornographers, and, above all, the anti-Christ Iranians.

Meanwhile, the older pious-looking chap next to Robertson—the guy wearing the Episcopal clerical collar—is softly singing, beseeching, "Jesus! Jesus!" It's a gentle, soothing, imploring chorus behind Shaman Pat.

Eventually Robertson begins to beg the Lord to strengthen and arm his people to deal with his enemies. The "Jesus! Jesus!" chorus increases in volume and tempo. Soon the two of them have worked up a voodoo rhythm. The cameras zoom in for close-ups of the audience, their faces twisted with awe and righteous self-pity. Soon the folks are holding hands, softly chanting and sighing the name of Jesus.

Hey, I've participated in as many trance experiences as anyone. I've tripped out to voodoo rites in Haiti. I've been mesmerized by Gnaoua drummers in Tangier. I've attended Navaho peyote ceremonies, Ken Kesey's acid tests, ganja funeral rituals along the Ganges, sacred mushroom chants in Oaxaca, Pan rites in the Rif mountains of Morocco. I've seen folks holding hands, softly chanting and sighing the name of Jerry Garcia. I've even participated in sunrise davening prayers with Hassidic rabbis.

So swear me in, bailiff, and I'll testify as an expert witness that the born-again rituals of our homegrown southern Pentecostals are authentic head trips, and that preachers such as Pat Robertson are performing the classic shamanic role of brainwashing.

The problem I have with these Bible Belt altered-statesmen has to do with their motive and cultural framework. When the power of the shamanic tripping is hooked to a confrontational, monotheistic religious dogma, you've got the potential for major mind games. Reverend Pat taps into the old "One God," Middle Eastern Numero Uno, who is congenitally jealous, possessive, and given to vengeful genocide if and when His monopoly is challenged. ("And the Lord was sorry that He had made man on the Earth, and it grieved Him to His heart," reads Genesis: 6. "So the Lord said, 'I will blot out man whom I have created from the face of the ground, man and beast and creeping things and birds of the air, for I am sorry that I have made them'.")

As I watch Robertson incite hatred of nonbelievers, I am reminded of those familiar television news scenes in which mobs in the streets of Tehran lash themselves with chains into frenzies of sorrowful rage against the Great Satan. Discounting superficial cultural differences, there do seem to be striking similarities between Robertson and the Ayatollah. They're both media shamans—electronic wizards who are able to use television to convey magnetizing charisma. And they both head highly efficient political organizations.

Come to think of it, Robertson and the Ayatollah are mirror images of each other. Their beliefs stem from the same monothe-

... our middle-aged leaders simply don't understand altered states of mind. They're neurological innocents. They never had to talk down a tripping college roommate. They're totally unequipped to handle cabinet-level kooks and White House zealots who use slick television advertising techniques to rave about their biblical revelations and millennium dreams.

ism. And when they look at each other, guess what they see: the Great Satan.

For instance:

1. They both present themselves as agents of God. Those who oppose them are, by definition, evil. They aim to create a theocratic state.

2. They both whip up hatred of nonbelievers—a condition that leads to holy-war crankiness. Their approach is divisive and confrontational.

3. As God's agents, they can allow no compromise with Satan. This leads to a profound impracticality. They can't be bothered with such prosaic human concerns as life, liberty, and the pursuit of happiness. They're engaged in an all-out Holy War against evil.

4. Their opponents are treated without tolerance or mercy. Robertson, for example, publicly wished for the deaths of Supreme Court justices Marshall, Brennan, and Stevens. (Scientific duty compels me to admit that all three justices were hospitalized within weeks after Robertson's curse. In fairness to the Ayatollah, I must also note that every American move against Iran has mysteriously backfired.)

5. They're both full of biblical sternness for unrepentant sinners. They're for the death penalty, punitive police action, a big military, and an aggressive foreign policy. They don't blink at nuclear weapons.

6. They believe that women should be subservient to men.

7. Both exhibit obsessive prudishness and a hatred of modern lifestyles; they believe in the censorship of books,

drama, music, movies.

8. They're committed to an apocalyptic vision. Both of them yearn for the end of the world, when God will reward His faithful.

9. They distrust science, Western culture, and secular education.

10. They appeal to the dissatisfied who feel that they've been left out of the secular mainstream. The American fundamentalists have been scorned by the mainline Protestant sects and ridiculed by such intellectuals as Sinclair Lewis, H. L. Mencken, and Garry Trudeau. Their followers include hardworking, God-fearing, small-town folk who bitterly resent the freedom of liberals, hedonists, and other urban followers of Satan.

11. They long for a return to a simpler, more ordered society.

12. They're intensely antihumanist. They see humanism as a satanic attempt to place worldly issues before the will of God.

13. They seek political power to further their religious aims. They're unconcerned with social and economic issues.

Robertson's platform doesn't seriously address nuclear disarmament, the budget deficit, racism, the agonizing conversion to a postindustrial society, the trade imbalance, and the environment. The Ayatollah is unperturbed by the slaughter of his young soldiers on the Iraqi front. They don't worry about social injustice and the fate of the Earth, because they're counting down to Armageddon. With only a few years left before the millennium, prayer in schools is obviously a key survival issue.

Since 1946 the Cold War has obsessed the planet's politics. Why did we support a monster like Ferdinand Marcos? Why are the Soviets wasting billions on an incompetent megalomaniac like Fidel Castro? Why are we in the Persian Gulf now? Why are the Soviets using toy bombs against Afghan children? It's because every country in the third world is a pawn on the red-black chessboard.

The American obsession with the Cold War came to a screeching halt in the mid-1960s, when the first waves of the baby-boom generation—76 million strong—started to hit college. The Dr. Spock people are the first post-Cold War generation. Winston Churchill and Omar Bradley are as alien to them as Ulysses Grant and General Jack Pershing.

The group initiations of the Spock kids occurred not at

I'll testify as an expert witness that the born-again rituals of our homegrown southern Pentecostals are authentic head trips, and that preachers such as Pat Robertson are performing the classic shamanic role of brainwashing.

Anzio Beach or Normandy but at Malibu Beach and Fort Lauderdale. They were the first postnuclear, the first postindustrial, the first electronic generation. Extremely individualistic, supremely self-confident, indulged, and ennobled by demand feeding, these affluent children of a doting adult culture are obsessed with such practical, down-to-earth matters as enriched sex, physical comfort, æsthetic style, and personal growth. Above all, they were and still are consistently antiwar and antidraft.

The 1976 election pitted a dependable Cold Warrior, Gerald Ford, against Jimmy Carter, who actually quoted Bob Dylan in his speeches. The election was a toss-up. The militant Bible vote was split. Carter, after all, was a born-again Southerner.

The election landslide of 1980 was produced by an alliance between fundamentalist Protestants, fundamentalist Catholics, and cold-war conservatives. The Reagan Revolution will surely go down in history as the most zany, irrational, unrealistic period in American history. Common sense has floated out the window. The national debt has exploded, the trade balance has collapsed, the industrial base has shrunk, the educational system has failed, and Reagan's ring-ding regime has launched military strikes in Beirut, Libya, Central America, Grenada, and the Persian Gulf, not to mention its highly publicized and ineffective War on Drugs. So what's going on here?

Oh, have you forgotten? It's Millennium Madness. Just a few more looney-tune years to go until A.D. 2000. Happens every thousand years.

Ronald Reagan, let us not forget, believes in the apocalyptic script. George Bush is an Episcopalian Christian. Can you imagine what Pat Robertson would do if he had the Pentagon and the CIA under his command?

How, you wonder, can these nitwits get away with this stuff? Why do the Democrats and the liberals and the moderate Republicans and other practical people sit by with dazed expressions and let harebrains like Pat Buchanan, Richard Secord, Thomas Clines, and Manucher Ghorbanifar run U.S. foreign policy?

Why? Because our middle-aged leaders simply don't understand altered states of mind. They're neurological innocents. They

> Mainstream America is now learning what psychedelic researchers learned in the early 1960s and what most baby-boomers learned in the 1970s: Religious, mystical, visionary possession states are powerful and wonderful—they open the doors of perception, polish our sensory lenses, shake up the autonomic nervous system, and get the hormones surging—but they're intimate and precious. They shouldn't be imposed on others. And above all, they should be kept out of politics. The real issue here is the separation of state and religious visions.

228   **TIMOTHY LEARY**   CHAOS & CYBER CULTURE ....

Oh, have you forgotten?
It's Millennium Madness.
Just a few more looney-tune years
to go until A.D. 2000.
Happens every thousand years.

never had to talk down a tripping college roommate. They're totally unequipped to handle cabinet-level kooks and White House zealots who use slick television advertising techniques to rave about their biblical revelations and millennium dreams.

The same thing happened in Tehran. The Iranian middle class and the technicians and the merchants watched with amazement as madman Khomeini whipped up holy-war passions.

Mainstream America is now learning what psychedelic researchers learned in the early 1960s and what most baby-boomers learned in the 1970s: Religious, mystical, visionary possession states are powerful and wonderful—they open the doors of perception, polish our sensory lenses, shake up the autonomic nervous system, and get the hormones surging—but they're intimate and precious. They shouldn't be imposed on others. And above all, they should be kept out of politics. The real issue here is the separation of state and religious visions.

As we approach the millennium, our survival could depend upon staying calm and cooling out the crazies among us. ☺

VIII.3.

WHO OWNS THE JESUS PROPERTY?

I've been trying to make sense out of the current flap about the film version of *The Last Temptation of Christ*. Why are fundamentalist Protestants attacking this movie inspired by a novel penned by a tormented Greek Catholic, adapted by a guilt-ridden Protestant, and directed by a moody Italian Catholic? Since they all claim to be sincere Christians, why all the rhubarb?

Here's my theory:
What we have here is a typical bunch of quarreling Christian sects—exactly the same noisy cast of characters who have been profiting from similar theological battles for two millennia. They've bick-

ered, century after century, about the trinity or the virgin birth or that always explosive topic, the personality, habits, and human/divine endowments of Jesus.

The sides in these well-publicized debates are usually drawn along geographic lines. In general, the people from North Europe tend to define Jesus and the women in his life as less emotional than people from the Mediterranean do. The Nordics want a Jesus like themselves, cold and repressed. The Southerners want a passionate, volatile Jesus—again, like themselves.

There is a fascinating parallel here with Islam. The angry born-again fundamentalists in Iran; the moderate Sunni and Saudi Arabs who are just trying to make a buck on the Mecca tourist trade and the oil wells, but who are forced to band together to resist the highly impractical Iranian militants.

This relativistic speculation cheered me up. It showed me, once again, how far our American Christians (and American Jews and Moslems) have evolved from their pesky counterparts in the Olde World. In the Middle East these theological differences are still being fought out with tanks and bombers and poison gas; in Northern Ireland, the dour Protestants and passionate Catholics have at each other with

guns and gelignite. Just like the Middle Ages, except for improved weaponry.

But here in the U.S. our sectarian Christians merely quarrel like talent agencies disputing who owns the screen rights to the Jesus Christ story. We're hassling over the ownership to one of the most valuable properties of all time. Look at the script: The birth in the manger. The walking on water. The loaves and fishes. The scourging of the money lenders from the Temple. (Well, on second thought, let's not stress that scene.) The betrayal by Judas. (I wouldn't mention the thirty pieces of silver, to spare Jerry Falwell's feelings.) The crown of thorns. The ever-popular Crucifixion Climax. The surprise-ending Resurrection. It beats *Indiana Jones*, doesn't it?

Our fundamentalists and television evangelists understandably insist that they have a monopoly on the Jesus Property. Of course, there's no shred of evidence to support this in any court. There's not a single paper anywhere that says the Christ family, Jesus, Mary, Joseph, etc., signed away these valuable docudrama rights to North European Protestants and their descendants in the right wing of the Republican party. Hey, these Johnny-come-lately Protestants didn't appear on the scene until fourteen centuries after the death scene went down. To be absolutely frank, the ancestors of these bad-tempered European Bible thumpers were running around bare-assed in bearskins, sacrificing virgins to Thor the Thunder God, when the origi-

> ... the ancestors of these bad-tempered European Bible thumpers were running around bare-assed in bearskins, sacrificing virgins to Thor the Thunder God, when the original Christ script was penned.

nal Christ script was penned.

The televangelists are obviously worried that their alleged monopoly on the $50 billion a year Christ Market will be threatened by passionate Latin and Greek versions that attribute Mediterranean humanity to Christ in contrast to the pale, blonde, plastic doll, blue-eyed killer version that they are peddling. The primordial Greek–Latin image of J. C. is too "human" and emotional for dogmatic Jerry Falwell or shy, onanistic Jimmy Swaggart, or sexually naïve Jim "Motel" Bakker.

In my scenario of these events, Jesus and Mary Magdalene and Peter the Fisherman and the rest of the rowdy gang would be laughing their haloes off at this grubby wrangling for the screen rights to their story. After all, the Jewish Jesus, or Yeshuah—the prototype, even older than Greek–Latin versions—seems to have been an easy-going Reform rabbi with a sly sense of humour, a genial, Hin-Jew rabbi like Ram Dass.

Anyway, if the Writers Guild takes an interest, they should demand residuals for Matthew, Mark, Luke, and John, those four hard-working, ink-stained wretches who penned this eternally interesting and controversial script. ◉

In general, the people from North Europe tend to define Jesus and the women in his life as less emotional than people from the Mediterranean do. The Nordics want a Jesus like themselves, cold and repressed. The Southerners want a passionate, volatile Jesus—again, like themselves.

> God is not a tribal father, nor a feudal lord, nor an engineer-manager of the universe. There is no God (in the singular) except you at the moment.... Since God #1 appears to be held hostage back there by the bloodthirsty Persian ayatollah, by the telegenic Polish pope, and the Moral Majority, there's only one logical alternative. You "steer" your own course. You and your dear friends start your own religion. The Temple, of course, is your body. Your minds write the theology. And the holy spirit emanates from that infinitely mysterious intersection between your brain and the brains of your team.

VIII.4.
HIGH-TECH PAGANISM
CO-WRITTEN WITH ERIC GULLICHSEN

THE CYBERPUNK AS MODERN ALCHEMIST

The baby-boom generation grew up in an electronic world (1960s to 1970s) of turn-on, tune-in television and personal-computing screens. The cyberpunks, growing up in the 1980s and 1990s, develop new metaphors, rituals, and lifestyles for dealing with the universe of information. More and more of us are becoming fuzzy-logic shamans and digital alchemists.

The parallels between the culture of the alchemists and that of cyberpunk computer adepts are numerous. Both employ knowledge of an occult arcanum unknown to the population at large, with secret symbols and words of power. The "secret symbols" compose the languages of computers and mathematics, and the "words of power" instruct computer-operating systems to complete Herculean tasks.

Knowing the precise code name of a digital program permits it to be conjured into existence, transcending the labour of muscular or mechanical search. Rites of initiation or apprenticeship are common to both. "Psychic feats" of telepresence and action-at-a-distance are achieved by selection of the menu option.

Young digital alchemists have at their command tools of a clarity and power unimagined by their predecessors. Computer screens are magical mirrors, presenting alternate realities at varying degrees of abstraction on command (invocation). The mouse or pen of the digitizing tablet is the wand, controlling the fire of the CRT/monitor display and harnessing the creative force of the operator. Spinning disk drives are the pentacles, inscribed with complex symbols, earthen tablets to receive the input of "air," resulting in the crackling intellectual electricity of the processor-chip circuitry programming. The RAM chips are, literally, the buffers ("buffer pools"), the water, the passive element capable only of receiving impressions and retransmitting, reflecting.

Iconic visual programming languages are a Tarot, the pictorial summarization of all possibilities, activated for divination by juxtaposition and mutual influence. It is a Periodic Table of Possibilities, the Western form of the Eastern I Ching. Traditional word-oriented programming languages—FORTRAN, COBOL, and the rest—are a *degenerate* primitive form of these universal systems, grimoires of profit-oriented corporations.

Detailed data-base logs of the activity of operating systems form the Akashic records on a microscale. At a macroscopic level, this is the "world net" knowledge base, the world-wide online hypertext network of information soon to be realized by the storage capacity of CD–ROM and the data-transmission capability of optical fiber—William Gibson's cyberspace "matrix."

Personal transmutation (the ecstasy of the "ultimate hack") is a veiled goal of both systems. The satori of harmonious human-computer communication resulting from the infinite regress into metalevels of self-reflection is the reward for immaculate conceptualization and execution of ideas.

The universality of 0 and 1 throughout magic and religion—yin and yang, yoni and lingam, cup and wand—are manifested today in digital signals, the two bits underlying the implementation of all digital programs in the world in our brains and in our operating disks. Stretching it a bit, even the monad, symbol of change and the tao, visually resembles a superimposed 0 and 1 when its curving central line is stretched through the action of centrifugal force from the ever-increasing speed of rotation of the monad.

CYBERRELIGION OF THE BABY-BOOMERS

By the year 2000 the concerns of the baby-boom generation will be digital or (to use the old paradigms) philosophic-spiritual.

During their teens the boomers went on an adolescent spiritual binge unequalled since the Children's Crusade. In their revolt against the factory culture, they reinvented and updated their tribal-pagan roots and experimented with Hinduism, Buddhism, American Indianism, Magic, Witchcraft, Ann Arbor Voodoo, Esalen Yoga, I Ching, Taoism, Exorcism of the Pentagon, 3-D Re-Incarnations, Love-Ins, and Psychedelic Celebrations.

Born-again Paganism! Pan–Dionysus on audiovisual cassettes. Mick Jagger had them sympathizing with the devil. The Beatles had them floating upstream on the Ganges. Jimi Hendrix

As Buddha, Krishna, Gurdjieff, <u>et al.</u>, have taught: The aim of your life is to take care of yourself so you can take care of others.

You and your friends can do anything that the great religions and empires and racial groups have done in the name of their God. And you're certain to do it better because . . . well, look at their track records. There's no way your Personal State could produce the persecutions and massacres and bigotries of the past and present. There's only one of you, and even with the help of your friends the amount of damage individuals can do is insignificant compared with that of a collective.

taught them how to be a voodoo child. Is there one pre-Christian or third-world metaphor for divinity that some rock group has not yet celebrated on an album cover?

ONTOLOGY RECAPITULATES THEOLOGY

The baby-boomers in their evolving life cycle seem to have recapitulated the theological history of our species. Just as monotheism emerged to unify pagan tribes into nations, so did some boomers rediscover fundamentalist, born-again Judaism and Christianity in their young adulthood. Even far-away Islam attracted gourmet blacks and ex-hippies like Cat Stevens. Bob Dylan nicely exemplifies the consumer approach to religion. For twenty-five years Dylan has continued to browse through the spiritual boutiques, dabbing on a dash of Baptist "born again," nibbling at Hassidism, before returning to his old-time faith of sardonic reformed humanism.

We can laugh at this trendy shopping around for the custom-tailored, designer God, but behind the faddism we find a powerful clue. Notice how Dylan, for example, preserved his options and tried to avoid shoddy or off-the-rack soulware. No "plastic Christs that glow in the dark" for Bob!

The real religion here is Evolutionism, based on the classic humanist, transcendental assumptions:

- God is not a tribal father, nor a feudal lord, nor an engineer-manager of the universe. There is no God (in the singular) except you at the moment. There are as many Gods (in the plural) as can be imagined. Call them whatever you want. They are free agents like you and me.

- You can change and mutate and keep improving. The idea is to keep "trading up" to a "better" philosophy-theology.

As Buddha, Krishna, Gurdjieff, *et al.*, have taught: The aim of your life is to take care of yourself so you can take care of others.

WITH A LITTLE HELP FROM YOUR FRIENDS

This generation, we recall, was disillusioned by the religions, politics, and economics of their parents. Growing up with the threat of nuclear war, the assassination of beloved leaders, a collapsing industrial system, an impossible national debt, religious fundamentalisms (Christian–Jewish–Islamic) that fanatically scream hatred and intolerance, acquired immune deficiencies, and uncomprehending neglect of the ecology, they have developed a healthy skepticism about collective solutions.

No wonder the baby-boom generation has created a psychology of individual navigation. Singularity. The basic idea is self-responsibility. You just can't depend on anyone else to solve your problems. You gotta do it all by yourself . . . with a little help from your friends.

A DO-IT-YOURSELF RELIGION

Since God #1 appears to be held hostage back there by the blood-thirsty Persian ayatollah, by the telegenic Polish pope, and the Moral Majority, there's only one logical alternative. You "steer" your own course. You and your dear friends start your own religion. The Temple, of course, is your body. Your minds write the theology. And the holy spirit emanates from that infinitely mysterious intersection between your brain and the brains of your team.

The attainment of even the suburbs of paradise involves good navigation and planning on your part. Hell is a series of redeemable errors. A detour caused by failure to check the trip maps. A losing streak.

Reward yourself for making choices that lead to friendship and pleasure. Build a cybernetic cycle of positive feed-

back. Only from a state of free selfhood can any truly compassionate signals be sent to others.

THE ADMINISTRATION OF A PERSONAL STATE

The management and piloting of a singularity leads to a very busy career. Once the individual has established herself as a religion, a country, a corporation, an information network, and a neurological universe, it is necessary to maintain personal equivalents of all the departments and operations of the bureaucracies that perform these duties.

This means forming private alliances, formulating personal political platforms, conducting one's own domestic and foreign relations, establishing trade policies, defense and security programs,

educational and recreational events.

On the up side, one is free from dependence on bureaucracies, an inestimable boon. (Free agents can, of course, make temporary deals with organizations and officials thereof.) And if countries have histories and mythic origins, why shouldn't you?

THE PERSONAL MYTHOLOGY

Search and research your very own genetic memory banks, the Old Testaments of your DNA–RNA, including, if you like, past incarnations, Jungian archetypes, and funky pre-incarnations in any future you can imagine. Write your very own Newest Testament, remembering that voluntary martyrdom is tacky, and crucifixions, like nuclear war, can ruin your day.

You and your friends can do any-

Write your very own Newest Testament, remembering that voluntary martyrdom is tacky, and crucifixions, like nuclear war, can ruin your day

> Intelligent post-humanists will not only store themselves electronically, but may do so in the form of a "computer virus," capable of traversing computer networks and of self-replication as a guard against accidental or malicious erasure.

thing that the great religions and empires and racial groups have done in the name of their God. And you're certain to do it better because . . . well, look at their track records. There's no way your Personal State could produce the persecutions and massacres and bigotries of the past and present. There's only one of you, and even with the help of your friends the amount of damage individuals can do is insignificant compared with that of a collective. Besides, you're children of the 1960s and 1990s. You're imprinted to want a peaceful, tolerant, funny world. You can choose your Gods to be smart, funny, compassionate, cute, and goofy.

"IRREVERENCE" IS A PASSWORD FOR THE 21st CENTURY

Human society has now reached a turning point in the operation of the digital programs of evolution, a point at which the next evolutionary steps of the species become apparent to us, to surf at will.

In the near future, the methods of information technology, molecular engineering, biotechnology, nanotechnology (atom stacking), and quantum-digital programming could make the human form a matter totally determined by individual whim, style, and seasonal choice.

The sanctity of our body image, along with the irrational taboos about sex and death, seems to be one of the most persistent anachronisms of industrial-age thought. The human being of the future may be a bio-computer hybrid of any desired form, or an "electronic entity" in the digital info-universe.

Human as program. Or human in programs.

Through storage of one's belief systems as data structures online, and driven by desired programs, one's neuronal apparatus could operate in "silicon" basically as it did in the meatware of the brain, though faster, more predictably, more self-mutably, and, if desired, immortally.

Intelligent post-humanists will not only store themselves electronically, but may do so in the form of a "computer virus," capable of traversing computer networks and of self-replication as a guard against accidental or malicious erasure.

> "What's on this CD?"
> "Ah, that's just boring, adolescent Leary. Let's go ahead and reformat it."

One speculation is that such viral human forms might already inhabit our computer systems. Cleverly designed, they would be very difficult if not theoretically impossible to detect. Current programs do not permit matching the real-time operation speed and parallel complexity of conventional brains. But time scale of operation is subjective and irrelevant, except for the purposes of interface.

Of course, there is no reason to restrict one's manifestation to a particular form. With ever-loosening physical constraints (through perhaps inescapable economic constraints), one will be able to assume any desired form.

Given the ease of copying computer-stored information, it should be possible to exist simultaneously in many forms. Running independently and cloned at each branch point, intelligence would persist in each of these forms. Where the "I's" are in this situation is a matter for high-tech pagans and digital philosophers. ◎

IX. EPILOGUE

BRILLIG IN CYBERLAND

BY WIM COLEMAN & PAT PERRIN

t was a void.

It wasn't darkness or silence. It was the absence of all sense. J. X. Brillig couldn't think in terms of blindness or deafness, because there was no such thing as sight or sound—and certainly not touch. She couldn't remember words like eyes and ears. Space itself had no meaning.

IX. BRILLIG IN CYBERLAND

BY WIM COLEMAN AND PAT PERRIN
FEATURING A CONVERSATION WITH TIMOTHY LEARY

"I guess this is what that first line of Genesis meant," thought Brillig. She floated through the void. She had no idea for how long. Time didn't mean anything, either.

Then came a voice: "Hey, Josie. Can you hear me?" The voice was warm and full of good humour.

"Sound!" thought Brillig. *"What a novel concept!"*

She heard herself answer: "Yes, I can hear you." She was surprised at the lightness, the lilting buoyancy of her own voice. She didn't yet know why. "Can you hear me?"

"Yeah, loud and clear."

"Good. Now maybe you can tell me where I am. Maybe you can tell me *what* I am."

The void was empty of sound again for a moment. Then the voice answered, "You mean you don't know?"

Suddenly, two human figures appeared in the void—two men, flickering and wavering, threatening to dissolve or collapse into a swirl of television snow. Brillig's reality had a weak horizontal hold. But it was a moderately convincing picture, as holograms go.

The man on the right was perched on an invisible stool, punching instructions into a keyboard that rested on his lap. He wore a cowboy hat, and was smoothly outfitted in black—but was it leather or some sort of synthetic? Optical fibers poked out of his head like an unruly mane of hair. At the ends of the fibers, tiny points of light danced around his craggy features. Brillig couldn't tell whether those were functional or not.

The one on the left was a tall, jolly fellow with silvery hair and Celtic features. He sported an enormous grin and mischievous eyes. He looked more than a little familiar.

"Can you see us, Josie?" asked the man on the left.

"Yes," said Brillig.

"Good. Do you recognize either of us?"

"I don't believe so," answered Brillig. "I'm not sure."

"Well, first off, let me introduce you to Upton Orndorf, database cowboy extraordinaire."

"Not so 'extraordinaire' just this minute, damn it," grumbled the cowboy, looking up from his console. "Something's not working right, here."

"Orndorf," thought Brillig. *"The name is familiar. Where have I—?"*

"And I'm Timothy Leary," said the tall, silver-haired gentleman. "Don't you remember me at all?"

Brillig's memory strained. "I remember headlines, news stories," she said. "I remember a Harvard psychologist getting mixed up with psychedelics and the counterculture during the 1960s, eventually getting into computer software and stand-up philosophy—"

Leary let loose a peal of laughter. "Whoa, you're way out of date."

"Please don't talk in riddles. I'm very confused here. The last thing I remember was swallowing a little capsule."

"When was that?"

"How am I supposed to know? It could have been minutes or hours or days. I don't even know what those words mean anymore."

"The year, Josie? What was the year?"

"Uh, 1994, I believe."

"You mean you don't remember anything past 1994?"

"No. Should I?"

Orndorf let out a wail of frustration. It was tough, gravelly, abrasive. "Holy shit! I broke through a wall of the blackest, meanest metaphor-chains in any inscape—to rustle a construct with a memory stuck back in 1994! I'm sorry, Leary. I guess I'm losing my touch." The fiberoptic lights whipped around his head as he shook it.

"But who am I?" asked Brillig. "What am I doing here?"

"You're a bio," Orndorf said offhandedly. Then he continued to Leary, "You should've read it, one simile just rolled into another and another and another. The oxymoron fence was easy, but then I ran into a cortázar continuity."

"What . . . what . . . who. . ." Brillig stammered frantically.

"You're supposed to be the recorded memory of Josephine Xaviera Brillig, one of the legendary pioneers of cyberspace," said Orndorf, a bit impatiently. "It was a serious marienbad, but I thought I'd broken out okay. Maybe it was eschered more than I thought."

"Are you telling me I'm not even *myself?*" cried Brillig. "I'm just a *memory?*"

Orndorf turned to Leary. "That's a problem with these bios," he said. "They think they're sentient beings."

"I resent that," cried Brillig. "If I *think* I'm sentient, then I must *be* sentient."

"That's another problem with 'em," Orndorf told Leary. "They're semi-stuck in the Cartesian paradigm. Like all those junior prosejockeys educated too spec—you know, majors and all that. No flex, no reflects."

"If I'm just Brillig's memory," Brillig demanded, "then what's happened to Brillig?"

"Brillig was remaindered," said Orndorf. He shivered. Tiny lights bounced. "I guess it could've just happened to me. I had a hell of a time getting back into this borgespath."

"What do you mean, remaindered?" Brillig kept futilely trying to pull at the hologram's arm.

"Remaindered. Discarded. Flat-lined, to use an older term," said Orndorf. "Do you understand brain-dead?" he asked when Brillig just looked uncomprehending. "Brillig died in the inscape, in cyberspace. Nobody knows why. That's why we did a re-release on you, to find out what happened. We didn't count on you being defective. We thought maybe you'd remember."

"Well, I don't remember," shouted Brillig. "I think this is all completely crazy. And what *is* cyberspace, anyway?"

"Relax," said Leary. "We'll fill you in on a few things. Where would you like to start?"

"Well, maybe you could give me an historical update." Brillig composed herself a bit.

"Gibson's the teller here," said Orndorf. "You'll have to grab that story line."

"What . . . who . . . " Brillig was sputtering again.

"**On** other planets, they've just been waiting around until we develop a global matrix brain or cyberspace entity that they can interact with."

"Maybe I can explain," chuckled Leary. "You see, it's now A.D. 2044. The culture, the habitat, the way of life right now was written very specifically and brilliantly back in the 1980s by William Gibson in his books, *Neuromancer, Count Zero, Burning Chrome,* and *Mona Lisa Overdrive.* Did you ever read any of those?"

"I'm afraid science fiction was never in my line," said Brillig, vaguely remembering a career involving the classics. She seemed stunned, docile.

So Leary continued. "Show her a map, Upton."

Orndorf punched some instructions into his board and the two men vanished. A great, holographic globe appeared, revolving in front of her. It was brilliantly detailed with familiar land masses—but instead of national boundaries, there were thousands, maybe millions of white lines, all radiating from various points around the world. An extraordinary number converged on the little island of Japan, which looked like a cluster of dazzling stars.

Brillig turned back to Leary, who was explaining the globe. "Politically, national states have diminished in power. The human species is basically organized into competing multinational corporations. There is no more large-scale warfare or national rivalry, because the multinational corporations won't allow it. It's bad for business. Way back when the Japanese started buying up most of America, they simply wouldn't have let the Russians bomb us, because they owned us. And of course, the American companies have formed conglomerate partnerships with the Swiss, and with the Japanese and the Chinese."

"Science fiction," Brillig mumbled, trying to look away from the image. "Is that where you got your, uh, new vocabulary?" she

> "Politically, national states have diminished in power. The human species is basically organized into competing multinational corporations. There is no more large-scale warfare or national rivalry, because the multinational corporations won't allow it. It's bad for business. . . ."

The intelligent groups now running things see the importance of diversity and plurality to allow an evolution of new creativity.

asked Orndorf.

"Gibson and some others defined a lot of terms we still use way back in the 1980s," Orndorf said. "But me, I take to the newniverse. It's based on fores who cogged the inscape."

Then the image changed. It looked like a 1980's newsreel—only holographic, multidimensional. Brillig gasped. "Didn't you say there was no more warfare?"

"Oh, there are still some conflicts here and there," said Leary. "Iraq and Iran are still fighting each other. But no one worries about the Persian Gulf. If Iraqis want to fight the Iranians, everybody lets them do it. It's the same elsewhere."

The hologram extended and wrapped around Brillig entirely. Jet fighters fired rockets at tankers. There were terrorist bombings. Leary explained, "Monotheists like Catholics and Protestants are still fighting each other in places like Belfast. Those kinds of conflicts are totally isolated; so they're just considered local customs."

Images of a riot swept by. Street punks surrounded Brillig, looking much like gang members of the 1980s, only with extraordinary innovations: electrical jacks and plug-ins built into their bodies, and weapons protruding from their flesh—switchblades that flashed from their fingers, forearms that concealed surgically implanted guns and launchers.

"And there still are street gangs in the urban centers," Leary continued amiably. "But they're high-tech street gangs, and so long as they're localized, people have the option to leave those areas if they want to."

Brillig cringed from the action around her. Despite their armaments, the cyberpunks fought each other mostly on computer screens and consoles, over networks and modems. Their plugs seemed more potent than their knives. Still, she was grateful when the scene changed again.

Now the view was from above. Brillig rushed high over the face of the Earth at unspeakable speeds, and as far as the eye could see was the interminable vastness of lighted cities merged together in enormous sprawls.

"The big cities are plastic fantastic. Both in the good and bad sense of it. But there still are places where you can get away into nature." Leary continued, "Instead of fighting over terrain—the Golan Heights, say—most of the competition is now commercial—among the big conglomerates. And what they're mainly fighting for is smart human beings. They're kidnapping smart human beings and high-tech secrets."

But Brillig was puzzled. "In 1994," she said, "a lot of us considered a world dominated by multinational corporations a rather frightening prospect."

Both Leary and Orndorf chuckled, disembodied sounds.

> "... they don't want warfare, because that's bad for business, and they want people to be prosperous, so they can buy stuff. And they don't want to interfere in your privacy. They don't care about your sex life or whether you take drugs or what you do alone, as long as you're consuming. The intelligent groups now running things see the importance of diversity and plurality to allow an evolution of new creativity."

"No, it's wonderful!" Leary explained. "It's a step ahead! Remember, they don't want warfare, because that's bad for business, and they want people to be prosperous, so they can buy stuff. And they don't want to interfere in your privacy. They don't care about your sex life or whether you take drugs or what you do alone, as long as you're consuming. The intelligent groups now running things see the importance of diversity and plurality to allow an evolution of new creativity."

But Brillig was swept with a wave of disorientation. "But— where are you? Where are we?"

"In high orbit," said Leary with a note of pride. "You see, the space migration I predicted way back in the 20th Century has just now begun. There are many permanent settlements in high orbit."

And now the scene included various objects hanging miles above the Earth, satellites cleanly diagrammed with computerized isometrics, eerily motionless in geosynchronous orbits. Her point of view zoomed in on a huge, wheel-shaped space station, whirling majestically above the Earth.

"But how do you get up here?" asked Brillig.

"By way of regular shuttles, like airlines. We call it 'going up the well.' Some of these settlements you see are industrial; others are scientific. But most of them are recreational. The one we're in, for example, is a bit like Las Vegas—an erotic vacation place, sort of a high-tech Club Mediterranean."

"Come on," Orndorf said. "Join us. Do it." And suddenly she was a hologram herself, with the curious physical illusion of being a body moving through space. She was with Leary and Orndorf inside the spectacular orbital playground where thousands of people strolled among shopping malls and health spas. Leary, still playing the garrulous tour guide, pointed out lakes, small forests, genetically engineered wildlife—and even a simulation of a mountain ski lodge.

How much of it was real, and how much holographic? Radiating from the center of the station was an astoundingly brilliant and convincing semblance of Sun, clouds, and blue sky. Were those real birds fluttering above her? She couldn't be sure. To the happy hedonists roaming the satellite, it surely didn't matter.

"Living in space is still considered somewhat adventurous, the way the Wild West once was."

"That was a little before my time," interjected Brillig.

"Most people are still living on the surface of the planet. But many very wealthy families have established their own private

realms up here, and there are some space colonies made up of religious groups and people forming new gene pools, people who enjoy the same lifestyle. There's one for vegetarian lesbians, for example."

Then they walked into a spa, where astounding medical feats were taking place. "Science has given every individual self-managerial control over almost every aspect of physical life," said Leary. "There are muscle implants. You can be any height you want, or any race you want. Plastic surgery and vat-grown organs are available; so everyone can have the body and the appearance that he or she wants."

The answer to a question began to dawn on Brillig. "And your outfit—" she began.

"Vat-grown leather," chortled Orndorf. "The best. No need for crocodiles to worry."

"Life extension can be achieved by means of hybernation techniques," continued Leary, "and there is cloning, too."

"So everyone . . . everyone will be . . . perfect?"

"No, not everyone is making use of all this, because the old monotheistic religions, which want to control people, are still operating. They don't want you to change your looks, because they think God wants you to look a particular way."

Suddenly, Brillig stopped cold. The sight of all these extraordinary transmutations brought something to mind. Something vague and indefinable had been bothering her since she had arrived—something about her name, the unusual lightness of her voice, some difference in her movements. And now she knew what it was.

"I'm a woman!" she cried with alarm.

"Of course you're a woman," said Orndorf. "What did you expect?"

"You don't understand! In 1994 I was a man! Joseph Xavier Brillig! That was my name! What happened?"

Leary and Orndorf laughed. "Son of a gun," chuckled Orndorf, his fiberoptic lights dancing. "You think you've really got somebody cogged! As far as we could figure, you'd always been a woman."

"No need for alarm," added Leary. "You just made a smart choice at one time or other. Women are now seen as the superior sex by far. The ascendancy of the male during the last five to ten thousand years of monotheism, feudalism, and all that has been completely changed. Today, it's just like William Gibson predicted. The women are incredibly powerful, strong, tough, sleek, attractive creatures. And we men are kind of dirty klutzes doing our best."

"It's the women who are the real poets," said Orndorf.

"With all this control over our bodies," mused Brillig, "people should be able to live virtually forever."

"Oh, certainly," said Leary.

"Unless they're dumb enough to get remaindered in cyber-

ANDY FRITH

Science has given every individual self-managerial control over almost every aspect of physical life . . .

"Basically, immortality is digitizing. The more of yourself you digitize, the more of yourself is going to be immortal. The more of your actions and memories you get digitized, the more immortal you're going to be. I was one of the first people to discover this. My claim to fame today is that there is more of me in digital form than of almost any other person from the 20th Century."

space," qualified Orndorf with a slight sneer.

"In general," Leary continued, "people who were born after 1946 have had a better chance at life extension than people born before that. The later you got born, the higher the probability that you had the option. Hybernation was a crucial factor."

And they stepped into an adjoining area, filled with rows of "coffins." Human forms could be seen vaguely through the transparent sides. One was being opened by a clinician, as a friendly group of bystanders watched. As the sleeper groggily awoke, she was warmly welcomed by her fellows.

"The life-extension transition was made within groups," Leary said. "At first, the idea of waking up as a stranger in a strange land surrounded by lab technicians was kind of scary. But in the 1990s, intelligent people got together—people who liked to live together and see each other as friends, and they did pretty much what the Mormons did long before them. They formed future companies. By pooling their resources, by pooling their support, by pooling their familial connections, their chances of being resuscitated were much greater, because they became part of a future family. Dying and re-animating are team sports. It was like the migration from the Olde World to the Newe World in the 16th and 17th Centuries. The Puritans went together to New England, and the Catholics went to Maryland. Different ethnic groups went together. You went with people who shared your belief. That's happened here, too. When you wake up from hybernation, you've got to be protected by your chronologically extended family—but not necessarily your *genetic* family."

"Then surely there are other folks from the late 1900s still around," said Brillig. She was eager to see some familiar faces. But Leary's response was a little cautious.

"Well, people who have been around since then were people who forecast these changes, and *arranged* for themselves to be here. All religions are against this sort of personal immortality. But some people saw the light. Ram Dass, for example, used to be very anti-tech, but he's always been very intelligent, and an opportunist in the best sense of the word. And when he saw how things were going, he came along—kind of reluctantly."

"Tell her the truth," said Orndorf, laughing. "You had to kidnap him and bring him along."

"Okay, that's true," said Leary, laughing. "It's always been like that with him. It took me a long time to get him to take psilocybin, and once he took psilocybin it was hard to get him to take LSD. And it was the same with computers. But he's still around, because he's part of the gang and we'll never leave him behind."

"But immortality! It's a terrifying idea," said Brillig with a shudder. She looked closely at Leary. "Isn't the boredom intolerable?"

Leary shrugged. "Well, obviously, if you're bored you hybernate. I wish I could have hybernated through much of the late

COURTESY OF DYNAMIC GRAPHICS, INC.

"Privacy is the evil of monotheism . . . basically, lettered writing is always about secrets."

20th Century. Whenever Republicans were elected, I would gladly hybernate for eight years."

"So death has become an unnecessary luxury!"

"Absolutely. The answer to boredom is not irreversible involuntary coma. We simply take a nap."

"But you'd wake up like Rip Van Winkle and have no idea what's happened—just like me!"

"Not true," said Leary. "We've got brain-information transfers, so that even while you're asleep you know what's going on."

"Only yours erewhoned," Orndorf added. "Shoddy workmanship."

"More and more of human intelligence is getting stored in living electronic form," said Leary. "Everything that a human being thinks or expresses can be electronically preserved. When you wake up in the morning you can jack your thoughts into your master program. Also, any important part of your life can be on video; so I can show you the highlights of everything that happened to me during the last ten years.

"Basically, immortality is digitizing. The more of yourself you digitize, the more of yourself is going to be immortal. The more of your actions and memories you get digitized, the more immortal you're going to be. I was one of the first people to discover this. My claim to fame today is that there is more of me in digital form than of almost any other person from the 20th Century."

"But death is so fundamental!" Brillig cried with incredulity. "Even our models of evolution and progress are based on organisms dying and clearing the way, passing their characteristics on to their offspring."

Leary scoffed. "These are primitive ideas, vestiges of when we had only one cave, say, and you couldn't have a hundred people living in that one cave—or in one tree, or on one plot of land. You had to die for the sake of the five kids who were supposed to inherit your plot of land, right? You see, everything is information now. Space is free; so the more the merrier. All the ethics and morals and sage principles of the industrial/feudal/land-machine world are totally overthrown in the info-world."

"Everything seems so communal," Brillig mused, "What about privacy?"

"Privacy is the evil of monotheism," Leary replied. "When literacy started, it was a code the Phoenician traders used, because they didn't want the Greek traders to know what the price was. And the Bible itself was a code by those cabalist guys who had that trick going; they were passing on information they didn't want anyone else to know. So basically, lettered writing is always about secrets."

Brillig felt an irrational wave of panic. "But surely you've still got books?" She turned toward Orndorf. "Why, you're bubbling over with literary references. Don't you read books?"

Orndorf barely seemed to understand the question. "Books? Hell, once we popped all the literature into the matrix, who needed books?"

But before Brillig could ask for an explanation, Leary had slipped into far-off reverie. "Back in the late 1980s," he said, "I remember talking to Spalding Gray. Wonderful, wonderful guy. He was a monologuist. I wonder what happened to him? He told me way back then that he was going to start writing. And I remember saying to him, 'Jesus Brown, why are you going to *write*? Why are you going to freeze your wonderful thoughts into lettered words?"

"He said, 'Well, I have to go through that stage, so I can recapitulate through to the human race.'

"I tried to explain it to him. I said, 'If you type "T–I–M" on a typewriter, that's just ink stained onto wood pulp, right? You can't change it. But if you type that on a computer keyboard, within seconds you can modem it up to a satellite, and a hundred million people can watch you type "T–I–M." ' "

"And do you know what he said to me? 'Maybe I don't *want* a hundred million people to see what I'm typing.' "

Leary chuckled. "You see that? That's your basic secrecy. Well, I respect that. If you want to keep secrets, make your own little code. A lot of people have kept on that way. The nice thing about human nature is that it's so perverse and so pluralistic, and so creative in both negative and positive ways, there will always be a lot of people who won't want to take advantage of all the things we've got—thank the Gods! Because those of us that do will be allowed to do what we like. It's like people in the 20th Century who didn't want to get stoned on drugs, and I always said, 'Great!' Those of us who did were all the freer for it."

But Brillig was still staggered by questions and perplexities. "What difference has all this really made?" she asked. "Are people any different, any better off—any *smarter*?"

> Essentially, there's a universe inside your brain. The number of connections possible inside your brain is limitless. And as people have learned to have more managerial and direct creative access to their brains, they have also developed matrices or networks of people that communicate electronically. There are direct brain/computer link-ups. You can just jack yourself in and pilot your brain around in cyberspace—electronic space.

"Lots," said Leary. "The level of intelligence has been tremendously increased, because people are thinking and communicating in terms of screens, and not in lettered books. Much of the real action is taking place in what is called cyberspace. People have learned how to boot up, activate, and transmit their brains. Essentially, there's a universe inside your brain. The number of connections possible inside your brain is limitless. And as people have learned to have more managerial and direct creative access to their brains, they have also developed matrices or networks of people that communicate electronically. There are direct brain/computer link-ups. You can just jack yourself in and pilot your brain around in cyberspace—electronic space."

The trio stopped and looked at one another. The surrounding orbital resort suddenly vanished. Brillig faced Orndorf and Leary again. There was anticipation in the air.

"So," said Orndorf after a silence. "Are you starting to remember or what? You were one of the legendary riders of the inscape. Want to try it again?"

Orndorf punched more instructions into the board, and Brillig felt an incredible sensation—as though she had done an

... An incredible sensation—as though she had done an extraordinary somersault from one reality into another. And suddenly she was plunging through an altogether different universe, careening among glorious, glittering geometric towers of light. The sense of space was extraordinary. Her mind swelled with incredible knowledge and perception. She had no voice or body, but she could still communicate ...

extraordinary somersault from one reality into another. And suddenly she was plunging through an altogether different universe, careening among glorious, glittering geometric towers of light. The sense of space was extraordinary. Her mind swelled with incredible knowledge and perception. She had no voice or body, but she could still communicate with Orndorf or Leary. Their thoughts had merged.

"What's this called?" she wondered.

"Myoelectric interface," she felt Orndorf answer.

"Like it?" she felt Leary ask.

"Like *it? It's* wonderful! *But where am I? What is this?"*

"Cyberspace—a consensual hallucination of all the world's information."

Brillig felt a twinkle of memory. She was back on her turf again—even if she still didn't quite grasp what it was. She was inside cyberspace, a world of pure information.

"What are those great towers of light?"

"Data banks. All the information of the world is now in them—and you gain access to them in cyberspace. All of the human signals that used to sell as books have been digitized and are now available and stored in these data banks—plus all the pictures, all the movies and the television shows—absolutely everything."

"Of course!" she began to remember as she swirled among the towers. *"These are symbolic receptacles of all the knowledge of the world!"* The thought thrilled her.

"There is tremendous competition and actual fighting over data bases," Leary continued. "For example, the Bank of Japan can't let the Bank of America into their data bases. So cyberspace is where all the action takes place. In a way, it's just like it used to be. Even back in the 1980s—can you remember?—trillions of dollars were exchanged every day in the computer network. These exchanges of money were all done by computer. Hundreds of billions of dollars were being moved around between Japan, Europe, America. I cite that as an archaic example of what's happening right now.

"And each of those towers is surrounded with ICE—intrusion countermeasures electronics—techniques of defending your base. That doesn't stop a lot of code rustling from going on."

Brillig felt herself swell with cybercosmic laughter. *"Code rustling! Sure, I remember. Legitimate accountants and CEOs work inside those towers, cowboys and rustlers like me work on the outside, busting in through layers of ice. A world of outrageous, high-tech adventure!"*

Her thoughts blended more and more with Leary's. "Everything is information," she felt him think. "Information is much more important than material goods. The politics of information, that's what we're talking about. So just as you had rustlers and cowboys in the Wild West, today you've got rustlers and cowboys and black marketeers in this info-world. Almost everything the Gods used to do, now the average person can do—change your body, change your mind, change your DNA code, clone, and also be part of the highly advanced wisdom center."

"And a part of a fantastic new mythology!"

"And a whole new theology, too," answered Leary's mind. "Once we established this information world, we'd also created a new intelligence entity—a superintelligence. People that operate at that level have formed networks of superintelligence."

Orndorf chimed in, "Even when we worked out the mathematics of recovering reality, it was more mysterious than we had expected. New story lines kept forming, beyond our programming."

Brillig tumbled through cyberspace, letting forth a cry of delight. *"Who'd ever want to go back?"*

Leary seemed to enjoy the question. "There's a real social conflict about that. The hottest political and social conflict now is between those people who want to spend *all* their time in cyberspace, and those who see it as very dangerous and addictive, who don't want their loved ones to leave them and spend more and more time in the info-world. Once you get into the info-world, there's no question that it's much more exciting than coming down and pushing a body around. So there is now, as there always will be with an

It wasn't just the flesh that tied you down. It wasn't just prosaic forces like gravity. The physical universe itself seemed cramped, claustrophobic—a realm of space-time bent by hunks of mass into gross finitude. It couldn't compare to an infinite ocean of uncut metaphor, a neuroelectric realm containing the absolute essence of literally everything.

intelligent species so genetically varied, a number of viewpoints. There are those who think cyberspace horrible, and those who consider their 'meat' existence slow and vulgar."

No, she couldn't imagine going back. It wasn't just the flesh that tied you down. It wasn't just prosaic forces like gravity. The physical universe itself seemed cramped, claustrophobic—a realm of space-time bent by hunks of mass into gross finitude. It couldn't compare to an infinite ocean of uncut metaphor, a neuroelectric realm containing the absolute essence of literally *everything*.

They passed beyond the man-made information monoliths, out onto the mysterious high seas of cyberspace. Brillig knew she had been to these parts before. But what had she found out here? Leary wanted to know the answer, too.

"According to Gibson's predictions, our planet now ought to be able to interchange messages with other species that have reached this level elsewhere. On other planets, they've just been waiting around until we develop a global matrix brain or cyberspace entity that they can interact with."

But it was Orndorf who came out and asked the crucial question: "Josie, before you came out here that last time, you told us you were about to connect with something, an extraterrestrial, extradimensional intelligence—an entity named Llixgrijb. No one else could do it. You went riding off into the inscape to make contact with Llixgrijb.

"Do you remember? Did you succeed?"

The question turned over and over in Brillig's mind. *"Llixgrijb . . . Did I succeed? . . . Do I remember? . . ."*

And she felt that presence again, a mind unlike any mind she had ever imagined, at once far away and inside of her, a mind from which she, the physical universe, and cyberspace itself seemed to emanate—a mind which contained all other minds. Could this be Llixgrijb?

But a force came down on her like a giant hand pushing her back. She felt herself moving out of cyberspace, backward through space and time, as if sucked into a terrible maelstrom.

"It's no use," she called to her companions. *"It's sending me back to the time I came from. It's sending me back to 1994. I'll have to wend my way back the way I came."*

She felt Leary's mind receding far into the future, sending one last message to her, saying, "It's all right. We understand. We'll miss you. But be sure to tell anyone back there in the 1990s who wants to know how we're getting along now to read William Gibson's stuff. It's a nitty-gritty, down and dirty, street-smart blueprint of how we're living and the options we have."

"And next time don't get remaindered," added Orndorf. "Watch your ways on the borgespaths." She caught a final glimpse of tiny dancing lights as the message from Orndorf's mind trailed away. ◉

X. RESOURCES

ANDY FRITH

TIMOTHY LEARY: CHECKLIST OF PRIMARY WORKS
• •
(WITH DATES OF FIRST PUBLICATION)

Multilevel Measurement of Interpersonal Behavior (1956)
Interpersonal Diagnosis of Personality (1957)
The Psychedelic Experience (1964). With Ralph Metzner and Richard Alpert.
Psychedelic Prayers (1966)
Start Your Own Religion (1967)
High Priest (1968)
The Politics of Ecstasy (1968)
The Declaration of Evolution (1970)
Timothy Leary, Appellant v. State of California (1970)
Jail Notes (1970)
Neurologic (1973)
Confessions of a Hope Fiend (1973)
Starseed (1973)
Terra II (1974)
The Curse of the Oval Room (1974)
What Does WoMan Want? (1976)
Exo-Psychology (1977)
Neuropolitics (1977). With Robert Anton Wilson and George Koopman.
The Intelligence Agents (1979)
Neurocomics (1979)
The Game of Life (1979)
Changing My Mind, Among Others (1982)
Flashbacks (1983)
Mind Mirror (1986; software)
Timothy Leary's Greatest Hits (1990)
Chaos & Cyber Culture (1994)

WORKS CURRENTLY IN PRINT ·

Mind Mirror (Mindware, 1986; software)
Info-Psychology (New Falcon Publications, 1987; revision of *Exo-Psychology*)
An Annotated Bibliography of Timothy Leary (Archon Books, 1988)
What Does WoMan Want? (New Falcon Publications, 1988; revised)
Flashbacks (J. P. Tarcher, Inc., 1990; additions)
The Politics of Ecstasy (Ronin Publishing, 1990; additions)
Timothy Leary's Greatest Hits (KnoWare, 1990)
The Game of Life (New Falcon Publications, 1993)
How to Operate Your Brain (Retinalogic, 1993; video)
The Psychedelic Experience (Citadel Press, 1993)

I. SCREENS

1. "How I Became an Amphibian" was first published in different form in *Timothy Leary's Greatest Hits* (1990).

2. "Custom-Sized Screen Realities" was first published in different form in *Timothy Leary's Greatest Hits* (1990).

3. "Imagineering" is previously unpublished.

II. CYBERNETICS: CHAOS ENGINEERING

1. "Conversation with William Gibson" is taken from "High Tech High Life" published in *Mondo 2000* (1989).

2. "Artificial Intelligence: Hesse's Prophetic *Glass Bead Game*" was first published in *Literature and Altered States of Consciousness*, a special issue of *Mosaic*, a journal for the interdisciplinary study of literature, Volume 19, Number 3/4 (Summer/Fall 1986).

3. "Our Brain" is adapted from talks delivered circa 1990, and first published in different form in *The (San Francisco) City* (August 1991).

4. "How to Boot Up Your Bio-Computer" was published in shortened form under the title "Digital Dependence" in the *Omni Whole Mind Newsletter* (1987). Reprinted by permission ©1987, Omni Publication Int'l.

5. "Personal Computers, Personal Freedom" was first published in *Digital Deli*, Ed. Steve Ditlea (New York: Workman Publishing Co., 1984).

6. "Quantum Jumps, Your Macintosh, and You" is taken from "Quantum Jumps, Your Commodore, and You" and "The Role of the Free Agent in the Computer Culture" published in *Guide to Computer Living* (October and November 1986).

III. COUNTERCULTURES

1. "The Woodstock Generation" was first published in *Timothy Leary's Greatest Hits* (1990).

2. "From Yippies to Yuppies" was first published in *High Society* (October 1985).

3. "The Cyberpunk: The Individual as Reality Pilot" was first published in *Mississippi Review* (1988).

4. "The New Breed" was first published in different form in *Timothy Leary's Greatest Hits* (1990).

5. "Electronic Cultures" is taken from "Hear Me Hear Me: How Home Media Designs Cultural Evolution" published in *Creem* (April 1993).

6. "The Next Twenty Years" was first published in different form in *Whole Earth Review* (Winter 1988).

7. "The Godparent: Conversation with Winona Ryder" is taken from "A Meeting of the Minds" published in *Interview* (November 1989).

IV. INFO-CHEMICALS & DRUG WARS

1. "Conversation with William S. Burroughs" is taken from "A Couple of Bohos Shooting the Breeze" published in *Mondo 2000* (1991).

2. "The Sociology of LSD" was first published in different form in *Psychedelic Reflections*, Ed. Grinspoon and Bakalar (New York: Human Sciences Press, Inc., 1983; "Some Superficial Thoughts on the Sociology of LSD"); material added from "Criminalizing the Natural and Naturalizing the Criminal," *Timothy Leary's Greatest Hits* (1990).

3. "Just Say Know: The Eternal Antidote to Fascism" was first published in different form in *American Book Review* (Nov.–Dec. 1989); reprinted in *Timothy Leary's Greatest Hits* (1990).

4. "Czar Bennett and His Holy War on Drugs" was first published in *New Perspectives Quarterly* (Fall 1989); enlarged with portions of the previously unpublished "The Solution to Drug Abuse" (1993).

5. "MDMA: The Drug of the 1980s" was first published in different form under the title "Ecstasy: Drug of the Nineties" in *Chic* (July 1985); reprinted as "Ecstatic Electricity" in *NY Talk* (August 1985).

6. "The Case for Intelligent Drug Use" is a fragment of an interview published in *Maclean's* (March 5, 1984).

V. CYBEROTICS

1. "Hormone Holocaust" first appeared in *Puritan International* (1987).

2. "In Search of the True Aphrodisiac" was first published in *Chic* (November 1985); reprinted in *Timothy Leary's Greatest Hits* (1990).

3. "Operation Sex Change" was first published in *Hustler* (October 1986).

4. "Digital Activation of the Erotic Brain" was first published in *Hustler* (February 1985); reprinted in *Timothy Leary's Greatest Hits* (1990).

VI. GUERILLA ART

1. "Pranks: An Interview," was first published in RE/Search #11: *Pranks!* Ed. A. Juno and V. Vale (San Francisco: RE/Search Publications, 1987). RE/Search Publications, 1232 Pacific Avenue, San Francisco, California.

2. "Keith Haring: Future Primeval" was first published under the title "One Rent in the Fabric Is All It Takes for Pandemonium to Sluice Through" in *Keith Haring: Future Primeval* by Barry Blinderman (Normal, IL: University Galleries, Illinois State University, 1990). Blinderman's work, *Keith Haring: Future Primeval*, which inspired the retitling of this article, is available in a new edition from Abbeville Press, New York.

3. "Robert Williams: Power to the Pupil" first appeared in different form as an introduction to Robert Williams's *Views from a Tortured Libido* (San Francisco: Last Gasp, 1993).

4. "On William S. Burroughs's *Interzone*" was first published in *Die Welt* (1990); an English translation was published in *Off the Wall* (1992); our current version is significantly revised.

5. "William Gibson: Quark of the Decade" was first published in different form in *Mondo 2000* (1989).

6. "How to Publish Heresy in Mainline Publications" was first published in *Trajectories* (1989).

7–8. *"Reproduced Authentic:* The Wizardry of David Byrne" and "Conversation with David Byrne" were first published in different form as "Two Heads Talking" in *Mondo 2000* (1992).

VII. DE-ANIMATION/RE-ANIMATION

1. "Common-Sense Alternatives to Involuntary Death" was first published as "22 Common Sense Alternatives to Involuntary Death" in different form as a KnoWare monograph (1988); in C. Hyatt, *Undoing Yourself Too* (1988); reprinted in *Timothy Leary's Greatest Hits* (1990) and in *Magical Blend* (April 1991).

2. "Hybernating Andy" was published in different form as "Andy Warhol's Secret Desire to Rejoin His Idol, Walt Disney" in *Mondo 2000* (1991).

VIII. MILLENNIUM MADNESS

1. "Backward, Christian Soldiers" was first published in *Hustler* (October 1985); reprinted in *Timothy Leary's Greatest Hits* (1990).

2. "God Runs for President on the Republican Ticket" was first published as "Robertson" in *Regardie's Magazine* (November 1987).

3. "Who Owns the Jesus Property?" was first published in *Trajectories* (Autumn 1988).

4. "High-Tech Paganism" appeared in a different version under the title "High-Tech Paganism and Digital Polytheism" in *Reality Hackers* (1988).

IX. EPILOGUE

"Brillig in Cyberland," by Wim Coleman and Pat Perrin, first appeared in the newsletter *The Jamais Vu Papers* (1988) and was reprinted in a book of that title (New York: Harmony Books, 1991).

LIST OF ILLUSTRATIONS

• •

THROUGHOUT THE BOOK:

Slogan buttons and computer icons on pages 9, 39, 40, 41, 54, 104, 122, 200, 218, 247 from the collection and archives of Vicki Marshall

Slogan buttons and event flyers on pages 40, 67, 102, 126, 169, 204, 236 from the collection and archives of Michael Horowitz

INTERGALACTIC PLACEMATS
Momentos from Brummbaer's Holidays in Cyberspace
Perfect for a 3:00 Brunch. For more Information write :
SATURDAY-AFTERNOON IN THE UNIVERSE
520 Washington Blvd., Ste # 114 , Marina del Rey, CA 90292

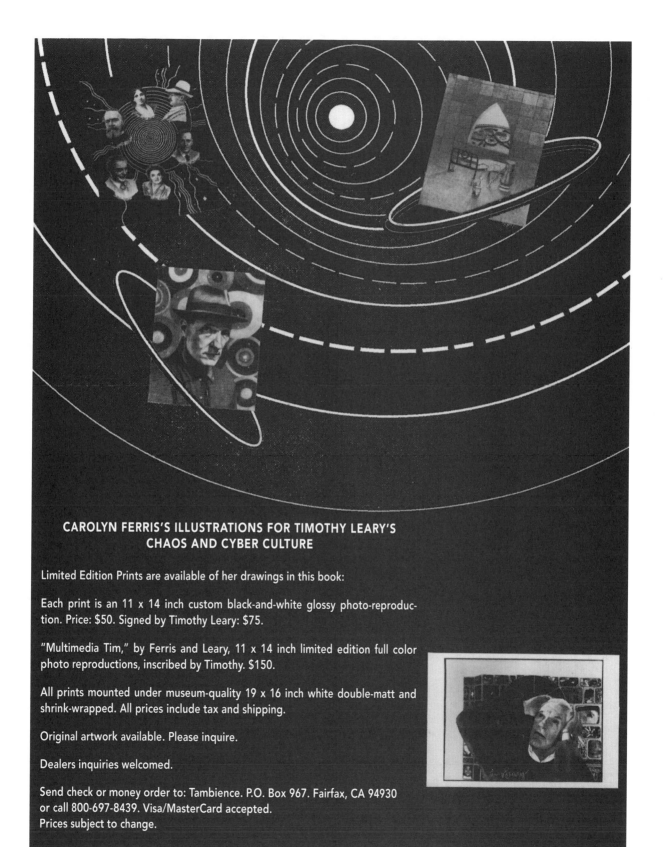

CAROLYN FERRIS'S ILLUSTRATIONS FOR TIMOTHY LEARY'S CHAOS AND CYBER CULTURE

Limited Edition Prints are available of her drawings in this book:

Each print is an 11 x 14 inch custom black-and-white glossy photo-reproduction. Price: $50. Signed by Timothy Leary: $75.

"Multimedia Tim," by Ferris and Leary, 11 x 14 inch limited edition full color photo reproductions, inscribed by Timothy. $150.

All prints mounted under museum-quality 19 x 16 inch white double-matt and shrink-wrapped. All prices include tax and shipping.

Original artwork available. Please inquire.

Dealers inquiries welcomed.

Send check or money order to: Tambience. P.O. Box 967. Fairfax, CA 94930 or call 800-697-8439. Visa/MasterCard accepted.
Prices subject to change.

Timothy Leary

SIGNED
BOOKS ☆ SOFTWARE ☆ TAPES

EXO PSYCHOLOGY	$15.95
FLASHBACKS	$15.00
THE GAME OF LIFE	$14.95
GREATEST HITS	$15.00
MIND MIRROR	$19.95
JUST SAY KNOW BUTTON	$2.50

FROM OUTTA
KNOWARE

11288 VENTURA BLVD #702 ▪ STUDIO CITY, CA 91604

US CHECK/MONEY ORDER
CA 8.25% SALES TAX
S/H $4 US; $8 FOREIGN
ALLOW 4–6 WKS DELIVERY

SASE FOR COMPLETE CATALOG

ANNOTATED BIBLIOGRAPHY OF TIMOTHY LEARY

A detailed listing of all of Dr. Leary's books, monographs, scientific papers, magazine articles, interviews, lectures, vinyl recordings, audiocasettes, videotapes, film appearances, software, posters, slogan buttons and bumperstickers from 1942 through 1986. Also included is a lengthy selection of works about Dr. Leary, and the legal briefs pertaining to his arrests, trials and imprisonments on four continents. *Over 1,200 entries, 304pp, with 50 items illustrated. Clothbound. $45 postpaid.*

SHAMAN WOMAN, MAINLINE LADY

The first anthology of writings by women about their experiences with mind-altering drugs. Over 60 writers explore the psycho-sensual-political landscape of women's drug experiences from mythic times to the contemporary shamanistic revival. Included are Sappho, Elizabeth Barrett Browning, George Sand, Charlotte Bronte, Louisa May Alcott, Edith Wharton, Isabelle Eberhardt, Billie Holiday, Anais Nin, Laura Huxley, Diane di Prima, Grace Slick and Patti Smith. *Profusely illustrated with portraits and rare graphic works. 8-1/2 x 11 inches, 288pp, $15 trade paperback or $25 hardcover postpaid.*

LYSERGIC WORLD/MONDO LYSERGICA

A psychedelic tabloid prepared for the 50th anniversary of the discovery of LSD. "Packed so full of history and trivia that it stands alone as a significant document"- *Factsheet Five*. "Absolutely incredible LSD newspaper printed in psychedelic colors" --*Freakbeat Magazine*. "Collectors, denizens of the underground, ravers, '60s nostalgia freaks, and the millions of psychedelic heads everywhere will all thoroughly enjoy browsing through *Mondo Lysergica*"--Terence McKenna. *16pp, 15 x 12 in., 50 illustrations. $5 postpaid.*

Send check or m.o. to: L-World
    40 Fourth St.-Suite 260
Petaluma, CA 94952

vic keller • studio
psych^erotica • p.o. box
193 • philo ca 95466
• (707)895-2919 •

Spiritual
Effects

Computer Graphics
Multi-media   Design

PH:415-896-5628 / FAX:415-896-5629

Chaotic Information from Ronin Books By Phone

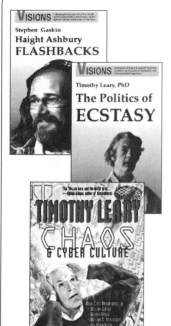

Chaos and Cyber Culture
Leary. 1994. Conveys Leary's vision of the emergence of a new humanism with an emphasis on questioning authority, independent thinking, individual creativity, and the empowerment of computers and other brain technologies.
0-914171-77-1   300pp.
CHACYB   **$19.95**

Politics of Ecstasy Leary. 1990. Leary's most provocative and influential early psychedelic writings and exploration of human-consciousness issues, containing many of his early pronouncements on the psychedelic movement of the 1960s.
0-914171-33-X   220pp.
POLECS   **$12.95**

Haight/Ashbury Flashbacks
Gaskin. 1990. Deeply personal account of experiences with psychoactive drugs during the "Summer of Love" written by one of the original Hippies. Glimpse the flower children & the transformational power—and dangers—of psychedelics.
0-914171-30-5   220pp.
HAIFLA   **$9.95**

Way Of The Ronin Potter. 1988. Cyberpunk career strategy. Developing potential by shedding specialization and getting off the fast track. Flowering rather than crisis, enthusiasm in place of burnout, and survival instead of obsolescence.
0-914171-26-7   242pp.
WAYRON   **$9.95**

Finding a Path with a Heart
Potter. 1994. Enjoy work while being creative and successful, how to take the lead in on-the-job projects as well as avocational pursuits, and how to follow a career path that brings meaning and satisfaction.
0-914171-74-7   288pp.
FINPAT   **$9.95**

Brain Boosters: Foods & Drugs That Make You Smarter Potter & Orfali. 1993. Make your mind work better. For professionals, business people, seniors, people concerned with Alzheimer's, students, athletes and party goers who want to improve mental permormance.
0-914171-65-8   256pp.
BRABOO   **$12.95**

Right Where You Are Sitting Now Wilson. 1982. How to have fun with your own head. "Prompts the cosmic with sex, coincidence, suspense, and flip humor." —Booklist
0-914171-45-3   207pp.
RIGWHE   **$9.95**

Illuminati Papers Wilson. 1990. Is all of history a vast conspiracy? Cosmic joke? Speaking through characters from his novels, Wilson presents his views on our future way of life. Liberate yourself and explore the New Social Order.
0-914171-44-5   207pp.
ILLPAP   **$9.95**

Sex Drugs and Aphrodisiacs
Gottlieb. 1980. An essential connoisseur's guide to herbs and potions traditionally associated with sensual pleasure. Chronicles the historical quest for aphrodisiacs. Includes discussions of various substances, as well as a history of sources, preparations, and effects. This hard to obtain cult classic is once again available.
0-914171-56-9   96pp.
SEXAPH   **$9.95**

Ecstasy: The MDMA Story
Eisner. 1989. Legal issues, psychotherapy, history, use, chemistry, illustrations, health risks, bibliography, index. "Remarkably complete, courageous and well researched work."—*American Book Review*
0-914171-68-2   228pp.
ECSTAS   **$17.95**

Marijuana Law Boire. 1992. Up-to-date comprehensive guide helps readers to reduce the probablity of arrests and to defend themselves from prosecution if arrested. Legal rights, searches, seizures, privacy, rulings, stories, dogs, cars, houses and more.
0-914171-62-3   128pp.
MARLAW   **$12.95**

Psychedelics Encyclopedia
Stafford. 1991. With a new foreword and an appendix on Ecstasy, this edition is an archive of the psychedelic age. Info on botany and cultivation; effects and pharmacology; LSD, cannabis, peyote, mushrooms, famous psychedelic users and events.
0-914171-51-8   420pp.
PSYENC   **$24.95**

(10% off with Money Order, Shipping add $3/order + $1/book, Credit Card check fee $3, CA residents add 8.5% sales tax)
☞ **FREE Catalog or VISA/MC orders call** ☎ **(800) 858 2665 • (510) 548 2124**
Ronin Books-By-Phone • Box 522 Berkeley CA 94701